IRAQ IN FRAGMENTS

Crises in World Politics

TARAK BARKAWI
JAMES MAYALL
BRENDAN SIMMS
editors

GÉRARD PRUNIER
Darfur—the Ambiguous Genocide

MARK ETHERINGTON
Revolt on the Tigris

FAISAL DEVJI
Landscapes of the Jihad

AHMED HASHIM
Insurgency and Counter-Insurgency in Iraq

IAIN KING & WHIT MASON
Peace at Any Price—How the World Failed Kosovo

ERIC HERRING • GLEN RANGWALA

Iraq in Fragments

The Occupation and Its Legacy

Cornell University Press
Ithaca, New York

Originally published in the United Kingdom by
C. Hurst & Co. (Publishers) Ltd, London

First published 2006 by Cornell University Press

ISBN 978 0 8014 4457 9

Printed in the United States of America

Librarians: Library of Congress Cataloging-
in-Publication Data are available.

Cornell University Press strives to use environmentally responsible suppliers and materials to the fullest extent possible in the
publishing of its books. Such materials include vegetable-based,
low-VOC inks and acid-free papers that are recycled, totally
chlorine-free, or partly composed of nonwood fibers. For further
information, visit our website at www.cornellpress.cornell.edu

Cloth printing 10 9 8 7 6 5 4 3 2 1

CONTENTS

ACKNOWLEDGEMENTS

We have accumulated many debts during the writing of this book and we are very happy to acknowledge them:

The UK Economic and Social Research Council funded the research (grant RES-000-22-0274), and we thank them for their flexibility. Joint thanks to Anne Alexander, David Gritten, Hannah Parrott and Elspeth Van Veeren for superb research assistance; to Jean Pretlove for her eagle-eyed administrative assistance; and to Michael Dwyer of Hurst & Co. for his vigorous support for this project. Thanks to the following for providing valuable comments on parts of the manuscript, or other support: Nadje Al-Ali, Falah Alkhawaja, Baher Butti, Ruth Blakeley, Simon Child, Tim Edmunds, Richard Garfield, Nathaniel Hurd, Kent Johnson, Colin Rowat, Anna Stavrianakis, Bill Robinson, Charles Tripp, Doug Stokes, Evan Hawker, Maria Petalidou and those who gave non-attributable interviews and feedback.

E.H. would like to thank Ruth Blakeley, Christine Davis, Bruce Herring, Tim Hetherington, Vernon Hewitt, Susanne Munro, Helen Redmond-Cooper and Doug Stokes for their support and friendship; John Munro, Siobhan Munro, Mark Karim and Olivia Karim for their patience and understanding while this book was being written; and Glen Rangwala for this productive joint project.

G.R. is especially grateful to Seb and Abi Wills, Kamil Mahdi, Sharif Nashashibi, Seymour Hersh, Ray Whitaker, Zaheer Kazmi, Mundher al-Adhami, Nathaniel Hurd, Robert Fisk, Eric Herring, Hans von Sponeck, Abbie Fielding-Smith, Alison and Per Klevnäs, Yezid Sayigh,

Sanjay Ruparelia and particularly Colin Rowat for all their encouragement, ideas and intellectual assistance. Without any one of the above, the arguments of the book would not be what they are. He would also like to thank William Morris, Brendan Simms, Shaikh Nasser bin Hamed and Tareq Ismael for providing the forums through which much of his research on Iraq has been carried out. Gratitude of a more general but no less extensive kind goes to Bryony Cobain, Geoff Hawthorn, the late Raj Chandavarkar, Mònica Badia, Charlie Jenks, Joy Labern, Graham Bash and Liz Watson.

An earlier version of parts of Chapter Two was published as Glen Rangwala, 'The Democratic Transition in Iraq and the Discovery of its Limitations', in Alex Danchev and John MacMillan (eds), *The Iraq War and Democratic Politics* (London: Routledge, 2005), pp. 160-180. An earlier version of parts of Chapter Five was published as Eric Herring and Glen Rangwala, 'Iraq, Imperialism and Global Governance', *Third World Quarterly*, vol. 26, no. 4/5 (2005), pp. 661-77. Thanks to the copyright holders for permission to draw on those publications. Thanks also to the United Nations for permission to reproduce its map of Iraq.

Bristol and Cambridge, June 2006   E.H. & G.R.

ACRONYMS AND ABBREVIATIONS

AIRP	Accelerated Iraq Reconstruction Programme
ARCENT	US Army Central Command
CENTCOM	US Central Command
CERP	Commander's Emergency Response Programme
CFLCC	Coalition Forces Land Component Command
CIA	Central Intelligence Agency
CIPE	Centre for International Private Enterprise
CJTF-7	Coalition Joint Task Force 7
CPA	Coalition Provisional Authority
CRS	Congressional Research Service
DCAA	US Defence Contract Audit Agency
DFI	Development Fund for Iraq
DoD	US Department of Defence
FPS	Facilities Protection Service
GAO	Government Accountability Office
	(General Accounting Office before July 2004)
GUOE	General Union of Oil Employees
HNCEBP	Higher National Commission
	for the Eradication of the Ba'th Party
IAMB	International Advisory and Monitoring Board
IAWG	Iraq Accountability Working Group
IBC	Iraq Body Count
ICDC	Iraqi Civil Defence Corps
ICG	International Crisis Group

ICP	Iraqi Communist Party
ICRSS	Iraq Centre for Research and Strategic Studies
IIA	Iraqi Interim Authority
IIACSS	Independent Institute for Administrative and Civil Society Studies
IIG	Iraqi Interim Government
IIGC	Iraq Inspectors General Council
IIP	Iraqi Islamic Party
ILCS	*Iraq Living Conditions Survey 2004*
IMF	International Monetary Fund
IMN	Iraqi Media Network
INA	Iraqi National Accord
INC	Iraqi National Congress
IRDC	Iraqi Reconstruction and Development Council
IRI	International Republican Institute
IRMO	Iraq Reconstruction and Management Office
IRRF	Iraq Relief and Reconstruction Fund
IRFFI	International Reconstruction Fund Facility for Iraq
ISFF	Iraq Security Forces Fund
ITG	Iraqi Transitional Government
KAR	Kurdistan Autonomous Region
KBR	Kellogg Brown and Root
KDP	Kurdistan Democratic Party
KIU	Kurdistan Islamic Union
KRG	Kurdistan Regional Government
LOGCAP	Logistics Civil Augmentation Program
MNC-I	Multinational Corps Iraq
MNF-I	Multinational Force Iraq
NDI	National Democratic Institute
OFF	Oil For Food
OIC	Organisation of the Islamic Conference

OPIC	US Overseas Private Investment Corporation
OPO	Office of Provincial Outreach
ORHA	Office of Reconstruction and Humanitarian Assistance
PCO	Project and Contracting Office
PMO	Programme Management Office
PNAC	Project for the New American Century
PRB	Project Review Board
PUK	Patriotic Union of Kurdistan
RIO	Restore Iraq's Oil contract
RTI	Research Triangle Institute
SCIRI	Supreme Council for the Islamic Revolution in Iraq
SIGIR	US Special Inspector General for Iraq Reconstruction
TAL	Transitional Administrative Law
TBI	Trade Bank of Iraq
TNA	Transitional National Assembly
UIA	United Iraqi Alliance
UNCC	United Nations Compensation Commission
UNDP	United Nations Development Programme
USAID	US Agency for International Development
WTO	World Trade Organisation

1

INTRODUCTION

When the US led the invasion of Iraq in March 2003, it expected to be able to establish a prosperous liberal democracy with an open economy that would serve as a key ally in the region. It also sought to engage Iraqi society in ways that would defeat any challenge to that project or US guidance of it. As it turned out, the project to remake the institutions of the Iraqi state has consistently fallen short of expectations, and the US has faced severe difficulties in its efforts to exert control and influence, both during the period of formal military occupation up to June 2004 and beyond. The purpose of this study is to describe and explain the US state-building project in Iraq and its legacy in the context of local, regional and global politics.

We conceptualise state building as the deliberate attempt to establish a centralised organisation in a territory, able to predominate in terms of political authority, coercive ability and control of financial capital. Clearly, the US has been the most powerful single actor in Iraq, and hence it has directed the process of attempted state building. This is not to say that the US has been able to impose its preferences — it has often failed to do so. Indeed, the drastic changes in direction in its approach to state building indicate how it has been baulked repeatedly in its attempts to determine that process. Moreover, the attempts by the US to retain control over the process in the face of multiple challenges have themselves been primary factors shaping the contours of post-invasion Iraq.

1

The central arguments of this study are that political authority in Iraq has fragmented along many axes — not just along Kurdish, Sunni Arab and Shi'a lines — and that the characteristics of the US state-building project have contributed significantly to that fragmentation. The US sought not simply to build a state, but to build a particular kind of state in a particular way, and to defeat armed opposition to that project more by force than by winning the battle of legitimation. The fragmentation of political authority in Iraq is not necessarily irreversible, but the project of 'reconstructing' Iraq has faced a series of major obstacles to the formation of a coherent state. For state building to succeed, the legacy of fragmentation must be addressed.

The US and the Coalition of states it has led have been consistent in declaring their commitment to the creation of a strong sovereign and democratic Iraqi state. Policies and actions which have not contributed to those ends have tended to be characterised as evidence of mistakes made in pursuit of that goal. However, conceptualising state building in Iraq since the invasion simply as the unfolding — or unravelling — of a project to establish such a state does not help very much in providing a framework with which to identify, categorise and explain the content of the US project in practice, or the nature of the state that is being formed. In this study we explore the concentration and fragmentation of political authority in national level politics, centre-periphery relations, coercion and capital.

Chapter Two argues that political authority in Iraq has fragmented, with the groups and militias that emerged after the US-led invasion throughout southern and central Iraq retaining forms of local power. Attempts by central government to reassert its primacy in political life, through strategies to build legitimacy, have been largely unsuccessful. The Chapter shows this in some detail in relation to provision of water and electricity services and generation of job opportunities. These failures were partly due to the insurgency, but also due to the hollowing out of the national political process by the US in its efforts to retain pre-eminence. The autonomy which had been established in northern Iraq in the wake of the 1991 war continued, excluding the Iraqi state from extensive involvement there. In the rest of the country, two mutually reinforcing trends emerged. The distance between the institutions of the state and Iraqi society encouraged Coalition reliance on strategies of coercion, conducted either by the US or by Coalition-supported Iraqi troops. Additionally, the US sought to retain its central role within the political process by balancing competing Iraqi political forces against each other, thus ensuring that any Iraqi actor aspiring to secure office had to coordinate with the Coalition authorities, which undermined any such actor's potential for nationwide popular legitimacy.

Chapter Three develops further the analysis of the fragmentation of political authority in terms of relations between central and local government. It shows that what has occurred is not a negotiated framework of decentralisation within an integrated state. Instead, a variety of rival local centres of authority has emerged with which the weak central authorities have had to interact and strike temporary deals. Through examples from al-Anbar, Karbala' and Basra, the chapter aims to show how local political leaders have achieved or sustained local power, and have enhanced centrifugal forces within Iraq's politics. Neopatrimonialism — the conduct of essentially private patron-client relations through the institutions of the state — is a feature of many states in the South, and it can have centralising effects in binding the population to state institutions. However, in Iraq it has not served to diminish local non-state power, for three reasons. First, significant sources of wealth and well-being lie outside the mechanisms of the state, and are deployed in patrimonial form, that is, cutting out the state from the formation of patron-client bonds. Second, patrimonialism in Iraq features a major role for external patrons (most notably Iranian ones). Third, Iraqi leaders, to a significant degree, have not required large client bases in order to secure state power: instead they achieved this through demonstrating their usefulness to the occupying powers and doing deals with other political parties. The Chapter demonstrates the interaction of these considerations with the growth in sectarianism within Iraq, particularly from late 2004 onwards.

Chapter Four examines the interaction of these national and local processes with the insurgency and counter-insurgency. The main argument of the chapter is that they have shaped each other in fundamental ways that have reinforced the trend towards political fragmentation. Without an adequate national process which all of the main groups of society see as legitimate, and without an accepted process of mediating national-local and intra-local disputes, the state is likely to face armed challenge. On the other side of the equation, counter-insurgency operations can be a way of containing an armed challenge until it is ultimately undermined by popular endorsement of an increasingly effective and legitimate state. However, the Iraqi insurgents have taken advantage of the flaws and vulnerabilities in the Coalition's state-building project in order to wreck much of it. When the state is ineffective and its legitimacy disputed, the US military has historically and doctrinally engaged in counter-insurgency operations which rely on armed coercion rather than political legitimation. In the centre and south of Iraq it has used force in ways that have alienated the population; it has acted with impunity, has made the population feel threatened by the 'security' forces, and has re-militarised the country in ways that have advantaged insurgents and also militias with little loyalty to the state. This has produced a downward spiral of state-society distance as Arabs (especially but not only Sunnis) have become increasingly alienated and coercion has been used to contain that alienation so that the state does not collapse.

Chapter Five considers how the condition of the Iraqi economy and its rearticulation to the global economy have shaped, and been shaped by, the Coalition's state-building project. In an effective national state-building project, the state is able to raise taxes, provide a regulatory framework for economic activity and services for the population, and represent the interests of that state in regional and global political and economic forums. The argument of this Chapter is that the Iraqi state has been unable to perform these functions because of the combined pressures of the transnational informal economy and insurgency undermining the state's control of the economy from below, and the US-led drive to open up the economy and configure the Iraqi state as an instrument of that process. The network of US-dominated and transnational decision-making institutions is operating, often at arm's length, to make the relevant elements of the Iraqi state integral and willing (rather than reluctantly subordinate) parts of the international state practices of global liberal governance. This process has made substantial if fragile headway even as economic reconstruction has struggled, corruption has flourished and the Bush administration has sought to keep US-based transnational corporations in a dominant position.

Chapter Six considers the legacy of the occupation for the Iraqi state in relation to five themes: the scope of its functions; its institutional capacity to carry out those functions; its autonomy from domestic society and foreign actors; its state identity (that is, adherence to the imaginative construct of an Iraqi state through which collective interests can be furthered); and the coherence or fragmentation of political authority. We thread these themes throughout this study, and in the conclusion elaborate further upon their meanings and the connections between them, both conceptually and in relation to the post-invasion Iraqi state. The state retains a broad range of functions despite the desire of the US to use the period of occupation to narrow that range (for example by privatising industry and eliminating state subsidies for fuel). The state's ability to ensure that the basic needs of the population are met is generally low and patchy. However, its performance in this area has not thus far been as negative (in terms of non-delivery of services or an active threat to the interests of the population through acts of repression or economic exploitation) as in a failed state. Its institutions generally have sufficient capacity for Iraq not to be considered a collapsed state either, with the defining characteristic of a collapsed state being minimal institutional capacity. Indeed, we argue in the conclusion that the institutions of the state have sufficient capacity to make them sites of struggles among a wide range of actors — Iraqi political parties, insurgents, militias, criminals and others — who seek to control them and their resources.

The central argument of Chapter Six and indeed this book is that the Iraqi state has been crippled because these struggles are occurring in the context of a fragmented state, that is, one in which actors dispute where overall political authority lies and there are no agreed procedures for resolving such disputes. As long as this is the case, fundamental limitations in the authority of the state will remain which technocratic mechanisms, such as training schemes for officials, narrow political fixes through elections and referendums, and coercive tools through military force and repression, have not been and will not be able to overcome. Successive post-invasion Iraqi governments have had little incentive to develop domestic constituencies to which they are responsive or to pursue nationwide legitimacy. Instead, they have had their power and survival tied to various non-state Iraqi networks and to various foreign patrons — principally US ones. Iraq's state identity remains a significant force for Iraq's citizenry, Iraqi political actors and the world at large, but it remains to be seen whether Iraq's political fragmentation can be overcome before the very idea of Iraq is extinguished for all practical purposes.

Before considering these themes, we first provide in this Chapter an account of the twists and turns of post-invasion Iraq. The account is broadly chronological while in places highlighting particular issues with the aim of communicating a broad sense of the overall trajectory of post-invasion Iraq in relation to our key themes. In the remainder of this Chapter we argue that the US has not pursued a consistent state-building policy. Instead, it has changed overall direction dramatically twice (rapid handover to an elected leader who was expected to inherit an effective state, then extended US occupation and the transformation of the state, and then short-term handover of some aspects of power to a partially rebuilt and reformed state). It has acted in reaction to developments in Iraq, in response to its own domestic political dynamics, and has tended to sacrifice state building in an attempt to retain control in the short term. We argue that this approach has been central to producing the fragmentation of political authority in post-invasion Iraq.

THE POLITICAL DYNAMICS OF POST-INVASION IRAQ

The vision before the invasion

The US approach to Iraq has its origins in the ascendancy of an alliance of neoconservatives and assertive nationalists in Washington under George W. Bush, elected president in November 2000. Contemporary US neoconservatives are characterised by advocacy of ambitious unilateral military and political intervention by the United States in promoting liberal democracy. Their strong rejection of cultural and moral relativism, and their tendency to portray past US foreign policy failings in terms of acquiescence to these perceived intellectual ills, translate into a morally-infused discourse of politics in which the US stands as a paradigm of the good and virtuous, while the tyrant stands for the forces of evil. As military power is taken as the fundamental determinant of relations between states, the willingness of the US to deploy its armed forces around the world for the sake of liberal democracy becomes, for them, the crucial determinant in world politics. Ivo Daalder and James Lindsay characterise neoconservatives as 'democratic imperialists' on this basis, a term that many of them would not shy away from using.[1] As US power is an exceptional force for good from their perspective, it is crucial to prevent its exercise from being hindered. Hence there are imperatives to avoid entanglement in alliances that would impose such limitations, and to preserve US military pre-eminence against potential challengers.

The neoconservative movement has had a presence in US political debate since the 1960s, with its first wave of exponents including Irving Kristol and Norman Podhoretz. However, its significance in contemporary affairs has come through its relationship with an older school of thought, assertive nationalism, which draws upon classical Realist conceptions of the pursuit of the national interest through the use of military force, and in which deterrence, containment and the balance of power stand as key concepts. Although neoconservatives are fundamentally opposed to these ideas, there is much that they can agree and have agreed with assertive nationalists about, including the importance of unilateral action, the value of military pre-eminence, and the priority of the military sphere over economic and social issues in understanding the configuration of world power. The cooperation that has existed between the two camps flourished under the Reagan administration in the mid-1980s, and it was under the auspices of Vice-President Dick Cheney and Defence Secretary Donald Rumsfeld — the two leading assertive nationalists aligned with the Bush presidential campaign in 2000 — that neoconservatives were either brought into the new administration or taken seriously as political advisers. Thus Paul Wolfowitz became Deputy Secretary of Defence, Douglas Feith was appointed Under Secretary of Defence for Policy, John Bolton served as an Under Secretary at the State Department, and Elliott Abrams acted as Special Adviser to the President. Outside the administration, neoconservatives such as Richard Perle and Eliot Cohen have sat on the Defence Policy Board which advises the Secretary of Defence, and their arguments have been disseminated through institutions such as the American Enterprise Institute and the *Weekly Standard* journal.

The strategic outlook of the neoconservatives in the post-Cold War world was first articulated in a draft 1992 Defence Planning Guidance paper, written under the stewardship of Paul Wolfowitz but actually drafted by Zalmay Khalilzad, who later served as US Ambassador to Iraq from June 2005.[2] Its basic argument was that the US was now in a position to secure its pre-eminence and use force unilaterally if necessary to prevent the rise of any power that might challenge that pre-eminence. Political uproar occurred when it was leaked to the press because it ran counter to the political optimism about the end of the Cold War and a financial 'peace dividend', included Western Europe and Southwest Asia as potential source of threats, and raised fears about what the US would do with that pre-eminence. Cheney, then Secretary of Defence, asked for it to be modified so that its focus would be altered, although the original ideas remained intact. The same themes were brought out in much the same form ten years later in the September 2002 *US National Security Strategy*, in this case drafted by Condoleezza Rice, then serving as National Security Adviser.[3] Rice was widely seen as an assertive nationalist rather than a neoconservative, and the extent to which ideas originally formulated by Wolfowitz could be re-presented under Cheney's auspices and later re-worked by Rice demonstrates the extent of strategic convergence between the policy camps.

Opposition to Saddam Hussein's rule over Iraq had become one of the chief focal points of the neoconservative movement over the course of the mid-1990s. For them, it represented the worst features of tyranny, not only in relation to the population resident under it, but also in the destabilising effects it was perceived to have externally. Iraq under the Ba'th Party was believed to constitute a long-term threat both to US dominance in the Gulf area and to Israel, prized as the model democracy in an undemocratic region, and thus the regime's removal was a priority issue.[4] In this call they were joined by many from the assertive nationalist camp, who believed in the importance of military dominance of the Gulf region for US interests. Through a series of articles and statements, neoconservative and assertive nationalist leaders placed relations with the Iraqi regime as one of the touchstone issues in US foreign policy.

Perhaps the best known such pronouncement was from the Project for the New American Century (PNAC), established in 1997. Its founding statement of principles was signed by twenty-five prominent leaders including Cheney, Rumsfeld, Abrams, Cohen, Wolfowitz and Khalilzad. In a report entitled *Rebuilding America's Defenses,* published in September 2000, the PNAC emphasised the centrality to US strategic interests of developing US military bases in the Middle East regardless of any dispute with Iraq or Iran:

[T]he US has for decades sought to play a more permanent role in Gulf regional security. While the unresolved conflict with Iraq provides the immediate justification, the need for a substantial American force presence in the Gulf transcends the issue of the regime of Saddam Hussein. … [E]ven should U.S.-Iranian relations improve, retaining forward-based forces in the region would still be an essential element in U.S. security strategy given the longstanding American interests in the region.[5]

Bill Clinton's policy since taking the presidential office in January 1993 had been to use sanctions and bombing to contain the Iraqi regime. However, pressure from assertive nationalists and neoconservatives mounted a strong challenge to this policy, culminating in the Republican-controlled Congress manoeuvring Clinton into signing the 1998 Iraq Liberation Act. This stated that: 'It should be the policy of the US to support efforts to remove the regime headed by Saddam Hussein from power in Iraq and to promote the emergence of a democratic government to replace that regime.'[6] This was to be achieved by providing weapons, military training and other assistance to designated opposition groups.

However, neither policy camp had developed the conceptual resources to focus on the question of what would come after the rule of Saddam Hussein. For neoconservatives, democracy was a universal good, and would be embraced by the Iraqi people. Michael Ledeen, a neoconservative commentator, wrote, 'If we come to Baghdad, Damascus and Tehran as liberators, we can expect overwhelming popular support.'[7] Although Ledeen has never held office, his views seem to have been shared by administration officials, and dovetailed with the famous criticism of Republican nationalists that the Clinton administration had wasted US money and energies by engaging in 'nation-building' across the world, a task which could instead be left to the local people themselves.

In September 2002, Cheney told the US Veterans of Foreign Wars in Nashville that:

Regime change in Iraq would bring about a number of benefits to the region. When the gravest of threats are eliminated, the freedom-loving peoples of the region will have a chance to promote the values that can bring lasting peace. As for the reaction of the Arab "street," the Middle East expert Professor Fouad Ajami predicts that after liberation, the streets in Basra and Baghdad are "sure to erupt in joy in the same way the throngs in Kabul greeted the Americans."[8]

He emphasised that, for these reasons, this was a period of opportunity as much as threat. This had much in common with the neoconservatives' line, but it did not incorporate their advocacy of actively promoting liberal democratic revolutions in Middle Eastern states other than Iraq. In his January 2002 State of the Union address, Bush declared that states such as Iran, Iraq and North Korea and their 'terrorist allies' constituted an 'axis of evil'.[9] He maintained that urgent action was needed to prevent them from acquiring weapons of mass destruction, but he also repeated the themes of opportunity and universal desire for freedom.

In the run-up to the invasion, the State Department led a large-scale 'Future of Iraq' project involving Iraqi exiles and many US government agencies (including the Department of Defence) to develop wide-ranging plans for state building.[10] Meanwhile, Feith established a rival Office of Special Plans within the Pentagon which also considered post-invasion planning, effectively supplanting the Future of Iraq project. This move mixed ideological hostility to anything coming from the State

Department with straightforward bureaucratic rivalry. On 20 January 2003 the White House came down on the Pentagon's side, and handed over to it responsibilities for Iraq after the invasion.[11] The Pentagon put a high degree of trust in the assurances of supportive exiled groups that they could act to bond a grateful populace to a benevolent occupier, and thus could act as leaders of a post-invasion government. In the words of one senior Coalition civilian official, the US political strategy at this stage 'relied upon two things: exiles and optimism'.[12]

The plan adopted by the administration was that the leaders of a group of six exiled and Kurdish groups that had allied with the Defence Department were to be installed as the leaders of a post-invasion government, which came to be called the Iraqi Interim Authority (IIA). The IIA would draft a new constitution and arrange elections for a new government, which would assume sovereign functions.[13] The democratic transition and the handover of power were thus envisaged as occurring simultaneously, and quickly. Defence Secretary Donald Rumsfeld, backed by Deputy Secretary of Defence Paul Wolfowitz and Secretary of State Colin Powell, put a timeframe for organising elections for the government in terms of months.[14] Ahmad Chalabi of the Iraqi National Congress (INC) was generally seen as the principal actor in this project.[15] In exile since 1958, Chalabi had been found guilty in Jordan of embezzlement after the collapse of the private bank he headed: his parallel banks in Lebanon and Switzerland were also closed down by the authorities.[16] His claims that the Ba'th regime had weapons of mass destruction, that US forces would be welcomed as liberators, and that he would be able to provide security and order after the invasion were taken as plausible by Defence officials who favoured an invasion.[17] They could also point out that he was a secular Shi'a and therefore, they assumed, capable of ensuring that the outcome of Iraq's Shi'a majority having the vote would not be a theocratic state. They did not think that US forces would be required to fight any kind of significant ongoing armed opposition, and expected that all of the costs of the invasion and reconstruction would be repaid from Iraq's oil revenues.[18]

As the administration's position was that a detailed project of state building was unnecessary in this case, the Office of Reconstruction and Humanitarian Assistance (ORHA), established within the Department of Defence under the directorship of Lt-Gen. Jay Garner to deal with civil affairs, was given a narrow mandate. Its focus was on dealing with the prospect of humanitarian crises that might arise from the invasion, such as population displacement, and with immediate reconstruction needs. It was not a mechanism of rule or an integrated administrative apparatus to manage a complex society, but a short-term holding operation until the IIA and its technocratic partner, the Iraqi Reconstruction and Development Council (IRDC), could take over. Soon after the invasion, the Bush administration realised that it could not escape the task of governing the country it had captured.

May 2003: Extended occupation to transform Iraq

The Iraqi armed forces collapsed quickly in the face of the invasion by a US-led Coalition which began on 20 March 2003. Saddam Hussein fled into hiding, Baghdad fell on 9 April and Bush declared major combat operations to be over on 1 May. The US military began planning for a staged reduction in US forces to as few as 30,000 troops by September 2003.[19] Nevertheless, developments in the politics of the occupation resulted in approaches that were difficult to reconcile with the goal of a speedy handover. In general, the Coalition was in a position of considerable political vulnerability within Iraq, given its status as a foreign occupying power. If a national political challenger to it were to emerge and win popular legitimacy, the Coalition's ability to maintain control would be highly limited. Thus a considerable part of the Coalition's work within Iraq was to prevent the emergence of such a challenger, whilst retaining an approach that was seen to favour political progress, and so undercut any arguments from Iraqis for achieving national self-determination through adopting an antagonistic or uncooperative stance.

These concerns were apparent in the process that led to the collapse by May 2003 of plans for the rapid transition from the ORHA to an elected Iraqi authority, via the IIA. Firstly, the unanticipated collapse of Iraq's public infrastructure and its urban security led to low levels of legitimacy for the Coalition administration. Ministry buildings in Baghdad were ransacked or destroyed by looters and by those seeking to make the administration of Iraq by the Coalition more difficult, leaving 17 of the 23 ministries unusable.[20] The ORHA itself was not designed to cope with this: it had, according to the senior British representative in Baghdad, 'no leadership, no strategy, no coordination, no structure, and [was] inaccessible to ordinary Iraqis'.[21] Political parties, tribal groupings and local militias forcibly installed or ejected mayors throughout southern and central Iraq, taking control of state buildings and finances in the process. Thus the militia of al-Da'wa al-Islamiyya (the Islamic Call), the historic vehicle of Shi'a radicalism, captured Nasiriyya, whilst the Supreme Council for the Islamic Revolution in Iraq (SCIRI), the more closely Iranian-aligned organisation, took possession of Ba'qubah and Majar al-Kabir through its militia. Other groupings — some specific to one town — also engaged in attempts to commandeer the local institutions of authority. The result was a set of turf wars. These began on 17 April 2003, when followers of Muqtada al-Sadr, son of the revered Ayatollah Muhammad Sadiq al-Sadr who was murdered in 1999, drove the Badr Brigades out of the poverty-stricken eastern suburb of Baghdad then known as Saddam City, to rename it Sadr City. Within days, the armed personnel of this movement had established strongholds in Kufa, Najaf and the Shi'a quarter of Samarra'. With the dissolution of the Iraqi army and the *de facto* (though unofficial) disbanding of police forces, the few remaining state officials who showed up for work were unable to retain any measure of control in the weeks that followed the invasion, whilst the Iraqi social order reconstituted itself in highly diverse forms in the south and centre of the country.

Secondly, after an unproductive set of meetings between US and UK officials and representatives of Iraqi parties in April 2003, it quickly became clear to many within the Coalition that these groups did not have the reach into Iraqi society that they had claimed previously. As the British representative at the conference in Nasiriyya on 15 April 2003, the first such gathering of Iraqi political parties after the invasion, later recounted, there was a 'sharp divide between exiles and survivors' at this event, with the latter group refusing to 'allow [their] future to be dictated by the exiles who had escaped to a life of relative ease outside Iraq and who, in their view, had lost touch with the people whose interests they claimed to represent.'[22] Furthermore, it became clear that there was little prospect of even the previously exiled opposition groups themselves cohering into a single force that would take its lead from the Coalition. Thus there was no single institution that could act as both a legitimator of and a successor to the Coalition.

Thirdly, the development of indigenous Iraqi political forces which took a more suspicious attitude towards the Coalition became apparent. Most notably, Sadr's movement, arising out of the slums east of Baghdad to take effective control over two million perceived malcontents, was a force of unpredictable vigour and prospects: US planners had not even been aware of its existence prior to the invasion. The risk that new political movements that the Coalition might not be able to coopt could make a bid for power at the national level was sharply felt.

Amidst these developments, the Bush administration concluded that there could be no speedy handover. Instead, it opted to engage in the direct and protracted governance of Iraq to transform its polity and economy. The ORHA was dissolved and replaced by the Coalition Provisional Authority (CPA), established in May 2003, whose administrator was L. Paul Bremer.[23] In contrast to the narrow focus of the ORHA, the CPA drew upon personnel with more of the expertise required for the overhaul of the full range of Iraqi ministries. 'CPA ministries' were run by senior advisers — in effect, ministers — from the Coalition and were based inside the CPA headquarters. These institutions were organisationally and geographically separate from the 'Iraqi ministries', which played a shadowing role to the CPA ministries until powers were turned over to them in stages during the first half of 2004.

With regard to Iraqi personnel, the prospect of an IIA was replaced with a proposal for an 'advisory council', subsequently strengthened after intense criticism from the Iraqi parties to become a 25-person Iraqi Governing Council (IGC), inaugurated on 13 July 2003.[24] Its membership was dominated by those who had spent the years preceding the invasion outside the rule of Baghdad, either in exile or in the Kurdish Autonomous Region (KAR).[25] Its six leading figures were two from Shi'a Islamist parties, two from secular post-1990 US allies, and two Kurdish leaders.

The two leaders of Shi'a-based parties were Ibrahim al-Ja'fari and 'Abd al-'Aziz al-Hakim. Ja'fari was leader of al-Da'wa, which was founded in the aftermath of the 1958 coup against the British-installed monarchy. It has been the bastion of Shi'a Islamism in the fight against secularism. Basing itself in Iran after the 1979 Iranian revolution, it tried to maintain some political distance from Tehran, only to splinter, with Ja'fari leading its London-based faction. Hakim meanwhile was second in command of SCIRI, and took over as its head when his predecessor and brother, Muhammad Baqr al-Hakim, was killed in the Najaf bombing of 29 August 2003. SCIRI was established in 1982 under Iranian auspices, originally to act as the provisional government of Basra in the event of that city being captured by Iranian troops during the Iran-Iraq war (1980-88). It has a substantial armed wing called the Badr Brigades (renamed the Badr Organisation in 2003).

Ahmad Chalabi of the INC and Iyad 'Allawi of the Iraqi National Accord (INA) had been closer to the US during the 1990s than the Shi'a parties, and had coordinated with it extensively. The INC was set up in 1992 as an umbrella organisation of all of the anti-Saddam opposition, with varying degrees of participation. Based in London and funded by the US, it was backed by the Pentagon but distrusted by the State Department, the Central Intelligence Agency (CIA) and the British Foreign Office, with relations deteriorating markedly after its plan for a coup in 1995 fell apart. In May 2004, the US cut off its $340,000 per month funding for the INC and raided its offices amidst allegations of corruption and supplying intelligence to Iran. The INA, composed mainly of former Iraqi Ba'thists and military officers, was the group partly created by the CIA in 1992, and favoured by the State Department. For some in Iraq, 'Allawi has been tainted by his past membership of the Ba'th party, his CIA links or both.

The leaders of the two dominant Kurdish parties were Mas'ud Barzani, leader of the Kurdistan Democratic Party (KDP); and Jalal Talabani, leader of the Patriotic Union of Kurdistan (PUK). Barzani and Talabani, both secular Sunni Kurds, had been able to operate in the north outside Baghdad's control during the 1990s, where they had built up stable bases of support and institutions, and both had large Peshmerga militia forces at their disposal.

The use of these party leaders and the indefinite postponement of national elections indicated that the US was attempting to bolster the positions of leaders whose standing among most Iraqis was weak, as part of a wider process of transforming Iraq. This process also involved a programme of mass de-Ba'thification — that is, sacking all senior public sector officials who had been Ba'th Party members (regardless of their status within the Party) as well as all senior Ba'th Party members in the public sector — and the announcement of a programme of US corporate-led privatisation and marketisation. The army was disbanded in order to eliminate it as a possible challenger, though some within the Coalition insisted that it had already effectively collapsed. Furthermore, the armed opposition was to be crushed by force, and it was assumed that all the various social forces — the political parties, the unemployed, the Kurds, Sunni Arabs, Shiʻa and others — could be marginalised or co-opted while the transformation occurred.

Developments were indeed fairly though not completely peaceful in the mainly Kurdish north of Iraq, as the *de facto* self-government which was established in 1992 continued. There was also relative calm in the south of Iraq, where Shiʻa Arab political forces were confident that they would soon attain a dominant political position in the new Iraq, because of their numerical superiority, following the anticipated rapid departure of most Coalition forces. Nevertheless, expectations of an easy victory for US forces were undermined quickly by a steady stream of attacks on Coalition forces, especially from June 2003 onwards. Twenty days of war during the invasion cost the lives of 138 US troops, while deaths of US forces in hostile and non-hostile incidents each averaged twenty per month in the first few months of the occupation, although the number of wounded increased steadily.[26] The military in Iraq, now anticipating its large-scale presence for the coming years, also reorganised itself in mid-June 2003: the Coalition Joint Task Force 7 (CJTF-7) was created, which reported to US Central Command (CENTCOM), led by Gen. Tommy Franks until July 2003 and thereafter by Gen. John Abizaid. CJTF-7 was led throughout its existence by Lt-Gen. Ricardo Sanchez, and it had operational control of all forces within Iraq, including forces from the UK, Italy, Poland, Spain (until April 2004) and South Korea.

Abizaid, at his first press conference after taking charge of CENT-COM, expressed the view that the insurgents were fighting 'a classical guerrilla-type campaign', but had not yet deduced that there needed to be a shift in strategy from simply mopping up residual fighters.[27] Although Coalition officials spoke of the area of attacks as 'the Sunni triangle', consisting of the territory from Baghdad west to Ramadi and north-west to Saddam Hussein's home town of Tikrit, the actual arena of regular violence was broader. It stretched across the governorate of al-Anbar up to and across the Syrian border; as far north as Mosul in the north-western governorate of Ninawa; into the city of Kirkuk in al-Ta'mim governorate; east into the governorate of Diyala (most notably in the city of Ba'qubah); and south into the governorate of Babil (mainly in the city of Hilla).

All the political elements of the transformation programme soon ran into trouble: there had to be some reversal of de-Ba'thification and the dissolution of the army in order to try to rebuild the state, privatisation and marketisation had to proceed much more slowly because of opposition within and outside Iraq and sheer problems of practicality, and many of Iraq's social forces, most notably leaders of the Shi'a majority, became increasingly agitated about the slow pace of the schedule for ending the occupation. Grand Ayatollah 'Ali al-Sistani, Iraq's most influential cleric, refused to meet Bremer, at least partly in order not be tainted by association with the occupation. Nevertheless, despite his avowed quietism — that is, his preference not to promote direct clerical rule — he has shown repeatedly that he can and will make major political interventions. He objected in June 2003 to the proposed multi-year occupation plan, with elections deferred far into the future, as 'fundamentally unacceptable'.[28] The Coalition was acutely aware that it could not survive widespread armed opposition by the Shi'i, who are usually estimated to make up about 60% of the Iraqi population. The Shi'i had been marginalised in Iraqi official political life, ever since the creation of the modern State in 1921 under the British mandate, in favour of members of the Sunni Arab minority, a situation reinforced by Saddam Hussein, who distrusted and persecuted the Shi'i and the (mainly Sunni) Kurds.

Between May and July 2003, no mass casualty car bombings or suicide bombings were recorded.[29] However, the tactics of some insurgents changed to what became a clear pattern in August, when suicide bombs destroyed the Jordanian Embassy in Baghdad and then another destroyed the UN headquarters in Baghdad, killing UN envoy Sergio Vieira de Mello and 21 others.[30] A little over a week later, SCIRI's leader Muhammad Baqir al-Hakim was killed along with dozens of others by a series of huge car bombs which exploded in Najaf. The general picture was one of a steady stream of attacks which showed no sign of abating, and with a new trend towards targeting of Iraqis and international personnel working with the Coalition. As a result, the number of US forces in Iraq, which had peaked at 148,000 in May and June 2003, could only be drawn down only slowly (and temporarily), and remained at around 85% of all foreign Coalition forces in Iraq.[31]

November 2003: accelerated handover and counter-insurgency

In September 2003, insurgents began a campaign of attacking all international governmental and non-governmental organisations and contractors and any Iraqis working with them and the CPA. Such attacks were very effective in forcing the withdrawal of international personnel from the country and forcing Coalition officials to stay within heavily fortified bases most of the time. In response to the problems it faced, the US switched abruptly in November 2003 to aiming for what became labelled an 'accelerated handover' to a new state. It also adopted a new counter-insurgency strategy which involved a major escalation of its use of force. On 12 November 2003, the US military launched Operation Iron Hammer in the Baghdad area, followed on 16 November 2003 with Operation Ivy Cyclone II using aircraft, tanks and artillery in and around Tikrit, Ba'qubah, Kirkuk and Balad.[32]

After Saddam Hussein was captured on 13 December 2003 near Tikrit, there was increased optimism in the Coalition.[33] An upbeat assessment by US Major William McCallister was being circulated within the CPA in January 2004. It declared that the Coalition's improved 'situational awareness' and intelligence, plus its superior firepower being applied through an increasing number of smaller scale attacks, were undermining the advantage which accrued to the insurgents from operating within a decentralised network.[34] McCallister asserted confidently that the population would gradually accept that their hardships were being caused by the insurgents and hence 'loss of public support for continued violence is inevitable' and the insurgency would 'wither'.[35] This analysis however neglected the impact of the US's heavy-handed use of violence and its high-handed attitude to public sentiment about the Coalition in central and southern Iraq.[36] In this sense, the Coalition was still losing ground to its opponents. In order to stand still, it was going to have to run faster, but the actions it took raised the question of whether it was running in the right direction.

The political track laid out by the US in November 2003 was that the IGC would propose a Fundamental Law — a provisional constitution — by 28 February 2004, which would require the approval of the CPA. This would be followed by a highly complex four-stage process. Firstly, the CPA, the IGC and municipal and city councils would each choose delegates to a committee for each of Iraq's 18 governorates. Secondly, those committees would select people for a system of caucuses, which would then, thirdly, select representatives to an Iraqi Transitional National Assembly (TNA) by 31 May 2004. Finally, this would select an Iraqi Transitional Government (ITG) which would 'assume full sovereignty' by 30 June 2004. At this point the occupation was to be deemed to have ended. This would give Bush the opportunity to claim in the campaign leading up to the presidential election in November 2004 that he had achieved his fundamental goal in Iraq. The next step was to be direct national election of delegates to a Constitutional Convention by 15 March 2005; the Convention would write a constitution to be approved in a national referendum. Following the referendum, and assuming that the new constitution was approved, national elections would be held for a new government to replace the ITG by 31 December 2005.[37]

The accelerated handover plan ran into serious trouble, partly for not being accelerated enough. Most importantly, Sistani demanded that direct elections should take place for the TNA, and before the drafting of a Fundamental Law. This would entail elections in mid-

2004 or sooner, at least a year and a half earlier than envisaged by the CPA.[38] The CPA argued that an election could not take place that quickly because it would need a national census which itself would take a long time because of security and fraud problems. Sistani's followers countered by arguing that voting based on ID cards, ration cards or a rough and ready census would be sufficient, but agreed to allow a UN mission led by Lakhdar Brahimi to determine whether this was a legitimate or practical mechanism. When that mission decided that elections held without a prior census would not be appropriate or workable, Sistani relented.[39] This was ironic as the national elections, when finally held in January 2005, were conducted on the basis of an electoral roll devised without a census and on the basis of the ration card system.

The CPA and IGC then proceeded to institute a Transitional Administrative Law (TAL) on 8 March 2004,[40] containing much the same process as laid out in the 15 November text, but replacing the complex system of caucuses that had been criticised by Sistani with a two-stage process: an Iraqi Interim Government (IIG) would be appointed to take over by 30 June 2004, and national elections to the TNA would take place in January 2005. The role of the elected TNA would then be to write the constitution. In the meantime, crucial political processes were also under way in the mainly Kurdish part of Iraq, and were deeply affected by the faltering national level processes.

Potentially explosive problems in the north

Kurdish political leaders had secured guarantees of federal government in the TAL, but their political goals concerned most crucially the areas that would come within the separate Kurdish region. They had long laid claim to the oil rich areas of Mosul and especially Kirkuk as parts of Kurdistan, against the objections of everyone else, including the Sunni Arabs, Turkmen and Assyrians. Escalation to large-scale violence between Kurds on the one hand and Turkmen and Arabs on the other in Kirkuk had been made more likely by the lack of a coherent and authoritative national level political process to address the issues in dispute. Around 750,000 people live in the city of Kirkuk, making it Iraq's fourth largest city, behind Baghdad, Basra and Mosul. Figures on its ethno-sectarian composition are rough estimates and vary widely, especially given the degree of migration and displacement. In October 2005 between one third and something over one half the city's residents were Kurdish, with the remainder equally divided between Arabs and Turkmen, plus a small number of Assyrian Christians. Turkey perceives itself as having a strong ethnic affinity with Turkmen and as being the guardian of Turkmen rights in northern Iraq. Many of the city's Arabs, largely Shi'a transported from the South, had moved to the northern region under the Arabisation policy of the central government, especially from the early 1970s onwards, a policy that also involved the forcible removal of 250,000 Kurds from Kirkuk.[41] The governorate produces around half of Iraq's oil, and so control over its future has been highly significant. As the *ancien régime* collapsed, many Arabs fled south as the KDP and PUK militias advanced with US special forces' support, fearing Kurdish revenge.

The CPA did little to address the legacy of Arabisation, in the belief that any decisions taken would be divisive and would involve a major commitment of its already highly inadequate resources. Immediately after the invasion, the US established a property dispute mechanism known as the Iraqi Property Reconciliation Facility (IPRF), contracted to the International Organisation of Migration (IOM). When attacks on IOM offices and staff began in July 2003, it curtailed its work drastically. Furthermore, the IOM was only charged with developing technical procedures when the heart of the issue was the principles which the technical procedures were meant to serve.[42] The IPRF was then replaced with the Iraq Property Claims Commission in January 2004. Although its offices opened to receive claims in June 2004, its funding was not made a priority and all issues of principle were deferred until after the taking of a new census, which did not occur.[43] The CPA only put larger-scale funds into non-contentious projects: in June 2004, Bremer authorised the spending of $100 million on the non-profit private Kirkuk Foundation to involve local leaders in intercommunal socio-economic projects.[44] The TAL in article 58 decided that a decision on the final status of Kirkuk should be deferred until the issues of the return of displaced Kurds and the resettlement of Arabs settled under the Arabisation programme were dealt with, a census taken and a permanent constitution agreed.

In the absence of authoritative decisions, some violence occurred but without large-scale clashes.[45] US forces ran Kirkuk in conjunction with PUK civil defence and police units and US local commanders, sometimes with the involvement of local officials. They made *ad hoc* property dispute resolution efforts, managed to prevent some evictions, and secured an effective agreement for a 50-50 sharing of the harvest.[46] Owing to poverty, the withholding of humanitarian assistance by the Coalition and limited encouragement by the KDP and PUK, the rate of spontaneous returns to Kirkuk by Kurds and Turkmen was low, which also helped to prevent tension from escalating.[47]

By 2005, the Kurdish parties were systematically planning and funding their own unilateral programme of Kurdish settlement in Kirkuk with villages mapped house by house using Google Earth. They argued that they had no choice because the Transitional Government had failed to carry out its responsibilities to promote return and resettlement.[48] The new constitution approved by nationwide referendum in October 2005 endorsed the provisions of the TAL, with return, resettlement and a census ahead of a referendum on the future of Kirkuk no later than the end of 2007. It also approved the principle of sharing of oil revenues between regions and the centre, which meant that incorporation of Kirkuk into a Kurdish federation in Iraq alongside Dahuk, Irbil and Sulaymaniyya would be hugely important.[49] The KDP and PUK expressed concern that the votes of Arabisation-programme Arab settlers and Turkmen would be sufficient to prevent this.[50] For their part, some Turkmen and Arabs alleged that vast numbers of Kurds who were not displaced by Arabisation were being sent to Kirkuk to shift the population balance and hence the voting balance, and that the Kurds took a role in inciting US attacks on the city of Tal Afar to cause its Turkmen population to flee.[51] They feared that a federation would be the prelude to a push for an independent Kurdistan, and even if that did not happen they largely opposed the prospect of living in a Kurdish-dominated federation.

Violence in Mosul, which — unlike Kirkuk — had an Arab majority, was only sporadic until the US assault on Falluja in November 2004, at which point the largely Sunni Arab police force of the city either resigned or joined the insurgents. Kurdish Peshmerga guerrilla forces were subsequently deployed to recapture the town.[52] Since then, violence has become more widespread in Mosul with insurgents and police on one side lined up against US forces, Iraqi army units and Kurds on the other. This pattern was repeated in many places across central and northern Iraq after Falluja, and the potential for catastrophic escalation in both Kirkuk and Mosul has been very high.

Within the KAR itself, the situation has been very different from the rest of country, with significant implications for state building in Iraq. North-eastern Iraq had been autonomous since the Gulf War of 1991. The Kurdistan Regional Government (KRG), created after elections held the following year, administered an area corresponding broadly to the governorates of Dahuk, Irbil and Sulaymaniyya, and also including parts of the governorates of Ninawa, al-Ta'mim, Salah al-Din and Diyala, but excluding both Mosul and Kirkuk. It has also been divided between the KDP based in Irbil and the PUK based in Sulaymaniyya, both broadly secular parties, with the PUK having an historical leftist stance. These two main parties and their smaller allies were unable to share power and engaged in armed conflict with each other intermittently through much of the 1990s. In 1996, the KDP even invited intervention by Iraqi government forces into Irbil to push the PUK out of the city, while the PUK allied with Iran against the KDP.

In 2005 the two rival parties were finally able to cooperate sufficiently well to reopen the Kurdish regional parliament, but they continued to run separate regional governments as they were unable to agree on a joint cabinet or the duration of its period of service before the holding of parliamentary elections.[53] The division was symbolised by the fact that the KDP local authorities in Irbil refused to allow Asia Cell, a mobile phone company based in Sulaymaniyya, to operate phone masts locally, and instead favoured Irbil-based Korek Telecom Ltd which is chaired by Sirwan Mustafa, a nephew of Barzani.[54] As a result, mobile phones which work in PUK-controlled Sulaymaniyya do not work in the KDP-controlled governorates of Irbil and Dahuk, and vice versa. Nevertheless, since the invasion the two parties have generally managed to put on a broadly united front in the pursuit of as much autonomy, territory and resources as they can secure for their region. In January 2006 they formally announced the unification of their government, with the process of merging institutions scheduled to take place over a period of 18 months, but it remains to be seen whether they will manage to make it function.[55]

Spring 2004: offensives against Sadr and in Falluja

While tensions simmered in the north, the US initiated two major escalations in its use of force in the spring of 2004, just before the broadcasting of photographs and video footage of torture and abuse of Iraqi detainees by US military personnel at the Abu Ghraib prison near Baghdad produced a worldwide storm of negative publicity. Over the month of April, US forces suffered over 120 combat dead and over 800 wounded. Although the number of US combat deaths fell back to around 60 in May, the number of wounded reached its highest ever level of 1,014.[56] The first offensive began in late March, when the US forces decided to take on Sadr and his militia, now named the Mahdi Army. Sadr had built up a stronghold of support in Sadr City, which the Coalition instead came to call al-Thawra (Revolution) district, reverting in part to its pre-1982 name (itself, ironically, an anti-imperialist slogan). From the outset, Sadr had called for an immediate end to the occupation. A parallel movement, al-Fadila (Virtue), was created by Shaykh Muhammad Ya'qubi in July 2003, also laying claim to the heritage of Ayatollah Muhammad Sadiq al-Sadr and espousing a campaign to reject the US military occupation. In July 2003 Sadr formally announced the existence of his Mahdi Army militia, and during that summer he sought, unsuccessfully, to wrest control of the shrine of Imam Husayn from Sistani, which would have given him access to major revenue as well as a powerful political base. In March 2004 Bremer revealed the existence of a warrant for the arrest of Sadr, his chief aide Mustafa al-Ya'qubi, and ten others for alleged involvement in the killing of 'Abd al-Majid al-Khu'i, head of the London-based al-Khu'i Foundation that had hosted meetings of the anti-Ba'thist opposition before the invasion; al-Khu'i had been killed on his return to Najaf in April 2003. On 28 March 2004, Bremer ordered Sadr's newspaper *al-Hawza* to shut down for sixty days for allegedly inciting anti-Coalition violence. Coalition forces began arresting Sadr's deputies and launching attacks on his offices.

Sadr responded by relocating next to the Imam 'Ali Shrine, one of the most holy Shi'a sites, in Najaf. The Mahdi Army and other Shi'a militias further asserted their control of Najaf and nearby Kufa, Karbala', Kut and Sadr City, and launched attacks in Basra. The US declared its intention to regain control of all of these places and Sanchez, acting on orders from Washington, declared: 'The mission of the U.S. forces is to kill or capture Muqtada al-Sadr'.[57] Nevertheless, the potential political explosion which could have resulted from a large-scale assault on the shrine cities of Najaf and Karbala' restrained the US forces. They engaged in lesser attacks which killed around 30 people at a time in various locations and caused significant damage to mosques. The US military command in Iraq, wary of Washington's command to kill or capture Muqtada, unofficially retracted that order within days of the wider combat beginning, and shortly afterwards officially retracted the warrant for his arrest.[58] In Karbala', Islamic militias, including the rival Badr organisation of SCIRI as well as the Mahdi Army, handed back 'control' of police stations only after the police reassured them that they supported the militias. Although Polish and Bulgarian troops were formally in charge, in reality they controlled nothing. The militias demanded the release of detainees, the departure of occupation forces from the city, and Iraqi-supervised city council elections.[59] Much of the US-Sadr combat revolved around taking and retaking buildings such as police stations. In the end the Sadr movement took heavy casualties and retreated to strongholds such as Sadr City where not even the *ancien régime*'s repressive apparatus had been able to crush them, and where they regrouped and rearmed and also recruited new members.[60]

In a deal brokered at the end of May 2004 by a group of Iraqi politicians calling themselves the Shi'a House, Sadr agreed to withdraw his forces from Najaf and in return the US agreed to end 'offensive operations' in Najaf and only patrol until local Iraqi forces could resume their duties. Neither side implemented the agreement fully.[61] By early June, US forces had killed more than 800 Iraqis in Sadr City alone in the space of nine weeks in their efforts to undermine the Mahdi Army.[62] The move against Sadr cannot be explained by intolerance of militias as such, as the Coalition was working with most of the other militias, some of which were run by members of the IGC. Officially, the US decided to try to crush Sadr because of his movement's growing political and armed opposition to the Coalition.[63] The decision may have been influenced by *al-Hawza*'s prominent coverage of Israel's assassination in Gaza of Shaykh Ahmad Yasin, the leader of the Islamist group Hamas, and Sadr's statement that he would act as the 'right arm' of Hamas in Iraq.[64] Its rationale was that it had become riskier to ignore Sadr than it was to take him on, but this view was based upon an assessment of the movement's abilities and level of organisation that turned out to be a grave underestimate. In late 2003 and early 2004, the Coalition had estimated that the Mahdi Army consisted of no more than 3,000 personnel, and that it could be forcibly disbanded if need be.[65] From April 2004, the Coalition concluded that this was a more substantial political force that it hoped to undermine or tame gradually.

Whilst the conflict between Coalition forces and the Sadr movement was beginning, a parallel conflict was taking place. The escalation in Falluja was not part of an overall strategic plan, either for dealing with the insurgency in mainly Sunni Arab areas as a whole or for dealing with them in combination with the Sadr movement. Instead, it was a locally-focused reaction to an event which took place on 31 March 2004: four US private security employees from the US firm Blackwater (which provided bodyguards for CPA Administrator Bremer) were killed and dismembered in front of TV cameras in Falluja. In the frantic internal consultations which resulted, the US Marines and the CPA wanted a slow, careful approach, but Bremer, Rumsfeld, Bush and Abizaid insisted that the city be taken, and taken immediately.[66] The following day Mark Kimmitt, Deputy Director for Coalition Operations in Iraq, announced that the Coalition would take 'methodical', 'deliberate', 'precise' and 'overwhelming' action with the aim of 'pacifying' Falluja and killing or capturing those who had killed and dismembered the mercenaries.[67] He asserted that Falluja would be 'pacified', as the 'hotspots' of Samarra', Tikrit and Ba'qubah had supposedly been (but had not been) already.[68] The US presented the retaking of Falluja as necessary action supported by most Iraqis to deal with 'fanatics', 'extremists' and 'terrorists' who were seeking to prevent the democratisation of Iraq.[69] Sanchez stated that he intended to launch an 'extremely precise' campaign to 'separate, isolate and destroy the enemy wherever we find him on the battlefield'.[70]

Within days, US forces had killed over 600 Iraqis and injured many more in Falluja and the insurgents had killed ten Marines, while the city of over 200,000 people remained in insurgent hands.[71] During a brief, partly-observed ceasefire, about one third of the population fled the city. For most Americans, the narrative of Falluja starts on 31 March 2004 with the killing and televised dismemberment of four US citizens, making the attempted retaking of the city a necessary and justified response. For most Iraqis, the narrative regarding US conduct in Falluja starts with the shooting of Iraqi anti-US demonstrators by US forces on 28 April 2003, 17 people being killed and at least 70 wounded, and then further US actions on 30 April which killed three more and wounded another 16, with no deaths or injuries on the US side. A Human Rights Watch investigation concluded that, while it was possible that US troops came under fire from members of the crowd, there was no clear evidence of this, whereas there was evidence to suggest that US troops acted with disproportionate force.[72] For anti-occupation Iraqis, the US forces had carried out another massacre in Falluja. Even Adnan Pachachi, a secular member of the IGC, said: 'We consider the action carried out by US forces illegal and totally unacceptable', and the IGC issued a statement demanding that the Coalition's 'collective punishment' of Falluja cease and offering to negotiate with what it called the 'leaders of the anti-coalition forces'.[73]

An intermittently observed truce was concluded between US forces and the Falluja insurgents in May 2004, and the US agreed to withdraw its forces. The Falluja Brigade set up as part of the truce agreement, led by former Iraqi Army officers and composed mainly of former insurgents, was meant to take control of the city, but it failed to do so because of continued insurgent opposition and because the line between the Falluja Brigade and the insurgents was blurred. Far from being an example of 'Iraqi-isation' (that is, the turning over of security duties to Iraqi forces), this involved the US conceding recognition to what was effectively a Sunni Arab communal militia.[74] The US failed to achieve any of its objectives such as defeating the insurgents, making them hand over their heavy weapons, arresting those who killed the US security employees, re-establishing Coalition control of the city, recommencing the reconstruction process or ensuring access for foreign workers. The city's tribal leaders became much less willing to work with the Coalition, and its Sunni clerics, always outspoken against the occupation, lost some control to the insurgents who managed to impose their control through checkpoints and patrols. Some of the insurgents took to enforcing their version of Islamic law by discouraging barbers from shaving off beards, forcing women's beauty salons to close and publicly flogging sellers of alcohol.[75] Insurgents continued to rule Falluja and in July 2004 Sanchez pronounced the Falluja Brigade to be a failure: 'It is not an experiment we want to replicate and it's definitely something that has not been effective in eliminating the safe haven for foreign fighters and extremists operating out of there.'[76] Despite the formal ceasefire and a reduction in the number of attacks on the Marines, fighting with insurgents in Falluja continued, and attacks by insurgents increased in the provincial capital of Ramadi west of Falluja.[77]

June-December 2004: Interim Government and the taking of Falluja

As the US conducted its counter-insurgency offensives in the spring of 2004, it also sought to achieve its goal of an accelerated formal political handover. In April, a month after the agreement on the TAL, Brahimi proposed that the IGC should be replaced by an Iraqi interim government of technocrats who would not be participating in the elections planned for January 2005. His assessment was that most Iraqis did not see it as legitimate to be ruled by the US via appointed politicians of the returning exiles' parties who had little support in the country. However, the IGC and the US rejected this proposal, and decided that the IIG would be made up of politicians. The IGC chose collectively to promote 'Allawi for the position of Prime Minister, and secured US agreement to this. The US appointed as President Ghazi Mashal Ajil al-Yawir, a Sunni Arab former member of the IGC. He was a minor figure without strong party connections who had spent the previous 15 years in exile as a businessman in Saudi Arabia. The US chose the remaining key positions from party officials: Ja'fari of al-Da'wa and Rowsch Shaways of the KDP were Deputy Presidents, Barham Salih of the PUK was Deputy Prime Minister. As Toby Dodge pointed out scathingly:

After describing IGC members as 'feckless' and incapable of reaching out to the wider Iraqi population [...], the CPA brought these same people back into government. By implication it entrusted them and their parties with the creation of Iraq's new state, and oversight of its evolving democracy.[78]

The handover arrangement was endorsed through UN Security Council Resolution (SCR) 1546 of 8 June 2004. It declared that the occupation would be over and Iraq would regain 'full sovereignty' by 30 June. The handover actually took place two days early and with no prior announcement, to avoid insurgent attack. Bremer immediately left the country and the CPA was dissolved. SCR 1546 approved the presence of Coalition forces and their use of 'all necessary measures' for security and stability, but stated that they were there only with the consent of the Iraqi government and should coordinate with it. However, Washington made it clear that the previous structure of the multinational force, with a US military commander taking the primary decision-making role in the security sphere, would remain in place.[79]

Many of the CPA's personnel and resources were transferred to the new US Embassy in Iraq, which in turn was responsible to the US Department of State. Among other functions, the Embassy has the role of allocating US funds to Iraqi projects. On the military side, CJTF-7 was replaced in advance of the handover, on 15 May 2004, by Multinational Force Iraq (MNF-I), under its Commanding General, George Casey. Operational control in Iraq fell to the Multinational Corps Iraq (MNC-I), under the command of Lt-Gen. Thomas F. Metz until February 2005, when he handed over to Lt-Gen. John Vines. Although US influence in Iraq continued via the military and the Embassy's funding and advisory role, the new US Ambassador to Iraq, John Negroponte, did not have the formal authority to rule by decree as Bremer had. In particular, he took a back seat when it came to political bargaining in the IIG. The hope was that indigenous central political authority and process would emerge as a result and thus undermine the insurgency.[80] The problem was that the IIG showed little interest in integrating Sunni Arabs into national politics, and US military offensives in mainly Sunni Arab areas further alienated them. Within days of the formal transfer of sovereignty, the Interim Government announced a new twin-track policy to deal with the insurgency. As a carrot, it offered an amnesty to insurgent 'footsoldiers' who had been 'misled', as Sabah Kadhim, spokesman and senior adviser at the Iraqi Ministry of the Interior, put it.[81] Extraordinarily, he said that fighting in opposition to the US was 'justified because it was an occupation force'. The amnesty, which was to last thirty days from 7 August, did not cover anyone who had killed or had committed unspecified 'major crimes'.[82] The vague offer amounted to little more than a call to the insurgents to surrender with no guarantees about what would happen to them, and the Coalition's continuing policy of arbitrary, indefinite detention was not likely to reassure. The amnesty ended with no evidence that anyone had responded to it.

The IIG also announced that there would be new sticks. On 6 July the Cabinet unanimously passed a national security law giving 'Allawi the power to declare a state of emergency, impose nationwide curfews, restrict movement, appoint military governors, and seize the assets and monitor the communications of suspects.[83] It excluded the power to delay the January 2005 National Assembly elections or to revoke the TAL. Exercise of the powers had to be approved unanimously by the Presidency Council comprising the President and Deputy Presidents, was limited to an initial period of 60 days with renewal every further 30 days, and could be refused by the Iraqi judiciary. Arrests required a warrant from an Iraqi judge and arrested persons had to be presented to a judge within 24 hours. Although US and British officials welcomed the national security law as something which would help against the insurgency, the Interim Government did not actually draw on those formal powers, apart from announcing occasional curfews. Those arrested by MNF-I would have none of the rights afforded to them under the national security law. Indeed, those arrested by Iraqi security forces were not afforded those rights as they were not being arrested under the terms of the new law. On 9 August, the IIG reintroduced the death penalty (which had been suspended by the Coalition) for murder, drug trafficking and the vague crime of 'endangering national security'.[84] Despite the desire for an image of strength that lay behind these measures, the passage of ineffective laws served only to make the government look weak, and US control of counter-insurgency operations made it appear irrelevant.

The two escalations of the armed conflict from April 2004 continued to resound through the remainder of the year. The US decided to confront the Mahdi Army again in summer 2004. On 2 August, US and Iraqi government forces cordoned off the al-Zahra district of eastern Najaf where Sadr's house was located. Two days later they arrested Shaykh Mithal Hasnawi, Sadr's representative in Karbala'.[85] Fighting soon began and spread rapidly to Baghdad. Within days, the Iraqi police claimed that over 1,200 militiamen had surrendered and the US military claimed to have killed 300 for three dead and twelve injured US soldiers: the Mahdi Army countered with the claim that it had suffered only one tenth of those losses.[86] On 9 August the commander of US forces in Iraq, General Casey, ordered the Polish-led element of the Multinational Force to give control of Najaf and Qadisiyya governorates to the US Marines because of the escalating clashes with the Mahdi Army, and called for all civilians to leave Najaf, thus signalling their intention to use force extensively in order to try to retake control of the whole of that city.[87] After a prolonged stand-off, a face-saving deal was negotiated under the auspices of Sistani by the end of the month, which formally provided for a mutual withdrawal from Najaf and tacitly brokered a *modus vivendi* between the Sadr movement and the Coalition forces across Iraq. This allowed the Sadr movement to consolidate its political position in Baghdad, and the deal led to members of Sadr's movement aligning themselves with other Shi'a parties in the run-up to January's elections and eventually taking positions within the new Iraqi government.[88] The Coalition, in accepting the deal, defused the threat of open revolt from within the Shi'a population, but also resigned itself to the continued and growing political challenge of the Sadr movement.

The US's next attempt at destroying an armed political challenge also failed. With the Falluja Brigade evidently unreliable, the US continued aerial attacks on targets in Falluja and tried to find ways of putting an Iraqi face on its actions. The US usually claimed that its attacks on Falluja were directed at suspected safe houses of the Jordanian terrorist Abu Mus'ab al-Zarqawi (himself killed in a US air strike on Ba'qubah on 7 June 2006), who had aligned himself with al-Qa'ida. In November 2004, the US finally launched an attack which captured Falluja by force. It claimed to have killed 1,200 insurgents, and it almost totally destroyed the city, causing nearly all of remaining inhabitants to flee.[89] Hundreds of civilians were also killed in the operation. Lt-Gen. John Sattler, commander of the 1st Marine Expeditionary Force in Iraq, asserted that that Coalition had 'broken the back of the insurgency' because the fall of Falluja meant that the insurgents had lost their safe haven and command structure, with the fighters of Zarqawi's network being 'scattered'.[90] This view was not shared more widely among US military or civilian officials. According to a leaked memo from the CIA station chief in Baghdad, the situation deteriorated for the Coalition after the taking of Falluja.[91] As Falluja was not surrounded, insurgents who wished to were able to leave and the focus of insurgent attacks, apparently boosted by a wave of new supporters, shifted to other locations such as Mosul. Iraqi insurgents had for the most part simply dispersed from Falluja, and, instead of fighting pitched battles, launched simultaneous attacks in many towns such as Baiji, Ba'qubah, Ramadi, Haditha and Tikrit.[92] The taking of Falluja hardened Sunni Arab opinion against the occupation, drove many to support the insurgency and caused the Sunni Iraqi Islamic Party to boycott the January 2005 TNA elections. Furthermore, the contrast between the effective truce with the Sadr movement and the destruction of Falluja contributed strongly to the perception among Sunni Arabs that the Iraqi state being sponsored by the US was increasingly rooted in a sectarian Kurdish-Shi'a alliance.

January-September 2005: Transitional Government and
new counter-insurgency operations

The January 2005 elections took place against a background of the Shi'a-led parties having agreed a level of cooperation between themselves, while the Sunni Arabs were more deeply disaffected than ever. Most Sunni Arab leaders promoted a boycott on the grounds that there could be no legitimate elections as long as Iraq was effectively still under US occupation. The boycott decision was announced during the Coalition forces' capture of Falluja. The parties organised around a conception of Shi'a identity focused on the gains they could make by cashing in on their numerical superiority in the elections. They coordinated to form a single list — the United Iraqi Alliance (UIA) — under the broad guidance of Sistani. The country was treated as a single constituency with seats allocated in proportion to votes received across the country above a minimum threshold. Few in mainly Sunni Arab areas voted: in al-Anbar the turnout was a mere 2%. The official turnout was 58% of registered voters across Iraq, although as there was a substantial increase in registration later in 2005, it is more likely that approximately 53% of eligible voters took part.[93] Out of the 275 Transitional National Assembly seats, the UIA took 140, the Kurdistan Alliance list (led by the KDP and PUK) 75, and the secular Iraqi List (primarily composed of 'Allawi's INA) 40. On the same

day, elections took place for the Kurdistan National Assembly and for councils for each of the 18 governorates.

Religious Shi'i and secular Kurds dominated the TNA, with only a handful of seats going to the various Sunni Arab political parties that had decided not to participate in the boycott. In the governorate council elections, SCIRI emerged as the dominant party of local government outside the Kurdish areas. By itself, it formed the largest bloc on the councils in five governorates including Baghdad, and stood as part of a joint slate which became the largest grouping in four other governorate councils.[94] The Kurdish parties won control of six governorate councils, managing to extend their rule to three governorates which had not largely been part of the KAR because of the Sunni Arab boycott in those areas.[95] Although Sadr did not formally endorse participation in the elections, his followers were on the UIA national list of candidates, and two supporters were appointed to head ministries in the Transitional Government — 'Abd al-Muttalib Muhammad 'Ali as Minister for Health and Salam al-Maliki at Transport and Telecommunications.[96] The Bush administration hailed the election as a triumph for Iraq and for democracy. However, leaders of other Arab States such as King Abdullah of Jordan and the Saudi Foreign Minister, Sa'ud al-Faysal, worried publicly about a 'Shi'a crescent' incorporating Iran, Iraq, Kuwait, eastern Saudi Arabia and Bahrain.[97]

In March 2005, Negroponte left Iraq to be Bush's nominee for the new position of National Intelligence Director, as post-election political deadlock in Iraq continued. It took until April for the wrangling over posts in the Transitional Government to be resolved, which was damaging to the credibility of the political parties involved. It was agreed that Talabani would be President while al-Yawir (who had set up a party list called The Iraqis which had won five seats) and 'Adil 'Abd al-Mahdi of SCIRI (in exile from 1964 onwards, in France and then Iran) would be the two Deputy Presidents. Ja'fari became Prime Minister and Chalabi managed to return to office as Deputy Prime

Minister and temporary Minister for Oil until the factions could agree
on a longer term appointee. The drift in US input into this process was
symbolised by the fact that Zalmay Khalilzad did not arrive to replace
Negroponte as US Ambassador to Iraq until late June, although he
sought to make up for lost time by vigorous involvement in the negotiations over the constitution.

When the number of attacks per day after the January 2005 elections subsided to an average of 45 per day, this was hailed as evidence
that the insurgency was on the wane. From April 2005, the number
climbed back up to 60 and then in May to 70 attacks per day, a third
higher than a year earlier.[98] From January 2005, the US shifted its
military emphasis away from patrolling and into increased investment
in the training of Iraqi security forces. This change of emphasis was
largely based upon the recommendations drawn up by retired General
Gary Luck, who was sent to Iraq in mid-January to conduct a full-scale
review of the military's role in Iraq.[99] As we show in Chapter Two,
spending was directed away from the development of Iraq's civil infrastructure and into Iraq's police and army. In the mainly Sunni Arab parts
of Iraq, throughout the spring and summer the US was also very active
militarily. It conducted repeated massive cordon and search operations
involving entire districts of Baghdad or entire towns in cooperation
with Iraqi units, and full-scale military assaults with tanks, artillery and
aircraft on town after town.[100]

Constitutional referendum and alienation of Sunni Arabs

The delays in forming the new government had an impact upon the
main purpose of the TNA, which was to draft a constitution by 15
August to be put to a referendum on 15 October. In full knowledge
that the chair of the constitutional committee would have considerable authority over the drafting process, protracted negotiations began
after the January elections that were only resolved by mid-May, with

the appointment of Humam al-Hammudi, a cleric from SCIRI, to the position. The first problem facing the committee was that while the TAL specified that it had to be made up of members of the TNA, given the nature of the election boycott the original committee included only two Sunni Arabs among its 55 members. Because it was obvious that a constitution drafted without participation from this group's members would lack legitimacy, 15 Sunni Arab politicians who were not TNA members were chosen in June to take part in an expanded committee.[101]

Despite this act of inclusion, the expanded committee rarely convened. In practice, drafting of the constitution took place through the chair's office, which one UN official described as being '100% SCIRI' in its make-up.[102] With the chair's office having the role of choosing the independent experts to bring in, arranging the sub-committees and setting the timetables for individual sections of the constitution, a high degree of leverage was given to this one political faction. A full text was presented to the full committee in early August, and a late effort was made to secure the agreement of the Sunni Arab members. This resulted in a few small changes being made to the earlier draft. Brinkmanship caused the 15 August deadline to be ignored, with a text agreed by the TAL and circulated publicly on 28 August. No Sunni Arab politicians endorsed the text.

The main matter in dispute was the relationship between the central government and Iraq's regions, a dispute in which the two main Shi'a parties, SCIRI and al-Da'wa, had shifted from favouring centralisation towards support for a high degree of local autonomy. The constitution specified that Iraq would be federal: a governorate would be entitled to declare itself a 'region' either singly or jointly with other governorates, and the region would be self-governing across a range of crucial spheres of activity, including maintaining internal security forces (articles 112-117).[103] Only seven tasks were reserved for the central (federal) government, including foreign policy, maintaining an army and fiscal policy. Most strikingly, in cases in which there was dispute between federal and regional government over the proper regulatory authority, the draft constitution specified that regional law would automatically have priority (article 111).

The potential for regional power was brought out most clearly in the constitutional draft on exploitation of hydrocarbon resources. Iraq's proven oil and gas reserves are located overwhelmingly in the northern regions (the Kirkuk and Bay Hassan fields) and in the far south (the north and south Rumayla fields) of the country: in 2003, just 1.1% of Iraq's total income from oil came from fields located in the four central governorates.[104] If revenue was to stay in the region of extraction, the governorates in which Sunni Arabs constitute a majority of population, with the exception of Ninawa (Mosul), would all be deprived of a significant share of the national income.

Partly to offset the resulting concerns, the text, after the August amendments, asserted that 'oil and gas remain the property of all the Iraqi people in all the regions and governorates' (article 108). However, the actual distribution of revenue was a more complex matter. For existing oil and gas fields, the revenue would be 'distributed fairly' by the federal government 'in cooperation with' the regional governments in which extraction took place. This distribution should also take into account 'regions that were deprived in an unfair way by the former regime or later on', for whom a 'quota should be defined' (article 109). Definition of future fairness and the nature of past unfairness, both of which would be crucial to the distribution of revenue, were not explained further in the constitution. For new fields, the constitution was even less clear, leaving open the possibility that the revenue could be claimed solely by the producing regions.

The role of religion in the state was also fudged. Article 2 stated that 'Islam is the official religion of the state and is a basic source of legislation' and that 'No law can be passed that contradicts the undisputed rules of Islam'; however, it also stated that no law could be passed that contradicted 'the principles of democracy' or 'the rights and basic freedoms' listed in the constitution. How these potentially clashing principles were to be weighted against each other was left unclear. The Federal Supreme Court was mandated to include 'experts in Islamic fiqh' or jurisprudence (article 89), but as with over 60 articles in the constitution, the potentially divisive issues relating to the broader theme were explicitly left to be stipulated by the legislature. In effect, this deferral of responsibility onto the legislature took away the potential for the constitution to provide institutional safeguards against the actions of the governing party or coalition, which the Shi'a bloc presumed it would control for the foreseeable future.

Four days before the 15 October referendum, Shi'a and Kurdish negotiators agreed to nine changes to the constitution, including a provision for a subsequent review process. This was sufficient to induce the Iraqi Islamic Party, but no other Sunni Arab political groupings, to support approval of the constitution. Copies of the earlier draft of the document arrived in Iraq only one week before the election and were not distributed widely. As a result, the public were being expected to vote on a constitution which they had not seen and which was not in any case settled. The amended text of the constitution was not available on either the government's or the drafting committee's website, and was only circulated as a single, authoritative document in English and Arabic by the United Nations Assistance Mission for Iraq in late January 2006 after further consultations with the major parties.

Against this background of uncertainty, the referendum was not simply a barometer of prior sectarian allegiance: it actively reinforced the trend towards sectarianism through the potential implications of its content. Most Sunni Arab politicians and clerics urged their supporters to vote to reject the constitution, although a few called for a boycott, especially in view of an ongoing military campaign conducted by US forces and the Iraqi army against the city of Tal Afar. The TAL had specified that a two-thirds majority of voters against the constitution in three governorates would be enough to veto it. Although this was included at the urging of the Kurdish parties (who sought it on the basis that it would give leverage to the three majority Kurdish governorates), Sunni Arab-led parties now sought to block the constitution using that provision. The potential for that was implicitly recognised when the TNA sought briefly to redefine the TAL to provide that a two-thirds majority of registered voters, not of actual voters, was needed in three governorates to act as a block, and only backed down under international pressure. In the event, despite the apparently small number of Sunni Arabs voting for the constitution, it was passed nonetheless: opposing the constitution were 97% in al-Anbar, 82% in Salah al-Din, 55% in Ninawa and 49% in Diyala. The last two of those governorates had narrow Sunni Arab majorities, and it seems that the two-thirds majority was blocked in both by their Kurdish and Shi'a minorities. Across the rest of the country, the supportive vote was high, with over 94% voting for the constitution in twelve of Iraq's eighteen governorates.[105]

Supporters of the constitution, including the US and Iraqi governments, portrayed this outcome as an improvement on the boycott of the January elections, arguing that the fact that objections were being registered through the ballot box indicated acceptance of the legitimacy of the process. However, it appears that voting 'no' was for the vast majority of Sunni Arabs — who, as we detail in Chapter Four, saw and continue to see attacks on Coalition forces as legitimate acts of resistance — a supplement rather than an alternative to supporting the insurgency. Indeed, the number of daily attacks continued to increase after the referendum was held.[106]

The US had from mid-2005 begun the gradual repositioning of its military units outside urban areas. By November, 15 of the Coalition's 110 bases had been transferred to Iraqi units, and another 13 closed down, many of which were within major cities.[107] Instead, the role of US brigades was now making forays into insurgent-held towns with the hope of then switching to helping Iraqi forces try to hold on to them. In practice, especially in al-Anbar, towns were entered with only the short-term goal of seizing suspected insurgents and weapons, and were then abandoned again to reasserted insurgent control. US officials claimed by this point that 91 Iraqi battalions could participate in combat, and that 24 could hold responsibility for areas of Iraq.[108] Nevertheless, only one battalion was able to operate entirely independently of Coalition support (a number which declined to zero early in 2006), with Coalition advisers and trainers embedded in each unit, providing the mechanism for Iraqi units to liaise with each other and with their operating bases.[109] Furthermore, there was a major increase in US aerial bombing.[110] US military power was propping up the government and the constitutional order. It appeared extremely unlikely that either would survive for long without that backing, and there was little reason to believe that the state was making progress towards independent military viability.

December 2005-June 2006: Deadlock over post-election government

In a confidential memorandum written in mid-2005, British Defence Secretary John Reid stated: 'There is a strong US military desire for significant force reductions to bring relief to overall US commitment levels', adding that the US Department of Defence and CENTCOM 'favour a relatively bold reduction in force numbers'.[111] In order to try to make this possible, the US sought to address the political marginalisation of Sunni Arabs. The US had promoted greater Sunni Arab participation in the constitutional drafting, and under Khalilzad, who took over as US Ambassador in June 2005, had a stronger role in promoting an accommodation between the Shi'a-led government and the insurgents. This new emphasis also reflected US fears that the new Iraqi government would shift its allegiance closer to Iran.

This promotion of accommodation was clear in the encouragement given by the US to the holding of a reconciliation conference in Cairo, held under the auspices of the Arab League, which included some who claimed to speak on behalf of the insurgency (a claim quickly disputed by some insurgent groups). In a similar vein, the US let it be known that it had started a dialogue with insurgents in June 2005 to see whether negotiations could lead to a lessening of violence. This strategy was also found in the extent of US criticism of four secret Iraqi Interior Ministry prisons that were discovered in November and December 2005, in which the SCIRI-run ministry had kept Sunni Arab prisoners in conditions of grave deprivation and appeared to have tortured them. Throughout late 2005 and into mid-2006, the United States kept up aggressive armed operations in areas in which the insurgency was strongest, presenting this as a necessary complement to the political process in trying to persuade the insurgents that it would not allow them to win by armed struggle. However, as we show in Chapter Four, there was no evidence that the insurgents had been persuaded, and a great deal of evidence that counter-insurgency operations were alienating Sunni Arabs from the political process. If anything, they appeared increasingly confident that they would be able to force a Coalition withdrawal, which they expected to be followed promptly by the collapse of what they see as a pro-Iranian sectarian Shi'a government.

This combination of declarations, conferences and US military operations provided the background to the 15 December elections. Many of the insurgent groups declared a ceasefire for the period of the election so that their supporters could vote in order to try to challenge Shi'a domination of the government and secure a timetable for the withdrawal of US forces. Al-Qa'ida in Mesopotamia and four other insurgent groups denounced the elections in a joint statement, but did not threaten to disrupt polling, as they had done previously.[112] Although Sistani remained officially neutral for the December election, he issued a communiqué that urged voters to choose religious candidates and to avoid 'weak' lists so as to avoid splitting the Shi'a vote - thus giving his tacit backing to the UIA once again.[113] The result of substantial Sunni Arab participation this time was that the other electoral blocs lost seats: the UIA won 128 of the 275 seats, down from 140 a year previously and ten short of the number required to form a government without allying with another list. The Kurdistan Alliance took 53 seats (down from 75). 'Allawi's secular Iraqi National List emerged with 25 seats (down from 40), the Iraqi Accord Front with 44 seats and the secular-leaning, mainly Sunni Iraqi Front for National Dialogue led by Salih al-Mutlaq with 11 seats. Together with the non-Kurdish parties representing small minorities in northern Iraq, a bloc led by the Sunni Arab-majority parties had 87 seats, substantially increasing its bargaining power.[114]

The basic electoral geometry remained the same as after the January 2005 polls: the Shi'a religious parties were dominant but were going to have to share power, either in a coalition to form a majority or in a government of national unity with all the other main political groupings. However, the Sadr movement now formed the largest group within the UIA — a good measure of the US failure to exert control, considering that less than two years previously US forces had sought to destroy it. Despite past experience of cooperation between the major parties of the National Assembly in the IGC and the governments led by 'Allawi and Ja'fari, serious difficulties beset the parties in trying to negotiate a new government. As after the January polls, al-Da'wa again pushed for Ja'fari to be Prime Minister, opposing SCIRI's nomination of 'Adil 'Abd al-Mahdi for this position. It won out among the UIA deputies by securing Sadr's support, but only by one vote. However, this time SCIRI did not relent, and continued to argue that 'Abd al-Mahdi would be better placed to lead a government of national unity, given his stronger relations with Kurdish, Sunni Arab and secular deputies than Ja'fari had. The US also leaned towards SCIRI in this respect. The result was protracted deadlock, with Ja'fari insisting upon the legitimacy of his nomination but unable to secure the necessary National Assembly majority. On 22 April, after two months of attempting to put a coalition together and under intense domestic as well as US pressure, Ja'fari stood down and allowed his deputy in al-Da'wa, Nuri al-Maliki, to take the UIA's nomination as Prime Minister.

The US had also opposed the Interior and Defence Ministries being led by sectarian parties, and found itself making common cause with Sunni Arab leaders on this issue. However, Hadi al-Amri, head of the Badr Brigades, argued that Shi'i had to retain control of those ministries because they were coming under attack daily. Maliki proposed a Cabinet to the National Assembly for approval on 20 May but had to leave the Interior and Defence posts unfilled. It was only on 8 June – nearly six months after the elections – that agreement was reached on this between the parties of the UIA, the other members of the governing coalition and the US. In the end, the Interior Ministry and the important position of National Security Adviser went to Jawad al-Bulani and Shirwan al-Wa'ili respectively, who had been leading members of Shi'a parties. However, they had to resign their membership of those parties prior to their appointment and Lt-Gen. 'Abd al-Qadir 'Ubaydi, a Sunni Arab, became Minister of Defence.

These two episodes illustrate the fact that US officials were now facing serious difficulty in exercising leverage over the entrenched positions of the parties, with those parties increasingly portraying themselves as the defenders of Iraqi democratic procedures against foreign interference.[115]

CONCLUSION

The December 2005 elections and the subsequent formation of a new government were meant to be the final act completing the building of the new Iraqi state by the US. Instead, the difficulties in forming viable governments were indicative of the extent of political fragmentation and the way in which political dynamics at the level of central government had moved out of US control. As we show in Chapter Four, into early 2006 the violence was still primarily anti-occupation and Iraq was some way from all-out sectarian civil war. Nevertheless, sectarian violence was increasing, with the destruction of the al-Askari Shi'a shrine in Samarra' on 22 February 2006, presumably by Sunni Arab insurgents, and the reprisals and counter-reprisals that followed. That trend has been exacerbated by the fact that the political process the US has sponsored is one which the vast majority of Sunni Arabs continue to reject, by the coercive counter-insurgency focused on mainly Sunni Arab areas, and by Sunni Arab perceptions that the state itself is sectarian. This Chapter has mapped how these themes of fragmentation, violence and sectarianism have impacted on the US project for Iraq. In doing so, it has aimed to demonstrate that the trajectory of post-invasion Iraq has not been the unfolding of a prior project or the gradual achievement of specific goals. Instead, the very nature of that project has shifted rapidly, and the way success has been defined has changed simultaneously: liberation, social and economic transformation, restoring Iraqi sovereignty, democratisation, military self-sufficiency and avoiding sectarian conflict have all functioned as the major objective for the US at some point during the three years since the invasion, and the tensions between these goals have led to a stuttering, often incoherent, political strategy.[116] In the next Chapter, we will look at how these approaches affected the character of the Iraqi state.

2

THE STATE – FRAGMENTING
POLITICAL AUTHORITY

The collapse of the Iraqi state in April 2003, with its central institutions ceasing to operate, represented more than just a short-term practical problem for the US-led Coalition which could be remedied through technical assistance. It also heralded the beginning of a multi-faceted struggle for control of the rebuilding of the state, and for control of particular state institutions. Furthermore, a wide range of actors, notably tribal, religious and militia leaders, asserted their practical autonomy from the Iraqi government even if they accepted the notion of the potential authority of an Iraqi state. Many of these actors outside the control of the Coalition have established forms of rule that have proved more resilient than many of the Coalition's own governing institutions.

The fragmentation of political authority was in some respects a welcome development to many. Within Iraqi society, with its incessantly suppressed peripheries, the opportunity to develop forms of rule outside Baghdad's stultifying grip was seized by those who held on to the instruments of local power. In their efforts to unseat the particular government being installed by the US, insurgents launched a campaign to prevent a functioning state from being re-established. Equally, once the Bush administration realised that it was not going to inherit a functioning state, it drew parallels with the reconstruction of Germany after 1945 and argued that Iraq's polity and economy could be rebuilt entirely from the bottom up. However, for a new state to be built, the localised or partial forms of rule that had emerged quickly after the invasion would have to be incorporated within it or, failing that, would have to be swept away.

This Chapter will discuss two closely interlinked processes: those of state building and state formation.[1] By state building, we mean the deliberate attempt by political agents to create the key characteristic of the modern state: a relationship of rule extending over a territory, supported by force that is exercised by agencies under the control of the ruling body and is the only form of violence considered legitimate by the population. This notion of state building includes the possibility that while the state is the formal site of final authority, it may be deeply integrated into international (that is, involving other states) and transnational (that is, involving non-state actors) sets of practices and power relations, which may be hierarchically ordered. Even if a population denies the legitimacy of the particular government that is controlling the state, it can still believe that the final arbiter should be the state, though controlled by a different government. The US placed considerable emphasis on the process of state building after 9/11, drawing upon the perception that the existence of a failed state — Afghanistan — allowed the flourishing of radical non-state organisations that could not be controlled through traditional mechanisms of inter-state pressure.[2] However, as we shall argue in this Chapter, the process of Iraqi state building was also a source of multiple inconveniences and hazards. As a result, state building was pursued inconsistently and often incoherently by the Coalition.

State building (the intentional project of creating a state) impacts upon but does not determine state formation (a process in which a state emerges independently of the intentions of any agents to create one). The strategies by which agents engage in conflicts and accommodations of power with one another may lead to the creation of a single site of political authority over a specific territory, even though no agent desired that outcome. Thus, in much of Europe, the centralised state was formed not as a result of deliberate schemes or with foresight of what would result, but through the acts of relatively small groups fighting off rivals in order to enjoy the advantages of power.[3] Our argument, and the reason for giving prominence to this distinction, is that the process of state formation in Iraq has operated with particular vigour independently of the deliberate process of state building; and that the latter process, paradoxically, has often proved counterproductive for state formation. Most importantly, the state has fragmented, in that claims of particular actors to exercise legitimate governmental authority remain fundamentally disputed, both in principle and in practice, and there are no clearly agreed procedures for resolving such disputes.

Iraq has long provided one of the best examples of a state that has remained largely external to society, in the sense that it has derived its power since its creation from sources not originating from its own population. In the royalist era, that source of power was the British; in the post-1953 period, the sources of the state's power have been located overwhelmingly in its revenues from oil production. Sami Zubaida's description of the modern Middle Eastern state applies particularly well to Iraq of the royalist (1921-58), 'Arifs (1963-68) and Ba'thist (1968-2003) periods: the state has acted as an imposition upon society, and is maintained through externally-derived forces and resources 'in an externalised and oppressive relationship to the social formation'.[4] The ruling class has only had close ties to a small geographical region of the country, which served as its seat of power, and has exercised authority over the remainder firstly by making uneasy alliances with local power structures, and then by manipulating local antagonisms to its own advantage. Iraqi political society was far from passive, with vibrant political movements coming to the fore especially during the early years of the Qasim era (1958-63), but its ability to limit the way the government acted — to protect itself, rather than the interests of the state — was highly circumscribed. At the state's disposal were

extensive powers of patronage, particularly after the land reforms of
May 1970 and the subsequent expropriations which allowed the state
to become the dominant landlord, and the nationalisation of the oil
industry in June 1972.[5] Iraq thus became a classic 'rentier' state, relying more on income gained through oil exports rather than on taxes
from the productive activities of its citizens through which it would
be enmeshed in a set of reciprocal obligations.[6] Through its combination of terror and enticement — *tarhib* and *targhib*[7] — the Iraqi state
has acted autonomously from and unidirectionally upon society; it has
rarely been steered to any considerable extent by it.

The impact of the externalised relationship has been, firstly and
most obviously, the comparative ease with which the state has resorted
to highly repressive means to control Iraqi society, as opposed to other
potential means of influencing the social formation. From the perspective of Iraq's rulers, the political and economic costs of oppression have
been low for much of Iraq's history. In addition, social forces that preserved the apparatus of the state, beyond the immediate self-interests
of the ruling clique, did not exist to any substantial degree. The size
of that clique was neither large nor stable enough to form a solid base
of support for an institutional order.[8] Remove the rulers and the state
would collapse.

The low degree of loyalty to the institutions of the state was demonstrated most graphically in the way in which the state's central bureaucracy and police melted away with the invasion. Even those officials who
had continued to take part in local administration and the enforcement
of order now rarely maintained their allegiance to the impersonal notion of the state, but often instead transferred their loyalty to sub-state
agents who were able to make a better claim to power. The old Iraqi
tribal chant about central government captured the sense of disen-
gagement of society from the state, in a way that took on particular
significance from April 2003: 'It is a flabby serpent and has no venom;
we have come and have seen it, it is only in times past that it kept us

in awe'.[9] With the venom — the Ba'th leadership — extracted by the Coalition, there was no longer a central state worth engaging with.

A number of officials and political commentators have attributed the post-invasion condition of disorder to the unusually low number of Coalition military personnel — less than 150,000 — who took control of Iraq after April 2003.[10] This can be compared to the number of NATO troops in Bosnia and Kosovo, in which there was approximately one soldier for every fifty inhabitants, a ratio that if maintained in Iraq would have resulted in a Coalition presence of over 460,000 troops.[11] One clear result of the comparatively low level of Coalition personnel within Iraq was their lack of ability to unseat those groups that had taken possession of key buildings and facilities around the country. Many of these groups went on to construct forms of localised rule that coordinated poorly, if at all, with central government. In some cases, this arrangement was formalised in terms of decentralisation. The clearest, but *sui generis*, example is the Kurdish Autonomous Region (KAR). This region has been left intact by the Coalition and subsequent Iraqi governments, and was given formal recognition through the Transitional Administrative Law (TAL) and the 2005 Constitution. The status quo was seen by the US as too entrenched to modify, and debate focused on the nature of the relationship between the (deeply divided) Kurdish Regional Government (KRG) and the rest of Iraq, rather than the form of internal rule exercised by the KRG.[12] There was also considerable emphasis in the discourse of US and UK officials on the value of decentralisation in Iraq, towards local councils and away from the previously overbearing hand of central government, and the CPA established its Local Government Programme to this effect.[13]

Nevertheless, in general, to portray the localisation of forms of rule as part of a structured process, managed and ordered in a coherent way through central government, is misleading. Rather, various groups — such as political parties, tribal networks, insurgents and local associations — which had taken control of particular areas from April

2003 were simply left in place, as the Coalition was unable to challenge them. Even when US forces retook those regions, they were not able to sustain a presence there, and were often replaced within a period of weeks by those they had sought to oust. This is not decentralisation, then, but a process of geographical fragmentation.

The extent of fragmentation became most palpable when the US military began describing parts of Iraq as 'no-go zones' for their patrols from early September 2004. Towns labelled in this way included Samarra', Falluja, Ramadi, Kufa and Latifiya.[14] The need for repeated incursions into these towns, discussed in more detail in Chapter Four, showed how incapable the US was of governing the towns, even if it was able to reconquer them by force. In the absence of US forces, these towns reverted to the rule of local leaders, such as leading cleric Shaykh Abdullah al-Janabi in Falluja.[15] However, even in lower profile cases, a *modus vivendi* was reached between local leaders and central government only through commitments from the Coalition not to interfere in the local governance of the area. Coalition military chiefs promised under agreements with self-appointed leaders in smaller towns, such as Hit and Majar al-Kabir, not to enter their areas.[16] In such regions, militias aligned with political parties, rather than with formal agents of the state, maintained their vision of order. In Basra, the streets were patrolled by members of the Badr Brigades and the Sadr militia, which styled itself the Mahdi Army;[17] in Samawa, the Badr Brigades and the armed wing of al-Da'wa ruled the streets, oscillating between mutual cooperation and confrontation;[18] and for much of the period following the invasion, the Sadr militia ran a system of courts, prisons and policing in Najaf, as it continues to do in Sadr City.[19]

The continuing existence of militias with a sizeable role in the ordering of Iraq through to 2006 reflects the Coalition's perception of the limits of what it could do. Forcible disarmament was mostly considered impossible, and no group could be expected to disarm voluntarily whilst others retained armed wings.[20] In many cases, the Coalition gave encouragement to armed militias to engage in activities that they would not be able to do. After the bombing of the Imam 'Ali mosque in Najaf on 29 August 2003, in which SCIRI's leader Muhammad Baqr al-Hakim and some 80 others were killed, the CPA's tone on armed militias changed from opposition to tacit acceptance. Bremer spoke of how organised militias would not have a role 'in the long run', but their members would be 'encouraged' to play a role in the CPA's security structures. He asserted soon afterwards that armed militias within Najaf 'were there with the full authority of the Coalition', though there was nothing to indicate that the militias would leave or disband should he re-scind that authorisation.[21] Over the ensuing weeks, party militias were out in force much more openly in Najaf and other areas of southern Iraq, and asserted their permanence in the months thereafter.[22] There were also repeated allegations that the Badr Brigades in particular took an active role in attacking individuals associated with the *ancien régime*, and that the Coalition at best turned a blind eye towards such activities.[23] The US broached the use of Shi'a militia in the struggle for Najaf in mid-2004, although eventually it did not use them,[24] but it did make use of Kurdish militia in Mosul to keep the city in order.[25] Although the CPA established a Transition and Reintegration Implementation Committee in June 2004 to oversee the disbandment of militias, it did not arrange for any funding for that Committee, and allowed it to wither away, seeing the militias instead as a useful tool against the insurgency.[26] Therefore, with the installation of the Ja'fari-led ITG from April 2005, the Badr Organisation — as the Badr Brigades had renamed themselves — was well placed to continue as a sizeable paramilitary force within the country. It now received encouragement from the Interior Ministry, which was now headed by a SCIRI official, to continue its activities.[27]

This form of geographical fragmentation was due not only to a comparatively low level of Coalition personnel, but also to its weakness in having to use non-coercive measures and coopt existing groups to bring order. The attempt to build a viable polity in Iraq involved bringing groups who were allied with the US at the time of the invasion voluntarily into the official framework of government, with their resources placed at the disposal of the state: allies of the Coalition had to be turned into agents of the state, transforming their local legitimacy into power delegated from the centre.[28] That this did not happen reflected the weak bargaining position of the Coalition in relations with Iraqi political movements. Association with the US would do little in assist these groups in developing a popular base, either in terms of their own legitimacy or in enhancing their knowledge of Iraq.

One form of the externalised relationship between the state and society is the absence of social sources of state power; a second form is the state's lack of ability to manage social forces coherently. An increase in the number of Coalition personnel might have kept official structures and buildings under state control better, but would not have substantially affected its ability to penetrate and manage Iraqi society; in many parts of Iraq, more US troops would have simply resulted in a deeper sense of hostility. The state under the Ba'th regime, by contrast, had a detailed knowledge of its internal fabric to bolster its repressive function, and an elaborate infrastructure to maintain relations of subordination. The initial act of distancing the state from society in this sense was the burning of the records held by the state apparatus, most likely a deliberate act of the departing regime, leaving relatively little for the new rulers of Iraq to use to remedy their initial ignorance of the society they had committed themselves to administering.

THE PROBLEM OF DISTANCE — STATE AND SOCIETY

The failure of the Coalition's initial strategy for reducing the distance between state and society was due partly to a misjudgement of the value of the interlocutors it had recruited, discussed above in Chapter One, and partly to a lack of proper appreciation of the problem it faced. The Coalition failed to appreciate from the outset how necessary it would be for the state to develop a complex engagement with society — that is, for the state to provide recognised channels through which the negotiation, implementation and evaluation of public policy could take place. US policy makers had a tendency to reduce the problem to one of how best to use Iraqi intermediaries, or to demonstrate Iraqi involvement to wider audiences. This attitude was revealed in the common expression of needing to put 'an Iraqi face' on its administrative activities, and can be shown through the example of the Iraqi Reconstruction and Development Council (IRDC). This body was formally established by the US Department of Defence (DoD) in late February 2003, and was made up initially of nearly 150 Iraqis mandated to direct the rebuilding of the structures of civil government after the ousting of the Ba'th regime. It was to be the technocratic wing of the bond with Iraqi society which was to complement the political wing that was the nascent Iraqi government. After initially being based in Virginia, its leading members were transported to Baghdad in late April 2003. The senior members of the IRDC were organised to hold positions in each of 23 Iraqi ministries and 18 provincial governments according to their professional abilities and fields of expertise. They were to work in close coordination with US and British officials in ORHA, advising the Coalition on the sectors they had detailed prior knowledge of. Thus an Iraqi-American oil company executive and energy consultant who had been based in Colorado, Muhammad 'Ali Zainy, was appointed as senior adviser to the Ministry of Oil. An Iraqi law professor who had been based in Sweden, Mundhir al-Fadhal, became senior adviser to the Ministry of Justice. An Iraqi-American professor of urology who had been resident in southern Florida, Sa'id Hakki, served as senior adviser to the Ministry of Health. These were individuals who had prior knowledge of the Iraqi sectors they were put to work in again: Zainy, Fadhal and Hakki had worked in their respective Iraqi ministries until the early 1980s in each case.

However, instead of directing the state apparatus in its interrelations with Iraqi society, IRDC members in most - though not all - sectors were provided with administrative rather than policy-making roles, implementing the orders of Coalition personnel. This limited nature of IRDC activity was perpetuated with the creation of the CPA. An institutional division was created. On the one hand, there was the 'CPA ministry', which was based inside the Republican Palace and made up of the Coalition personnel under the CPA senior adviser, who had decision-making authority. On the other, there was the 'Iraqi ministry', with the remnants of, and the small number of new recruits to, the Iraqi central bureaucracy, based inside the old ministry buildings and assigned the role of implementing CPA ministry decisions. Zainy, who resigned from the IRDC in September 2003, complained that he had been delegated subordinate responsibilities and had been restricted to acting as little more than 'a go-between to convey American orders to the ministry'. Other members of the IRDC spoke of being excluded from policy discussions, and being confined to the vetting of remaining staff for their prior political affiliations.[29]

The reluctance to place into decision-making roles individuals who had close personal and family linkages with Iraqi society, especially in the eight months after the start of the occupation, can be explained partly by the low level of trust between those individuals and the DoD. Although many IRDC members had had long-standing contacts with personnel from Coalition governments, their institutional existence began less than a month before the invasion, and this institution was untested for both its competence and its affiliation. Nevertheless, the fact that the requisite time and effort had not been put into developing trust between Coalition personnel and expatriate Iraqi administrators shows how little thought had been given to the problems that would be associated with a state that remained external to society. To put it another way, the Coalition assumed, falsely, that an Iraqi face on state building could substitute effectively for Iraqi ownership of state building.

A further theme that became more significant through the latter half of 2003 was the extent to which personnel within some branches of the state had to extract themselves from society in order to maintain their official positions.[30] Coalition personnel already required military escorts to leave the Green Zone (the heavily-fortified area of Baghdad containing the main headquarters of the Coalition and Iraqi officials), and these were only infrequently available to middle ranking staff. As a result, only a minority visited the Iraqi ministries over which they had decision-making authority on a regular basis, with decreasing numbers willing to do so after the attack on the UN compound on 19 August 2003. With some of the insurgents targeting Iraqi personnel who worked in the Green Zone and within the IGC, the ability of those Iraqis who kept their official positions to maintain a close interaction with society without jeopardising their own security was stretched considerably. The murder of SCIRI's head Muhammad Baqr al-Hakim in the bomb blast at the Imam 'Ali mosque on 19 August and the fatal shooting of Aqila al-Hashimi on 20 September, less than ten weeks after being appointed to the IGC, ensured that the prospects for fluid inter-action between the senior personnel of the state and Iraqi society were cut off. The IGC and senior officials cooperating with the Coalition shut themselves away inside what used to be the Ministry of Industry and Military Industrialisation within the Green Zone, or in separate security compounds such as al-Shaheen hotel on Masbah Street, often keeping them as their main places of residence within Iraq. The result was highly limited interaction between Iraqis cooperating with the Coalition and Iraqi society.

Moreover, whilst the Coalition was willing to provide protection to senior Iraqi officials and their families (or, as was sometimes the case, to enable those families to relocate abroad), it did not offer such protection to lower level staff. As a result of the series of death threats and attacks made upon local translators, the Coalition preferred to use translators from outside Iraq, primarily Arab Americans. This had two consequences.

Firstly, many CPA personnel, not to mention military patrols, had to do without translators in their engagements with Iraqi society and personnel. The number of Arabs who had not been resident in Iraq but who were willing to serve with Coalition personnel inside Iraq was relatively low, particularly given the unpopularity of the invasion with most of the population. Thus, middle-ranking Coalition officials in CPA ministries were frequently able only to consult with staff from Iraqi ministries or prominent figures from Iraqi society whose English was sufficient for those purposes, regardless of their seniority or expertise.

This inefficiency in interaction converged with a second consequence: even when translators were available, they lacked the ability to act as intermediaries. Coalition military personnel who had served in Bosnia-Herzegovina drew a stark contrast between that situation and their Iraq experiences. In Bosnia, local translators gave regular informal accounts to NATO service personnel of local grievances, anxieties and rumours, and were able to converse freely with local officials and members of the population to gain a nuanced perspective on their beliefs. They also acted as a constituency supportive of NATO within much of Bosnian society, dispelling rumours and lessening suspicions. In Iraq, the translators, many of whom were second or third generation Arab Americans, lived alongside Coalition personnel, and thus did not develop any better an understanding of local opinion than non-Arab Coalition personnel, and were usually treated with as much suspicion as that group.[31] In these most elemental ways, the personnel of the state were always detached from the society they were ruling over, and became increasingly so over time.

We shall discuss in Chapter Three why the US reversed its initial policy of holding elections soon after the toppling of the Ba'th regime. One effect of this abandonment of elections was that in the aftermath

of the invasion there was no direct mechanism for conveying Iraqi preferences and pressing them on to state authorities. In place of a more
direct form of access to the range of Iraqi viewpoints, the Coalition
used alternative methods to access and influence public opinion from
the summer of 2003. In early July 2003 the CPA Governance Office
— in coordination with the Office of Transition Initiatives of the US
Agency for International Development (USAID) and the State Department's Office of Research — made the decision to provide funds and
resources to establish the Iraq Center for Research and Strategic Studies (ICRSS). This body, formally independent although working under
contract from US governmental agencies, was headed by Sa'dun al-
Dulaymi, a former security officer in the Iraqi armed forces. Dulaymi
had defected in 1991, and had been advising exiled opposition groups
and US agencies — unsuccessfully, as it turned out — on strategies
for the dealing with Iraq's armed forces during the occupation. He was
later appointed Minister of Defence in the Transitional Government
from April 2005. The ICRSS went on to conduct three opinion surveys
in collaboration with the CPA and the State Department later in 2003,
as well as quality of life surveys from October onwards.[32] A separate
organisation with Iraqi staff, the Independent Institute for Administrative and Civil Society Studies (IIACSS), conducted a series of extensive
opinion polls from November 2003 that were devised and funded by
the Washington-based International Republican Institute (IRI), working on behalf of a semi-official US agency, the National Endowment for
Democracy (NED).

To supplement the statistical data from opinion polls, in August
2003 the Coalition military recruited a team of eleven Iraqis who
would work with eight US personnel to collect information from local newspapers and other documents in circulation, to produce a daily
intelligence briefing, called the 'Baghdad Mosquito'. As part of this
gathering of information, a set of trusted local Iraqis, acting without
the knowledge of their neighbourhoods, would be brought into the

Coalition headquarters every week to inform military analysts of the political discussions that they had participated in or overheard during the course of the week. The information from these two sources would be compiled into a weekly document that was circulated widely among policy makers and military officials, entitled 'What's the word on the streets of Baghdad?'[33]

The Coalition military also paid particular attention to mosques in Baghdad. A psychological operations team from the US military would be sent to the vicinity of every significant mosque in the city for Friday prayers, to listen to the sermon broadcast through the loudspeakers. This allowed Coalition personnel to categorise each mosque with a red, yellow or green light. The red light was a signal that the preachers at the mosque should be visited by Coalition personnel with a warning. If the mosque retained its red light after the following Friday, the standard procedure was to detain the relevant preacher.[34]

Whilst through the latter half of 2003 and 2004 the Coalition built up a significantly greater knowledge of Iraqi society and popular politics, many problems remained in this regard. Intelligence gleaned through the Coalition military was often not provided to civil affairs personnel, and vice versa: the separation of command chains, discussed further in Chapter Three, impacted negatively upon the Coalition's ability to make an integrated analysis of Iraqi political developments. There was a severe problem in transmitting information through the Coalition system, arising from the *ad hoc* nature of arrangements made in Iraq. One CPA Governorate Coordinator described to us how on arriving in the region over which he was to try to exercise rule in October 2003, he 'inherited not a folder' from his predecessors to induct him into his new environment.[35] These problems were only partially remedied by the end of 2004, with the military still citing an 'intelligence gap' that hindered its ability to identify the societal mechanisms of support for the insurgency.[36]

Larry Diamond, who served as Senior Adviser to the CPA on governance issues from January to April 2004, later described the problem in these terms:

Crippled by a severe shortage of American officials fluent in Arabic (as well as the steady loss of Iraqi translators to intimidation and assassination), and distanced from Iraqi society by formidable walls of security, the CPA never adequately grasped Iraqi preferences, hopes and frustrations.[37]

The number of Coalition officials who spoke in interviews of this distance between the mechanisms of governance and Iraqi society indicates that this was a widely held perception.

The Coalition sought to use the media to influence public opinion, but its efforts were slow in developing. Bremer, in drafting his first strategic plan for the CPA in July 2003, included 'strategic communication' — that is, shaping the understanding and evaluation by key audiences of US policies — as one of the five 'pillars' around which CPA action would be oriented. However, according to the CPA's Director of Planning, this pillar was dropped from the final version of the plan because 'the resources to implement it were unavailable'.[38] Strategic communication was only reintroduced as a pillar from December 2003, when the CPA redesigned its strategy around the forthcoming transition and dissolution of the CPA scheduled for June 2004.

The slow pace at which a strategy was developed can be seen in the pattern of interaction with the Iraqi media from 2003. Television serves as the most significant source of news for the vast majority of Iraqis. In a nationwide survey carried out by Gallup in March and April 2004, 57% of Iraqis said that they did not read the newspapers at all, while more than 76% watched TV every day.[39] *Al-Sabah*, a Coalition-sponsored newspaper in Baghdad, reached around 50,000 people out of a city population of 5 million.[40] Despite its potential value as a means of influencing popular perceptions, US policy initially favoured the dismantling of the centralised state broadcasting network, with US commanders in some areas helping to set up new local TV and radio stations.[41] However, from mid-2003 the CPA-sponsored Iraqi Media Network (IMN) made a concerted effort to rebuild a national broadcast network, in some cases at the expense of new, local media outlets which US personnel had been instrumental in creating. For example, in May 2003, US troops seized control of the TV station in Mosul.[42] Over the next two months, the 101st Airborne Division provided funding to refurbish Mosul TV; re-named Channel 7, the TV station was relaunched July 2003. This time, US troops took a direct role in programming, rather than simply airing announcements. The US Army's 22nd Mobile Public Affairs Department created the Arabic language 'Iraqi Freedom News' and ensured the programme was broadcast at least four times a week. However, within weeks, the CPA asserted its control over the station, and brought it within the Iraqi Media Network to give it direction from Baghdad.[43]

The Iraqi Media Network struggled to gain the level of credibility attained by its competitors, even though its reach was more extensive. Its main TV channel, re-branded al-Iraqiya in November 2004, was received by 84% of homes, in contrast to approximately 33% having access to the satellite stations al-Jazeera, based in Qatar, and al-Arabiya, based in Dubai. It carried official statements from the CPA, including a weekly television address by Bremer broadcast on Friday evenings, to put over the Coalition's account of events. Nevertheless, according to a survey carried out by the State Department in August and September 2003 in seven Iraqi cities, only 12% of households with satellite access said they watched the IMN station, and only 6% named the channel as the one they 'trust the most'.[44] Across all households, a later survey found that only 21% of viewers accepted a description of al-Iraqiya as 'objective', in contrast to 39% describing al-Arabiya and 35% describing al-Jazeera in this way.[45] These problems were compounded with a generally low level of resources and capabilities available to al-Iraqiya. Unlike the satellite stations, it did not undertake live broadcasts until October 2003, its broadcast signal was often weak and difficult to receive, and its staff were poorly paid in comparison with what was on offer from international broadcasters, so that there was a high turnover of personnel.[46] Al-Iraqiya was thus ill-equipped to take on the difficult job of bridging the gap between senior Coalition personnel — neither Bremer nor the CPA's two senior spokespersons spoke any Arabic — and Iraqi society.

Anecdotal evidence also suggests that the pan-Arab satellite channels had a much greater appeal than al-Iraqiya. Kate Butler, who delivered a training course for Iraqi journalists from Basra on behalf of the BBC World Service Trust in August 2004, recalled that her students all turned first to the satellite channels for news:

TV is by far the most popular source over radio and newspapers. All of them say they regularly depend on Al-Jazeera, and Al-Arabiya for their news - they are very suspicious of Al Iraqiya [...] all feel it is a mouthpiece for the Americans and the new government.[47]

In view of the low level of credibility of al-Iraqiya from late 2003, Coalition military and civilian officers began to interact with the Arab satellite broadcasters to a much greater extent, despite their considerable initial mistrust of these outlets. At its inception, the CPA press office contained only two Arabic speakers out of its ten staff, and none of its personnel had prior links to or experience with the mainstream Arab news stations. The Coalition eventually hired a Cairo-based Arab consultancy firm to help build better links with Arab broadcasters, but only after seven months of the occupation, during which the relationship was confrontational at best.[48] It was only in 2004 that the Coalition managed to monitor the Arab satellite stations closely, and be on hand to provide them with contrary viewpoints.

With the new Iraqi newspapers, US Central Command authorised a programme, seemingly beginning in June 2004,[49] to pay Iraqi newspapers to take unattributed articles written by US psychological operations officers. The programme was conducted by members of a contracted private company, the Lincoln Group, but was under the close supervision of Multinational Corps-Iraq.[50] According to reports referring to unpublished official documents, about a thousand such articles were published over the next eighteen months, in 12 to 15 Iraqi and other Arab newspapers, with payments to newspaper editors ranging from $40 to $2,000.[51] A second channel to influence media coverage was the Baghdad Press Club, founded by the US military in 2004, which reportedly paid Iraqi journalists from both print and broadcast sectors sums up to $50 each to cover stories related to US-led reconstruction projects.[52] This point is relevant here as it indicates that the Coalition had such difficulties in putting its arguments across in a consistent and transparent way through the Iraqi media that it decided to resort to subterfuge and concealment of authorship as a mechanism of influence.

One Coalition military commanding officer, based in southern Iraq during 2004, described to us the effects of the poor relationship with the Arab satellite broadcasters. According to him, Coalition personnel felt aggrieved that al-Jazeera or al-Arabiya would broadcast claims about the conduct of Coalition personnel without bringing CPA personnel on as well to challenge those claims. One example was a claim on Arab satellite stations that US forces had destroyed the golden dome at the shrine to Imam 'Ali Ibn Abi Talib in Najaf during the clashes of August 2004 with the Mahdi Army. Correctly or not, Coalition personnel considered that spontaneous demonstrations resulted from these claims. The Coalition, which had not established channels of access to the satellite broadcasters to challenge these claims, had to find other mechanisms to put over its position, such as leaflet drops from aircraft and meetings with local tribal leaders. These measures however were deeply unreliable and had at best a delayed impact: the commanding officer estimated that Coalition soldiers had killed 600 to 700 Iraqis in riots during the six-month period he was based in the governorate, and blamed these riots on claims broadcast by Arab satellite networks. The claims made by Coalition officers indicate the scale of the practical difficulties that the Coalition attributed to its inadequate ability to influence Iraqi society. The Coalition also failed to convince Iraqis of its view that responsibility for the deaths of those it killed lay with others.

FAILURES OF COMPLEX ENGAGEMENT
WATER, ELECTRICITY, EMPLOYMENT

For the Iraqi state to become effectively socially engaged, it needs to do more than establish reliable channels of communication with the population. Given the degeneration of Iraq's social infrastructure, particularly since the imposition of UN sanctions in 1990, the state had to act as the primary service provider to society. The problems of reconstructing the state so that it could re-establish that role after its post-invasion collapse have often been attributed by political commentators in the US and UK to the damage caused by the insurgency, petty crime and organised criminal networks.[53] However, a range of difficulties have also been caused by the political priorities of the occupying powers, and these have been only partially related to those factors often cited. We will give three examples of sectors which the new Iraqi state failed to develop effectively in order to integrate itself into Iraqi society: water, electricity and employment.

The water sector provides an example of a set of reconstruction and development programmes that consistently failed to achieve their expected results. In January 2004, the CPA estimated that the water network was still only working at 65% of its pre-invasion level.[54] According to the estimates of the CPA and the State Department, the proportion of Iraqi citizens who received potable water fell from 55-60% pre-invasion to 40% eighteen months after the invasion.[55] At the time of the June 2004 handover the CPA estimated that 90% of the Iraqi population would have access to potable water through the completion of US-funded projects over the following two years; however, evaluations of the likely impact of these projects had fallen considerably by September 2005, with only 50-60% thought likely to receive potable water when the projects had been completed.[56] In a USAID survey in February 2005, over half of the respondents rated their water supply as poor or fair, and over 80% rated their sewerage and wastewater disposal as poor or fair.[57] The reasons for this failure to meet expectations thus need examination.

The insurgency has clearly caused severe problems in completing water and sanitation projects within the expected timeframe. Work had to stop on the construction of a wastewater plant in central Iraq for almost two months in early 2005 because of threats from insurgents against the agency contracted to build the plant.[58] However, this is a problem particular to a certain model of reconstruction, in which foreign contractors had a leading role. Although Iraqi employees and subcontractors working in the water sector have often been subjected to intimidation, the politicisation of the development process through the contracting out of key services meant that the insurgents quickly understood the value of targeting projects that they could portray as dominated by foreign interests.

The Iraqi institution previously responsible for developing the national infrastructure, the General Company for Water Projects, was barred from bidding for water contracts with the CPA because of pre-invasion US regulations prohibiting the use of Iraqi state-owned enterprises as contractors. It may be because US corporations could benefit from a situation in which they were in an optimal position to serve as contractors that there was no political incentive to remove those prohibitions after the invasion. Bechtel National Inc. was awarded the contract for managing the reconstruction of Iraq's water supply system, the result being excess costs for foreign workers and importation of materials that were actually available locally. For the expansion of the Sharkh Dijlah Water Treatment Plant, according to the *Washington Post*, Bechtel 'spent four months studying the General Co. plans, concluded they were adequate, modified them slightly, city officials said, reissued orders for parts from the same supplier, and basically did what was being done before.'[59] In consequence, the water treatment facilities scheduled by the Iraqi company for completion in mid-2003 were due under the new schedule to be opened only by May 2004. With numerous delays, the plant remained closed, and had not opened by the time Bechtel's third quarterly report for 2005 on the water sector in Iraq was issued. USAID, the contracting agency, reported in July 2005 that the project was 70% completed.[60]

A range of further problems hampered the effective development of the water sector even when projects were completed. The US Government Accountability Office (GAO) found that out of the $200 million of US funds spent on completed water and sanitation projects by June 2005, approximately $52 million had been spent on projects that were either not operating or operating below capacity.[61] Problems in recruiting and re-hiring plant personnel caused consistent staffing shortages. Bechtel estimated that water and wastewater plants had only one-third of the staff they required, which meant that plants intended to function continuously had to be shut at night.[62] There was a high level of staff turnover, and management problems meant that chemicals and supplies, present in some parts of the country, were often unavailable at plants in other areas. This indicates that very large expenditure was unable to overcome the specific problems of foreign management of these projects in that environment.

A similar pattern exists in the continuing difficulties of the electricity sector, which was given priority status by the CPA. Out of the approximately $18.44 billion allocated as supplemental appropriations for the Iraq Relief and Reconstruction Fund (IRRF) by Congress for fiscal year 2004, $5.56 billion was committed to the electricity sector. This was the largest block of funds devoted to any sector and was over seven times the funds allocated to health care ($793 million).[63] This reflected a sense within the CPA that maintaining electricity supplies would be crucial in preventing economic collapse and the resultant political unrest.[64]

The CPA produced a series of plans to renovate the electricity sector. Under the *ancien régime*, Iraq had been generating 4,400 megawatts (MW) of electricity at peak times of the day. However, Baghdad had priority in terms of supplies, often receiving electricity round the clock. The first objective of the CPA from June 2003 with regard to electricity was twofold: to repair the existing infrastructure, and to remove the priorities that existed for some areas under the Ba'th — that is, to allocate electricity equitably.[65] This was followed, from mid-August 2003, with an attempt to boost generation to pre-war levels of 4,400MW by October, and to reach 6,000MW by 1 June 2004. Bremer went further, declaring in October 2003 that if Congress allocated the requested resources for the IRRF, as it duly did, then 'we expect to produce enough electricity for all Iraqis to have electrical service 24 hours daily'.[66]

It took a long time for any of these targets to be reached. Although the CPA managed to raise electricity generation from 3,200 megawatts in June 2003 to 3,900MW by October 2003, its target for that month was 4,400MW. Moreover, levels fluctuated around the 4,000MW mark for the next eight months, going no higher than 4,300MW in mid-February 2004. In the week at the start of June 2004 during which generation was planned to reach 6,000MW, it stood obstinately at under 4,200MW.[67] Although there were notable increases in power generation by October 2004, production once again had fallen by January 2005 to around 3,600MW.[68] US officials later shifted to evaluating electricity generation in terms of average electricity production over the day, rather than just peak production. By this measure, Iraq had produced 98,000 MW-hours (MWh) before the conflict. In March 2004, the CPA set a goal for electricity generation as 120,000 MWh.[69] The Iraqi power sector had not reached this goal by 2006; instead, the State Department simply lowered the goal to 110,000 MWh in June

2005, which it then said it had reached.[70] The level of power generation fell beneath this target again a week later, and had not regained it by the start of 2006. Overall, three years down the line, electricity production was hovering around pre-war levels.[71]

The extreme slowness and frequent failure of the CPA to meet its generation projections have often been attributed to the destruction and theft of parts of the electricity infrastructure by guerrilla organisations and private criminal organisations. Some have speculated that sabotage of the electricity network was a particular objective of insurgents.[72] Although the insurgency clearly has had a direct effect upon the operation of some power stations, its impact was exacerbated by the role that foreign contractor companies have had in re-establishing Iraq's electricity system. The contractor companies have been in general extremely hesitant to place their personnel in situations of potential danger. As one former CPA regional coordinator recorded, the security standards of some contractors were so 'unrealistic [that] … it made them unreliable'.[73] In practice, this meant that some engineers would not spend more than thirty minutes at any one power plant; that a significant amount of funds would go on supplying up to six bodyguards to each official;[74] and that major contractors would pull all their staff out during sensitive periods, often for a periods of weeks at a time.[75] Where military or paramilitary personnel could not go, electricity stations stagnated. For example, a power station in Maysan governorate, built by the German electrical company Siemens, was left idle when the Coalition military formed an agreement with the town council not to enter the town. Siemens personnel refused to enter the town without a uniformed armed escort after the April 2004 disturbances, and so the relatively minor problems that prevented the power station from becoming operational were not fixed.[76]

Furthermore, the weakness of the bureaucracy that now managed Iraq took its toll. The Ministry of Electricity was beset with problems of inadequate planning, and the CPA failed to ensure the timely delivery of necessary parts, material and specialised labour. Two senior officials who had a direct role in the organisation of Iraq's electricity network throughout the CPA period labelled this 'the primary cause of the disappointing maintenance program'.[77]

Two political decisions were also highly relevant to the electricity programme. Firstly, the CPA decided to build a particular type of power station that could be opened quickly, in order to demonstrate its dynamism through the successful completion of large-scale projects, as well as to use the increased electricity supply as a mechanism to legitimise its rule.[78] As a result, it chose to construct power stations powered by gas combustion turbines, which could be completed in four to eight months, or to re-fit existing power stations with this technology. Gas stations were preferred over steam turbines fired by crude oil, Iraq's standard form of electricity generation before, which would take at least two years to build.[79] The contract for the larger power stations went to Bechtel Inc, who constructed gas turbine stations in Baiji, south Baghdad and Kirkuk among other places; the smaller projects were left to three other US corporations (Washington Group International for northern Iraq, Fluor Corporation for central Iraq, and Perini Corporation for southern Iraq).

The major problem with building gas-fired power stations was that there was limited availability of suitable natural gas inside Iraq. Iraq had not previously created an effective gas collection system from its oil wells, its gas fields were undeveloped, and its pipelines were in a considerably worse condition than the oil equivalents. As a result, there was a persistent shortage of gas supplies for these new or newly fitted power stations. Iraqi plant managers ended up using low-grade oil to fuel the gas combustion engines, which resulted in low efficiency. Plant maintenance costs increased threefold, resulted in frequent equipment failure, decreased the life-span of the generators by 60-70%, and decreased the power output of the turbines by up to 50% even when they were operating. A review conducted by the Iraqi Ministry of Electricity found that 65 out of the 123 gas combustion turbine units — 53% of the entire capacity — were out of operation on the day of investigation. One would usually expect no more than 10% of units to be out of operation for scheduled maintenance.[80]

The second political choice made by the Coalition was to strive for equitability in electricity distribution, a goal it did not achieve. The CPA planned to concentrate electricity generation in the more stable south of the Iraq, and to transmit the required amounts northwards to Baghdad via high-voltage transmission lines. However, this process could only work if it had the general compliance of the population in the areas that hosted the large power stations, which was found to be lacking. The transmission network was frequently attacked, seemingly not by anti-occupation insurgents, but by those who sought to retain locally-produced electricity for their own governorates. The lines northwards from Nasiriyya were consistently sabotaged, which allowed the southern region to have continuous electricity, whilst denying equivalent amounts of power to central Iraq. In some cases, saboteurs left signs reading, 'Stop sending our power to Baghdad'.[81] The result was a near-reversal of the situation that had existed under the *ancien régime*: in March 2004, Basra was receiving electricity for 24 hours a day, and was keeping its main roads illuminated overnight, whilst central Iraqi provinces received much less: Salah al-Din had power for 11 hours per day, Babil for 12 hours, Baghdad for 14 hours.[82] Nevertheless, as the network was continually, albeit temporarily, rebuilt, Basra would frequently go back to having 12 hours of electricity per day or fewer.[83] By July 2005, the network had once again reversed its inequality of distribution in favour of Baghdad which was receiving an average of 14.4 hours per day of electricity, whilst south-central governorates received between 6 and 8 hours a day.[84] However, the tug-of-war against Baghdad was soon resumed by the governor of Basra province, Muhammad Musabih al-Wa'ili.[85] In January 2006, the situation in Baghdad had deteriorated even further, with the city receiving only 2.6 hours a day of electricity compared with a national average of 10.3 hours per day. Some central areas of Baghdad, such as Bab al-Mu'atham, were receiving no electricity at all for more than a month at a time in mid-2006.[86]

The fate of the Iraqi electricity sector from April 2003 onwards demonstrates well the way in which the centrifugal forces of highly mobilised local movements combined with the political priorities of a foreign administration working through the framework of a weak bureaucracy to hinder the development of a key state building project. The water and electricity sectors indicate how the state did not establish itself in the role of a service provider, a key method of cooption for the modern state. The third sector that states have frequently used to structure the lives and activities of its citizens in a relatively non-coercive way has been that of employer, and this was a route that the CPA-led state again attempted to take. CPA officials envisioned that through the process of engaging large numbers of Iraqis in the labour market, they would acquire a position of social influence, with the Iraqi workforce acting as a stabilising force within society.

The theme of employment had already been brought to the fore by the de-Ba'thification programme and the dissolution of entities associated with the *ancien régime*. These two processes were launched in the first two orders issued by the CPA. De-Ba'thification meant exclusion from public sector employment of those who had been in the top four ranks of the Ba'th party, and Ba'th party members of any rank within the top three layers of management, subject to discretionary exemptions.[87] Up to 30,000 individuals, including people who had sought a role in the public sphere and career advancement rather than acting as ideological supporters of the *ancien régime*, were dismissed from their positions as a result.[88] The entities dissolved in the CPA's second order included the army, the ministries of Information and Defence and all Iraqi intelligence services, and a figure of 400,000 left unemployed by this measure was widely reported.[89] The direct impact of these two orders, particularly in the development of the insurgency, has been widely discussed, and will be returned to in subsequent chapters. Both measures were in large part tacitly rescinded over the following few months, but the point here is that the CPA began its rule of Iraq with a programme to dismantle organisations that were also some of Iraq's biggest employers prior to the invasion, and its reputation suffered accordingly. The Iraqi Union of the Unemployed kept a round-the-clock encampment outside CPA Headquarters in Baghdad and maintained it for 45 days until it was forcibly dispersed and its leaders arrested.[90] The CPA would need to find ways of providing formal sector jobs to Iraqis to attain a steering influence over Iraqi society.

The CPA initially projected that it would be able to engage 100,000 new workers per quarter through a national employment programme, and launched the 'Hundred Thousand Jobs' Programme for engaging the unemployed in civic works programmes to operate through the Ministry of Public Works.[91] However, delays in establishing the national employment programme meant that only 9,100 new jobs were created in the public works sector during the first seven months of occupation through a pilot project for this programme.[92] The number employed on new public works jobs had increased to nearly 77,000 by March 2004, when the programme was closed down. Even taking into account the Iraqis newly employed in the security sector, the number of new jobs created in the first eleven months of occupation was only 44.5% of the Coalition's initial projections for this period.[93] Subsequent programmes of the CPA's Programme Management Office (PMO) — renamed the Project and Contracting Office (PCO) when it was brought under the auspices of the US Embassy after June 2004 — all served to increase employment, particularly from November 2004 onwards. The PCO had begun over 1,000 construction projects across Iraq by December 2004,[94] and over 150,000 Iraqis were employed in projects administered by the US Government throughout the period from March 2005 until mid-June 2005, when numbers declined. This was in contrast to only 60,000 Iraqis employed on such projects in November 2004.

This increase in the numbers of Iraqis employed through this route was the result of rapid creation of smaller-scale projects that were less visible than earlier schemes. After January 2005, these were usually organised through Iraqi ministries, albeit with funds from the PCO.[95] However, the projects involved only a small minority of the Iraqi labour force. By December 2004, only 23.4% of a sample adult population was in full-time employment, with a further 13.8% in part-time employment. Over 40% of a polled sample cited unemployment as one of the three main issues for concern, a significantly higher total than for any other issue.[96] According to the *Iraq Living Conditions Survey (ILCS) 2004*, out of Iraq's total working age population of 16.45 million, only 6.03 million (37%) were employed.[97] This does not mean that the remainder should all be classified as unemployed, as 59% of the working age population were not seeking paid work, for example being engaged in child rearing or domestic work. However, the ILCS notes that the percentage of the working age population who were part of the labour force, whether employed or seeking work, had fallen over time in Iraq — from 41% in 1977 to 35% in 2004. Only 13% of women of working age were part of the labour force.[98] This can be seen as part of the Islamisation of society, which will be addressed more thoroughly in Chapter Three. More generally, hopes of the state acting as an employer have led to frustration, particularly among the educated, as the ILCS reports:

A large number of workers are discouraged and have given up looking for work, believing there is none to be found. In total, 1,359,000 Iraqis are either unemployed or discouraged workers, yielding an unemployment rate of 18.4 % when including the discouraged workers, and a core unemployment rate of 10.5 %. The unemployment rate (including discouraged workers) among young persons is 33.4 %, and reaches an astonishing 37.2 % among young men with secondary or higher education.[99]

What explains the substantial delays and limited impact of the PMO/ PCO in engaging the labour force in the processes of state building? One major problem was the delays caused by competition between parts of the US administering structures for control. The PMO/PCO was a major element of the US programme in Iraq — its entire budget was $12.6 billion, or 68% of the entire US allocation for Iraq's reconstruction.[100] This high level of resources for a new organisation, which was thus without an established place in the US political process, turned it into an arena for bargaining between different factions. The PMO/ PCO was part of the CPA, but reported independently to both the Department of Defence and the State Department. It worked substantially through CJTF-7 and later through Iraqi ministries, but was dependent upon the US Congress for its budget. This left it vulnerable to a multiplicity of conflicting pressures without clear procedures on how to resolve them. After it was created in September 2003 to administer Iraqi funds for reconstruction, the Department of Defence sought from December 2003 firstly to reduce its budget to $1.9 billion — barely 10% of what it had been established to administer — and then to turn over a substantial part of its work to USAID or the Army Corps of Engineers. Additionally, the issuing of the first $5 billion of contracts was put on indefinite hold. According to his public affairs assistant, the head of the PMO, David J. Nash, wrote to his staff threatening to resign. The continuation of the PMO, and Nash's own position, were saved largely through feeding of articles to the news media about the threat to the reconstruction process.[101] Nevertheless, the overall level of funding was reduced and new delays introduced in order to cope with a new factor thrown into the reconstruction process — the announcement in November 2003 that the CPA would dissolve itself by the end of June 2004, which meant that contracts already negotiated with those involved in Iraq's reconstruction would have to be reworked.[102]

The problem of disbursing funds effectively did not just come from battles with the Pentagon. The US Congress insisted on maintaining oversight to a degree that many officials in Iraq rejected. As Hilary Synnott, Regional Coordinator for CPA South from July 2003 until January 2004, wrote:

[T]he CPA's accounting practices were tightened due to questions in Congress about possible irregularities and alleged improprieties. This led to a stark contrast between, on the one hand, Bremer's repeated, and surely justified, injunctions to spend money and create jobs and, on the other, delays caused by constantly changing rules for bidding and accounting for funds to conform to the multiplicity of US government requirements.[103]

The result was grave delays in the contracting process which underlay the formal process of Iraq's reconstruction, and the low level of disbursement once the awarding process had actually begun. The Pentagon only began awarding contracts out of Iraq Relief and Reconstruction Fund (IRRF) funds from the US taxpayer for reconstruction projects in March 2004, almost six months after the allocation was made, with only companies from Coalition countries initially able to bid for primary contracts. It was somewhat unsurprising that at a networking event organised for Iraqi businessmen shortly afterwards by the CPA, the participants complained of lack of clarity surrounding the reconstruction process.[104] Only $366 million of the $18.4 billion — less than 2% — of the funds allocated by Congress in October 2003 had been spent from the IRRF by 22 June 2004, six days before the handover. This is in contrast to the $19 billion spent from the Development Fund for Iraq (DFI) out of the $20 billion available; the DFI, funded from Iraq's oil export earnings, was not subject to the same degree of external competition for control, and so was relied upon by the CPA for its expenditure.[105] The result, however, was that significant amounts did not go into the programmes specifically designed for Iraqi job creation, which were to be implemented by the PMO out of IRRF funds, until after the June 2004 handover. By May 2004, only 104 of the 2,300 projects planned by the PMO had even begun.[106]

Although funds began to be disbursed on a larger scale after the formal handover of sovereignty, problems of coordination between different parts of the US administrative structures continued. A separate programme, the Commander's Emergency Response Programme (CERP), had been established to focus on local, small-scale projects, and enabled brigade- and division-level commanders to spend up to $50,000 and $100,000 respectively for reconstruction projects of their choice. Though they were highly dispersed and without strong central coordination, and thus of variable quality, the effectiveness of these programmes was in general high, disbursement was good compared to the IRRF (up to March 2004, $222 million of $549 million had been spent) and a comparatively high level of employment resulted, with over 20,000 Iraqis employed on projects funded by the CERP throughout the first half of 2005. According to one official US assessment: 'Tactical military commanders say the benefit received from CERP funds far outweighs the amount provided and are finding that funding minor efforts such as repairs to houses and buildings are helping to stabilize areas in Iraq.'[107] Nevertheless, when the International Crisis Group analysed the operation of the programme in Iraq, it found that its activities were largely under-funded and commanders were struggling to find the additional resources needed, relying upon seized assets and Iraqi oil revenues.[108] Hesitations about devolving significant amount of money away from CPA headquarters may well be partly responsible for these difficulties.

These problems were compounded by the weakness of established channels through which funds could be distributed for job creation. There have been frequent reports of how US military personnel would travel through parts of Iraq, handing out wads of notes — presumably from CERP funds — to seemingly worthy causes, in the absence of formal mechanisms for determining local needs. One journalist, walking with US troops around Yusufiyya, reported that 'commanders were carrying thousands of dollars to give to good citizens who promised to fix things in their village. An official at the local water treatment works got $900 to help him with his generator, while someone at the school down the road was pleasantly surprised to have 10 crisp $100 bills thrust into his hands.'[109] This approach, justified with the counter-insurgency slogan of 'winning hearts and minds', seems to have been taken particularly in areas, and at times, of unrest. One officer in Tikrit described measures such as paying villagers to clean out a ditch or to repair a local swimming pool as a strategy of 'economic warfare'.[110] A former CPA Governance Coordinator for a southern governorate described how US troops went into local organising bureaus of the Sadr movement in the aftermath of the conflict in April 2004, and offered well-paid jobs to anyone willing to give up his or her membership of the movement.[111] This degree of *ad hoc* organisation has existed because of the weak nature of the Iraqi governing bureaucracy, incapable for most of the country of translating centrally designed projects reliably into operational programmes for employment. A governance officer with the CPA related this point well:

There was just no system, governmental system in place that you could just rely upon. So, every group that was providing funding was just providing money and was sometimes sketchy as to how the funds were being managed in their disbursement and use.[112]

There were further specific failures with employment programmes. On 22 April 2004, the CPA launched the Accelerated Iraq Recon-struction Programme (AIRP) with a $500 million budget, designed to 'deliver high value services for communities with critical needs, and provide employment opportunities for a number of struggling communities'.[113] Despite its generous budget, the AIRP employed at a maximum 17,600 Iraqis. The number in employment through the programme actually decreased by over a quarter, to 12,900 employ-ees, during the anti-Sadr offensive in August 2004, and fell to less than 10,000 by the end of the year.[114] Furthermore, as funds were disbursed more consistently through the PMO/PCO, the sectors to which they were mostly allocated — oil and electricity — whilst highly important, were relatively small employers. In contrast, the agricultural sector was a significant employer, accounting for the employment of 27% of those in the age group 15-25.[115] However, it was not until October 2004 that the US authorities began specific funding for agriculture aimed at expanding private sector agribusiness throughout Iraq, and only $3 million out of the $100 million allocated to this sector from the IRRF had actually been spent by July 2005.[116]

All three service sectors discussed above — water, electricity and employment — include examples of the problems faced in creating a state able to adopt non-coercive mechanisms for managing Iraqi society. Other sectors display the same problems and the same negative outcomes. In January 2006, 63% to 74% of Iraq's diesel, kerosene, benzene and LPG were being imported (a significant deterioration compared with earlier periods). Even with these imports there were severe shortages.[117] There are frequent reports of Iraqis spending days queuing to fill petrol tanks, with family members taking turns waiting in the car. As a result fuel shortages have constituted a major source of frustration with the Coalition, and rumours readily spread that the shortages are caused by the Coalition stealing Iraq's resources.[118] 25% of the population (6.5 million people) were dependent on food rations in September 2004, while 2.6 million of them were forced by poverty to sell part of their food rations in order buy other basic necessities such as medicine. Food shortages between the invasion and the end of 2004 resulted in a doubling of acute malnutrition among children under five,[119] particularly in the South.[120] 27% of children were suffering from chronic malnutrition in September 2004 and the figure was roughly the same in late 2005.[121]

In summary, because foreign corporations have been central to the project of state building there have been a range of inefficiencies, inabilities and vulnerabilities that have stymied that project considerably. Prioritisation of these corporations and Coalition decision-making compounded the low capacity of the Iraqi state apparatus, which was unable to re-establish the administrative structures able to assess conditions and implement programmes that could in turn form the basis of the state building project. Coherent Iraqi ownership of the various sectors of state service provision has not been promoted with any vigour. As a result, the resources of the new Iraqi state have themselves become arenas for competition in which the actions of elements of the US government and local Iraqi agents to maximise their own benefits from the rebuilding process have substantially derailed its overall impact.

As we have argued, the state building project involves trying to turn the allies of the rulers into their agents, through a blend of coercion, cooption and legitimation, preserving the locally-based legitimacy of those agents but with their political authority delegated from the centre. The highly limited successes of the Iraqi state in becoming socially engaged means that many of the tacit allies of the US at the start of the occupation, such as much of the traditional Shi'a leadership, have often not actually been drawn into becoming agents of central government as hoped, but have preserved a highly conditional and occasionally antagonistic relationship with it. This stance is best illustrated through a quotation, by no means unusual, from 'Ali Shakr, a Shi'a secondary school maths teacher from al-Thawra district (Sadr City): 'Before this war, I was waiting for the Americans to come — and now I feel sort of cheated. All this talk about rebuilding Iraq, and all we see is a couple of light coats of paint. And they say they renovated Iraq.'[122]

BALANCING POWER, STRIVING FOR CONTROL

With most of the population not coopted into the process of state building, and with the weakness and unreliability of available channels to influence Iraqi political trends, the CPA and the Coalition more generally had to concentrate on how to maintain their position of centrality within the Iraqi political arena. Autonomous political dynamics were at work within Iraqi society which left the authority of the Coalition open to challenge, with potentially grave repercussions for the US's international standing. This led to the CPA and Coalition forces taking repeated measures that tended to entrench Coalition rule in Iraq, either sidelining domestic political actors or ensuring their dependence upon the Coalition, often at the expense of their legitimacy in the eyes of wider Iraqi society.

A legitimate Iraqi political centre would have entailed continual negotiation over, and challenge to, the Coalition's presence in and plans for Iraq during the transition and afterwards. This would have been highly noticeable in the military sphere: the oversight of Coalition military actions by an authoritative Iraqi national institution would almost inevitably have led to their curtailment, as greater caution would have been needed to avoid risking Iraqi lives. Significant constraints on the counter-insurgency methods of Coalition forces would have resulted. The Coalition's capacity to hold the keys to political authority gave the military the ability to preserve their security as they saw fit — a feature that remains a key requirement of the US armed forces for perceived political and strategic reasons. The US thus needed to manage and balance competing Iraqi political processes in order to maintain its unofficial retention of the levers of state power, particularly given the hostility of (as we show in Chapter Four) most of Iraq's population to a continued role for the Coalition military inside Iraq.

Therefore, in order to retain its pre-eminence within Iraq, the Coalition had to forestall the creation of an autonomous rival centre of political power, which would have necessitated some degree of oversight of, and compromise over, its actions. The US believed from late 2003, and especially after the January 2004, mass demonstrations called by Sistani's representatives, that a Najaf-based Shi'a leadership had coalesced, and would stake a claim to political power that the US could not challenge directly for fear of open revolt throughout southern Iraq.[123] On the one hand, the US calculated that it would need to acknowledge the legitimacy of the Shi'a claim for power, through acceding to the demand for elections that would translate a numerical majority into political superiority. On the other hand, it sought to ensure that this superiority would not seriously threaten US autonomy in decision-making.

The process of balancing internal political forces so that the US could retain pre-eminence did not stem from a carefully planned official strategy. It emerged as a product of many separate decisions taken by the US in seeking to preserve its autonomy from Iraqi political forces. It can be most clearly seen in the structuring of appointments to the Iraqi governing bodies, particularly the 25-member IGC. Although the IGC was accorded the authority to appoint ministers and issue decrees, its ability to function as a significant political actor was limited. Its nine major figures, appointed initially to operate as rotating presidents, came from antagonistic political factions, and they did not act in a unified way subsequently. One of the most important initial tasks given to the IGC was to establish a committee to draw up a constitution, but it was unable to reach agreement over the method of choosing the drafting committee; its failure to act decisively in this regard led to its constitutional role being supplanted by the 15 November 2003 plan.[124] The lack of coherence was also demonstrated in the way the ministers were selected: instead of selection by collective agreement, each member of the IGC was accorded the right to choose one minister, and the result was a 25-member cabinet to mirror the IGC. Many members of the IGC were heavily dependent upon the Coalition for their status; their access to the CPA provided many of them with an ability to gain leverage over the institutions of government, which they could use to improve their political positions. As a result, few within the IGC were willing to risk their good relations with the CPA in order to take a position critical of it, until the Falluja assault in April 2004, as it was nearing the end of its period of office. As their positions in national policymaking came from their appointment by the CPA, they did not carry the authority to challenge the CPA's decisions in the name of the Iraqi people, but only in the name of their own parties. Thus whilst the creation of the IGC was portrayed by the US as the advent of 'representative government' in Iraq, it can also be understood as forestalling the emergence of a cohesive and authoritative Iraqi political body.

Similarly, the provisions of the TAL of 8 March 2004 served to prevent any one political grouping from attaining a position of dominance. The TAL required a two-thirds majority in the National Assembly to elect a presidency council (article 36A) and, in the absence of unanimous agreement of the presidency council, to pass legislation (article 37) and to select a prime minister (article 38A). The high threshold necessary for the adoption of the permanent constitution (article 61C), and the implicit agreement that the three-person presidency council would be made up of a Sunni Arab, a Shi'a and a Sunni Kurd, together served to prevent any one group or leader — however popular — from being able to speak with the authority of the Iraqi people, and thus potentially challenge the US in their name. Inevitably, the stymieing of Shi'a political power through the TAL was disliked by the Najaf-based leadership, who conceived it as undemocratic and whose relations with the Kurdish leadership — arguably the biggest victors of the TAL — were left in crisis; but the Coalition ensured that the benefits to be achieved through it for the Shi'i were enough to offset the risks of outright rebellion.[125] By dropping the endorsement of the TAL from the draft of a text placed before the UN Security Council, for what became Security Council Resolution 1546 (8 June 2004), the US was able to demonstrate to the Shi'a leadership that its balancing process would sometimes tilt in their direction too, despite vigorous Kurdish protests.[126]

In addition to this process of internal balancing through forestalling the emergence of cohesive central institutions in official Iraqi political life, the US also undertook to ensure that those institutions were themselves offset by alternative forces within the sphere of governance. The overall authority of the IGC was itself frequently questioned, and Coalition officials indicated to journalists that they did not rule out dissolving it.[127] Ministers appointed by the IGC from September 2003 often faced a process of being marginalised, with their decision-making authority left unclear with respect to the CPA Senior Advisers appointed to each of their individual ministries. Two examples illustrate this process.

Haidar Jawad al-Abadi of al-Da'wa, Communications Minister from September 2003, was in repeated conflict with the CPA over the jurisdiction of his ministry. Abadi was more critical of the CPA's approach than most ministers, contradicting the CPA's stance on the goal of privatisation and strongly opposing the US military assault on Falluja in April 2004.[128] Abadi's ministry had awarded three Middle Eastern consortia two-year licenses to operate a mobile phone network in October 2003, but the CPA asked for the signing of these deals to be postponed, and the US Department of Defence ordered an investigation into how these licenses were awarded, because of allegations of bribery.[129] Whilst this investigation was ongoing, the jurisdictional dispute spread to the broadcasting sector in January 2004, when the US awarded a contract to a US manufacturing company, Harris Corp., to run Iraq's national broadcasting service in conjunction with two Arab companies. This time, Abadi claimed that he had not even been consulted over these contracts, and threatened to revoke them.[130] The CPA then established in March 2004 two autonomous organisations — the Iraqi Media Network and the Communications and Media Commission — which assumed roles that had been held by the Communications Ministry.[131] Neither of these two bodies could simply be dissolved by the IIG under the provisions of the TAL. One CPA official told the *Financial Times* that these bodies were created specifically to prevent Abadi from carrying out his threat to cancel licenses awarded by the Authority.[132] Finally, in April 2004, after the CPA closed down *al-Hawza*, the newspaper of the Sadr movement, Abadi criticised the act and claimed that he, as Communications Minister and thus with responsibility for the Iraqi press, should have been consulted.[133]

A second example is that of Nuri al-Badran, who served as Interior Minister from September 2003 until he resigned in April 2004. There were frequent disputes between Badran's office and the Coalition over the appointment of chiefs of police in individual governorates. In Maysan governorate, one senior Coalition military official described Badran's choice of police chief as 'incompetent', and the Coalition refused to support his appointment. Despite Badran's continued objections, he was, in the words of the Coalition official, forced 'to eat humble pie'.[134] In Wasit governorate, the CPA Governance Coordinator raised frequent criticisms of the police chief and his deputy, but considered that these officials had 'invisible protectors' inside the Ministry of the Interior, who promoted them despite the Coalition's misgivings about them. Nevertheless, the Governance Coordinator took the step of dismissing these two officials, despite acknowledging that this had been done 'in the teeth of opposition from the Ministry of the Interior'.[135] Badran claimed that he was asked to leave his position on 8 April 2004 by Bremer, although he asserted that Bremer made this request because he did not want both the Interior and Defence ministries to be headed by members of the Shi'a community.[136]

These examples indicate that, despite a process in which Iraqi officials were portrayed as having increased responsibility for governance, in cases of dispute the Coalition tended to overrule and marginalise officials who sought to act as autonomous decision-makers. This approach was adopted less often but did not disappear after the formal handover of June 2004. The IIG came into office with the major plan, supported by both Prime Minister Iyad 'Allawi and President Ghazi al-Yawar, of offering an amnesty to those who had been members of the insurgency but who had not killed other Iraqis.[137] However, it became clear quickly that the US Ambassador in Iraq opposed an amnesty for those who had been involved in attacks on US personnel, and the amnesty law that was eventually promulgated in August only dealt with minor offences.[138] Similarly, when 'Allawi attempted to appoint his ally Qassim Da'ud as his national security adviser as his tenure was about to begin, he found that Bremer had already appointed Muwafaq al-Rubiy'i to that position for a five-year term; Da'ud had to settle for the position of Minister Without Portfolio.[139] After four jails operated by the Interior Ministry were publicly reported in November and December 2005 as holding prisoners without charge, many appearing to have been starved, beaten and tortured, the US military in Iraq criticised the Iraqi Government for being ambivalent about the existence of militias, and announced that it would take over the role of prison inspections and require the Iraqi police forces to consult them before engaging in raids in the Baghdad area. The US military made these decisions despite acknowledging that the Interior Ministry was unhappy with them.[140] These episodes demonstrate that, in aspects of Iraq's governance that related to the security sphere, the US continued to assert its pre-eminence in decision-making after the formal handover, a position which it claimed the UN Security Council had endorsed in conferring authority on the multinational force 'to take all necessary measures to contribute to the maintenance of security and stability in Iraq'.[141] Nevertheless, from mid-2004 the US was less able to constrain the powers of central government through internal balancing: it retained the levers of financial controls and military force, but the Coalition had lost the central role in Baghdad's politics that it had once had.[142]

The US also sought to limit the authority of central government through balancing its power with that of regional actors. Once again, this was not dispersal of power through an integrated hierarchy, but fragmented power. There was a significant turn towards the use of tribal shaykhs, who became an alternative power base of the Coalition. This was not a new strategy for Iraq: under the League of Nations mandate, the British administrators had used tribal leaders — whose status had been weakening under the impact of large-scale migration to the cities, land reforms and the changing economy — as rivals to the monarch, as a method of limiting Faysal I's ability to campaign against the continuation of the mandate.[143] Additionally, the Ba'thist regime had used tribal leaders as a mechanism for social control as the central state lost its major sources of revenue with the imposition of UN economic sanctions in 1990. Judicial functions, tax collection and the enforcement of law were all to a considerable extent devolved to tribal figures, some of whom were appointed on the basis of often tenuous claims to traditional leadership while others had sworn an oath of allegiance to Saddam Hussein in 1991.[144]

Both of these tactics were employed to different extents by the Coalition, with the CPA creating an Office of Provincial Outreach (OPO) to deal with tribal affairs in December 2003. The CPA often channelled resources through tribal shaykhs, who then acted as intermediaries between the population and the occupation authorities. In Ramadi, for example, the Coalition military supplied tribal leaders with arms permits and gave jobs to their nominees, to guard power lines, for police work and as construction labour for example.[145] In return, tribal leaders reported to the CPA on local affairs, including the presence of looted material and wanted individuals. Tribal leaders also negotiated the release of prisoners and operated a tribal justice system in parts of the country.[146] A number of US military commanders took tribal shaykhs as their central point of contact within their areas of responsibility.[147] As a mechanism of social influence, then, tribal leaders were perceived as particularly useful to the Coalition. Alan King, deputy director of the OPO, stated, after meeting around 2,500 tribal leaders, that he had 'found that the sheikhs have the ability to exert a certain amount of influence and are key communicators, but I do not suggest that they control members of their tribes.'[148] The tribal leaders in turn affirmed their ability to act to reduce crime in their localities, thus asserting their role in activities usually reserved for agents of the state.[149] In January 2004, as discussed in Chapter Three, tribal representatives were allocated between 10 and 23 places out of approximately 40 members on each council.[150]

Tribes were often in direct competition as focuses of loyalty with political parties and the IGC that the parties dominated. Tribal leaders often spoke disparagingly of the role and legitimacy of the IGC, and vice versa. The former CPA Governance Coordinator of Wasit brought this point out well:

Although there were areas where the [tribes and parties] overlapped politically, these groups generally disliked one another; each competed for power, and neither would share it. [...] The tribes believed they embodied all that was good about Iraq and Iraqis. Their chiefs described themselves as men of chivalry and tradition, whose lineage stretched back over centuries. They were men of the law, who administered discipline in their clans and communities; they were friends to the Coalition; and, most importantly, they were men of their word. To the political parties this was nonsense: in the modern world the tribes were an irrelevance, anxious only to perpetuate a self-aggrandising feudal order of resolute self-interest. Something new was needed — perhaps secular, perhaps religious but certainly devoid of tribal influence.[151]

By making extensive use of tribal structures, therefore, the Coalition was providing a counterweight to political parties which dominated central Iraqi politics; indeed, its turn to the tribes for support occurred in late 2003, when relations with the IGC were at a low ebb.

We have argued so far that the Coalition both autonomously and in tandem with Iraqi governing institutions made intermittent efforts to recreate the basis of state authority after its collapse that accompanied the invasion, but was hampered by a number of interlocking factors. The weakness of the Iraqi state institutions meant that the programme for state building was susceptible to appropriation and substitution by non-state agents for private ends. The internationalised and contractor-led nature of governance and administration left the US stymied in its programmes to transform Iraq, with private corporations unwilling to expose their personnel to security risks, and a degree of competition among external agencies for the high level of available resources in which political struggles in Washington, not the effectiveness of those agencies in Iraq, proved decisive. Without a mechanism to structure the state building programme, either from within or without, its progress was halted or even went into reverse — as shown by the low degree of success in the attempt to make the state a primary service provider.

The key mechanisms by which the institutions at the disposal of the Iraqi state have engaged with Iraqi society have thus been the forcible actions of the US military, the extensive role of private security firms, and, particularly from January 2005 onwards, the building up of the Iraqi security forces, whose actions the US sought to direct. This result has not been an outcome intended or expected by policy makers in the US or by their allies. The Pentagon, and Secretary of Defence Rumsfeld in particular, had consistently argued against the need to base a large US military force inside Iraq. CENTCOM had originally intended to reduce US forces in Iraq progressively after the ousting of the Ba'th regime, projecting in May 2003 a reduction to as few as 30,000 troops by September 2003. As it turned out, there were still 133,000 US troops in Iraq in March 2006.

Walter Slocombe, who has had a career alternating between US legal practice and working for successive presidents in the DoD, was given the role within the CPA of creating the New Iraqi Army. He intended that army to be solely for the purposes of defence against external enemies, and to have no role in internal security and stabilisation. CPA Order 22 which established the New Iraqi Army stated specifically that the army 'shall not have, or exercise, domestic law enforcement functions, nor intervene in the domestic political affairs of the nation'.[152] Slocombe decided that the Iraqi army would be 'much smaller' than before the invasion, referring to Iraq before March 2003 as a 'grotesquely over-militarized society'.[153] The CPA adopted a policy not to allow a Ministry of Defence to be re-established until after Iraq had formally adopted a permanent constitution.[154] Nevertheless, within a month of the establishment of the New Iraqi Army, the Coalition made the decision to create the Iraqi Civil Defence Corps (ICDC) — originally as a 'temporary institution', but later becoming a permanent force under the new name of the Iraqi National Guard (ING) — whose purpose would be 'to counter organized groups and individuals employing violence against the people of Iraq'. Since then, the types of Iraqi armed forces have proliferated, with at least eleven different official security forces or sub-forces in existence by mid-2004.[155] The CPA changed its policy on a Ministry of Defence, devising the framework for the new ministry by November 2003 and formally creating it in March 2004.[156] By January 2006, the personnel of official security forces — 227,000 from the Iraqi Security Forces, 138,000 from the US military and 21,000 from other countries — inside Iraq stood at 386,000.[157] This is 99% of the level of Iraq's armed forces of approximately 389,000 full-time personnel in February 2003,[158] which Slocombe referred to as a 'grotesquely over-militarized society'. With at least 20,000 private security guards also in Iraq,[159] the number of armed personnel in Iraq in 2006 exceeded that prior to the invasion.

As well as in the number of personnel, the emphasis on the re-militarisation of Iraq can be seen through the levels of resources devoted to the preservation of the US military presence in Iraq, the building up of Iraqi armed forces, and the expenditure on private security. Expenditure on US forces in Iraq amounted to approximately $5.1 billion per month through 2004, or $61.2 billion annually.[160] Of the expenditure from the IRRF, substantially more funds were allocated to security and law enforcement than to any other sector by April 2005: $5.0 billion was allocated to this sector, or 27% of the IRRF.[161] This total came after a reallocation of resources, largely decided upon in September 2004: in April 2004, the allocation to the security sector from the IRRF was $3.2 billion, or 17% of the fund.[162] If spending on prisons and the protection of facilities is included in the calculations, the allocation to the security sphere in 2005 amounted to 33% of the IRRF.[163] Money originally slated for public works projects was diverted, and projects had to be cancelled. For example, in the water and sanitation sector funding from the IRRF, originally projected at $4.6 billion in November 2003, had been reduced to $2.6 billion by July 2005; this led to the cancellation of some projects and a lack of funds to repair water plants that had been built or rebuilt.[164] Similarly USAID cancelled two electrical power generation orders worth $15 million in March 2005 in order to allow for security costs.[165]

The expenditure on military and paramilitary forces, and the number of personnel associated with these spheres, have been the central manifestation of the Iraqi state. The Iraqi population in the centre and south know the state primarily as the army helicopters that fly overhead; as the concrete walls constructed around army installations; as the US military vehicles that occupy and block main roads; and as the recruiter of young men for army service. They know it much less as the effective provider of goods or services. We examine the opinion poll evidence of these perceptions at length in Chapter Four. The US started out with the intention of de-militarising the Iraqi state and then found the need to reverse that process. The expansion of the total military force inside Iraq has come about not through a preconceived plan, but as part of the reactive efforts of the US and its Iraqi allies to preserve through coercion the institutions they had created, given their high degree of externalisation from society and the extent of the challenge posed by the insurgency.

Analyses of state building in the South have often argued that such states tend to be heavily militarised owing to the characteristics of the post-colonial state, such as its low degree of internal cohesion, the disputed legitimacy of its borders, and its easy permeability to external actors.[166] The military acts as the mechanism not only for the preservation of regimes with low levels of legitimacy, but also for producing cohesion, defending borders and excluding external actors. The result is a state which may be powerful in the military sphere, but which has low levels of capability and legitimacy in other spheres, such as service provision. This analysis applies to post-invasion Iraq in that extensive remilitarisation has taken place. However, remilitarisation of the state is not being carried out nationally in order to defend it better against external actors. It is being directed principally by an external actor, the US, as we detail in Chapter Four. Indeed, such external penetration and integration, most obviously characteristic of the colonial state, has also been characteristic of the US's extensive involvement with the armed forces of other states during and beyond the Cold War, with such activities receiving a major boost in the wake of 9/11.[167] Some of that effort is aimed at excluding involvement by external actors such as the Iranian Revolutionary Guards, foreign jihadists and criminal networks. However, it is mainly aimed at dealing with domestic opposition to the form of state which the US has established. However, the problem is not only the high degree of militarisation, but also the fragmentation of the mechanisms that control the military and paramilitary elements: from the Coalition force commander to the individual ministries to non-state actors, such as political parties, tribes and militias. Without authoritative state institutions to adjudicate between these militarised fragments, they may end up asserting their claims to power increasingly by large-scale force of arms against each other.

CONCLUSION – SHORT-TERM CONTROL VERSUS STATE BUILDING

The Coalition has prioritised trying to retain short-term political control in Iraq. Sir Jeremy Greenstock, the UK's Special Representative to Iraq, put this point concisely: 'This place has to be controlled, and I think this is an area where Bremer has got it exactly right, has shown that he's boss.'[168] The Coalition has felt it necessary to do this to ward off the threat to its control not only from the insurgents but also from Iraq's other political actors, whose motivations and ambitions Coalition officials have by their own admission never adequately understood, particularly those of a religious character.[169] The US has feared that even those actors who have been prepared to work with the occupation might take Iraq in directions inimical to perceived US interests. In this context, the US decided to try to retain possession of the key levers of state power and to limit the emergence of a coherent Iraqi state until it could ensure that that state would be safe for US interests. The fundamental problems with this have been that the legitimacy of the Coalition presence has been undermined, a state is emerging in which political authority is fragmented, and the Coalition is losing control anyway.

Failure to achieve either control or state building became apparent very quickly. It has been symbolised by the fact that, since early in the occupation, CPA personnel and foreign contractors have rarely travelled to or spent significant amounts of time on the projects that they were administering because of the security risks involved. Spatially, the Coalition took over a central area of Baghdad's al-Karkh area for its main headquarters — the Green Zone, later renamed the International Zone — in order to assert its rule at the historic focal point of power. In order to do this safely, it closed off the 14th of July Bridge, which had been a major transport link between the two halves of Baghdad across the Tigris river, for almost the entire period since the invasion. The area has been surrounded with concrete slabs, tanks, armed checkpoints, razor wire and chain link fences. As a result, movement through central Baghdad has been paralysed. This has not been a feature likely to endear the Coalition to Baghdad's five million residents, not to mention those Iraqis who reside within the expanded boundaries of the Green Zone.[170] In addition, Coalition personnel extensively uprooted trees along the banks of the Tigris in Salah al-Din governorate to prevent guerrillas using the ancient lime, orange and pomegranate trees and date palms as shelter from which to launch attacks on US vehicles on the adjacent road.[171]

The actions taken by the US to try to preserve its control of Iraq have been at the persistent expense of the legitimacy of its presence. Furthermore, the process of balancing Iraqi political forces in ways that have fragmented political authority has left the US without the ability to create a state that engages effectively with the social and political dynamics of Iraqi life. The prioritisation of short-term goals — including meeting individual deadlines such as those for the June 2004 handover, the January 2005 elections and the October 2005 constitutional referendum, preventing the losses of Coalition lives by heavy use of force, and forestalling the emergence of cohesive oppositional Iraqi political forces — represented in crucial respects not a method of state building but refusal to engage in it. This process of prioritising the maintenance of short-term control over development of a project for creating a coherent state has impacted heavily upon the nature of political competition in Iraq, as we show in the next Chapter.

3

GOVERNANCE – CENTRE AND PERIPHERY

In Chapter Two, we discussed the relationship between the state and Iraqi society in the aftermath of the 2003 invasion, and showed how the Iraqi state has been external to society in two ways: it has had a low degree of embeddedness in social ties, and it has not been able to penetrate society adequately to steer societal forces to a significant extent. As a result, the Coalition and its allies in Iraq have relied heavily upon coercion and re-militarisation.

This Chapter will look at a parallel set of relationships — between the population, on the one hand, and the personnel of the state and political groupings that have participated in the structures of governance on the other. How did office-holders themselves interact with Iraqis? How did constituencies form among Iraqis for policy makers and personnel to access? To what extent were the actions of the state's personnel geared to the achievement of collective goals rather than individual interests? How have professional political actors in Iraq gone about building support bases, and what has been the impact of this process? We will examine these questions with particular reference to the relationships between the institutions of the central government and those of Iraq's local governing structures. As we will argue, although this set of relationships was sometimes consensual or cooptive, since 2003 they have involved a high degree of contestation and conflict, and this has affected Iraq's political process.

In popular discourse, both within Iraq and in Coalition countries, these questions have been discussed primarily through the prism of Iraq's democratisation. The sporadic local elections held in some parts of Iraq in 2003-04 — and particularly the national elections held in January and December 2005 — have formed the basis for many acclamatory discussions of a transformation in the relationship between office holders and individual Iraqis. Whilst we will discuss the electoral process in some detail below, we will set it in the context of a more general analysis of Iraqi politics. Drawing upon the arguments of Chapter Two, we will argue that a transformation of government — from autocratic to democratic — impacts upon society only insofar as there is a state for the government to rule through. When that state is weak and the process of state-building is hindered by factors outside the control of government, as in the case of Iraq, the competition for political power cannot easily be based upon the development of alternative policy programmes. Instead, it tends to situate itself more in neopatrimonial relations between officials and non-officials, and these relationships entrench and prioritise sectarian political practices. However, in the case of Iraq, sectarian politics is not simply localised in the parochial affairs of the mosque or the tribe but is highly permeated by external actors who provide the resources and often much of the impetus for wider antagonistic relationships. Firstly, however, to situate this discussion, an account of the formal apparatus of governance in Iraq, and an analysis of its operation, is necessary.

THE STRUCTURES OF COALITION GOVERNANCE

Since the deposing of the Ba'th in 2003, the structure of governance in Iraq has not only changed frequently; in addition, its *ad hoc* character has meant that a description of the institutions is a highly imperfect guide to its actual operation. The key institutions, on the Coalition side, were two-pronged: civil, with the lead institutions being the ORHA followed by the CPA and then the US Embassy; and military, consisting of CJTF-7 followed by MNF-I. Both civil and military prongs were organised regionally as well as centrally. The Coalition divided Iraq from the commencement of the occupation into areas of responsibility for different military divisions. After beginning with four sectors, by late 2003 the Coalition military was organised into six sectors: North, which incorporated Ninawa (Mosul) governorate as well as the three clear Kurdish-majority governorates; North Central, incorporating Salah al-Din, Diyala and al-Ta'mim (Kirkuk) governorates; Baghdad; West, consisting solely of al-Anbar governorate; Central South; and South East. All were under overall US command, except for Central South, under Polish command, and South East, under British command, with responsibility in individual governorates devolved further to other military forces in both these cases.

For the CPA, separate offices were established throughout Iraq from July 2003. A 'Regional Coordinator' was appointed to each of four different areas, initially matching the military sectors: Central, based in Baghdad; North, based in Arbil; South Central, based in Hillah; and South, based in Basra. As well as the Regional Coordinators there were individual 'Governorate Coordinators', one for each of Iraq's eighteen governorates, whose responsibility it was to implement CPA programmes locally. They were meant to work in cooperation with Regional Coordinators, but reported directly to Bremer. Each Governorate Coordinator led a 'Governance Team', which included a Political Adviser, Programme Officers, Iraqi advisers, and military personnel to provide technical assistance (the 'Governance Support Team').[1] These Governance Teams also included contracted personnel, most notably from the North Carolina-based Research Triangle Institute (RTI), who were hired by USAID in April 2003 to run a local governance programme, and whose role it was to act as mentors to Iraqi officials. These administrative structures remained in place until the CPA dissolved itself (when some regional offices became US consular hubs), despite the reorganisation of the military sectors. CPA regional and governorate offices were in principle entirely independent of military commands, and there was no straightforward fit between the nationality of the Governance Coordinator and the military command in individual governorates. For example, the CPA Governance Coordinators in al-Ta'mim (Kirkuk), Dhi Qar and Wasit were all British, whilst the military forces were American, Italian and Ukrainian respectively. Contractors also had a separate chain of command, further complicating administrative relations.

Hence there were two major arrangements of Coalition power within Iraq, each of formally equal status, but with separate personnel and different chains of command. For a coherent framework of governance, there would need to be close horizontal cooperation between these two sets of institutions. Furthermore, there was a considerable dispersal of power to separate military units, national forces or civil officials throughout the country. For national programmes to be implemented effectively, a high level of joint action would be required between these bodies, organised through a centrally-administered bureaucracy able to exercise consistent hierarchical power.

The Coalition did not seriously address these two structural obstacles. A persistent problem was that the two sets of Coalition institutions in Iraq, not linked by any formal hierarchy, were highly unequal in terms of number of personnel, availability of expertise, level of organisation and resources. Whilst the CPA had less than 600 US staff in the country at any one time plus an additional few hundred staff from other Coalition countries,[2] CJTF-7 and its successor organisations had over 150,000 personnel at their disposal for most of the period from mid-2003 through to 2006. This numerical imbalance was reflected in numbers dispersed around Iraq: in Wasit governorate in late 2003, for example, there were 1,600 CJTF-7 troops, part of the Ukrainian brigade, but the CPA staff numbered four international personnel, and this would rise by mid-2004 to just eight.[3] In al-Anbar, the discrepancy by November 2003 was even greater: 20,000 military personnel from the US 82nd airborne division, but just one CPA official, Keith Mines.[4] As a result, Governorate Teams were not able to place advisers inside the branches of ministries within the governorates in the way that the CPA had senior advisers for the central ministries, and so were not able to steer individual sectors to any significant extent.[5]

In addition to the problem of low numbers on the civil side, many Coalition personnel commented negatively on the low level of expertise amongst staff seconded to the CPA from government ministries. This was a particular problem for the US, where inter-agency disputes and the common perception that the Pentagon had 'won' Iraq for itself contributed to a more widespread unwillingness of other government departments to allow their best staff to be transferred under the DoD's wing to Iraq. The US Department of Justice, for example, allowed only two of its personnel to be sent to Iraq, despite a request for twenty.[6] Robin Raphel, the CPA's Senior Adviser on Trade, put this point particularly bluntly:

[I]t was very obvious to me that we [ie, the CPA] couldn't do this, we could not run a country that we did not understand. We were a bunch of amateurs largely except for the engineers, and even they didn't have a professional means to interface with the Iraqis, so they were missing … It was very much amateur hour to me, with all respect.[7]

Owing to these gaps, the CPA made use of personnel seconded from the military. One official estimated that 200 civil affairs officers were integrated into the CPA in *ad hoc* ways.[8] The perception within the US Government that Iraq policy belonged to the Pentagon did change from late 2003, as both the State Department and the US National Security Council took on a significant role in policy-making over Iraq, facilitating greater cooperation between branches of government. The element of contestation was nonetheless significant: Washington's policy towards Iraq was often the product of interdepartmental bargains or temporary ascendancies within the US political arena, with the Pentagon's stock generally in decline from the end of 2003 and the State Department remaining untainted by policy failures. The culmination of this process was the transfer of responsibility to the State Department for the funds apportioned by Congress for Iraq's reconstruction in December 2005.[9]

The CPA's vulnerability to the changing politics of Washington, and its reliance upon other government agencies for many of its staff, can be contrasted with CJTF-7 and MNF-I, which had a full range of personnel in civil affairs, intelligence and planning fully integrated into their operations, and whose chain of responsibility was clear throughout. The military's practical capabilities were enhanced by its comparative ease of mobility: whereas CPA officers would need to bargain, sometimes laboriously, for military escorts if they wanted to leave CPA headquarters in order to visit programmes for which they were responsible, the military was already set up with the facilities necessary to undertake regular patrols. This factor, added to the established hierarchies and budgeting procedures within the military in contrast to the *ad hoc* and contested nature of decision-making within the CPA, meant that funds could be allocated much more quickly to projects in Iraq by the military than by the civil side.[10]

Finally, CPA personnel had in general shorter tours of duty in the country than military officers. A considerable number of the CPA's personnel, particularly earlier on, were in Iraq for 90-day stints, not leaving enough time to develop expertise or organisational familiarity; this meant that a considerable amount of time was devoted to educating newly arrived staff. A CPA Regional Coordinator also noted how from late 2003 contracted technical staff were often not replaced after their three month stints were over, since the CPA's mission was scheduled to terminate in June 2004; this meant that key service and maintenance tasks were not carried out.[11] This can be contrasted again with the military personnel, who usually spent periods of twelve months inside Iraq and whose positions were filled immediately on leaving the country through the coordinated system of rotation.[12]

This imbalance in numbers, capabilities and experience meant that, after a period in which there was an informal and often unclear realignment of the balance of responsibilities between the two sets of institutions, the Coalition military became the *de facto* senior agency to the civil administration.[13] However, this also meant that the military brought with that status its own range of methods and priorities, in which concepts derived from the proclaimed 'war on terror', rather than from civil administration, became preponderant.[14] In short, coercion rather than political and economic development became the primary *modus operandi*. Because of the separation of chains of command, CPA officers were sometimes unable to access information and resources that were available to the military owing to its greater capability, and which were required for effective governance. One CPA Governorate Coordinator gave the example of how military intelligence collected within the governorate for which he was responsible was not made available to him, and how he was unable to task the military to collect information relevant to the CPA's political objectives from its sources.[15]

The second range of difficulties with the Coalition's organisation inside Iraq concerned the central authorities' coordination of action between geographically dispersed components of various institutions. This framework of analysis applies both to the CPA and to CJTF-7 or MNF-I, as well as to the external US authorities to whom they were responsible. In this respect, too, the military again showed itself to be a more coherent body. On the whole, the chain of command operated fairly consistently from the Pentagon to the commanders in Baghdad to the separate divisions in each of the six sectors. There were a few exceptions to this general pattern. Military commanders in different sectors did sometimes take diverse approaches to issues involving governance, particularly with respect to the installation and operation of local councils. The approaches taken by non-US Coalition forces in the

Central South and South East sectors were clearly different from those taken by US forces in the rest of Iraq, as discussed in the next Chapter. Although disputes between central command and local units have been rare, the case of the Falluja assault of April 2004, described in Chapter One, illustrated one such struggle. Finally, some of specific practices of abuse and torture inflicted on prisoners in Iraq showed lack of direct control over specific units: this is an issue we will return to in Chapter Four. In general, nevertheless, there was a robust centralised system of command and control in operation for CJTF-7 and MNF-I, in which the autonomy of local commanders existed within a framework that was centrally designed.

This arrangement contrasted with the civilian administration, in which coordination between the centre and the regions was often poor, and there was frequent contestation for control by its different levels. Much of this can be explained by the *ad hoc* nature of the CPA, as the ill-defined and shifting responsibilities for separate institutions generated competition over who should have the lead in undertaking particular tasks. For example, some of the offices of the four Regional Coordinators attempted to retain a management role over the eighteen Governorate Coordinators, instead of merely concerting action with them, and the CPA headquarters was unable to mediate effectively in these inter-institutional struggles.[16]

The difficulties of establishing an effective system of central direction were compounded by the CPA's generally limited knowledge about local processes. The CPA's priorities were with national and international strategy, constitution drafting, the stabilisation of the Baghdad region, and relations with the national leaderships of Iraqi political parties. CPA headquarters did not devote much of its energy or its personnel to engaging with, and giving direction to, governorate offices.[17] There were practical obstacles stemming from poor facilities for communication between the Authority's headquarters and the governorate offices, as the CPA never developed a secure communications system and its

Governorate Coordinators had to use commercial email services to pass information to and from Baghdad. The only secure communications system in Iraq by the start of 2005 was that of the military.[18] As a result, sensitive information could only be passed between civilian governorate officers and Baghdad when those civilian officers travelled to military bases, which were often at some distance away from CPA offices; or at meetings between headquarters staff and governorate officers, which were rare owing to the dangers of travelling.[19]

The result was that many local governance teams operated largely autonomously from central CPA control. One Deputy Governorate Coordinator in Maysan and later in Dhi Qar governorates told us: 'Baghdad has largely been defined by the lack of instruction which it gave us - my experience is that we all did pretty much our own thing'.[20] The Governorate Coordinator in Wasit described how that governorate 'was operating in almost complete independence by late 2003'.[21] The Regional Coordinator for CPA South up to January 2004 was more sanguine in referring to this region having had a 'judicious degree of independence' from Baghdad's rule.[22]

The relative autonomy of the local civil administrators, however, also meant that CPA headquarters took policy decisions in collaboration with the administration in Washington without receiving input from its local coordinators or foreshadowing those decisions to them, though the decisions impacted greatly upon governorate activity. The clearest example was the decision of 15 November 2003 to bring forward the handover so that it would occur by the end of June 2004; this was reached through consultations between Bremer and policymakers in Washington, although it was formally an agreement between the IGC and the CPA. It meant that Governorate Coordinators would have to hand over all of their responsibilities to Iraqi councils in fewer than eight months. Given that many councils were not functioning at all at the time of the 15 November plan, it changed to a great extent the focus of the Governorate Coordinators' work and meant that many plans for the creation of other local institutions had to be abandoned.[23] The plan also contributed to the abandonment of many of the other projects that the CPA was working on, such as projects to overhaul the food rationing system, demobilise party militias and privatise state-owned factories.[24] This demonstrated that the fracturing of the CPA decision-making process was not purely geographical but also sectoral. Similarly, CPA local officials had little input into the decisions over the companies that the Authority's headquarters or US governmental agencies awarded contracts to, even though they would be the officials with whom the contractors would have to work within Iraq.[25]

The comparative weakness of the Coalition civil bureaucracy, both centrally and in Iraq's regions, and its lack of institutional coherence meant that Coalition leaders were left with two conflicting inclinations. On the one hand, they needed increasingly to look for Iraqis to take control of governance, given the lack of CPA capabilities. They could not postpone or draw out the process by which Iraqi officials were appointed to positions of responsibility, and had to make these appointments before developing a good working relationship and a basis of trust with those officials. On the other hand, Iraqi political organisations were more able to commandeer the Coalition's resources and guide its action for self-seeking purposes, and so the Coalition was reluctant to allow power to slip away from it. The next section of this Chapter examines how the Coalition sought to reconcile these two impulses.

CENTRE AGAINST PERIPHERY

The nascent Iraqi administration both at the national level and at the local level in southern and central Iraq can be seen to have employed two different types of personality to engage in governance — the established political party and the embedded local leader. Although the contrast should not be drawn too sharply, there was in general a difference in the approaches taken by and towards these figures.

On the one hand, there were political organisations that had developed or matured in exile, such as the INA, SCIRI, the major branches of al-Da'wa and the Iraqi Islamic Party (IIP). These organisations had national leaderships and preexisting international networks of alliances (and enmities), but their organised bases of support inside Iraq were highly limited at the start of the occupation, owing to the effective repression of these parties by the Ba'th regime. The Kurdish and other northern Iraqi ethno-nationalist parties were in a clearly different position, as they had had a stable base in the autonomous northern enclave since 1991. However, for the Arab-dominated parties aspiring to state leadership, their introduction or reintroduction to Iraq in April 2003 provided a new opportunity to organise themselves amidst their primary constituencies.

On the other hand, the individuals already in place inside Iraq in 2003 who held positions of social and political power prior to the invasion sought to retain those roles. With the de-Ba'thification process removing from the official political contest many of those whose links with the *ancien régime* had been institutionalised within the party or the national government, this left in place figures such as tribal shaykhs, religious clerics, bureaucrats, council leaders and police chiefs. All of these had some degree of existing authority, and they exercised that authority through institutions that they sought to protect. The political parties were a threat to these roles, and this threat could be dealt with through a number of techniques — amalgamation, cooperation or conflict. The structure of this contest in southern and central Iraq manifested itself in different guises: rural versus urban, traditional versus modern, and particularly local versus national. The changing role of the international forces within this contest, as the Coalition sought to utilise multiple levers for exercising its control, and as regional states gave their backing to different forces within the country, altered its balance significantly.

At the national level, priority in US policy-making was given to the political parties. An example can be seen in the extent to which the political parties were represented on the IGC: 18 of out of its 25 members were or had been in leadership positions in political parties. Although the Coalition attempted to balance the IGC in terms of the ethnic and sectarian background of its members, the IGC was not structured in terms of regions: it included no Iraqis from the governorates of Salah al-Din, Diyala, Wasit and Dhi Qar — all governorates in which insurgent groups later took root — but it contained five Iraqis originating from al-Ta'mim (Kirkuk) governorate.[26] Few Iraqis from any region other than Kurdistan with status as regional leaders had a role on the IGC; out of its eighteen Arab members, only six had had some status as local leaders prior to the invasion.[27] None of these six served within the initial nine-person rotating presidency, which was made up exclusively of those strongly associated with the major political parties. The IGC can thus be considered to have been primarily representative of the US-aligned parties of Iraq; it was not representative of the country's regions.

Through their new roles, parties represented on the IGC were able to establish themselves in Baghdad. Through the IGC, each party was able to secure control for itself over one or more of the government's ministries, which led to sectors of public life being appropriated for factional purposes. An example is the role of the INA in the management of internal security before the formal handover in June 2004. Iyad 'Allawi, the INA's leader, was able through his position on the IGC to appoint Nuri al-Badran, the INA's spokesman, as Interior Minister. 'Allawi himself was able to take the chair's position in the IGC's Supreme Security Committee, whose operational direction was left to Ibrahim al-Janabi, the INA's former representative in Amman. A close associate of the INA, General Muhammad Abdullah al-Shahwani, who had led the INA's coup attempt in 1994, was appointed Director of Intelligence in April 2004. In this way, INA members held all the major national positions relating to internal security, and were able to appoint and dismiss local officials on this basis, a process checked only by the Coalition's erratic oversight.[28] The US acted more generally to secure the positions of each of the parties represented on the IGC. It allocated properties in Baghdad that had formerly belonged to the Ba'th Party or to state institutions and had been dissolved after the invasion to these parties: the INC took the Iraqi Hunting Club in al-Mansur district, the ICP took a former Mukhabarat building on Shari' Abu Nuass, al-Da'wa took Sindbad youth centre, and so on.[29] The US also invested considerable resources in Iraqi political parties: the State Department and USAID contracted the National Democratic Institute (NDI) and the International Republican Institute (IRI) to implement a training and assistance programme for Iraqi party officials that began in 2003. NDI and IRI carried out an assessment of Iraqi parties in early 2004, and focused their spending on entities that they considered, according the NDI, to be 'moderate religious and secular parties'.[30] In the run-up to the January 2005 elections, they channelled $30 million from the State Department to parties they considered to be 'democratically oriented', which constituted 40 out of the 111 entities running in that election.[31]

Despite the IGC's lack of authority, discussed in Chapter Two, the significance of the IGC structure to its member parties was considerable. Without a popular base in the country, many of the parties considered that the only way they could develop the material and human base necessary for their own political development would be to remain within the structures of central government. This was apparent in the creation of the IIG in June 2004. Whilst Sistani favoured an elected replacement to the IGC and Brahimi supported a technocratic replacement, its leading members instead chose — with US consent — an interim government in which its dominant parties continued to take all the highest positions apart from that of the figurehead presidency.[32]

The parties represented on the IGC thus captured the institutions of central government for themselves.

However, alongside the operation of the IGC, the Coalition was beginning to establish systems of local government which took a different path initially from that of national politics. Two key facets of Coalition local government initiatives were in tension with each other: promoting the autonomy of local actors from national level Iraqi political actors, and trying to retain Coalition control over how they exercised that capacity. The measures the Coalition adopted to address this tension were to put a stop to the local electoral processes that had begun in a disjointed way immediately after the fall of the Ba'th regime, and to use the power of appointment to decentralise power to local actors who seemed likely to follow Coalition preferences.

In the first weeks of the occupation, direct elections for local councils were held in some districts of Baghdad, such as al-Adhamiyya on 3 May 2003,[33] and 300 local 'delegates' selected the Council in Kirkuk on 24 May 2003.[34] Although neither set of elections was untroubled, both resulted in councils able to claim some measure of democratic legitimation. Practical arrangements were made to hold direct council elections in some of the main predominantly Arab cities of Iraq, such as Najaf and Samarra', in June, with US officials involved in initiatives to register voters, prepare ballot boxes and encourage participation. However, this round of local elections scheduled to take place across Iraq was cancelled in mid-June when the CPA was created.[35] Furthermore, few attempts were made to prepare for elections: there were no processes to register voters, train election observers or establish an electoral commission; and no moves were made to establish regulations on party financing or campaigning. Despite the considerable latitude under which CPA Governorate Coordinators acted, they were given forceful guidance that no elections should be held. It was underlined to Iraqi political actors that a process of selection, not election, was occurring at the local level, and that the councils had an advisory rather than a decision-making role.[36] The process of producing elected local councils had ground to a halt, and instead the CPA took to appointing leaders already perceived to be in positions of local authority.

With the 15 November plan, and the need for the CPA to pass on local administration to Iraqi councils, the Coalition placed much emphasis on forming operational councils at the local level. From late 2003 onwards, the CPA began a process of diversifying the local councils, establishing a consistent arrangement of municipal, district and neighbourhood councils for towns, and district and sub-district councils for rural areas. The Council for each of Iraq's eighteen governorates was expanded to approximately forty members, a process known as 'refreshment'. Although elections were held in a number of regions, there was little in the way of common procedures. One arrangement promoted within the CPA — called the 'Muthanna model', after the governorate in which it was pioneered — was to reserve 12 seats each for tribal representatives, members of political parties, and officers of civic organisations, together with two seats each for women and clerics, with the members of each category selected through caucuses or structured voting arrangements. However, no other Governorate Coordinator adopted the Muthanna model in its entirety; instead, each promoted arrangements that he saw as most suitable in his locality.[37] A former senior CPA official referred to this situation as 'eighteen different arrangements for local government in each of the eighteen governorates'.[38] This lack of common standards inevitably led to a perception that when local elections were held (for example, in Dhi Qar province),[39] it was because the CPA was confident of the success of pro-Coalition figures, in contrast to locations in which elections were not held or were cancelled abruptly (as in Basra in mid-February 2004).

More commonly, arbitrariness reigned. In Baghdad, for example, the arrangements for local councils and their meeting procedures were copied directly from Colorado, simply because the CPA's senior governance official with responsibility for Baghdad happened to be a former mayor of a Colorado town.[40] The CPA retained the authority to alter the composition of the Baghdad councils at its discretion,[41] and used the 'refreshment' process to remove council members whom the Authority had itself appointed but who were later deemed unsuitable.[42] The CPA also apportioned to itself the role of excluding anyone, at its discretion, from a position on a local council if it judged that they had, *inter alia*, 'publicly espoused political philosophies or legal doctrines contrary to the domestic order and rule of law being established in Iraq'.[43] In summary, the Coalition sought to retain a high degree of formal control over local political processes, but had severe limitations in its own personnel and expertise for making and implementing decisions: some of those functions, inevitably, would need to be contracted out to Iraqis.

The second feature of the Coalition's official plans for local government, decentralisation, was implemented in a way that aimed to skew it towards pro-Coalition actors. USAID had signed a $167 million contract with the RTI on 11 April 2003 to 'strengthen local administrations, civic institutions and processes'.[44] In practice, however, this was in many cases not the coordinated devolution of power, but the fragmentation of the Iraqi state as analysed in Chapter Two. There was often an attempt to formalise the positions of *de facto* local leaders, enabling them to win out over their competitors for power through giving them access to the resources of the local administrative structures and police forces. This was done in order to bring local power-holders within Iraq's official life and thus under the CPA's overall guidance. Thus whilst the Coalition retained hold of the funds that enabled Iraqi administrative structures to function, both before and after the June 2004 handover, it had to secure agents with the capacity to exercise control at the local level. The discourse of decentralisation was used in many cases to legitimise strengthening the power of local leaders, who often had not derived their existing positions from any association with the political parties that were pre-eminent at the centre, but through a network of tribal, social, religious and professional contacts. However, the process of bringing those local leaders within the Coalition's framework of governance also had the effect of radically changing their standing within their regions, as the periphery as well as the centre became heavily permeated with tensions arising from the international contest over the control of Iraq.

THE PRIMACY OF LOCAL POLITICS
AL-ANBAR, KARBALA', BASRA

The Coalition's efforts to retain control of state building produced some common outcomes in local governance, as can be seen from an examination of local governance in three very different parts of Iraq: al-Anbar, Karbala' and Basra.[45] The first included the main centres of the insurgency in mainly Sunni Arab areas, including Falluja, Ramadi, Haditha and al-Qa'im. The second and third cases are Shi'a-majority governorates, though Basra city in particular has substantial Sunni and Christian populations. Whilst Karbala' as the birthplace of Shi'ism is the premier shrine city, with an historically significant role for the *'ulama* in steering the affairs of the region independently — a 'self-governing semi-alien republic' according to the British reports during the Ottoman era[46] — Basra provided Iraq's best example of mercantile cosmopolitanism, nationally and internationally integrated, and with strongly nationalist sentiments frequently on display throughout the 20th Century.[47] Despite these differences, in all three cases, as we show below, the Coalition strove to promote local leaders who were not also national level political players, while those and other local leaders themselves actively developed their own ability to resist subordination to the Coalition and to Iraqi national political actors. The overall outcome has been the primacy of diverse local political dynamics which has been a critical obstacle to the emergence of a coherent Iraqi state.

In al-Anbar, the Coalition focused on bringing the leaders of the 'Ali Sulayman family of the Albu Assaf tribe, the leading grouping within the extensive Dulaym set of tribes that reside mostly around the Upper Euphrates, into a central role in the administration of the territory. The Coalition took Shaykh Majid 'Abd al-Razzaq 'Ali al-Sulayman, a Ramadi-based chieftain, to be 'shaykh of shaykhs for the Al Anbar province'.[48] This category was not in use among members of the Dulaymi or other tribes in al-Anbar before, and was to a considerable extent an invention of the Coalition; the major claimant to this title prior to the war was Saddam Hussein, who accorded himself this position in March 1991.[49] Furthermore, tribal organisation in al-Anbar was by no means a self-contained traditional sphere that encompassed the activities of its members and excluded other social and political identities. Nevertheless, it was one among many competing structures of authority in al-Anbar that could be bolstered and put to use by the Coalition; and for the tribal chiefs, it was an opportunity to assert their pre-eminence in local politics.

The attempt to promote a tribally-organised political structure for the post-invasion politics of al-Anbar began with a meeting of tribal leaders from and allied with the Dulaym shortly after the fall of the Ba'th regime, which allocated the governorship of al-Anbar to 'Abd al-Karim Birjis 'Izz al-Din al-Rawi, a former police chief and ally of Shaykh Majid. This appointment was duly recognised by the Coalition, and Governor Birjis retained his position for the next fifteen months. A new Council with 42 members was created in July 2003, with both Governor Birjis and Shaykh Majid on the appointments panel;[50] according to the senior CPA official in al-Anbar, 70% of the council seats were taken by tribal leaders.[51] Shaykh Majid was given the vice-chairman's position on the governorate council. He also created an al-Anbar Tribal Chieftains Council as an independent organising vehicle, and claimed that the tribe acted as the key organising instrument for al-Anbar: 'Here people obey the tribe above all else. The tribal sheikh is the true political leader.'[52] This political power was backed with patrimonial benefits: within weeks of the invasion, Shaykh Majid was contracted by the US to be its supplier of cement for the rebuilding of an airfield.[53]

The dominance of local leaders over those with national alliances continued even after the Coalition carried out by decree a 'refreshment' of the Council in January 2004: only three of the 41 positions in the new council were given to representatives of the national political parties. Although Shaykh Majid had been aligned with the INA since 1996, and had been in exile during the years leading up to the invasion, his significance as a political actor came not from any role in the INA, but from his position within the Albu Assaf tribe.[54] The composition of, and Coalition support for, the governance structures in al-Anbar thus represent an attempt to uphold the dominance of the local over the national.[55]

The subcontracting of governance and the benefits of patronage to local agents is hardly a novel tactic in cases of foreign occupation. Nevertheless, by placing a high degree of reliance upon specific individuals who were engaged in local struggles for pre-eminence, the Coalition found itself sucked into entrenched contests over which large sections of the governorate's population could be mobilised. This was a possibility recognised by the Coalition. To offset the political dominance of the 'Ali Sulayman, another of the Dulaym tribes, the Albu Alwan, headed by Shaykh Hamid Albu Alwan, were allowed to secure primary control over the local police in al-Anbar. Shaykh Hamid's construction company was also awarded a contract to tear down the local Ba'th Party headquarters, even though this cost the Coalition $15,000 more than other commercial bids, in order to keep him on side.[56] Even so, the newly acquired official standing of the 'Ali Sulayman drew their opponents — including leading members of the Albu Alwan —[57] into a process of challenging not only the local Council but also its support base, the Coalition. When an agreement was reached in November 2003 between the Coalition and the Governor for US forces to vacate the governorate capital Ramadi, and to hand over control to council officials, Shaykh Majid's house was subjected to a bomb attack that killed his nephew. A second bomb attack in February 2004 led to Shaykh Majid leaving the country to go into exile in Jordan, where he continued to receive death threats.[58] As for Governor Birjis, three of his sons were kidnapped and held, to force him to resign his position and make a public apology for acting in concert with the US. He acceded to these demands, and gave up political control of al-Anbar in August 2004.[59] Al-Anbar went through a succession of five appointed or self-proclaimed governors over the next ten months, with police chiefs and tribal leaders engaged in a struggle for local power that led not only to the kidnapping and killing of one Governor after just eleven days in office but also to the effective disbanding of the governorate's police force and its replacement by forces drawn predominantly from Iraq's Shi'a population.[60] Local political struggles had become enmeshed with national and international conflicts, displacing the attempt to transform a *de facto* hold on power into devolved authority.

A quite different outcome, but a similar set of issues, can be seen in the politics of Karbala'. In contrast to al-Anbar, the collapse of central authority in Baghdad did not result in widespread disorder there, and Karbala' in its role as a shrine city was able to support the vast influx of hundreds of thousands of pilgrims for the Ashura ritual there from 19 April 2003, just two weeks after the city fell to US forces. In contrast to many areas of Iraq, national politics intruded strongly into Karbala's street politics from the beginning of the occupation, and were the primary ingredient for one substantial set of competitors for local power. A struggle between the Sadr movement and the followers of Sistani for control over the mosque attached to the shrine of Imam Husayn, one of the most prestigious venues in the Shi'a world, became violent in

July and again in October 2003 when the Sadr movement reneged on an agreement to alternate the leading of Friday prayers with Sistani's representatives.[61] This was part of a broader struggle between the two forces that took place across much of Shi'a Iraq, with the Sadr movement attempting to displace the authority of what it saw as the 'silent jurisprudent' — the quietist-led seminary of Najaf (*al-hawza al-ilmiyya*) in which Sistani was pre-eminent — and replace it with the model of the 'speaking jurisprudent', the activist model of the cleric living under tyranny, developed by Ayatollah Muhammad Sadiq al-Sadr, Muqtada's father. The Sadr movement put this model of the 'speaking jurisprudent' to use in becoming an organising force behind criticism of, and later armed conflict with, Coalition forces based in Karbala'. SCIRI and a rival Shi'a clerically-led party, the Islamic Task Organisation, also placed significant emphasis on the politics of Karbala', and tried to rally their supporters there immediately after the invasion in order to demonstrate their power in the new Iraq. Thus Karbala' became a venue in which national and international political battles were played out in the competition to steer the overall course of the Iraqi state.

Nevertheless, Karbala' was more than a sacred arena in which national and transnational political forces engaged with each other; it also had its own political actors with distinctively local political interests. The fall of the *ancien régime* left an intense competition for political power in which three local leaders with different political bases all declared themselves Governor in the first weeks of the occupation: Muhammad Husayn al-Nasrallah, who was selected by a panel of 30 local tribal leaders and clerics; Yusuf al-Habubi, who claimed the support of the Shi'i seminary; and Mudhur al-Hakim, who told reporters that his claim to the governorship had been recognised by the US forces.[62] Instead of picking one of these three, the US installed an unaffiliated town notable, 'Ali Kammuna, in early May 2003. Kammuna was a member of the family that had been the historic leaders of Karbala' during the Ottoman era.[63] The US was thus selecting local notables rather than those with national standing as its intermediaries with the governorate's population, and making possible a reassertion of purportedly traditional power. Kammuna resigned two months later, but his replacement, Akram al-Yasiri, was dismissed by the CPA early in 2004, after publicly criticising the behaviour of US troops, and he in turn was replaced by Sa'd Sufuk, the head of the Mas'ud tribe.

During the governorships of Yasiri and Sufuk, the tension between local and national political actors became more overt. The local Council's membership was overhauled by the US twice, with both stages criticised not only by the Sadr movement but also by Sistani's followers. 'Abd al-Mahdi al-Karbala'i, Sistani's agent (*wakil*) in Karbala', announced at the first stage in November 2003 that he had withdrawn his support from the Council;[64] and then, when the Council was 'refreshed' and a new governor appointed in February 2004 at the instigation of the CPA Governorate Coordinator, he called on its members to resign, claiming that the 'refreshment' process had 'undermine[d] the powers of the religious authority'.[65] He was backed by the Islamic Task Organisation in this call.[66] Sa'd Sufuk, appointed as Governor in February 2004, issued an order prohibiting unlicensed demonstrations in an attempt to forestall a counter-mobilisation against his appointment by national parties. This led to SCIRI joining in the criticism: its radio station, Sawt al-Mujahidin, claimed that 'such decisions issued by the Governor of Karbala' who is appointed by the occupation authorities, cast doubts on the Governor and raises a lot of question marks around him.'[67] Sufuk remained in more violent conflict with the Sadr movement — the Mahdi Army attempted to seize his office on 4 April 2004, and he in turn called upon US forces to drive the Sadr movement out of Karbala'.[68]

The disputes between local and national forces did not end with the process of Coalition appointment. The January 2005 governorate elections, taking place alongside the national elections for the Transitional National Assembly (TNA), were won overwhelmingly by SCIRI, which secured 34% of the vote, in contrast to its nearest rival, the Fadila (Virtue) Party, with 7%.[69] The Council then appointed 'Aqil Mahmud al-Khaz'ali as Governor on 14 March, with the backing of the Council members from the SCIRI faction.[70] Given SCIRI's power at the centre, as the most highly organised faction within the United Iraqi Alliance that held the majority of seats in the TNA,[71] it might have been expected that this convergence would alleviate tension between local governance and the central state. However, the two quickly came into conflict, with Khaz'ali and the Karbala' Council challenging in particular the authority of the Minister of the Interior, Bayan Baqir Solagh Jabr — a key leader of SCIRI himself — to establish two local commando units which had been in preparation from May 2005. The Karbala' Council unilaterally dissolved these units in June, and established its own force with 1,600 personnel under its exclusive direction.[72] Khaz'ali further ordered the closure of the local office of the Interior Ministry, alleging interference in the affairs of the governorate, and dismissed the chief of police, Maj.-Gen. 'Abbas Fadil al-Husayni, who had been appointed by the Interior Ministry. Khaz'ali upheld this decision despite Solagh's order for Husayni to be reinstated.[73]

This series of disputes between the Governor and the political forces amongst the Iraqi Shi'i that were contending for power at the centre indicates two features. Firstly, the Coalition sought to transfer local power to individuals who did not have national standing, and thus were unlikely or unable to use that power to lead a challenge to their legitimacy as occupying powers. The Coalition did not select individuals with prior affiliations to the major religious or political networks, despite the loyalty of many of Karbala's residents to Najaf's seminary and the evident popularity of SCIRI, demonstrated in the January 2005 governorate elections. Secondly, though, the conflictual relationship between centre and periphery cannot be seen solely as a result of Coalition strategies of distributing clients in various positions of power as part of a divide and rule strategy. As the escalation of tensions after

March 2005 indicates, a developed sense of the legitimacy of local interests had crystallised, to be enforced by local power holders against a weak centre that lacked the authority to override regional decisions. The holding of and struggle for local power thus constituted a political dynamic that had priority over national political struggles.

A third example that will clarify the strength of the periphery in comparison to the centre is that of Basra. This case is clearly different from those of al-Anbar and Karbala', in that Basra headquartered the only military zone — Multinational Division (South East) — that was under overall British command. The British let it be known from the outset that their approach would be different from that of US forces. Nevertheless, the process of selecting local leaders to take administrative positions took a similar course initially. Four days after securing military control over the governorate on 7 April 2003, the British command selected a local tribal leader, Shaykh Muzahim al-Tamimi, to head a thirty-member council to administer the governorate. This appointment was similar to the tactic adopted by the US in appointing leaders who asserted traditional authority, thus both coopting and bolstering local power-holders.

However, this appointment generated a series of violent protests, with local demonstrators claiming that the Shaykh was a former Brigadier-General in the Iraqi army with close links to the Ba'th party, and opposing his stated intention of keeping former members of the Ba'th party within the council's members and staff.[74] These protests seem to have been mounted by a mixture of local organised groupings spurred by tribal rivalry and national political factions creating openings for local control by excluding the former Ba'th-aligned political elite from positions of power. The British assented to the protests by the end of May in dismissing Shaykh Tamimi, but did not agree to vigorous demands for a free election for the Governor's position. Instead, they sought to appoint a committee of local technocrats who would be dependent on the Coalition for their authority.[75] A compromise deal was reached by late June: a 27-member 'Interim Governorate Council' for the province was appointed, and it chose Wa'il 'Abd al-Latif, a judge who also served as a member of the IGC, as Governor.[76] This arrangement was endorsed, crucially, by Sayyid 'Ali 'Abd al-Hakim al-Musawi al-Safi, Sistani's *wakil* in Basra.[77] In this way, the British command installed a set of leaders who were independent of Iraqi political parties, so that their authority rested upon their alliance with the Coalition, but behind whom a well-organised social movement could embed itself further into the life of the region. By the following year, the British commander in the region was acknowledging that the presence of his troops in Basra was entirely dependent upon Sayyid 'Ali's goodwill.[78]

The involvement of followers of Sistani in the legitimation of the Council also gave opportunities to political parties whose local branches had good relations with Sayyid 'Ali to take official positions within Basra. However, these parties — principally SCIRI — were open to direct challenge in a way that Sistani, who was for many above political criticism, was not. This became increasingly clear in July 2004 when Wa'il 'Abd al-Latif moved to Baghdad to take up a cabinet position and his successor, Hazim Tawfiq Aynashi, was assassinated. Hassan Rashid, a former head of intelligence of SCIRI's paramilitary wing, the Badr Brigades, took over the governorship, whilst Badr Brigades members took up positions within the governorate's police force. This move prompted the Sadr movement to respond, sensing a concerted effort to exclude it through commandeering a key mechanism of social control: members of the Mahdi Army engaged in a programme of mass counter-enrolment. Over the coming months, there were widely varying estimates of who had won this battle over Basra's police force: some commentators claimed that ex-Badr Brigades members made up over half the police force, whilst others asserted that three-quarters of policemen were loyal to Sadr.[79] Basra's Chief of Police admitted that he could trust no more than a quarter of his own force to follow his orders.[80]

Although well known beforehand, the political struggle over Basra's police force received international attention in September 2005 when police officers apprehended two British undercover Special Air Service soldiers after they tried to shoot their way out of a police checkpoint.[81] In the day before this event, tensions had increased owing to the arrest by the British of three Mahdi Army leaders. British forces destroyed a substantial part of al-Jamiyyat police headquarters in southwest Basra to secure the soldiers' return and around 150 prisoners escaped. In riots and demonstrations that followed, British troops killed four Iraqis and injured 44 more. The British claimed that they were justified in their action because the Interior Minister had ordered the soldiers' release and the local police had refused to release them. Lu'i al-Batat, the Deputy Governor for Basra, argued that the British had violated Iraqi sovereignty and suspended cooperation with them, and the city's chief anti-terrorist judge called for the arrest of the British troops on suspicion of committing 'terrorist acts', with some reports saying that the troops had explosives with them. The Governor of Basra province, Muhammad Musabih al-Wa'ili, called the raid 'barbaric, savage and irresponsible'. These events and the competing narratives associated with them — legitimate rescue of soldiers from militia-infiltrated police or violation of sovereignty by occupying forces refusing to follow legal procedures — show fundamental conflict over the operation of a key site of local authority.[82]

In parallel to this struggle for control of the police force, party officials used it to win control over sectors of Basra's society and so bring them under party dominance. This was found most overtly in the enforcement of codes of social morality under the guise of Islamisation and the use of violence as a tool of silencing or eliminating challengers and critics, both of which appear to have been carried out by party militia members and police working in concert.[83] For example, when Sadr's militia attacked picnicking male and female university students in March 2005, the police force, despite having a sizeable presence at the scene, did nothing to stop the militia from beating the students, and according to some eyewitnesses even joined in the attack.[84] More generally, there was pronounced competition between the militia of the Badr Organisation and the Mahdi Army for dominance of Basra's streets, breaking out briefly into violent conflict in August 2005.[85]

The influence exercised by individual political factions over the means of violence in Basra is, however, not simply a case of national battles for power being played out at the local level. This is because a straightforward hierarchy between national party leaders and local officials has not existed. The Sadr movement split nationally between the two figures each of whom claimed that Ayatollah Muhammad Sadiq al-Sadr had left his mantle to him: Muqtada al-Sadr, leader of the Mahdi Army, and Shaykh Muhammad al-Ya'qubi, founder of the Fadila Party. Both factions nonetheless cooperated in Basra. Fadila took part in the governorate elections there in January 2005, and had the support of Mahdi Army members in its campaign. It won 21% of the vote, coming second to the 'Islamic Basra' slate that included SCIRI and al-Da'wa, which won 33%.[86] However, subsequently it managed to put together a coalition with minor parties that gave it 21 out of the 41 seats on the governorate council, and thus won the governorship position for a party member, Muhammad Musabih al-Wa'ili.[87]

Although Musabih remained aligned with both Sadr and the Fadila Party, he also demonstrated his independence from both on a number of occasions, sometimes on issues of key national significance. For example, he was a keen supporter of a high degree of decentralisation and of the southern governorates joining together to form a single administrative unit. From May 2005 onwards, he led consultations between the governors of three southern governorates, Basra, Dhi Qar and Maysan, on formation of an autonomous region within Iraq, with Basra as its capital, that would keep a much greater share of its oil revenues for itself.[88] These proposals were vigorously opposed by both major wings of the Sadr movement, which favoured a strong national government under Shi'a leadership.[89] Nonetheless, Musabih engaged in a public campaign to win support for an autonomous southern region, adorning the streets with banners and placards to encourage decentralisation. He underscored this campaign by deliberately withholding electricity supplies from Basra power stations to Baghdad, as described in Chapter Two. This approach, pursued by Musabih despite the disapproval of the faction of which he was part, indicates that the struggle to secure and build local power bases was of greater significance than the attempt to secure allegiances with national political actors or build a cohesive national movement. Local leaders' push for autonomy from central government was also apparent in the September 2005 incident with the two undercover British soldiers, mentioned above. Whilst Prime Minister Ja'fari was affirming that nothing had changed in relations between the UK and Iraq, Basra's Council, including Musabih and members of Ja'fari's own party, voted unanimously to suspend all cooperation with the British until apologies, guarantees of non-repetition, and compensation were forthcoming for the destruction of the police station.[90]

General points can be drawn out from these three examples of local governance in Iraq, despite the very different conditions of these regions, for example their differing levels of political violence. All three examples show how the Coalition, in establishing new structures of local government in the period from April 2003 to June 2004, did not seek to use or bolster Iraqi political parties as intermediaries with local populations. As the RTI official in charge of establishing local government later explained, 'there wasn't much room or scope given for political party activity' in Iraqi local affairs.[91] The US official who took on mayoral responsibilities for Baghdad from May 2003 to March 2004 explained that 'the philosophy which was inculcated [to local officials] was that local government is non-partisan'.[92] In some governorates, Council members were formally prohibited from acting as representatives of political parties during council sessions.[93]

This arrangement had the effect of preventing unified challengers to the Coalition from emerging, and of frequently setting local officials against national Iraqi bodies and ministries, which were dominated by the political parties. It also provided initial disincentives to political parties to organise a structure of offices and candidates at the local level: if there was little opportunity to secure local power through formal electoral competition in the periphery, local organisation lost its main function. This began to change with the move towards governorate elections in January 2005 (in which, as the cases of Karbala' and Basra showed, electoral competition could result in securing local power). However, as the national election was organised on a single constituency basis — in which the national share of the vote directly translated into a number of seats in the transitional assembly — parties' motivation for organising local apparatuses geared up for electoral competition was again diluted. The parties remained institutions concentrated and often closed away in the arena of the central state's functioning, able to make populist appeals to the wider population for support, but with few dependable links into the country outside the Green Zone.

The substitute actor in the regions became the local leader who held a prior position of power but whose authority was nonetheless independent of that of the *ancien régime*. This category was made up of those with claims to traditional authority, such as clerics and tribal shaykhs, and those in charge of relatively untainted state institutions, such as police chiefs. Whilst a number of these individuals made pragmatic alliances with political parties, they remained independent political actors, and often took different stances on key issues, as all three examples above demonstrate. These officials were given formal positions by the Coalition, which also tried to strengthen their local power bases, for example by distributing contracted funds through their private sector institutions. However, this approach ensnared the Coalition within local power struggles which were often unanticipated and poorly understood by them. The struggles were most apparent over control of key social institutions, such as prestigious mosques, the local police force and the governor's office.

With the parties dominant in the central state institutions and embedded local leaders in charge of regional institutions, a set of conflicts between centre and periphery became a major part of Iraq's political dynamic. This involved regular contestation over the legitimate scope of the authority of central ministries, particularly over the right to appoint local officials of each ministry. These were contests in which the Coalition, before and after the handover, was unable to mediate. Owing to the weakness of the Coalition's regional political institutions and their limited ability to coordinate effectively with the central instruments of Coalition rule, as recounted earlier, it was ill-equipped to provide a structure through which tensions between the region and the centre could be channelled or resolved.

Central Iraqi agents were sometimes able to assert the authority of the central state. In charge of the national ministries, they often engaged in a vigorous process of providing orders to local ministry offices, counteracting the official policy of decentralisation that had placed them under direction of the local councils.[94] Before the handover, the reassertion of ministerial power went largely unopposed by CPA headquarters, which often found it easier to coordinate with the IGC and its constituent parties than with its own governorate offices.[95] The IGC managed to dissuade the CPA from establishing a decentralised governing structure, thus leaving the ministries under its control with budgetary powers and the ability to appoint, promote or fire local staff, often on the basis of their party loyalties.[96] In Wasit, for example, the Ministry of the Interior refused to allow the Governor to dismiss the Chief of Police even though his senior officials had been involved in an attack on the Governorate Coordinator's compound.[97] After the handover, Iraqi parties were able to mobilise their militias to challenge and threaten local officials, particularly if they were also in charge of the relevant central government ministries. Thus SCIRI, which held the Interior portfolio from April 2005, was able to use armed members of the Badr Organisation to seize control of police forces in 'Amara, Diwaniyya and Nasiriyya in mid-2005. In the latter case, militias simply broke into the police chief's office whilst he was abroad and installed a new head, who was then duly confirmed in his position by SCIRI's Interior Minister.[98] In Baghdad, around 120 members of the Badr Organisation broke into the city mayor's office on 8 August 2005, announced that he had been removed from power, and installed in his place, on a purportedly temporary basis, one of its own officials, Husayn al-Tahan.[99] The Council of Ministers gave its *post hoc* endorsement of this move later in the month.[100] The ousted mayor, 'Ala al-Tamimi, told journalists, 'I was removed by gunmen because I am a secular technocrat with no ties to SCIRI and not backed by a militia.'[101]

In these attempts to assert control over local leaders, however, the institutions and parties of the central state were often countered by regional officials who, as the Basra example showed, took up a discourse of decentralisation and federalism as a way of asserting their own power against the challengers. The promotion of federalism in Iraq has come from a number of different sources, most notably through the KRG from October 1992.[102] It was even taken up by SCIRI's leadership — which had since its inception opposed federalism — in August 2005 in the debates surrounding the drawing up of an Iraqi constitution. However, in Arab areas of Iraq, the issue of federalism has been most insistently pressed by local leaders as a way to delegitimise the actions of the central authorities since the conflict between the centre and the periphery started taking shape.[103] A series of tensions between the institutions of the central state and those of the periphery developed under the occupation, and the occupation authorities were not capable of managing them. The result has been an ongoing set of conflicts, often violent in nature, which are unlikely to be amenable to solution through the passing of laws or constitutional provisions, but can only be resolved through one set of institutions effectively supplanting the other as the site of ultimate authority.

PATRIMONIALISM, PARTIES AND EXTERNAL FORCES

The preceding section discussed the extent to which national and local institutions of governance have been in contestation with each other, and demonstrated why understanding these contests is significant for appreciating the political dynamics of post-invasion Iraq. However, it left open the question of how populations themselves have been brought in as actors into the politics of Iraq. Their agency has been far from marginal. From the mass demonstrations of January 2004, which forced the abandonment of the 15 November plan, to the widespread participation in armed militias, to the January and December 2005 elections, the participation of those outside the narrow categories of politicians and insurgents has been extensive.

This section will look at the incorporation of the population into the political process through an examination of the neopatrimonial character of the Iraqi state. Although analyses that emphasise the significance of political patronage have been common in studies of the post-colonial world,[104] this section will also highlight the distinctiveness of the Iraqi case, due to the intense role of international actors in shaping its political processes.

The Weberian concept of patrimonialism is that of personal loyalty to a ruling individual on account of his or her traditional status. This concept has been assimilated into the standard scholarly apparatus with a variant, that of loyalty arising out of the material rewards that a patron dispenses to a client. In both cases, the relationship is a personal one, maintained by reciprocal exchanges of favours of either material or moral forms between people who are unequal in the sector relevant to the exchange. For example, a wealthier or higher status individual secures the loyalty of poorer or lower status individuals in return for material or status rewards.

This form of patrimonialism is distinct from but closely related to situations in which the loyalty of clients is no longer based exclusively upon personal relationships, but is conducted instead through the formal mechanisms of the state. This is neopatrimonialism: it is the exchange that takes place within traditional patrimonialism but conducted instead within and through the modern apparatus of the state. Officials dispense favours to particular individuals or groups through the state institutions that they are in charge of, in return for popular backing for those officials, for example through votes, bribes or participation in mass demonstrations. The state retains a formal pretence of allocating public funds and services on a fair basis, but its officials are steered in their actions by their desire to capture a clientelistic base which secures them in personal positions of power or wealth: the neopatrimonial state 'dissimulates the private while simulating the public'.[105]

Analysts of neopatrimonialism generally agree that it is most likely to arise when a particular group controls access to critical resources, and can deliver them, either directly or through brokers; when patrons require the service of clients for their own positions of power or wealth; when the client group is unable to unite or inhibited from uniting to confront or bargain with the patron group; and when there is a weak ethic of public allocation. These conditions are most frequently met in poor societies in which the contests for political power are central to the allocation of resources as the state is disproportionately wealthy compared to society. For example, it is most likely in rentier economies, in which the state obtains its main income from external sources — such as minerals sales or aid — and the population is largely dependent economically upon the state's allocation of those funds. These factors appear *prima facie* to apply to Iraq since the invasion, and Dodge among others has discussed Iraq in these terms.[106] We will argue that Iraq does have a number of neopatrimonial characteristics, but there are two important ways in which

Iraqi politics has diverged from being a purely neopatrimonial state. First, many of the patron-client relationships are not channelled through the Iraqi state, and hence are patrimonial rather than neopatrimonial. Second, there is a major role for non-Iraqi patrons, most notably Iranian ones (as we show below) and others through the transnational informal economy (as we show in Chapter Five). Third, Iraqi political parties have had their need for neopatrimonial Iraqi clients reduced dramatically by the fact that they have often been able to secure access to power by doing deals with other political parties.

Neopatrimonial state

Regarding the neopatrimonial aspects of the Iraqi state, clearly one key mechanism by which national parties attempted to gain a client base has been through disbursing benefits to supporters. In this respect, parties were aided by a general absence of regulation to limit the role of political parties or restrict their financing. In the absence of a state which could act as an effective service and security provider, as discussed in Chapter Two, the benefits that could be distributed by parties were in great demand: the aspiration from potential clients for would-be patrons was thus in place. Most obviously, through the existence of the armed militias, the political institutions were able to provide security and jobs to their supporters. Through gaining control of the institutions of government and installing leading officials, political parties could seek to direct resources to themselves and to supportive populations.

This ability of parties to commandeer state institutions was most notable in the handover of Iraqi ministries to officials selected by individual IGC members in September 2003. As one Pentagon official based in Baghdad noted, IGC members chose 'their sons or brothers-in-law' to become ministers, sometimes literally as well as figuratively.[107] With ministers given wide latitude to appoint their staff, the result was often the packing of a ministry with party and personal affiliates who would then leave when the minister lost his or her position. The political parties were instrumental in re-establishing some of the ministries: Col. Philip Dermer, the US official responsible for creating the new Ministry of Defence, found that he had to look to the parties in order to find suitable staff members for the ministry, the joint force headquarters and the upper echelons of the military itself.[108] Ministries thus became directly aligned with political parties: posters of Shi'a clerics were placed prominently inside the Ministry of Education building and female employees of ministries run by some Islamist parties, such as the Transport Ministry, were forced to wear the *hijab* at work.[109] As organisational bodies, ministries were weakened by being transformed into the agents of parties rather than neutral bureaucracies. Despite having control over the budgetary allocations to regional ministries, they often lacked the capacity to govern their sectors adequately.[110] Sometimes this process of party alignment also set one ministry against another, with wider political battles translated into inter-ministerial disputes and vice versa. For example, there were persistent disputes through the summer of 2005 between the Electricity Ministry, which was run by 'Abd al-Muhsin Shlash, the head of a monarchist party, and the Oil Ministry, run by Ibrahim Bahr al-'Ulum, aligned with the Shi'a Islamist parties. Both required each others' output in order to function, but each publicly blamed the other for not providing enough supplies. These disputes led to continual bargaining over the trade between the ministries, and on occasion to both ministries stopping supplies to each other. The Electricity Ministry also blamed a number of governorates for using more electricity than their share, claiming that these governorates were not cooperating with the Ministry.[111]

This case shows how Iraq has fragmented not only geographically, but also sectorally. With different parts of the state machinery acting against each other, Iraq provides an extreme case of what Joel Migdal has referred to as 'dispersed domination'.[112] When the components of the state coordinate with one another ('integrated domination'), the state is able to position itself at the centre of processes of creating and maintaining social control. By contrast, in situations of dispersed domination, many significant political processes take place outside the arena of the state — between and within political parties, amongst independent social agents such as tribes or neighbourhoods, and often transnationally. In the case of Iraq's electricity, these different arenas all became significant: the Islamist parties made an effort to oust Shlash;[113] people across Iraq turned increasingly to private generators, purchased either collectively or by local non-state leaders; and electricity purchases from Iran and Turkey became highly significant to Iraq.[114] The Iraqi state had lost much of its centrality to the electricity sphere.

A second method for parties with representation in the IGC to secure a client base was to act as brokers between local populations and the CPA. For example, one significant form of party recruitment took the form of employment brokerage. Employment with the institutions of, and foreign contractors for, the state was much in demand, particularly given the extent of unemployment and insecure employment. Perhaps the most straightforward route to priority consideration for employment was to obtain a letter of recommendation (*tazkiyya*) from one of the CPA-aligned parties.[115] Such letters could be obtained either by joining the party, or by making a substantial payment to it.[116] According to one report, parties who had cultivated the CPA's trust, presumably through cooperation in local administration and pacification, were more able to act as vetting agents for it; *tazkiyya* from one of the Shi'a Islamist parties was the most effective of all.[117] In some areas, local parties held particular sway: Arabs in Kirkuk reported that they would need supportive letters from the Kurdish parties to obtain public sector employment.[118] This brokerage was not always so explicit: educational institutions in southern Iraq would be more likely to employ members of the Badr Brigades even in the absence of direct pressure, knowing that this would help them retain the militia's support for their work.[119] A working group of a number of US government agencies involved in the water sector in Iraq found in early 2005 that in water and sewage treatment plants the installed Iraqi 'operations managers were often political appointees with little or no water sector experience'.[120] Through both direct and indirect routes, therefore, the parties were able to secure the loyalty of individuals by providing them with much-needed possibilities of employment.

Political sponsorship of this sort has been particularly important for recruitment to the new security forces, which remains a popular route to employment for many from the party militias as well as from disbanded armed forces and the intelligence apparatus of the Ba'th era, despite their frequent targeting by insurgents. The ICDC drew upon the personnel of the militias as well as tribally-organised armed groupings, and undertook joint operations with Coalition troops.[121] The Facilities Protection Service (FPS), established to guard ministries and government infrastructure, was made up of individuals recruited by and responsible to each participating ministry or governorate. With individual ministries under the *de facto* control of political parties, militia members may simply have been transferred to the ministry controlled by the relevant party. This would explain why the FPS was severely overstaffed, unlike the other security forces: in January 2004, it had 97,200 members, in contrast to the projected force level of 50,000.[122] A private military company, Erinys Iraq, contracted to guard Iraq's oil facilities was closely linked to the INC, and recruited heavily from its militia.[123] Thus the new security forces contained shadow networks of faction within them: the boundary between the arms of the state and the activities of political parties was weak.

The INA was initially the most successful party in recruiting a new political base from the old Iraqi army and Ba'th apparatus, building upon its members, many of whom were senior officers within Iraq's security apparatus before 1991. The INA made clear its opposition both to the extent of de-Ba'thification and to the disbanding of Iraq's armed forces; it also hosted a regular programme on its radio outlet specifically for former members of the armed forces.[124] It won control over both the IGC's Supreme Security Committee, through its long-standing links with the CIA and the Interior Ministry in the round of negotiations over the apportionment of portfolios in late 2003, holding primacy in the security field until Iyad 'Allawi was replaced as Prime Minister in April 2005. This allowed it to provide employment on a large scale to those who sought advantage through its offices.[125] A similar model of employment took place at the local level: in Nasiriyya, for example, the city council which was dominated by SCIRI decided to establish a new police battalion by giving each council member the right to appoint seven members.[126] This move, replicated in slightly different forms in other Iraqi towns, has meant that police forces in which members retained loyalty to individual parties and council members have been able to enrich themselves in return for appointments, both classic features of neopatrimonialism. By late 2005, SCIRI had used the Interior Ministry, which it had controlled since April of that year, to integrate its militia into the police forces. The army had relied upon the transfer of personnel from the Kurdish Peshmerga to boost its numbers, as was demonstrated by the 'special tally' of the December 2005 elections, made up overwhelmingly of votes cast by the security forces, in which the main Kurdish slate won 45% of the votes.[127] This would indicate that the Kurds, approximately 20% of the population, constituted around half the army.

Furthermore, former members of the Ba'th Party often needed to secure the support of the political parties to ensure their reintegration into the labour market. After the de-Ba'thification order of 16 May 2003, those excluded from employment needed to apply to the CPA to regain a role. However, responsibility for assessing applications shifted to institutions established by the IGC in November 2003, with the creation of its Higher National Commission for the Eradication of the Ba'th Party (HNCEBP), commonly known in English as the de-Ba'thification Commission.[128] This body and its subsidiary institutions were made up of the appointees of ten political parties, who were given a direct role in choosing which individuals to allow to return to work and to serve as prospective members of local councils.[129] There was therefore a strong incentive for many Iraqis — particularly from upwardly mobile sectors of society — to become affiliated with one of the political parties within the IGC, primarily the INC, whose members held both the HNCEBP's overall chairmanship under Ahmad Chalabi and its operational directorship under Mithal al-Alusi. It retained the directorship for most of the period of the Interim Government, in which the INC did not have a role. During this time Prime Minister 'Allawi made an unsuccessful attempt to shut the Commission down as part of his policy to bring the de-Ba'thification process to an end.[130] When Chalabi returned to government in April 2005, he resumed chairmanship of a reconstituted HNCEBP and another ally of his, 'Ali al-Lami, was appointed to the directorship.[131]

Acting as an autonomous arm of the state under the guidance of INC members, the de-Ba'thification Commission came into repeated conflict with other government branches. Those conflicts were resolved through *ad hoc* compromises or remained unresolved in a highly unclear legal environment. For example, the attempt by the Commission to remove a judge, Sa'id al-Hamashi, from the Iraqi Special Tribunal in January 2006 due to allegations of prior Ba'th Party membership, after the panel had already been sitting for almost three months, partly succeeded: Hamashi was moved to a separate court despite initial statements from the tribunal that he would be taking up the position of Chief Judge after his resignation of Rizgar Amin from this position.[132] The Commission's attempt to exclude 185 candidates from standing for election in December 2005, however, failed: the Board of Commissioners of the elections authorities simply announced that it would not abide by the HNCEBP's decision, and permitted those candidates to stand, persevering in this stance despite subsequent objections from the HNCEBP.[133] The power of particular factions over sectors of the state's activities, and the extent to which their struggles over power were conducted rather than resolved through official channels, were thus demonstrated.

As well as acting as employment brokers in a job-poor environment, it appears that some of the political parties also sought to act as intermediaries for international and Iraqi contractors in their relations with the CPA. Allegations of Coalition favouritism to corporations promoted by members of the IGC were widespread after mid-2003. Wider attention focused on a $327 million contract for supplies for the new Iraqi army that was awarded to a consortium created by a former business partner of Chalabi, but that was by no means the only such alleged case.[134] Parties may have consolidated their positions by building alliances with supportive corporations. The INC, which held the chair of the IGC's Economic and Finance Committee and which appointed the Ministers of Finance and Trade, was again particularly well placed to do so.[135] In May 2005, Chalabi took on the chairmanship of a six-member Supreme Contracts Committee, which had power to vet every contract between government institutions and private corporations worth more than $3 million.[136] This committee met 36 times in its first six months, with Chalabi claiming it had 'succeeded in putting an end to corruption in 98 percent of the big contracts in Iraq'.[137] The authority and reach of the committee nonetheless demonstrated again the lasting hold of one faction over a sector of public life.

There was thus extensive use of patron-client relationships in structuring the political arena. The boundary between public and private spheres was continually blurred and often erased completely, with the staff of ministries, police forces and security services dependent upon and thus loyal to factional leaders who exercised their power through their private, not their official roles. Because oversight by either the Coalition or, after June 2004, the central government was minimal, and the administrative framework weak, local governors could appoint staff personally beholden to them, rather than those best qualified for the jobs.[138] This loyalty was demonstrated most notably when US military commanders ordered Iraqi battalions into combat during 2004, and found that two battalions refused to move into Falluja and five would not take part in the assault on the Mahdi Army in Najaf. Most probably these refusals occurred not because of incompetence or fear, but because the battalions were drawn from parties that held strong reservations about the US military attacks, and gave direct orders or implicit signals to their clients in the Iraqi armed forces not to participate.[139] This appropriation of organs of the state by private institutions indicates that the Iraqi state does have strong neopatrimonial characteristics.

Externally penetrated patrimonial society

Although the Iraqi state has significantly neopatrimonial characteristics, patrimonialism within Iraqi society also plays a major role in Iraqi politics, and that patrimonialism features a major role for external patrons.

To elaborate upon the first of these points, many of the patron-client bonds that structure Iraqi political action are not routed through the institutions of the state, and some do not even have the state as a central actor in sustaining them. In contrast to the use by parties of *tazkiyya* for their members to secure employment at a government ministry, many Iraqis have obtained services through non-state institutions such as independent religious bodies, external agencies and informal economic actors. The logic of patron-client relationships has remained strong in these cases, and has been instrumental in bringing political participation, but as they were not routed through state institutions they should be considered as examples of patrimonial bonds, not neopatrimonial ones. For example, in Shi'a parts of Iraq, the network of mosques, *husayniyya*s (Shi'i community centres), foundations and personnel have acted to provide medical care, social order, funding and schooling, but have retained their vigorous autonomy from state institutions.[140]

This is not merely a point about appropriate classification. Neopatrimonialism has the effect of binding populations to the personnel of the state, who in turn have a clear incentive to maintain the authority and dominance of the state institutions of which they are part, even if this is for purposes of personal gain rather than public benefit. Iraqi neopatrimonial linkages work on this basis too: ministers have to sustain the overall control of their institutions over the appropriate sector of public life for them to be a source of employment to their loyalists. However, purely patrimonial linkages cut out the state; those involved have no interest in sustaining the authority of its institutions, and often undermine it in crucial ways. For example, the use of armed militias and tribal courts to maintain local order may be popular as a mechanism to reduce local crime, but it also directly challenges the central role of the state as having the authority to judge according to its own laws and enforce them. This major role for patrimonial, as opposed to neopatrimonial, bonds can be contrasted with the Ba'thist era, which across the periods of economic growth, war and sanctions retained tight control of the levers of patronage, thus atomising the population and subordinating it to state actors.[141]

Furthermore, non-state patrons are not purely indigenous, but are deeply enmeshed in and partially constituted by international actors and processes. The nature of Iranian involvement in Iraq has been one of the most politically charged issues since the invasion: those who have alleged large-scale covert Iranian moves to destabilise Iraq, for example by using *agents provocateurs* or sponsoring insurgents, include US Defence Secretary Rumsfeld, Iraq's interim President and Defence Minister and prominent Saudi-owned newspapers.[142] Reliable evidence in each case has been lacking, often conflating the transborder movement of previously exiled Iraqis with Iranian infiltration, and imputing the actions of Shi'a political parties directly to the Iranian government.

Although evidence exists of the transport of weapons into Iraq from Iran in July 2005, there has been little to suggest that this was not part of the general high level of smuggling taking place between the two countries, outside the purview or knowledge of either government.[143]

However, placing the multiplicity of Iranian governmental and quasi-governmental actors within a framework of patrimonial relationships with Iraqi clients has greater explanatory potential and plausibility than the accusations of a monolithic external agent fomenting an internal insurgency. Iranian involvement in Iraq's political development after April 2003 was highly multifaceted, with extensive movements of population, funds, information and goods across permeable borders. Locating an analysis of these movements within a study of patrimonialism seeks to place them within the context of power relations of various forms, in which not only the identities of both the client and the agent, but also the extent and type of the former's power over the latter are primary questions. The Iranian involvement in Iraq illustrates the competing role of the institutions of an external state, with the Ministry of Intelligence and Security, the Iranian Revolutionary Guard Corps, the Ministry of Foreign Affairs and the Supreme National Security Council all engaged in attempts to develop support bases inside Iraq. These institutions have provided material support to a variety of tribal leaders, militias, local notables, political parties, individual mosques, neighbourhood councils and autonomous welfare organisations.[144] Furthermore, sectors of the Iranian state have been able to cut off Iraqi actors' access to resources, for example by exercising more stringent border controls on smuggling or by dissuading Iranian pilgrims from travelling to the Iraqi shrine cities. Both actions, practised by the Iranian government over the period since the invasion, have served to entice Iraqi agents into closer coordination with particular factions in Tehran so as to protect access to key resources. The relevance of the Iranian government in this respect was acknowledged by the Bush administration in November 2005, when it authorised its ambassador in

Iraq to open negotiations with Iran with a view to cooperation as US forces reduced their numbers inside Iraq.[145]

The different centres of authority in Tehran were caught up in competitive bidding for clients, and thus unable to give a single political direction to those drawing upon the resources of the Iranian state. As a senior leader of al-Da'wa said in October 2004:

Iran does not have a single line. There are different centres of power: the Pasdaran, the supreme leader, the president. And you can't really know who is who, who is making the decisions. Sometimes you can be dealing with a senior official who agrees to something, but then he turns out not to have the power to implement it, and the agreement falls apart.[146]

This picture of multiple patrons is further complicated by the diversity of forms of brokerage relationship. Few if any Iraqi religious and political actors were simple conduits of values or resources originating in Iran. Some commentators have emphasised how many of Iraq's Shi'a leaders were politically socialised in and integrated into Iranian political networks before 2003, and have used this fact to point to the emergence of a resurgent and cohesive Shi'a political movement — a 'Shi'a crescent'.[147] Iranian models of government have clearly had some influence on Iraq's Shi'a politicians: the creation of the 'Martyrs' Foundation' (*mu'asasa al-shuhada'*) in article 104 of the 2005 Iraqi Constitution, replicating the terminology of its well-known Iranian equivalent, illustrates this. However, it would be a mistake to underplay the autonomy and pragmatism of Shi'a social and political movements in Iraq, most of which have been keen to distance themselves not only from ideas of a single political authority — a shared jurisprudent (*faqih*) — common to both Iraq and Iran as supported by Ayatollah Khomeini, but also from the distinctive Iranian model of 'guardianship of the jurisprudent' (*wilayat al-faqih*) that results in clerical rule.[148] This distancing process has been particularly notable for the Sadr movement, which originally located its source of religious authority in Ayatollah Kadhim al-Ha'iri, a former leader of al-Da'wa based in Qom in Iran, who opposed having separate *faqih*s for Iran and Iraq. Nevertheless, the Sadr Movement maintained separate institutions inside Iraq from the offices for Ha'iri's *wakil*s. By mid-2004, both Sadr and the Fadila Party had broken with Ha'iri, and sought a distinctively Iraqi leadership for the seminary in Najaf.[149] Furthermore, the highly structured decision-making process and intense striving for a rigorous theological grounding within the Iraqi Shi'a religious leadership insulate it to a considerable degree from the straightforward pressures of patron-client exchanges. Religious authority, therefore, will not serve easily as the moral glue for patrimonial relations.

This lack of a single political agency directing the actions of Iraqis who are only partially integrated into Iranian patrimonial networks is not taken into account by analyses that focus on observations of the high degree of symbolic penetration of Iran into southern Iraq. Whilst the frequent display of pictures of Khomeini in Basra does indicate the salience of patrimonial networks over which the Iraqi state does not exercise overall leverage, it does not indicate precisely which other seat of authority has captured this position. There are multifaceted networks of patronage in southern Iraq, in which transborder relationships are significant but not exclusive, and the Iraqi state, political parties and religious authorities are all major players. Nevertheless, the intertwining of patrimonial and neopatrimonial connections within Iraq means that state agents do not have the centrality and binding power often associated with more straightforwardly neopatrimonial networks. Instead, loyalties have been structured in more diffuse, disjointed and interpenetrated ways, and are unlikely to develop in direct parallel with the interaction of state officials with local populations. State officials, in short, are in a weaker position in making a claim on citizens' loyalty.

Parties, clients and the Coalition

The binding of citizens to the state has been weakened further by the fact that Iraqi official actors at the state level have rarely needed clients in order to retain positions of authority. Neopatrimonialism only has a role when both those with access to resources and those without would benefit significantly from an exchange, typically involving resources for loyalty. However, mass loyalty has been only one mechanism — and at times, only a secondary mechanism — for political actors in Iraq to gain or retain political power, and utility for the Coalition and the ability to make deals with other political parties have often been more important.

Between July 2003 and June 2004, political participation was structured solely on the basis of cooperation with the Coalition: groups that could demonstrate their relevance to the Coalition were in demand, and were thus appointed to positions on the IGC. Political positions on issues involving central administration were developed by such groups largely on the basis of such positions' utility to the Coalition, and not in order to contest or rethink policy. Once a representative of each of the major parties had been appointed to a position on the IGC, and had thus also secured the ability to appoint a minister when the cabinet was established in September 2003, there was little to be obtained through official channels by attempting to win over sectors of the population. The demonstration of abilities in this sphere could not result in the formal transfer of more resources to the party as those resources were held by the Coalition, which had already fixed the roles of each of the parties for the period of occupation. The official payoffs for action in recruiting a large number of clients were disproportionately small when compared with the effort necessary.

Similarly, from June 2004 to January 2005, political power in Baghdad was largely determined by inter-party bargaining. 'Allawi secured the prime ministerial position by securing votes within the IGC, and by encouraging Washington to back his stance. His personal popularity amongst the Iraqi population, which was close to nil, was largely irrelevant to this process: one poll conducted in late June 2004, conducted just as 'Allawi was taking up his position, found that just 1.6% of Iraqi would have supported him in an election.[150] Despite having minimal support, 'Allawi was still selected by IGC members as Prime Minister, which demonstrated that a client base outside the Green Zone was not necessary to achieve power. This would explain why only 6.5% of the Iraqi population acknowledged that they had been approached by a political party or grouping in the period between April 2003 and June 2004.[151]

The national elections of January and December 2005 did demonstrate that a substantial support base amongst the population was significant in the competition for political power, providing the incentive for political parties to exercise neopatrimonial relations. However, the system of electoral lists substantially offset this incentive. That process was encouraged by the US, which had originally pushed for all the parties within the IGC to be on the same so-called 'monster list'.[152] Although the parties did not end up agreeing to such a list, because all the major political entities from each of Iraq's Kurdish and Shi'a communities formed united groupings, they did not need to compete with one another for clients, but instead held close to a *de facto* monopoly of the political representation of their respective communities.

Most of the major Shi'a-led parties, including SCIRI, different branches of al-Da'wa, and al-Fadila, joined to form the UIA for the two elections.[153] The Sadr movement gave implicit backing to the UIA in the January elections, and approximately 20 of its members took positions on its list, although Sadr himself maintained an official stance of supporting a boycott (other supporters organised a separate list).[154] It participated fully in the December 2005 UIA list. Sistani acted as the glue which held together the Shi'a political parties, ensuring that the major parties did not need to compete against each other and thus disrupt each others' client bases. A vote could be cast for the UIA as a communal obligation. The UIA could thus be confident that it would secure the votes of the overwhelming majority of Shi'a voters. A similar process took place amongst the Kurdish political parties, with the two major parties joining with smaller entities to form the Kurdistan Alliance.

The actual competition for political pre-eminence amongst Iraq's Shi'a thus took place within the closed-door discussions of the UIA rather than through an open political contest. The group of parties within the UIA engaged in an intense debate during October and November 2004 about the order of names on the list, which would affect the proportion of seats that each party would hold as part of the overall number won by the Alliance. In the end, the committee established by the parties agreed that approximately 12% of the seats won by the UIA would go to SCIRI members, 18% would be divided between the different branches of al-Da'wa, 10% would go to those aligned with Fadila and Sadr, and 10% to the Shi'a Political Council, itself established as an alliance between the INC and independent personalities.[155] In advance of the December 2005 elections, for which a list of candidates for every governorate was necessary, the negotiations within the UIA led to a different balance of power: out of the UIA candidates elected, 23% of seats went to SCIRI, 20% to the branches of al-Da'wa, and 35% to the two branches of the Sadr movement.[156] The remainder in both cases was allocated to smaller parties and non-partisan figures. In one sense, then, the crucial mechanism of allocating seats to parties was already fixed between most of the largest parties before the election actually took place. Moreover, it seems unlikely that the agreed allocation between different parties within the UIA was simply based on a calculation of perceived popularity. The leading figure of the Shi'a Political Council on the UIA list in the January 2005 elections was Chalabi, whose popularity as registered in Iraqi opinion polls had been minimal. Despite this, a grouping emerged with 14 members in the new assembly as a result of the election, and was able to ensure that Chalabi was appointed as one of Iraq's Deputy Prime Ministers. Similarly, the increase in members of the Sadr movement elected in December 2005, to make it the single largest bloc in the National As-

sembly, was unlikely to have been a simple reflection of any increase
in popularity since January 2005. Instead, it resulted from its changed
strategy in relation to the other Shi'a parties, moving from overt competition to wary compromise.

The extent of the dominance of these two lists — the UIA and
the Kurdistan Alliance — within their own sectarian and ethnic communities was apparent from the election results. In January 2005, the
UIA won the largest share of votes in each of the nine governorates
with a large Shi'a majority, such as Dhi Qar (80.9%), Babil (79.3%),
Muthanna (77.1%), Qadisiyya (74.8%) and Basra (70.2%).[157] In eight
out of these nine governorates, the share of the UIA vote increased in
December 2005, the only exception being Babil (which also has a significant Sunni Arab minority). In six governorates (al-Najaf, al-Qadisiyya, Wasit, Maysan, Dhi Qar and al-Muthanna), the UIA achieved
over 80% of the vote in December 2005; in Karbala' and Basra, the
UIA obtained 76.1% and 77.5% of the vote respectively. The Kurdish
Alliance was even more dominant, achieving over 90% of the vote
in the three governorates in which there is a clear Kurdish majority
in January 2005, and only slipping below that threshold to 87.2% in
Sulaymaniyya in December 2005.[158]

The only arena in which parties that had a similar scale of resources
and a level of organisation in competition against each other was in
the Sunni Arab community in the December 2005 elections, in which
the Iraqi Accord Front (itself made up of an alliance between the IIP,
the list of Adnan al-Dulaymi and others), the Iraqi National Dialogue
Front, the Reconciliation and Liberation Party of Mish'an al-Juburi and
the INA-led Iraqi National List strove for pre-eminence. The Dialogue
Front, headed by Salih al-Mutlak, and the Iraqi National List both presented themselves as non-sectarian parties ('Allawi himself is of Shi'a
origin), although both appear to have achieved their strongest results
in Sunni majority areas. Although 'Allawi's list, then called simply the
'Iraqi List', had won some votes among the Iraqi Shi'a community in

January 2005, it had a fairly distinctive client base within that group, of urban secular-oriented Shi'a. With few mechanisms of local organisation, it also relied heavily on media campaigns backed by US and British financial support.[159] That vote declined even further in December 2005, winning no more than 12% in any governorate except Baghdad.

Outside the areas in which Sunni Arabs were the majority, the opportunity for open political competition in December 2005 was restricted not only by the unequal nature of the contest in terms of resources, but also by the repression of smaller groups that were emerging. The Kurdistan Islamic Union (KIU), the only Kurdish party with an historical lineage to stand outside the Kurdistan Alliance, suffered from armed assaults on six of its offices in northern Iraq on 6 December 2005, shortly after announcing that it would stand as a separate list. The attack by unidentified personnel on the KIU office in Dahuk killed four of its members, including a member of the party's leadership.[160] In Basra, one journalist reported how '[v]irtually all the opposing candidates [to the UIA] in Basra are cowering inside their offices and say they are terrorized by a campaign of intimidation by Shiite extremists'.[161]

In summary, inter-party competition had only a marginal role in the January and December 2005 national elections outside the Sunni Arab areas. For those groups with a client base, the list system enabled them to avoid having their patrimonial and neopatrimonial relationships opened to political competition. Patrimonialism can be a highly competitive phenomenon, with would-be patrons seeking clients to strengthen their positions against other patrons, especially in the struggle for office. The effect of competition is to weaken the patron's hold and bargaining power. However, the circumstances of Iraqi parties made them especially wary of competition: SCIRI and the leading wing of al-Da'wa had recently returned from exile, and were already challenged over their new client bases by embedded local leaders. The Sadr movement, also part of the UIA, meanwhile had the opportunity to make substantial inroads into the client base of the exilic parties, but had suffered under two waves of US-led assaults in April and August 2004. For them, to compete against the exilic Shiʿa parties for support when those parties were potential protectors against future Coalition attack would make little sense.

Therefore, seeking a support base within the country was not necessary for political groups to secure power in Baghdad. Instead, the ability to make deals at the centre — for example, to provide goods to other parties such as external actors' engagement, institutional resources or expertise, in return for a slice of the political proceeds — can be another route to political power. This emphasis on succeeding in negotiations within the governing institutions rather than capturing support bases within the country was reinforced by the structures of the TAL and the 2005 constitution, both of which required two-thirds majorities in the assembly on the most important votes. The result was a tendency towards forming grand coalitions at the centre, with cabinets consisting of more than 30 members and prolonged debates over appointments that have paralysed the assembly's business for weeks and even months at a time. For example, a speaker was only nominated to Iraq's Transitional National Assembly 62 days after elections to it in January 2005, and it took 35 more days before a full government of 38 ministers and members of the presidency council was confirmed. During this time, the ability of the TNA to engage in serious debate about the future and problems of Iraq was minimal.

Since Iraqi politicians had become trapped in the game of making alliances and agreements at the centre, the level of engagement with, and responsiveness to, popular pressures was limited. Parties formed ruling coalitions to sustain their hold on power, and thus retain their relevance, and did so without a common purpose of social or economic transformation. Meanwhile, with the retrenchment of patrimonial bonds, loyalty was increasingly transferred to other sites, away from those competing for power at the centre and towards non-state political agents. In sum, we have shown in this section that Iraqi political parties have tended to exercise both neopatrimonial and patrimonial forms of rule in a way that has in general enabled them to capture a specific client base or control over sectors of Iraqi public life, but still have comparatively few incentives to engage in the detailed cultivation of a popular support base. The final section of this chapter examines how the forces of patrimonialism and neopatrimonialism have interacted with the rising sectarianism that has been fuelled by the initial collapse of the state immediately after the invasion, and also by aspects of the state building process.

SECTARIANISM AND THE STATE

So far in this Chapter, we have argued that the weakness and disjoint-edness of the Coalition civil structure within Iraq were particularly pronounced in its regional management, and that this left extensive room for indigenous actors to commandeer the political arenas and resources of regional administration. These local actors often stood in opposition to national political parties, who were increasingly drawn into the politics of deal-making in Baghdad at the expense of furthering their integration into the networks and byways of local politics. The struggle of many of the local actors to assert their dominance against attempts by the centre to reappropriate power for itself took the form of a formal discourse of autonomy or decentralisation, with local loyalties being stressed at the expense of national ones. In this section, we will examine the nature of Iraqi sectarianism and show its relationship with the political process underway in the country.

Before a more detailed examination of the extent of sectarian discourse and its political impact, it is worthwhile to make two clarifications. Firstly, our analysis rejects primordialist conceptions of Iraqi sects; we do not accept that the significance of sectarian membership in the construction of Iraqis' identities has been constant over Iraq's history. Whilst sectarian self-identifications have had some salience in the past, other forms of self-description have often been as strong if not more so: the tribe, clan, city quarter, guild, class, nation-state and transborder ethnonational groupings have all been strong claimants on loyalty in the past.[162] Intermarriage, and the resultant mingling of identities, have all been features of Iraq's past. The new salience of specific claimants on identity arises from a conjunction of social, political and ideological factors in the modern world, such as local grievances arising out of the capture of the Iraqi state by Arabised Sunni officials and officers in the post-mandatory period, the worldwide growth of Shi'a activism, and the weakened ability of the Iraqi state after 2003 to act as a vehicle of citizens' loyalty. None of these factors is immutable.

Secondly, the new sectarianism in Iraq's politics is not simply a reflection of pre-existing popular opinion. Instead, it arises from a complex weaving of institutional rivalries, new political ascendancies and international priorities that has given new force to sectarian claims within Iraq, without direct regard to the proportion of people who would endorse those claims. Polling organisations in general record weakly-held sectarianism. For example, polls held from August to September 2003 showed that only 29% of Iraqis believed it important or very important that a leader should represent 'my sect'.[163] A poll a year later found that only 4.5% of Iraqis took as their most important consideration, in choosing a party to vote for, that it should be from 'my religious group' (a further 7.4% took it as their second most important consideration).[164] In contrast, a majority gave answers that indicate statist rather than sectarian attitudes: 79.1% agreed in a March 2004 poll that there should be 'one unified Iraq with central government in Baghdad' (as opposed to 18.6% who thought there should be 'a group of regional states');[165] 56.6% said in July 2004 that they favoured 'a strong central government in Baghdad' (as opposed to 37.8% who chose one of three looser models offered to them);[166] and 64.2% in October 2004 responded that 'strengthen[ing] central control over Iraq's regions' would most improve the current situation in Iraq out of four constitutional options (in contrast to 12.3% who chose one of two options for forms of decentralisation).[167] These attitudes seem to have continued even after the October 2005 constitutional referendum, in which the federal structure of Iraq was accepted. In a poll a month after the referendum, 70% of the sampled population favoured 'one unified Iraq with central government in Baghdad', with only 18% supporting 'regional governments and a federal government in Baghdad'.[168] By late 2005, then, the proportion of the population articulating sectarian allegiances and supporting regional devolution remained small: Iraq's federalisation did not occur by virtue of popular pressures across Iraq.

This is in strong contrast with the alignment of post-invasion Iraqi politics, with all the major parties and groupings except for the INA structured largely on ethnic or sectarian bases. SCIRI, the branches of al-Da'wa and the two wings of the Sadr movement, whilst sometimes publicly cooperating with Sunni Arabs and Kurdish organisations, draw their membership and leadership overwhelmingly from the Shi'a community. The parties or groupings that Sunni Arabs have demonstrated support for, such as the IIP, the Association of Muslim Scholars led by Shaykh Harith al-Dhari and the 'Iraqis' list put forward by interim president Ghazi al-Yawir, have been entirely run by Sunni Arabs. The only significant exception, as mentioned, is the INA, led by a Shi'a (Iyad 'Allawi) but with a prominent number of both Sunni Arab and Shi'a supporters in mixed urban areas, particularly in Baghdad and Basra where it won 52.5% of its entire share of votes across the country in January 2005 (these regions contributed 30.8% of the overall number of votes cast). To win support from the Kurdish population, the major parties all proclaim Kurdish national rights as a key part of their political identity. It is not only formal political parties that have become based solely in one sect or ethnic grouping: as one journalist records, 'Most universities have only two major political student associations: a Shiite Muslim one and a Sunni Muslim one.'[169] Iraqi political movements that are not rooted primarily in one ethnic or sectarian group have formed since 2003, but none has yet made a significant political impression or achieved mass support.[170]

Until late 2004, few of the leaderships of these parties or groups resorted to language that directly challenged the value of other sects or the desirability of working with their representatives. There were groups that set out to incite a large-scale armed struggle between the groups, such as Tawhid wa Jihad (which became al-Qa'ida in Mesopotamia) of Abu Mus'ab al-Zarqawi. However, reports indicated that its anti-Shi'a rhetoric was not well received initially by Iraqi-led Sunni Arab insurgents, many of whom sought to work with Sadr, and who justified their involvement in or support for attacks on Shi'a leaders on the grounds of those leaders' alleged collaboration with the occupation rather than through the denigration of the Shi'a community as a whole.[171] Instead, there was a consistent call for joint action to solve the problems set out for Iraq, whether those were conceived as arising from the occupation or from the insurgency. For example, in April 2004, as the US-led assaults on Falluja and the Mahdi Army were beginning, a large demonstration of approximately 200,000 Sunni Arabs and Shi'a was held at the mosque of Umm al-Qura (Mother of Villages, a Qur'anic name for Mecca, previously called the Mother of All Battles) in Baghdad. The demonstrators chanted 'Long live Muqtada, long live Falluja, long live Basra, long live Karbala', emphasising unity between the two sects' sense of vulnerability and grievance.[172] Nevertheless, this was clearly organised as a joint project of two groups that saw and portrayed themselves as distinct from one another. The demonstration's organisers were the Sadr movement and the Association of Muslim Scholars, both of which grounded their authority in principles specific to the Shi'a and Sunni sects respectively. Therefore, whilst political organisation in Iraq since the invasion may not reveal antagonism between the sects, it has in general indicated that members of the different sects have largely taken part in political organisations that are specific to those sects: the sect has become the basis of the new political community.

The reasons for this discrepancy between the initially non-sectarian expression of political identity by the population in polling surveys and the sect-based nature of political groupings are worth exploring. We will now look at two explanations that seem intuitively plausible: that the parties that took control were already of a sectarian hue; and that the different politics of Sunni Arabs and Shiʻa come from the different problems that they have faced since the invasion. Although both explanations provide insights, neither of them is sufficient to explain the extent of sectarian politics within Iraq in the aftermath of the invasion.

Firstly, as with many Islamist parties that evolved in situations of intense political oppression, groups such as the Sadr movement, the IIP and the wings of al-Daʻwa that remained active in Iraq during the Baʻth era were only able to organise through networks of religious institutions, such as mosques and (for the Shiʻi) *husayniyya*s. Many parties that were formed or grew in exile before 1990 were heavily influenced by the need to find a state sponsor for resources and a base. In this regard, Iran became the key state, which in turn had a heavy role in reorganising groups based within its territory along principles that conformed to its interpretation of Shiʻa Islam. Those groups included SCIRI, many of the external branches of al-Daʻwa, and the Islamic Task Organisation. As a result, political groups took on characteristics and leaders specific to the religious networks through which they were operating. The situation changed from 1990, with Jordan, the UK and US most actively providing channels for non-sectarian groups such as the INC and INA to pursue means to overthrow the Baʻth regime, but these groups did not have the opportunity to build a support base inside Iraq before 2003. Furthermore, some of these groups took on a sectarian character subsequently; the INC, for example, amalgamated itself into the Shiʻa Political Council in May 2004, thus confining its potential support base to one sect only. Therefore, almost all the major Arab political parties inside Iraq since the occupation have had strongly sectarian pathways of development. The salience of sectarian divisions was further entrenched with the Coalition policy of making political appointments to the IGC and other senior positions on the basis of estimated proportions of different sectarian and ethnic groups within Iraqi society, a practice that many Iraqis called *al-muhasasa* (sectarian apportionment),[173] a term taken from Lebanese discourse. For example, a suitable Sunni Arab leader had to be found for the presidential position from June 2004, to complement the Shi'a Prime Minister; and the Iraqi Communist Party's leader was able to gain a position in the IGC by virtue of his Shi'a background, despite the party's historically strong anti-sectarian rhetoric. Sunni Arabs and Shi'a now had to sell themselves on the basis of sectarian identity if they wanted employment from the Coalition; political leaders had to become sectarian entrepreneurs.

However, these conditions generate only very incomplete explanations of the significance of sectarian allegiances in Iraq after the invasion. In particular, although relatively few Iraqis espouse explicit sectarianism, the views of Sunni Arab and Shi'a members are highly divergent on many political matters not directly related to the relative positions of the major sects, and this cannot be explained plausibly by the nature of the parties or the way in which senior jobs have been allocated. For example, a poll from October and November 2004 found that 54% of those living in Sunni-majority regions said they felt 'not very safe' or 'not safe at all' in their neighbourhoods. In contrast, in Shi'a-majority areas, 74% in the mid-Euphrates region and 60% in the south, both of which have predominantly Shi'a populations, said they felt 'very safe'.[174] Moreover, the starkness of this division has increased over time: by November 2005, 80% of Shi'a felt safe in their neighbourhoods, whilst only 11% of Sunni Arabs did.[175] A poll conducted in November and December 2004 found that 61.7% of Iraqis in the south and 71.3% of Iraqis in the mid-Euphrates region thought that Iraq was 'headed in the right direction', but only 18.9% in Sunni-majority regions affirmed this.[176]

A second, alternative, explanation for these differences in attitudes, then, is that the conditions in the predominantly Sunni Arab and Shi'a regions have been different. This is indicated by polling questions that ask not about attitudes but about situations. A September 2004 poll found that 18.9% of those living in predominantly Shi'a areas said that someone in their household had been directly affected by serious violence since the invasion, compared with 33.1% of those in Sunni-majority regions who reported this.[177] An equal number of those in Sunni regions (35% each) said that they were better and worse off economically since the invasion in response to an October 2004 poll. This compares with 59% of those in the mid-Euphrates region who said they were better off and 14% who said they were worse off; and 61% in the south who claimed they were better off while only 9% said they were worse off.[178] This finding is reinforced with the results of the *ILCS 2004*, which showed that incomes in four of the six central, largely Sunni Arab, governorates of Iraq were lower in 2003-04 than the national average. It also showed that households in those governorates had more assets in general than the national average, whilst the average household in every southern governorate had fewer assets.[179] Since assets indicate past wealth, the results clearly indicate a reversal in the relative economic standing of the southern and central governorates.

In terms of services, in March and April 2004, 40% of those in Sunni areas reported no clean water over the past four weeks, a marginal deterioration (from 38%) from the period before the invasion. This was worse than for Shi'a regions, in which 29% of respondents reported a lack of clean water, which was an improvement on the period before the war when 42% recollected this problem occurring.[180] Therefore, one straightforward explanation for the different political trajectories of Sunni and Shi'a communities, and hence their alignment with separate factions, has been the different conditions under which they have been living. These differences arise partly from the varying approaches used by Coalition forces in regions with Sunni Arab and Shi'a majorities, and partly from the varying socioeconomic starting conditions. This explanation coheres with the form of analysis frequently adopted by commentators on Iraq: that, since the Sunni Arab minority was greatly advantaged under the Ba'th regime, the widespread opposition from this community to the occupation can be traced to the greater equalisation in access to resources. The Sunni Arabs, in other words, resent the loss of their dominance.[181]

Whilst this account has some validity, it also contains significant problems. It is by no means clear that Sunni Arab populations across the country were advantaged under the Ba'th regime. Economic wealth was concentrated in specific areas of Baghdad and Salah al-Din governorates, inflating calculations of average incomes for central Iraq.[182] When access to services is measured, the difference between the sects is much smaller. For example, a similar proportion of residents reported problems with electricity (83%) and water (38%) before the invasion in areas outside Baghdad that had a Sunni Arab majority as in areas with an Arab Shi'a majority (80% and 42% respectively).[183] There was a striking difference in recollections of political freedoms before the invasion, with 82% in Shi'a areas speaking of being afraid to worship compared with 28% in Sunni areas outside Baghdad.[184] However, it would not be plausible to see this as the basis on which political organisation has existed post-invasion, since no more than 5% in either sect have reported restrictions on religious rights since then; so neither sect has distinctive political problems to address in this field which would impel separate political institutions.

A further problem with explaining the sect-based bifurcation of political organisations in Iraq on the basis of the differences in their social conditions is that, notwithstanding these differences, similar proportions of the members of the two sects actually share an extensive range of political beliefs. There were very similar proportions of Sunni Arabs and Shi'a with positive and negative impressions of the CPA's performance (15% versus 54% respectively in Sunni Arab regions, 16% versus

46% in Shi'a regions, outside Baghdad).[185] Polling also showed similar proportions wanting the Coalition to leave immediately or to stay longer (65% versus 27% in Sunni Arab regions, 61% versus 30% in Shi'a regions, outside Baghdad);[186] and wanting a special role for religion in the Iraqi government or believing state and religion should be kept separate (44.3% versus 46.0% for both sects).[187] When presented with a list of countries that Iraq could model its government upon, the same choice scored most highly for both Sunni Arabs and Shi'a — the United Arab Emirates (the choice of 50% of Sunni Arabs, 34% of Shi'i).[188] There is no inherent reason why political organisation in Iraq could not have crystallised along the lines of these issues, with the major political contest occurring, for example, between parties supporting the separation of religion and government and those wanting a strong religious influence on government, instead of along sectarian lines.

The primary reason for the sect-based alignment of political groupings and the heightening intensity of conflict between the sects, we argue, rests in the collapse of the institutions of the Iraqi state and the reconstruction of their fragments along sectarian lines. A stated tendency of people to join religious organisations during periods of conflict has often been applied to the Iraqi context, and given a psychological edge. Adnan al-Pachachi, for example, spoke of how he 'came back to Iraq with the assumption that these religious and sectarian tendencies were not that strong. But in times of trouble, people tend to go toward religion and the religious parties make use of that very skilfully.'[189] However, with significant economic and organisational power resting in groups that have a basis in sectarian structures, political explanations may be more useful. Without a state that is capable of providing basic services, the opportunity for patrimonial and neopatrimonial relations to form is considerable.

Alongside the fragmentation of governing structures, forms of discourse that emphasise the political significance of values specific to one sect have been apparent across much of Iraq, conveyed by indigenous actors who have sought modes of justification for their rule and for political programmes that stretch beyond their immediate locality. Patrons who seek to retain client groups over extended periods of time have to find ways to turn transactional relationships into moral bonds by incorporating patrimonial ties into a set of social values. This is what allows a pattern of credit and expectation to arise, to be employed and valorised by both patron and client.[190] Clientelistic ties thus become multifunctional, often with personal, religious, economic and political facets that are mutually reinforcing. In this way patrimonial and neo-patrimonial ties are embedded more deeply into Iraqi life through a 'social glue' whose ingredients are political programmes, appeals to tradition, welfare programmes and religious direction.

Local political actors who have attempted to install themselves as autonomous centres of power, against Baghdad's centralising institutions, cannot use nationalist discourse to this effect. The hallmark of nationalism is the overriding allegiance to a powerful central state, and this is directly contrary to the interests of local leaders. The most noticeable alternative discourse in Arab areas of Iraq that justifies state authority but does not subordinate the periphery to the centre is that of sectarianism. Alongside and often in tandem with embedded local leaders, religious venues have become the primary arena through which an individual's interests and grievances can be presented and acted upon.

Many of those grievances are rooted in the violent conditions of post-invasion Iraq. With many police forces lacking an effective and impartial command and control structure, and with weak judicial structures, the mechanism sought for judgement, retribution and punishment has often been that of the militia organised through a sectarian group, aligned either with a political party or with a set of local religious institutions. As the examples above showed, militia members are often located within police forces, able to guide police action for factional purposes. The militia member also often acts as the neighbourhood informant — the *alasas* — who watches for outsiders and follows them while they are in the neighbourhood. In the mixed areas of Iraq in particular, the use of these militias against perceived violations of group interests has been especially disruptive, and has served as a basis for Iraqi discussions of the possibility of civil war or mass population movements to separate out the sectarian communities. Thus, in Hamdan, south of Basra, the killing of five Sunni men in September 2003 was blamed on a militia from al-Da'wa, which may in turn have been related to local allegations of a 'Wahhabi' presence in the town.[191] In the absence of an effective official investigatory force, the truth about the allegations both of al-Da'wa's involvement in the killings and of extremist infiltration will remain unknown, and this will sustain the incentives for communal organisation and polarising the groups. A similar pattern can be seen in many other mixed villages and neighbourhoods of Iraq; the police and security forces are in the hands of groups based upon sectarian allegiances, and this serves as a key factor in broader communal organisation along these lines.[192] Retribution thus organises itself around sectarian lines: for example, after a Shi'a student was murdered for celebrating the January 2005 election outcome, Shi'a students attacked Sunni Arab students and academics on the campus of Baghdad University.[193]

This condition of great uncertainty in southern and central Iraq, without a state to act as a basis for civil order, has been the key factor in the rise of inter-sectarian violence from late 2004 onwards. The heightened discourse of fear, often based on unsubstantiated claims, has been apparent in the Iraqi news media. For example, Karbalanews.net published an item in November 2004 entitled 'Shi'is are bought and sold in Latifiyya';[194] taxi drivers had reported that leaflets had been distributed in Latifiyya offering the drivers a reward of $10,000 for kidnapping Shi'a clerics. The site said that lower rewards were offered for the capture of Iraqi soldiers ($3,000), Iraqi policemen ($2,000) and 'ordinary Shi'i Iraqis' ($1,000). Some media take a bluntly sectarian approach. Alnajafnews.net, a popular website which one report claimed belonged to the office of Sistani's son-in-law and representative Jawad al-Shahristani,[195] published an article in January 2005 accusing the Sunni Arabs of 'refusing to support any democratic or pluralist project in Iraq', as if all Sunni Arabs were of one mind.[196] Such collective condemnation, rare in the print media and on major broadcast outlets until late 2004, had become widespread by the end of the year.

From early on after the invasion, then, the institutions of violence were dominated by the organisations and networks with most power in society — political parties, tribes and mosques. This has been the seizure of the fragments of the state, usually by sectarian entrepreneurs, primarily the Shi'a parties and sectarian leaders. The capture by SCIRI of the Interior Ministry in April 2005 was the key to this process, and the perception that the Shi'a parties had taken over the Interior Ministry and Defence Ministry forces in southern and central Iraq and were using them to operate 'death squads' against the Sunni Arabs became widespread.[197] These perceptions were partly confirmed by independent findings which we review in the next Chapter. Equally, however, control of these forces by Shi'a groupings was perceived as valid by many members of that community as a legitimate tactic of defence against Sunni Arab attacks.[198] Endemic, unresolved and unpunished violence has been a uniquely powerful tool in reshaping Iraq along sectarian lines.

For their opponents, the alliance of Shi'i with the US has cast the Coalition in the role of building a Shi'a state from the wreckage of its centralised predecessor. In November 2004, the Shi'a cleric Iyad Jamal al-Din told al-Arabiya satellite television that he supported the US-led attack on Falluja, speaking of the 'dens of terrorists and Saddam's supporters who know only violence in Falluja'. Sheikh 'Abd al-'Aziz al-Dulaymi, a prominent Sunni preacher, responded: 'We won't forget the weak stance of the Shia [during] the aggression against Falluja [...]. The Falluja crisis revealed the poisonous nature of the Shia.'[199] After the formation of the Ja'fari Government in April 2005, Sunni Arabs commonly attributed US-led military operations to the sectarian policies of the parties in the UIA. An example is the way the Association of Muslim Scholars attributed the offensive carried out in Tal Afar in September 2005 to 'a deep-seated sectarian grudge', whilst the Sunni mayor resigned, calling it a 'sectarian operation'.[200]

CONCLUSION

The inadequacy and incoherence of the Coalition's ruling structures, especially on the civilian side, led it to look for Iraqi political actors whose actions it hoped to be able to direct. It tried simultaneously to develop Iraqi institutional capacity and to control it, by engaging with political parties at the national level and a variety of local leaders while trying to balance them against each other. A crucial defect of this strategy has been that local leaders have been able to assert, in principle and in practice, their primacy over national level political parties. The coherence of the state has been further undermined by the use of the state to conduct neopatrimonial relations, by extensive patrimonialism which has competed with the state as a provider of benefits to Iraqi society, by foreign involvement in those neopatrimonial relations, and by the fact that Iraqi political parties have concentrated on acquiring control of elements of the state by doing deals with the Coalition and each other.

The fragmentary nature of the Iraqi state, partial as a mechanism of order and weak as a service provider, has been instrumental in the alignment of populations with groups rooted in principles specific to a sect. In this sense, then, the state machinery has lost its position of being capable of authoritative action across the breadth of Iraqi society. With power lying in the peripheries of the state, structured and restructured through multiple channels of patronage and increasingly distant from the official seat of decision-making, sectarianism has become the main principle of political organisation. In a play on words used by Talib al-Shatri, a regular commentator for an Iraqi news web-site aligned with Sistani, this is not only *tashyi' al-dawla* (the funeral of the state); it is also *tashayyu' al-dawla* (state Shi'ism), in which the identity and economy of the state are the possession of a movement that gains its vigour by dissolving central authority.[201] As we show in the next Chapter, the fragmentation of political authority has been a crucial factor in preventing the Coalition from winning the battle of legitimation against the insurgency.

4

INSURGENCY AND COUNTER-INSURGENCY

The US has been unable to draw the various elements of Iraqi society into cooperating actively with and participating in its state-building project in ways that would not challenge its control of the project's broad parameters. We showed in Chapter Two that its efforts to bridge the gap between state and society within these constraints by establishing channels of communication and influence and providing services largely failed. It has resorted to a range of strategies to trade off control and effectiveness — sectarian balancing, creating institutions but limiting their authority, playing off the centre against the periphery, playing off political parties against tribes and other embedded leaders, and demilitarisation followed by re-militarisation. As we explained in Chapter Three, the outcome has been a lack of a truly national, integrative political process which subordinates the local. This in turn has promoted neopatrimonialism, sectarianism and unregulated national-local political conflict. In other words, when the US has had to choose between trying to build a state and trying to retain control, it has mostly chosen the latter. It has ended up achieving neither, as increasing amounts of power have been accumulated by neopatrimonial, sectarian and clashing actors: to the extent that a state exists in Iraq, it is one characterised by fragmented political authority.

The insurgency and counter-insurgency are shaping and being shaped by these dynamics. There is a great deal of uncertainty about aspects of the insurgency, and we survey the main issues below, in relation to the theme of how it is challenging the US-led state-building project and whether it is offering an alternative to that project. It is not a coherent single movement and in this sense there are multiple insurgencies rather than a single insurgency. The insurgents are clearly united about at least one thing — wrecking the US-led state-building project — and they have made a great deal of headway towards that goal. For its part, the approach of the US to counter-insurgency has relied heavily on coercion (that is, violence and a variety of repressive means).

Counter-insurgency theorists have criticised the US for alienating the population by acting as if it was involved in a scaled-down and slightly modified conventional war. They argue that the primary emphasis should be on achieving victory politically by securing legitimacy among the population — winning hearts and minds, as the standard phrase goes — rather than trying to defeat the insurgents through the use of coercion. They attribute what they perceive as the failure to adopt the right strategy to an organisational culture within the US military and a broader US strategic culture, which prioritise fighting conventional wars against conventional opponents.[1] In addition, it is routinely observed that the constant strain on soldiers, knowing that they could come under attack from what feels like any direction at any moment, will make some treat the entire population like the enemy. The insurgents themselves often use brutal tactics which can make extreme measures by the Coalition seem justifiable to some, in the same way that insurgents regard their actions as justified by Coalition brutality.

We agree that the US approach to counter-insurgency in Iraq has been influenced by a strategic and organisational bias towards a conventional war approach. Although this is more the case with the Army than the Marines, and although extensive efforts are under way in the US military to learn lessons and adapt training, these criticisms still apply. And operating in a hostile and unpredictable environment does reinforce tendencies towards harshness and violence by Coalition soldiers. However, we argue that these points are insufficient to explain the theory and practice of US and British counter-insurgency within (and indeed beyond) Iraq. In this Chapter we show that US counter-insurgency doctrine has elements that emphasise coercion as well as elements that emphasise legitimation. We argue that the failure at the political level to bridge the gap between the state and society — the use of strategies which prioritise attempts to exert control over state-building, and the lack of an integrative national political process — have been fundamentally important in shaping policy towards the insurgency. As the political process has not generated sufficient legitimacy, in central Iraq especially, to influence the population to back the Coalition against the insurgents, the US military has relied on coercion, as it has historically when propping up a government which could not otherwise hold on to power. The reverse dynamic has also been in operation: the more that coercion has been used, the greater the gap between state and society has become. This has been shown clearly in opinion polls, as we discuss in some detail below, with lack of approval of the state linked directly, although not exclusively, to the conduct of the counter-insurgency campaign. The nationalist dimension has meant that when insurgents cause casualties, people often blame the Coalition's presence and actions for provoking the attacks instead of the insurgents for carrying them out.

Nor has the British approach in the south been superior, as is often supposed. The atmosphere has been relatively calm there compared with the centre not because the British have secured legitimacy among the population, but because failure to bridge the state-society gap at national level has resulted in them abandoning for the most part efforts to control the political process locally. This is not successful state building and counter-insurgency but a decision not to engage in them. The position of British forces in the south has always been highly precarious. They have been able to remain only because they are tolerated, they are tolerated because they are doing little to interfere in the competition between the political forces there, and when they do interfere their position becomes even more precarious.

THE INSURGENCY AS WRECKER OF COALITION STATE BUILDING

The insurgency is clearly primarily Iraqi in personnel and resources, although it benefits from Iraq's porous borders and includes foreign volunteers. Iraq has nearly 4,000 kilometres of borders, shared with Jordan, Syria, Turkey, Iran, Kuwait and Saudi Arabia. These and Iraq's relatively small coastline are mostly unguarded and unmarked. Insurgents can move money, goods, personnel and weapons back and forth at will (links between the insurgency and the transnational informal economy are explored in Chapter Five). Despite the many allegations that have been made about the role of the Iranian and Syrian Governments in supporting the insurgents, the evidence of either government's involvement in creating and sustaining the insurgency does not exist. We addressed Iran's role in Chapter Three, and whilst Syria has allowed Iraqi supporters of the insurgency to collect and disburse funds from its territory, it has also been active in preventing cross-border raids.[2] Whilst neither Syria nor Iran perceives it to be in its interests for the US project in Iraq to be a success, equally they do not perceive it to be in their interests for Iraq to become an arena for an open-ended conflict. The insurgency appears to support itself mainly from Iraqi sources — donations, smuggling and funds left over from Saddam Hussein's regime — and has access to hundreds of thousands of tons of weapons and explosives left over from the Ba'thist era and left unguarded, as well as new weapons from the Coalition's floundering efforts to establish Iraqi state security forces.[3]

Estimates of the number of insurgent fighters are inevitably very much approximations: many engage in training and fighting only sporadically, and are either not organised formally or organised into secretive cells. In November 2003, Coalition commander Gen. Abizaid claimed that the number of insurgents 'does not exceed 5,000'.[4] US officials revised their estimate upwards in July 2004 to about 20,000 fighters, and this remained the figure offered publicly by US officials through to 2006.[5] Other estimates were often larger: off-the-record briefings put numbers at up to 31,500 fighters, whilst the Director of Iraq's intelligence service, General Muhammad Abdullah Shahwani, claimed that there were 40,000 'hard-core fighters', with 160,000 additional part-time fighters and people in support roles.[6] US estimates have been complicated by the claims about numbers of insurgent fighters that they have killed or captured: the US Commander in Iraq, Gen. George Casey, estimated in January 2005 that Coalition forces had killed or captured 15,000 insurgents during the course of 2004; and Gen. Jack Keane, former Deputy Chief of Staff of the US Army, claimed in July 2005 that 50,000 insurgents had been captured or killed during the first six months of that year alone.[7] As these figures are almost as high as, or higher than, the official estimates of insurgent numbers, this would mean that Coalition forces had killed large numbers of people who were not insurgents, that insurgent numbers were actually much higher than any of those estimates, or that there had been many new recruits, or some combination of all three. Whichever was the case, the insurgency has proved that it can survive and indeed strengthen.

The US has tried to categorise the insurgency into discrete groups. In October 2004, for example, CENTCOM gave an estimated total of 19,000 insurgent fighters, divided between 10,000 former regime elements, 5,000 criminals and religious extremists (who were inexplicably categorised together), 3,000 pro-Sadr fighters and 1,000 foreign fighters.[8] Such taxonomies are misleading in that individuals with very different motivations can be in the same insurgent group, and all of the different, even apparently contradictory, motivations can reinforce each other in the minds of individual insurgents. To complicate matters further, the line between insurgents and those who are motivated by personal criminal gain while flying a nationalist, ethnic or religious flag of convenience is also very blurred. These ambiguities and complexities have helped to soften the divisions between the groups and encourage overlap and cooperation between them. As one Mahdi Army member in Najaf said: 'I came for the defence of Islam ... Moqtada is a nationalist and he demands the right of the Iraqi people and the rights of the poor. He is the only one who didn't betray the people and cooperate with the Americans.'[9] This statement combined notions of Islamism, nationalism, social rights, economic rights and loyalty. Nevertheless, especially with the accommodation of the Sadr movement in the UIA coalition since late 2004, the groups oriented around Shi'a identity have not been a significant part of what is usually labelled the insurgency, even though their relations with US-led forces have frequently been violent. Shi'i have had a role within this insurgency, but it is predominantly and increasingly Sunni Arab.

Estimates of the proportion of non-Iraqis in the insurgency in 2004 and 2005 clustered around the 4-10% range.[10] When Coalition forces capture people who are indisputably insurgent combatants, they are rarely non-Iraqi. While the vast majority of those detained by the Coalition are not proven to have had any involvement with the insurgency, detainee figures also show foreigners to be a rarity. For example, the CPA's Arabic website in July 2004 listed more than 10,000 detainees and only 1% were indicated as being non-Iraqi.[11] In November 2005, the Coalition claimed 3.8% of detainees were foreigners.[12] In July 2004, Brig.-Gen. John Custer, Director of Intelligence for CENTCOM, described the notion that there were thousands of foreign fighters in Iraq as a 'big myth' (one often propagated very extensively by the Coalition in justifying its uses of force, as well as by Iraqis who do not wish to believe that beheadings and horrific attacks on civilians are the work of their fellow citizens). He also said that there was little evidence of an al-Qa'ida presence in Iraq, and that Zarqawi's role in Iraq had been exaggerated.[13] Since then, al-Qa'ida in Mesopotamia has become more prominent in that many suicide bomb attacks on Coalition and government targets are claimed in its name. This lends it significance beyond the sheer number of its members; it is quite likely that other groups launch attacks but then claim responsibility for them in the name of al-Qa'ida in Mesopotamia to create confusion and avoid political costs. Al-Qa'ida in Mesopotamia also became increasingly Iraqi in image and apparently in personnel in 2005, and was prominent in insurgent debates (mainly conducted via the internet) about goals, strategy and tactics.[14] In early 2006, Iraqi Interior Minister Bayan Jabr estimated that there were no more than a few hundred al-Qa'ida foreign fighters in the country.[15]

US officials have often suggested that the insurgency comprises essentially two elements — a centralised and pre-planned operation by the Ba'th regime (or an *ad hoc* strategy by Ba'thist 'remnants' and 'dead-enders'), supplemented by an uneasy alliance with foreign jihadists inspired by or organised through al-Qa'ida in Mesopotamia. In September 2002 Tariq Aziz, then Deputy Prime Minister, threatened a guerrilla war: 'People say to me, "You are not the Vietnamese; you have no jungles and swamps to hide in." I reply, "Let our cities be our swamps and our buildings our jungles."'[16] In December 2004 the then Iraqi Interim Interior Minister Falah al-Naqib claimed that the insurgency was centralised with a unified and mainly Ba'thist command based in Syria.[17] This is also the conclusion that pro-Ba'thist websites based outside Iraq, but with virtually no traffic from inside Iraq, want to encourage.[18] However, initially the insurgents emerged primarily from personal, family, geographical and sectarian links, and from personal, tribal, sectarian, Islamic, Arab and nationalist resentment at the myriad humiliations of the fact and conduct of the occupation. Former regime connections were mostly secondary and indeed often regarded as very much a hindrance to the cause, with the insurgents generally ignoring or condemning Saddam Hussein.[19] No evidence has been found that the *ancien régime* planned for an insurgency to follow its own toppling.[20] In

May 2003, the month after the end of formal combat, only eight US soldiers were killed in hostile incidents, rising to 18 in June and 30 in July.[21] This is not the level of casualties one would have expected from a pre-planned insurgency.

After the early period of spontaneous, *ad hoc* operations, greater coordination and coherence gradually emerged. By 2006, regular and extensive public statements and internal discussions conducted via the internet were predominantly in the name of four bodies — al-Qa'ida in Mesopotamia, the Islamic Front of the Iraqi Resistance (al-Jabha al-Islamiyya lil-Muqawama al-'Iraqiya), the Islamic Army of Iraq (al-Jaysh al-Islami fil-'Iraq) and the Partisans of the Sunna Army (Jaysh Ansar al-Sunna) — with at least nine other less prominent groups also having a public profile.[22] Uncertainty remains as to how many 'brigades' issuing statements in the names of these four bodies are actually fully part of them. However, each of them is increasingly internally coherent in terms of functional and geographical organisational subdivision, with increasing numbers of joint operations and statements. The word 'occupation', while an international legal term used by the Coalition as neutral and descriptive, for most Iraqi Arabs denotes something highly humiliating, resonant of imposition, coercion and the brutal and illegal Israeli occupation of Palestine.[23] All the insurgent bodies claim to be engaged in patriotic, Islamic and non-sectarian resistance (*muqawama*) against occupation (*ihtilal*) and a Christian Crusade (*harb salibiyya*).

None of the insurgent groups has claimed responsibility for any of the massacres of Shi'i that have occurred — indeed, no one has claimed responsibility for such attacks. The insurgents themselves often blame them on *agents provocateurs* from Iran, the US, Israel or the Shi'a Arab community seeking to discredit the resistance. It may be that the attacks are secret operations by one of more of the main insurgent groups, or they may be the work of small numbers of people acting in an uncoordinated and spontaneous way against the wishes of those groups. The circumstances of many of the attacks, such as those in the wake of the bombing of the al-Askari shrine in February 2006, suggest a motivation based on revenge. Statements from al-Qa'ida in Mesopotamia have denied vigorously any claim that they are seeking to foment Sunni-Shi'a civil war, and asserted that a letter purporting to be from Zarqawi advocating this is a fake. All of the insurgent groups accuse the US of backing Shi'a sectarian forces, which they often claim are ultimately under Iranian direction. They maintain that the goals of the US are to keep Iraq weak in order to gain control of its oil, attack Islam and further the goals of Israel. Such perceptions seem absurd to the US, which insists that its goal is to liberate and democratise Iraq, while some Iraqi Shi'i complain bitterly that the US is seeking to deny the Shi'i the political fruits of their electoral victories. Despite the claims of the insurgent groups that they are non-sectarian, they rely solely on Sunni Arab rather than Shi'a clerics for advice and emphasise broad Salafi Sunni religious themes focusing on correct personal behaviour as a good Muslim, in which Shi'a Islam can be but is not necessarily regarded as a betrayal of the faith.[24] The Salafi theme underlines the point that the insurgency has not been driven by a Ba'thist ideology, which has historically been highly inimical to Salafism. In advocating attacks on all heretics (*rawafidh*) who collaborate with the 'Christian Crusaders' and routinely referring to the main Shi'a parties in this way, al-Qa'ida in Mesopotamia's message in particular appears effectively sectarian.

The insurgent groups have not articulated separate or joint state-building programmes of their own. They have not advocated Sunni Arab dominance, the return of the Ba'th to power or a unified broader Islamic state as their objective. Their focus has been on forcing the withdrawal of Coalition forces, and they have argued that the government security forces would quickly collapse should Coalition forces leave. Despite reports of limited contacts between the Coalition and the insurgents, the public statements and internet discussions of the insurgents show growing confidence of achieving victory. They expect to so by inflicting costs on foreign forces that will force their with-drawal, preventing the normalisation of daily life, attacking the government's new security forces and staging large high profile attacks as demonstrations of strength and ability to strike at will. They have also put major efforts into making the case that their cause is just and their means legitimate, while arguing that those of the occupiers and the government are neither. For example, the tactic of videotaped beheadings was dropped in 2005 when its value in scaring off participation in the reconstruction appeared to be outweighed by the costs to the legitimacy of the insurgents. Instead, they present their US and Shi'a opponents as being brutal, sectarian and in an alliance of convenience.

The primary focus of the insurgency has been upon disrupting the project of state building on anti-occupation grounds, rather than upon attacking Shi'a targets, although the anti-occupation attacks have often been highly indiscriminate. The Pentagon reported consecutively in October 2005 and February 2006 that 'approximately 80%' and 'almost 80%' respectively of all attacks by insurgents were upon Coalition forces.[25] The Non-Govermental Organisation (NGO) Coordination Committee in Iraq calculated that 75.3% of insurgent attacks were on Coalition forces and civilian personnel in the period from September 2003 to October 2004, with 6.8% on Iraqi security forces. In the period from January to July 2005, 65.5% of such attacks were on Coalition forces and 12.1% on Iraqi security forces.[26] US military casualties totalled 2,158 dead (1,690 in hostile incidents) between 1 May 2003 and 6 March 2006.[27] Between them, other Coalition countries lost 206 troops up to March 2006, and 4,219 Iraqi police and military were killed.[28] Around 258 non-Iraqi contractors plus some 45 other foreign civilians were killed up to 28 August 2005, and this ensured that reconstruction projects would find it hard to continue.[29]

Humanitarian non-governmental and inter-governmental organisations have been forced to scale back their operations or operate from outside Iraq, often based in Jordan. They have been targeted by insurgents on the grounds that they are not neutral humanitarians but legitimisers of and collaborators with the occupation. All of southern and central Iraq, including Baghdad, has become extremely unsafe for the Coalition, and for all foreigners and any Iraqis working with the Coalition or the state in any way, with severe consequences for state-building. As the focus of the insurgency has been on international actors, it is misleading to characterise the conflict as being a case of low-intensity civil war, as both USAID and 'Allawi have done,[30] and as others increasingly came to do after the bombing of al-Askari shrine in February 2006; it has remained primarily an international conflict throughout.

Some Sunni Arab organisations such as the Iraqi People's Conference of Adnan al-Dulaymi and the IIP have taken the position that the insurgency would end if Sunni Arabs were given a full and appropriate role in the state-building process, if significant amendments were made to a constitutional arrangement which they have portrayed as likely to lead to the break-up of Iraq, and if military operations in Sunni Arab areas were suspended.[31] In contrast, the consistent position of all of the main insurgent groups is that their rejection of participation in state-building is unconditional as long as there is a foreign, especially US, military presence in Iraq. However, it is far from clear whether the insurgent groups would hold this line with sufficient practical support among Sunni Arabs if Shi'a-led political parties made the concessions which groups such as the IIP have demanded.

In trying to deal with the insurgency, the Coalition was faced with the choice of emphasising state-building through coercion or through legitimation. From early on, the US chose to emphasise the former.

The remainder of this Chapter describes that choice, explains the reasons for it and indicates its implications for the Iraqi state.

COUNTER-INSURGENCY –
COERCION VERSUS LEGITIMATION

In public during the early part of the occupation, the Coalition generally portrayed its opponents as a tiny handful of Ba'thist 'dead-enders' with nothing to lose and hoping to wreck the reconstruction, and as foreign al-Qa'ida-related or -inspired Islamic terrorists. As late as the spring of 2004, in the midst of a major escalation of the conflict, Coalition spokesperson Dan Senor asserted that the insurgents had the support of only 3 to 5% of the population while Gen. Ricardo Sanchez, as US commanding officer in Iraq, dismissed the armed opposition as merely 'a small group of criminals and thugs'.[32] In private, by the early autumn of 2003 the Coalition was considering alternative analyses of the armed opposition and how to deal with it.[33] Coalition military strategists concluded that they were facing an organised insurgency — that is, an armed and organised campaign to overthrow the form of rule that the Coalition was trying to establish - rather than remnants of a defeated state, and a British Army lieutenant-colonel devised a counter-insurgency plan in order to deal with it.[34]

One of the past cases from which the Coalition drew lessons was the Briggs Plan, a British operation in Malaya which lasted overall from 1948 to 1960, with its most intense phase lasting from 1950 to 1952.[35] This has long been regarded in the British and US armed forces as a paradigmatic example of successful counter-insurgency.[36] Five mutually reinforcing principles for success in counter-insurgency, based on a comparison of Malaya and Vietnam, were developed by Robert Thompson, who was a high level military adviser in both conflicts as well as being a theorist.[37] The government, according to these principles, should 'have a clear political aim: to establish and maintain a free, independent and united country which is politically and economically stable and viable', act strictly within the law, have an overall plan, prioritise the political rather than military defeat of the insurgents, and secure its base areas first. The second to fifth principles are effectively means of achieving the state-building goal set out in the first. Whether or not these principles represent an accurate depiction of actual British policy in Malaya is not relevant here. Our concern is with the extent of their application in Iraq.

John Nagl, a high profile figure in Coalition counter-insurgency policy, endorsed and adapted Thompson's principles. As a US Army major, he wrote a doctoral thesis also comparing Malaya and Vietnam, which he turned into a book.[38] US Army Chief of Staff Gen. Peter Schoomaker wrote a foreword to it and gave copies of it to all US Army generals. Between September 2003 and September 2004, Nagl was third in command of a tank battalion in Khaidiyah near Falluja, before moving on to become a lieutenant-colonel and military assistant in the office of the Deputy Secretary of Defence, and was slated to command a tank battalion in 2006. He presented his views to the leading US establishment thinktank, the Council on Foreign Relations.[39] Nagl's principles of successful counter-insurgency are that it should achieve the national goal of victory, set realistic national goals, subordinate military action to political goals, and use minimal force and structure its forces so that the population feels protected and not threatened by the counter-insurgent forces.[40] This approach involves giving priority to defeating the insurgency politically by ensuring that the government secures the active support or passive acquiescence of the people. This is victory through isolating rather than annihilating the insurgents.

In response to the Iraq conflict, the US Army produced in 2004 its first ever manual on counter-insurgency, which was distributed to all its officers, and updated its manual on counter-guerrilla warfare (we will discuss the distinction between insurgents and guerrillas below).[41] Previous manuals written in the early 1960s were mainly for US special forces in Vietnam, and some in Iraq have been using the Marine Corps' *Small Wars Manual* from 1940. In some places, the US Army's formal doctrine does articulate a perspective of counter-insurgency being an instrument to enable an increasingly legitimate state to protect a free society. Its counter-guerrilla handbook states that counter-insurgency involves 'a full range of measures used by a government to free and protect its society' including 'building viable institutions (political, military, economic, social) that respond to the needs of the people'.[42] The government needs to win the support of the people 'through providing them with security and showing an honest effort to correct those conditions which cause dissatisfaction.' It asserts that counter-guerrilla operations without 'balanced development of the country and mobilisation of the populace against the insurgents' will not succeed. The political defeat of the insurgency by undermining its support among the population is stressed as key, rather than the military defeat of insurgent combatants, with the former always to take priority over the latter. The counter-insurgency manual concurs in stating that the aim should be the achievement of 'the end state established by the President' by providing security for the population, developing host country political institutions and the services they provide, eliminating the ability of insurgents to exploit grievances by addressing the concerns of the population, and using comprehensive information from local sources. In all of this, '[t]he support of the people ... is the center of gravity' and success depends on 'the willing support and cooperation of the populations directly involved.'[43]

Viewed from a legitimation perspective, US actions, especially in the centre of Iraq, would seem to be irrational or mistaken: the US has broken every rule in the counter-insurgency book if the aim is to build a state which has vigorous popular support. The US undoubtedly prefers to be in a situation in which a pro-US state has popular support and is able to deal with any armed challenge using its own forces rather than US ones. Its search for localised forms of political participation in Iraq while it tried to create a state that would operate within broad parameters acceptable to it reflected that preference. However, a preference is not to be mistaken for a requirement; we argue that, despite these considerations, the US military's counter-insurgency actions have been consistent with the US's doctrine and practice when its goal is to impose an unpopular form of rule on an unwilling society or section of society. Hence its counter-insurgency actions based on coercion have not been merely irrational or mistaken, even if they prove in the end to be ineffective. US doctrine states:

Commanders must be prepared to operate in a broad range of political atmospheres. The host country's form of government may be anything from an absolute, and not too benevolent, dictatorship to a democracy struggling to establish itself, or anything in between.[44]

The manual continues:

No matter what political atmosphere prevails in the host country, the brigade commander must engage the guerrilla with every asset at the commander's disposal. He must realize that democratic principles may not be immediately applicable. However, he should act within the limits of his authority to improve the circumstances of the government he was sent to support. Any incidents of deep-rooted corruption, gross inefficiency or violation of human rights should be documented and reported to higher headquarters. The commander can also offer other alternatives to accomplish the same objective. *It is the responsibility of the US Government to influence the host government's attitude toward democratic principles; it is not the responsibility of the commander.*[45]

There is a contradiction between endorsing potential armed support for an absolute, malign dictatorship and the doctrinal claim that the core mission of counter-insurgency is backing a government's efforts to promote a free society and institutions which respond to the needs of the people. While the Iraqi Government was eventually elected in a relatively free fashion, doctrinal endorsement is still provided for supporting it despite its failure to establish its legitimacy among most of the Sunni Arab population of Iraq, many of its Shi'i and some of its Kurds.

The doctrinal contradiction between coercion and legitimation can be seen in what the US counter-insurgency manual lists as intelligence indicators of 'enemy activity'. These include 'Increase in the number of entertainers with a political message', 'Increase of political themes in religious services', 'Circulation of petitions advocating opposition or dissident demands', 'Attempts to discredit or ridicule national or public officials', 'Characterization of government leaders as puppets and tools of foreign intervention forces', 'Accusations of brutality or ineffectiveness', 'Distribution of clothing to underprivileged or minority classes by organizations of recent or suspect origin', 'Agitation against government projects and plans', 'Emergence of new leaders among the population', 'Unusual gatherings among the population', 'Increase of visitors (for example, tourists, technicians, businessmen, religious leaders, officials) from groups or countries hostile to the United States or opposed to the current intervention', 'Communications between opposition groups and external supporters', 'Increase of disaffected youth gatherings', 'Appearance of many new members in existing organizations such as labor unions', 'Refusal of population to pay or unusual difficulty to collect rent, taxes or loan payments', 'Increased antigovernment or mission force rhetoric in local media', 'Widespread hostile media coverage of even minor criminal violations or incidents involving mission force personnel', 'Nationwide strikes', 'Closing of schools' and 'Student unrest'.[46]

Insurgents could promote or join in such activities, but there is no recognition in the manual that any of them could equally be regarded as entirely legitimate activities in a free or unfree society. Instead, they are interspersed among a long list of indicators of a developing armed insurgency such as 'receiving military training in foreign countries', 'Assassination or disappearance of government sources', clandestine manufacture of arms and ammunition, 'terrorist acts', 'murder ... [or] kidnapping' of officials, 'theft of weapons' and 'Attacks on patrols'. The blurring of the line between armed and peaceful political activity in this way encourages the treatment of any kind of political opposition in a repressive fashion. The blurring is continued in key definitions. The counter-insurgency manual defines an insurgency as an 'organized movement aimed at the overthrow of a constituted government through use of subversion and armed conflict'.[47] The US counter-guerrilla handbook defines resistance as 'an organised effort by some portion of the civil portion of a country to resist, oppose, or overthrow the existing government' and says that 'an insurgent organization can be considered a type of resistance organization' because it too 'seeks to overthrow the established government'. The counter-guerrilla handbook states that 'The guerrilla is the overt combat element of the insurgent organization'.[48]

Therefore, in circumstances in which a sizeable portion of the population rejects a form of rule, military doctrine provides a strong predisposition for US personnel to respond to the expression of popular grievances, peaceful dissent and armed opposition with repressive measures. The US and Britain have a long history of engaging in counter-insurgency for repressive purposes, either directly or in conjunction with military, paramilitary and militia forces in other states.[49] Central aspects of the conduct of the US and those it has backed in Iraq — such as imprisonment without due process, disappearances, torture, impunity and indiscriminate use of force — are characteristic of the coercive counter-insurgency it has been involved with in places such as Vietnam, Central America, Colombia and Afghanistan.

Where the active support of the population or a large section of it is not sought or achieved, passive acquiescence must be enforced if the government being imposed is to survive. Despite the elections of January and December 2005, the ruling authorities that emerged would be unlikely to survive without the backing of US forces, owing to the weakness and questionable loyalty of the state's armed forces. In these circumstances, the repressive side of US counter-insurgency doctrine comes to the fore.

The counter-insurgency manual states, 'The insurgent's primary target is the people; therefore counter-insurgency must separate the insurgent from the people and their resources' through 'population and resource control'.[50] The distinctions between those who oppose the insurgents, those who are neutral, those who support them and those who are insurgents are crucial if counter-insurgency is about protecting the population from insurgents. The US Army acknowledges this but also states that 'it is nearly impossible for US forces to accurately identify friend from foe from disinterested.'[51] The temptation is to treat all civilians, or at least all adult or adolescent male civilians, as enemies, potential threats or objects to be denied to the enemy. Col. Jan Horvath of Army's Combined Arms Doctrine Directorate, who led the joint team from the US and British Armies and US Marine Corps which produced the revised US counter-insurgency manual, felt able to say during an interview in November 2004 for a pro-US military website, apparently without fear of recrimination:

…we must still root out the counter-state infrastructure in Fallujah using population [and] resource control. [That's a] mechanism to collect social and economic intelligence… The Nazi's Gestapo and the Eastern European communists were the best at this. Without becoming tainted or infected by their methods and attitudes, we have picked up some of their systems and processes.[52]

In this context, people become objectified. As Horvath said — inaccurately as it turned out — after the US-led offensive to retake control of that city: 'We still own the people of Samarra'.[53] According to Mark Etherington, CPA Governorate Coordinator for Wasit, the attitude of the US 'allowed Iraqis to be de-humanised in their eyes'.[54] Any counter-insurgency policy which does not have as its paramount characteristic the protection of the population and is aimed at forcing a government upon them that they do not support tends towards this approach. From 1967 to 1975, the CIA sought through what it called the Phoenix Programme to undermine the Vietnamese insurgency by targeting those suspected of supporting it politically as well as materially, by means of terrorism, torture, assassination and indefinite detention without trial.[55] Over 20,000 Vietnamese were killed in the process. US counter-insurgency policy in Iraq has not escalated to the degree it did in Vietnam, but there are parallels, including hints of a covert assassination campaign.[56]

All of the coercive counter-insurgency measures discussed in this chapter have been defended by the US as legal. This is another indication that the strategy being used is not the product of the system going wrong or making a mistake that contradicts its counter-insurgency doctrine (even though mistakes have been made in carrying it out). It is in line with US counter-insurgency theory and practice in the context of propping up an unviable government and continuing an unpopular occupation. In such circumstances, there will be a strong predisposition to use force in ways that alienate the population, and that is what has occurred in Iraq, as we now discuss.

Use of force which alienates the population

In counter-insurgency focused on legitimation, minimum use of force needs to be calculated in political terms, and specifically in terms of ensuring that force is kept down to a level that will win the support of the population or at least not alienate it. Operations to kill or capture insurgents are counterproductive if their political effect is to increase the insurgency's recruitment and resources overall. Indeed, this is a key dynamic on which insurgents rely. 'Mopping up', to use the euphemism, can take place only when insurgent fighters have lost their political base. In military terms, this means generally avoiding using large conventional formations, as they will tend to operate in conventional style, with use of force which will seem to the population to be completely disproportionate. The US counter-guerrilla handbook states that the level of force used should be appropriate to the threat and activity, justifiable in the minds of the public in the host country and in the United States, the minimum necessary to accomplish the mission, with maximum benefit for the population and with full compensation for damage done.[57] The counter-insurgency field manual is more equivocal. It refers to the need to balance not alienating the population through excessive use of force against not leaving US forces vulnerable or encouraging insurgents through insufficient use of force.[58]

In practice, the US has interpreted minimum force to mean the minimum amount of force necessary to achieve specific military missions while keeping immediate US casualties as low as possible, even at the risk of alienating so many people that US casualties are in the end higher. In the first few days of its initial assault on Falluja in April 2004, the US military killed at least 600 Iraqis. Of the dead, US Marine Lt-Col. Brennan Byrne stated:

What I think you will find is 95 percent of those were military age males that were killed in the fighting. The Marines are trained to be precise in their firepower … The fact that there are 600 goes back to the fact that the Marines are very good at what they do.[59]

Subsequent research from the NGO Iraq Body Count (IBC) showed that at least 572 of around 800 reported dead were civilians, 308 of them women and children.[60] It is true that US forces could have been much more indiscriminate and could easily have killed thousands rather than hundreds of people. However, the political costs are substantial when aircraft and helicopter gunships are used to carry out attacks in a city. The use of snipers was also a significant feature of the US attack on Falluja. To many this was not proof of precision, but an indication that US forces were targeting civilians or drawing no distinction between civilians and combatants.[61] Whether or not insurgents try to shield themselves among the civilian population, US forces are blamed by many Iraqis as being responsible for the casualties, and the dead and injured have friends and relatives who are likely to seek revenge.

As Sanchez left Iraq in July 2004, he said the lesson of Falluja was that the US should use 'massive force' rather than 'precision strikes' should it re-enter the city.[62] Mark Etherington wrote in his memoir of his time in Iraq as CPA Governorate Coordinator for Wasit:

> If the British argued that U.S. methods in Fallujah, for example, were counter-productive, American officers I met were adamant that if they had only been allowed to "flatten" the city, they might have broken the insurgency. In purely military terms it is difficult to decide who was right, and there is no evidence that a more gentle approach would have worked.[63]

In November 2004, the US military did flatten the city and did claim to have 'broken the back of the insurgency', but was proven wrong.[64] Reference by Etherington to the 'purely military' misses the point that military action is meant to serve political ends. The US military emphasises force protection in a counter-productive way. Firepower has quickly been brought to bear against anyone who might turn out to be a threat, in order to protect US forces. The problem is that as a result many innocent Iraqis get killed, and this produces more support for the insurgency and more deliberate attacks on US forces.

There has also been a low priority on rehabilitating those displaced. As a result of the assault on Falluja, 203,000 people (around 80% of city's residents) fled their homes.[65] Less than one quarter of those displaced had returned by April 2005, little reconstruction had taken place, and control on movement into and out of the city was tight. Only 200 people had been paid for the destruction of their homes (they were given $2,000 from a $100 million US military fund for compensation and reconstruction).[66] Insurgent attacks resumed, while the US relied on Iraqi army units composed exclusively of Shi'i and Kurds from other parts of Iraq who dared not spend time in the city off-duty. Intelligence officers of the 1st Marine Expeditionary Force argued that the number of insurgents would continue to grow and that they would return to Falluja, especially if troops were redeployed elsewhere.[67] In November 2005, the US Marine officer responsible for Falluja characterised the situation as one of no progress.[68]

The best force protection is a population which is on your side. British military chiefs urged the US without success to concentrate less on short-sighted force protection and more on preventing Iraqi casualties, although by summer 2005 British aircraft had begun to fly missions in support of large-scale US conventional force operations.[69] Certainly, there is no guarantee that minimum use of force would have produced popular support, because popular allegiances are shaped by much more than this alone. However, as we discuss below, public opinion poll evidence shows that the population has been alienated by the way the US has used force. Lt-Col. Frederick P. Wellman, a member of the team training Iraqi security forces, conceded in June 2005 that: 'We can't kill them all. When I kill one I create three.'[70] Yet there has been no basic change in the way US forces conduct themselves in Iraq, even if there has been a shift of emphasis towards more reliance on aerial bombing, which increased over 50% in the five months from November 2005 onwards.[71]

The over-inclination of the US to mount offensive operations in response to challenges or suspicions — in military jargon, being 'too kinetic' — has been adopted most frequently when attempting to deprive the enemy of a sanctuary and securing control of 'base areas' (population, economic and communications centres), cornerstone principles of counter-insurgency doctrine.[72] Nevertheless, the Iraq case has shown the drawbacks of that approach. After the second assault on Falluja in November 2004, insurgents spread out to neighbouring towns and appear to have recruited more supporters. This is why US forces, backed by militias, then moved on to Ramadi and were sent in November 2004 to Mosul.[73] Hence Mosul, another 'base area' that had been relatively calm, was destabilised by the assault on Falluja. In December 2004, Horvath claimed that military operations following the new doctrine had ensured Coalition control of Samarra'.[74] In fact, attacks on US forces in this city of 220,000 people quickly resumed and continued unabated.[75] The US military then commenced attacks such as the one on suspected insurgents in the western desert town of al-Qa'im in May 2005, which in turn produced hundreds of displaced people.[76] The offensives continued throughout 2005 and into 2006, with US forces surrounding entire towns such as Siniyya north of Baghdad with sand barriers miles long in a futile effort to control the population and prevent attacks by insurgents.[77]

Attempting to secure the base areas primarily by force has not succeeded, as is most clearly indicated by the fact that the US and its allies could not control much of Baghdad three years after the invasion. This kind of outcome, which is the norm, led Casey in June 2005 to characterise the flaw in the attempts to eliminate sanctuaries as 'the Pillsbury Doughboy idea', meaning that pressure on the insurgency in one place just makes it more prominent elsewhere: 'Like in Baghdad ... We push in Baghdad — they're down to about less than a car bomb a day in Baghdad over the last week — but in north-center ... they've gone up.'[78] Despite this realisation, Casey continued to carry out these operations in towns such as Tal Afar in western Iraq. US forces moved to recapture this town from insurgents in September 2004, but as soon as they left the insurgents re-established control. In September 2005, US and Iraqi forces attacked again, killing hundreds, with thousands fleeing the town before the attack. According to US Army Maj.-Gen. Rick Lynch, Deputy Chief of Staff for MNF-I, 'Tal Afar is just one piece of an overarching operation. We are not going to tolerate a safe haven anywhere in Iraq.'[79] In what purported to be a response, al-Qa'ida in Mesopotamia launched coordinated suicide bomb attacks in Baghdad which killed around 100 people.[80]

The Coalition has not sought to keep track of the number of Iraqi deaths caused by the invasion and its aftermath, but this task has been taken up by others. Extrapolating from a sample of households, a study published in *The Lancet* estimated that 98,000 more Iraqis died violently and nonviolently between the start of the invasion in March 2003 and September 2004 than would otherwise have been anticipated had the invasion not occurred. No attempt was made in the study to distinguish between combatants and non-combatants. *The Iraq Living Conditions Survey* carried out by the Iraqi Ministry of Planning and Development Cooperation in cooperation with the UN Development Programme (UNDP) sampled over twenty times as many households as the *Lancet* study. It concluded that 24,000 Iraqis — combatant and non-combatant — had died as a result of combat up to May 2004. The study reported 95% confidence that the figure was between 18,000 and 29,000, with children below 18 years of age comprising 12% of the total.[81] IBC uses a very different methodology. It surveys news media reports and eyewitness accounts and focuses on confirmed civilian deaths. As IBC notes, this approach produces an underestimate to the extent that civilian deaths are not reported reliably by its criteria or not reported at all. From the beginning of the invasion up to 19 March 2005 IBC found nearly 25,000 violent civilian deaths, 37% (9,250) caused by Coalition (including Iraqi, but in nearly all cases US) forces, 9% (2,238) caused by 'anti-occupation forces', 36% (8,951) by criminals and 18% (4,476) by unknown agents.[82]

Focusing on the period of the insurgency alone covered by the study (1 May 2003 to 19 March 2005), IBC's figures suggest that the insurgents have killed up to twice as many civilians as Coalition forces. Of nearly 18,000 violent civilian deaths for which there were reliable reports, 14% (2,388) were caused by US-led forces, 30% (5,237) by insurgents and unknown agents, and 51% (8,894) by criminals and 6% (1,047) by 'shared causation' (such as crossfire).[83] However, civilian deaths caused by Coalition forces are less likely to be reported than those caused by insurgents because the Coalition has often been the only source of information for journalists, and thus is not susceptible to checking of its claims, particularly claims that those killed in military operations were insurgents.

The US *Quadrennial Defense Review 2006* prepared a draft study on 'irregular warfare' in May 2005. Although omitted from the final report, its account of strategy in Iraq is revealing: 'There was a strong focus on raiding, cordon & search and sweep op[eration]s throughout: the one day brigade raid is the preferred tactic ... [the] focus is on killing insurgents, not protecting the population'.[84] We have argued that this approach is not the result of inadequate adherence to US military doctrine, but the direct result of applying the coercive aspects of that doctrine. The costs have been significant in terms of Iraqi lives, the viability of US military operations and Iraqi public support. This last point is illustrated by the way in which Iraqis, when insurgents launch attacks that deliberately or incidentally kill civilians, have often directed their anger at the US. In the next section, we will look at how Coalition forces have not placed themselves within a structure of accountability, further diminishing Iraqis' sense of security.

Impunity, the law, and popular attitudes

Winning over the population is assisted greatly if the authorities establish the rule of law and operate within it, according to Thompson.[85] From this perspective, any supposed advantages gained in operations against insurgents by disregarding the law are far outweighed by the cost to popular support for the government. The law should not be applied arbitrarily or unfairly, the line between legality and illegality should be clear, and the state should also only pass laws that it can enforce, otherwise it looks hollow. Thompson argued that the state must be accountable in the civilian courts rather than military tribunals, especially with regard to detention, and trials must be public so that justice is seen to be done and so that the case against the insurgents is known. The current US counter-insurgency manual states explicitly: 'A successful counter-insurgency depends ultimately and initially on a legitimate and effective HN [Host Nation] justice program integrating law enforcement, the judiciary, and a penal system.' It continues by laying down that 'counterinsurgency operations must conform to the law' and that 'the very goal of counter-insurgency operations is to help maintain law and order'.[86]

One of the difficulties in the Iraq case has been in knowing what constitutes operating within the law. In terms of the dynamics of the insurgency, what matters is popular perception of the extent to which the Coalition is operating within the law and the insurgents outside it.[87] The position of the Coalition was not helped when even the US-appointed IGC felt the need to condemn the April 2004 US attack on Falluja. IGC member Adnan Pachachi said: 'We consider the action carried out by US forces illegal and totally unacceptable', and the IGC issued a statement demanding that the Coalition's 'collective punishment' of Falluja cease and offering to negotiate with the insurgents.[88]

The most widely publicised example of the counter-insurgency operating outside the law took the form of the abuse and torture of detainees. The humiliation and torture by a group of US personnel of Iraqi detainees at the Abu Ghraib detention centre near Baghdad have been extensively discussed elsewhere.[89] In respect of our argument, the key aspects are how the US policymakers did not take action to stop abuse once they were aware of it, or to punish abusers until after worldwide negative publicity had been generated, starting with the photographs first shown on 29 April 2004 by CBS News. The internal US Army investigation, led by Maj.-Gen. Antonio Taguba, highlighted in March 2004 the extent of prisoner abuse in Abu Ghraib. It found that Maj.-Gen. Geoffrey Miller, the commander of the US prison in Guantánamo Bay, had recommended making detention guards in Iraq subordinate to military intelligence, so that the conditions of detention would be those most conducive to the extracting of maximum information from the prisoners.[90] Taguba found that such arrangements were likely to lead to the use of torture. Despite this, Miller was appointed in April 2004 to take charge of all US detention centres in Iraq.

Furthermore, the US did not take effective action when the International Committee of the Red Cross (ICRC) told it repeatedly throughout 2003 and into 2004 that torture and mistreatment were rife in Coalition prisons. The ICRC report of February 2004 indicated in detail virtually all of the aspects of torture contained in the Taguba report. It drew attention to many other cases of mistreatment, not just at Abu Ghraib but throughout Iraq, committed also by the Iraqi police. It found that mistreatment was widespread but not systematic for those suspected of criminal offences. However, it found that those suspected of security offences or thought to have intelligence value were ill-treated systematically.[91] The ICRC indicated that some members of military intelligence had told them such behaviour was part of their standard operating procedures.[92] The fact that the US did not take serious action despite being fully informed by the ICRC, until a public scandal broke, indicates the extent to which US prisons in Iraq operated in a culture of impunity in which there was little chance of legal redress for mistreatment.

This evaluation is applicable not just to the condition of detention facilities, but to the wider process of arrest and detention. The ICRC found a 'consistent pattern' of 'brutal behaviour during arrest' in Baghdad, Basra, Ramadi and Tikrit.[93] The standard pattern was that soldiers arrived at night, broke down doors, caused damage during the search, shouted orders, used violence and threats indiscriminately, flex-cuffed and hooded suspects, sometimes arrested all adult males even if ill or handicapped, and took people away without allowing them to dress properly or take basic necessities including medicine. Detainees were generally not informed of the reason for their arrest or allowed to ask, and sometimes family members — including females — were held hostage as a means of forcing suspects to cooperate.[94] Property including money and cars was confiscated without receipt, which made it look to the owners like theft. Although the Coalition runs a system of compensation via General Information Centres, there are only nine in Baghdad, one in Mosul and none for the rest of the country, and lack of receipts makes claims difficult.[95] The ICRC also found that those carrying out arrests routinely did not explain who they were, which base they were from, what the reason was for the arrest, where those being arrested were being taken and when they would be released. When people were arrested away from their homes, the lack of a proper system of notification meant that families tended to find out the whereabouts of arrested people when notified by others who had been arrested, or notified by the Red Cross, or when family members scoured the country. As a result, people under arrest effectively 'disappeared' for weeks or even months, with families worrying that they might be dead.[96] There is no evidence that arrests have become less brutal. Two US military interrogators, Josh Casteel and Tony Lagouranis, have reported independently that, since the Abu Ghraib scandal, torture and abuse of detainees (such as burning or breaking of bones) has taken place routinely and on a large scale, but now occurs in detainees' homes, remote locations or military divisional holding areas. While these acts were not authorised, there was no response from higher authorities when they were reported.[97]

Iraqis have few protections against arbitrary detention. Security detainees — those detained under 'imperative reasons of security' — have made up around two thirds of the detainee population. In February 2006, 14,229 individuals were officially being held by MNF-I and a further 6,457 by the Iraqi Ministries of Defence and the Interior, out of a total of 29,565 detainees.[98] Detainees of MNF-I are meant to be released once it is concluded that they are of no intelligence value and are not a threat to Coalition forces. The remainder — suspected criminal detainees — can be released if they are deemed to have no intelligence value and are not a threat to society, or may be handed over to Iraqi criminal jurisdiction. Not only are the release criteria extremely vague and therefore difficult to meet, detainees deemed by the Detainee Release Board to meet the criteria for release were, according to the Taguba Report, 'routinely' still kept in prison.[99] CPA Memorandum Number 3 directed that those held by the Coalition must be brought before a judge within 90 days, but this is routinely ignored and many detainees were denied access to family, lawyers or judges.[100] The Release and Review Board, composed of members of MNF-I and the Iraqi Government, was established in August 2004 to review the detention of security detainees, and was examining up to 250 cases per week by late 2005, according to the Iraqi Human Rights Ministry.[101] Whilst this demonstrates a level of commitment to bringing a structure to the security detention system, the rate of review means that each detainee would have their case examined only every nineteen months on average. In December 2005, after secret jails operated by the Iraqi Interior Ministry were discovered, a US spokesperson announced that MNF-I would stop transferring detainees to the Iraqi security forces, on the grounds that their conditions of detention were deemed inadequate. As a result, the number of detainees held by MNF-I rose by 23% in the period from October 2005 to February 2006, so that even more prisoners were outside the jurisdiction of the Iraqi legal system.[102]

Regarding the Iraqi legal system, the Iraqi Central Criminal Court was established by the CPA in June 2003 to deal with cases involving threats to the stability and security of Iraq, including activities against Coalition forces.[103] By August 2004, it had sentenced 49 people to terms of six months to thirty years in Iraqi prisons, and had acquitted six more.[104] CENTCOM described it as an 'Iraqi national court' in which '[a]ll judges, prosecutors and defense counsel are Iraqi'. However, state-appointed defence lawyers have only minutes to prepare and very limited access to evidence, and as their payment is $33 per case they have no financial incentive to request a postponement or to appeal. Of six trials watched by a journalist in July 2005, all lasted less than an hour for even the most serious of cases and most of the accused were convicted, with one receiving a sentence of twenty years.[105] In another case, an entire trial (including judicial deliberation and delivery of verdict) of four suspected of assassinating a senior Iraqi intelligence official lasted two hours, with three men sentenced to death and one to ten years in prison.[106] Furthermore, if the US authorities dislike the verdict they ignore it. This attitude was exemplified by the statement by CENTCOM referring to acquittals of defendants occurring 'due to lack of sufficient evidence to prove their crimes.' When Iyad Akmush Kanum was acquitted by the Court of attempted murder of Coalition troops, the US returned him to Abu Ghraib prison rather than release him. According to Michael Frank, Deputy Special Prosecutor for MNF-I: 'Iraqis who have been detained as a security threat can still be detained until firstly the coalition leaves or secondly they are considered to be no longer a threat'.[107]

Oversight measures instituted in relation to the formal transfer of sovereignty have generally been weak. On 27 June 2004, the CPA formally established the Joint Detention Committee (JDC) so that the Interim Government and the Coalition could liaise on detainee issues, and to ensure that there would be clear criteria for detention, the location of detainees would be tracked, and detainees' families would be kept properly informed.[108] On the same day the CPA established the office of the Iraqi Ombudsman for Penal and Detention Matters, to which Iraqis could complain about any aspect of detention.[109] The Ombudsman is to be an Iraqi national who is meant to be allowed to demand documents and statements and interview witnesses from Coalition forces and to recommend actions including the award of compensation. The provisions stated that the Ombudsman could be denied documents and witnesses for operational or 'legal' reasons, and would not be permitted to investigate matters prior to 27 June 2004. The JDC was only created in December 2005, and by early 2006, an Ombudsman had still not been appointed. Initial detention decisions are made by a single US military lawyer, while reviews of detentions are held in secret. Families of detainees are not informed of proceedings, detainees have no access to independent legal counsel and detention periods are potentially unlimited. Even though three quarters are eventually released without charge, most are held for over three months.[110]

In addition to the threat of arbitrary imprisonment, innocent Iraqis have very limited prospects for redress for personal injury or property loss and damage from the actions of the Coalition and/or foreign security contractors.[111] CPA Order Number 17 gave Coalition forces immunity from prosecution in Iraq: instead, they would be subject only to the domestic law of their own country. That position was extended to the post-occupation period, as is standard practice for the US with regard to the status of its forces abroad.[112] Outside combat, US forces destroyed at least twenty-five houses, claiming that insurgents lived in them with their families. Although this seems to have been a locally initiated and short-lived policy, the US military defended these actions and there has been no redress.[113] By November 2003 there had been 10,402 claims against the US military, and it had paid out $1.5 million in compensation for death, injury and damage, but there had been no prosecutions of US soldiers for illegally killing Iraqi civilians, and no independent investigations. For compensation to be made, the US military insists that death or damage must be in a non-combat situation (a highly ambiguous category), with $4,421 being the average payment for a civilian death, and $2,500 sometimes given as a 'sympathy' payment. Of 4,611 claims, three-quarters were turned down.[114]

With Coalition forces there are limited opportunities for redress; with foreign corporate security forces there are practically none. Under the Bush administration, privatisation of the military accelerated rapidly, with the aims of saving money and promoting privatisation as a matter of ideological principle.[115] Around fifty have been killed, with hundreds wounded and some being taken hostage. The US has declared foreign corporate security staff to be immune from prosecution under Iraqi law and answerable only to the laws of their countries of citizenship. Around 20,000 private security personnel from around sixty companies, mostly based in the US, operate in Iraq.[116] A US Army internal investigation found that their staff, recruited from around the world, tend to be inadequately vetted.[117] Interrogators provided by private contractors are suspected to have been among those who participated in and encouraged the torture at Abu Ghraib.[118] In June 2004, the US-based Center for Constitutional Rights (CCR) filed a lawsuit against the US companies Titan Corporation, which provided translators for Abu Ghraib, and CACI International, which provided interrogators, in a class action on behalf of Iraqis. The CCR argued that these corporations 'conspired with US officials to humiliate, torture and abuse' detainees in Iraq.[119] There is no overall Department of Defence process of managing, overseeing and reviewing the performance of private contractors who undertake a wide range of tasks, including security (such as guarding buildings and convoys and training troops), intelligence, law enforcement and criminal justice functions in Iraq.[120] Overall, there are insufficient safeguards against abuses, and the practical barriers for Iraqis seeking redress against such contractors are large.

While people in southern Iraq are at much less risk from the actions of US forces or foreign corporate security contractors, they still face problems in ensuring that British forces are accountable to them. The British Government admits the involvement of its forces in killing 37 civilians since 1 May 2003, but there have probably been many more cases, as soldiers are themselves unsure about how many people they have killed.[121] Decisions as to whether or not to investigate the killing of civilians by British soldiers are left solely to the local commanding officers, although the Government is considering the transfer of these powers to the British military police. Only 18 of the 37 deaths were investigated by the military police, and those investigations were secret, with families being told little or nothing about the progress or outcome of the investigations, or even that they were being conducted. Amnesty International has identified cases which seem to have involved the use of force in breach of relevant international standards but which have not been investigated.[122]

There is a system of compensation but it is problematic. The level of compensation for an unjustified or accidental killing of an Iraqi civilian has been set on the basis of Iraqi law as interpreted by an Iraqi judge, generally at 2,000,000 Iraqi dinars (US$1,405). Between 1 May 2003 and 5 January 2004, twenty-three claims had been made, with seven being rejected, thirteen still being investigated and three met. To receive the money, the recipient must sign a form saying that it is a 'full and final settlement'. Where the British authorities decide that there is no liability under English law, *ex gratia* donations are sometimes made for humanitarian reasons or according to local custom. There is considerable dissatisfaction with the compensation process: the claims offices are not easily accessible, the criteria are not explained clearly, there are long delays in processing, and details of the grounds for decisions are not provided. A perceived lack of consistency in applying the criteria, and the fact that payments tend to be negotiated with clan representatives instead of immediate families, have led to suspicions that the decisions are influenced by calculations about the impact of decisions on British forces' relations with political and tribal interests.

The British NGO Public Interest Lawyers has pursued forty cases of torture and killings by British forces in southern Iraq.[123] As a result of this legal action, the British High Court ruled in December 2004 that the European Convention on Human Rights (ECHR) applied to those held in the custody of British forces in Iraq, and that the Convention had been violated by British forces in respect of the right to life and freedom from torture and the requirement for independent investigation. However, it found that shooting by British forces 'in the field' did not fall within the purview of the ECHR, and this implied a much lower level of safeguards prior to completion of an arrest. The Court of Appeal ruled in December 2005 that the applicable condition was whether the individual had their liberty restricted by British forces, within a prison or not. On this ground, it found that the ECHR did not apply to Iraqi civilians who had been shot in the street in Basra by British forces. These judgements therefore made limited advances in extending accountability and the rule of law to the conduct of British forces.[124]

The transfer of formal sovereignty did not improve the situation significantly with respect to the rule of law, and the Iraqi police and armed forces contribute in important respects to the insecurity of the population. According to human rights NGOs and the US State Department, they routinely carry out arbitrary arrest and detention, improperly detain children, deny access to family and legal advice, use torture and gain forced confessions.[125] The lack of adequate oversight is compounded by the sectoral fragmentation of Iraqi state institutions. From the formation of the ITG in April 2005, a struggle existed between the Ministries of the Interior and Justice over the control and oversight of detention facilities.[126] Both have operated separate jails, with the Interior Ministry also holding prisoners at undeclared centres and subjecting at least some of them to torture. Although judges, acting with the authority of the Justice Ministry, have the constitutional power to order the confinement or release of suspects, obedience from Interior Ministry officials has been sporadic at best. In Mosul, for example, judicial orders were issued for the release of hundreds of detainees from Interior Ministry jails in late 2005, but the Ministry refused to abide by them.[127] The Human Rights Ministry was not able to act as an effective intermediary, as the position of Human Rights Minister was the only cabinet position left unfilled in the ITG. This splintering of authority also spread to relations with the Coalition: in April 2006, it was revealed that the Interior Ministry had refused to deploy the thousands of members of the police force trained by the US/UK-led Civilian Police Assistance Training Team (CPATT) in the preceding three months.[128] The attempt by individual ministries to obtain power for themselves, and the absence of effective restraints upon this, has meant that police on patrol in southern and central Iraq have been under the direction of a ministry strongly aligned with and permeated by SCIRI and the Badr

Brigades. This has not been a factor conducive to confidence in the impartiality of the police among the non-Shi'a population.

Counter-insurgency, re-militarisation and embedded insurgents

The actions of the Coalition and the Iraqi Government show that in practice they attach little importance to the rule of law as a means of reassuring the population and winning its positive support. Such an approach has made it difficult to persuade people not merely to support the Government but to risk their lives for it. Yet US counter-insurgency doctrine stresses as a 'basic premise' that this is what must happen:

> To prevent the overthrow of a government friendly to the US or to provide security while a new government is established, US forces may be required to engage in combat, either unilaterally or with multinational or HN [Host Nation] forces. As quickly as possible, though, HN military and police must assume the primary combat role. A long-term US combat role may undermine the legitimacy of the HN government and risks converting the conflict into a US-only war. That combat role can further alienate cultures that are hostile to the US.[129]

The development of 'host nation forces' was dependent upon the success of the policy of 'Iraqi-isation' as the US labels it (the British term is Iraqification): that is, the transfer of responsibility for security to Iraqi government forces from US forces. Based in part on the 15 November 2003 plan, this transfer was designed to take place in four stages. In the 'mutual support' first phase, the Coalition was to establish the necessary conditions for the transfer. Iraqis were to take local responsibility for security in stage two and regional responsibility for security in stage three, and national responsibility, with the multinational force limited to 'strategic over watch', in stage four.[130]

In order to implement its 15 November plan, the Coalition produced in December 2003 a detailed chart called 'The Security Sector Sychronisation and Development Matrix'.[131] It mapped out a timeline across every major sector from January 2004 to December 2006. Its top line included a formal request for NATO support in April 2004; disarmament, demobilisation and reintegration of militias in July 2004; a reduction in US force levels in November 2004 (perhaps coincidentally, the month of the US presidential election); 'full Iraqi sovereignty' in mid-November 2004 at the earliest; the liberalisation of fuel and electricity prices in January 2005; a transition to a NATO/Multinational force in February 2005; and a phased withdrawal and drawdown of US forces plus rebasing, exercises and prepositioning of equipment as of June 2005. The dates and the proposed actions listed were intended to be a means of promoting coordination rather than a fixed timetable, and particular elements such as the request for NATO support were included as options.[132]

The significance within this plan attached to the drawdown of US forces has been echoed in the State Department's framework for US policy in Iraq. From 20 July 2005 onwards, the State Department had in its weekly status report organised its presentation according to 'the seven key areas identified as pillars of US government policy in Iraq'. The first of these 'pillars' has been the 'transition to security self-reliance', the others being support for freedom and democracy, provision of essential services, establishing a foundation for a strong economy, promotion of the rule of law, maintenance of international engagement and support and promotion of 'strategic communications'.[133]

Coalition efforts at Iraqi-isation have been belated, half-hearted, ineffective and even counter-productive. There have been few places or occasions where they have achieved the goal of phase two or even phase one of the November 2003 plan. The US re-established the Iraqi Ministry of Defence in late March 2004, adding the new army to the other Iraqi security forces: the police, the Iraqi Civil Defence Corps (ICDC), the Department of Border Enforcement and the Facilities Protection Service (FPS). All of the security institutions were allocated counter-insurgency roles, with various new forces being created.[134] However, initial low pay levels — in the autumn of 2003, starting pay was $60 per month for soldiers and $80 for police officers — plus lack of any evidence of a US willingness to permit Iraqi senior ranks or politicians to have any significant decision-making role contributed to low morale and high resignation rates.

When the US moved against Falluja and the Mahdi Army in April 2004, these Iraqi security forces fell apart. Depending on the region, ICDC force levels fell between 30% and 82% in mid April, and combined police numbers in Falluja, Najaf, Karbala' and Kut fell from 2,892 officers to 23 in one week.[135] Iraqi security forces failed to turn up for duty, declared neutrality and refused to engage the insurgents, or joined them to fight on the same side. Furthermore, the Coalition's very limited efforts at screening of recruits had little success in preventing the existence of what one might call embedded insurgents, who covertly or even openly use the weapons and skills given to them against the Coalition. According to Etherington:

When we found, in May 2004, that a senior police officer had directed rebel rocket fire on to our compound during the Sadr rebellion and been wounded taking part in the ensuing assault upon us, his chief confided in me with due gravity that he had "spoken very toughly" to him and the officer had promised not to do it again.[136]

The US military attributed the collapse of Iraqi security forces to lack of training and equipment. Certainly, they were very short of both.[137] The CPA said that the shortage of equipment was due to problems with contractors, slow allocation and release of funds, and lack of contracting expertise in Baghdad. However, as we argued in Chapter Three, since many of these forces had been recruited through Iraqi political parties which themselves did not support the April 2004 assaults, the Iraqi forces' lack of effectiveness was probably due more to the influence of factional networks than to inadequate technical capacity.

In response to the April 2004 desertion and rebellion fiasco, the Coalition sought to accelerate equipment acquisition, improve training (involving NATO), recruit experienced former Ba'thist military personnel and recruit units with people from more of a mix of localities.[138] The ICDC (relaunched in July as the Iraqi National Guard, with its merger with the army announced in December) and other non-combat Iraqi security services were close to or over their intended quotas of personnel by late June, but all remained very short of training and equipment.[139] Once pay levels were increased, the security institutions provided one of the few routes to a good income (police pay was $207 per month in July 2004) in a context of desperate poverty and extremely high unemployment.[140] In November 2004, in the face of insurgent attacks the Mosul police force collapsed from 2,000 to 50 police officers, and the Iraqi army in the area and the police force in Samarra', disintegrated to the same degree.[141] Although Iraq's security forces totalled some 120,000 on paper in January 2005, the Coalition calculated that only 5,000 could actually be relied upon in combat, and of 135,000 police, one third did not show up for duty at all.[142] With the increase in spending on security forces, described in Chapter Two, by March 2006, the official figure of Iraqi counter-insurgency forces had grown to 240,000, with 53 battalions of 800 men (increased from 36 in November 2005) assessed as able to take the primary role in operations, but with none at all (down from one battalion in November 2005) able to operate without US assistance.[143]

The main reason Iraqi security forces are extremely reluctant to fight is sometimes lack of training and equipment, but it is usually lack of loyalty. Apart from seeking to serve their state and society, people join the Iraqi security services to earn money, to serve particular sections of society and, in some cases, to gain intelligence and weapons for the insurgency, and not to serve the US or Britain. The security forces have primarily become instruments of sectarian, not national, politics, because most of the recruitment has been done on a communal basis. Recruitment tends to be based on lists of people and militias provided by political parties, tribal chiefs, provincial governors and notables.[144] This has applied particularly to the police forces, run by the Interior Ministry: the State Department commented in March 2006 that '[m]embers of sectarian militias dominated police units to varying degrees and in different parts of the country'.[145] In Chapter Three we argued that this was reinforcing the neopatrimonial aspects of the Iraqi state and the wider trend towards sectarianism. Our point here is that these neopatrimonial and sectarian characteristics mean that there has been little prospect of such forces displaying the loyalty necessary to be effective in counter-insurgency operations, unless perceived neopatrimonial and sectarian interests happened to coincide with those of the Coalition.

Nor had the goal of switching to a combination of NATO and Iraqi forces been achieved even by June 2006. NATO agreed only after vigorous internal disputes to train Iraqi security forces, and only established a training mission in Iraq in June 2005. Its aim was to train 1,500 Iraqi military personnel per year, just over 1% of the projected armed force level of 131,000 soldiers.[146] Although not negligible, NATO's role has clearly been small. In March 2006, 26 countries other than the US had a total of 20,000 troops in Iraq, which represents a slow decline in the number of countries and troops.[147] As a result of problems on all fronts, the number of US troops in Iraq reached record highs of 155,000 in February 2005 and 160,000 in November and December 2005, before being reduced to 133,000 in February 2006.[148] The original expectation at the time of the invasion — that US forces in Iraq would be drawn down to 30,000 by September 2003 — became an ever-receding dream despite occasional optimistic noises.[149] In similar fashion, a prediction in July 2005 by the commander of British forces in southern Iraq, Maj.-Gen. Jonathan Riley, that control of Maysan and al-Muthanna provinces would be handed over to Iraqi forces in 2005 and Dhi Qar and Basra provinces in 2006 was undermined in September 2005 by clashes not only with the Mahdi Army but also with the police in Basra.[150] There have been some apparent successes, such as the handing over by US forces to local Iraqi control of the mainly Shi'a holy cities of Najaf in August and Karbala' in September 2005, with US forces relocating to bases outside the cities.[151] However, Najaf remains too dangerous for foreign contractors to visit and, as we showed in Chapter Three, Karbala' is the site of political conflict between the Karbala' City Council and the Interior Ministry over control of the security forces, with the Ministry failing to impose its authority.

With formal Iraqi forces so fragile, the US allied itself with or actively created a variety of new militias, as described in Chapter Two, and paramilitary forces. The Coalition called the new militias that subsequently emerged late in 2004 'irregular brigades' (as militias are deemed illegal), and they have not been brought fully under the direction of the Iraqi Government or the Coalition. Instead, though they receive government funding and operate in conjunction with the Coalition, they are the personal forces of individual shaykhs or government ministers and tend to be tribal and sectarian.[152] The 'Wolf Brigade' was created in October 2004 by a military leader of SCIRI who used the *nom de guerre* of Abu Walid, and who recruited personnel from Sadr City. They came to prominence when they were given their own television programme, 'Terrorism in the Grip of Justice', broadcast on the US-funded al-Iraqiyya network, in which their detainees proclaimed their own guilt.[153] They were prominent in the offensive to retake Mosul in December 2004, and Abu Walid claimed that they had 2,000 personnel.[154] After numerous allegations of violations of human rights, the US military announced in December 2005 that they were now named the 'Freedom Brigade'.[155] Other such units include the Muthana Brigade set up by 'Allawi, the Defenders of Khadhamiyya (a Shi'a militia under the control of cleric Husayn al-Sadr), the Second Defenders of Baghdad Brigade chosen by Shaykh 'Ali Sha'lan of the Al Shamr tribe in southern Iraq, and two mainly Shi'a militias developed by the US Marines — the Iraq Freedom Guard and Freedom Fighters — which have been deployed in al-Anbar province. The US is supporting some of the militias and paramilitaries with counter-insurgency experts such as James Steele, who was a US adviser to the El Salvador government, which ran militia death squads in its dirty war against civil society and armed insurgents alike in the early 1980s.[156]

The US has decided to work with the militias and paramilitaries because of the disadvantage it perceives in having a large part of its army tied down in Iraq. This was made most explicit by General Myers, in his warning to Congress in May 2005 that the ongoing operations in Iraq made it difficult for the US to engage in other major conflicts.[157] Public opinion polls show clearly that most Iraqi Arabs also want US forces to leave, but not for the reason given by Myers.

Iraqi Arabs: from sceptical to hostile

Attitudes to the Coalition have been consistently and fundamentally different in the north of Iraq compared with the centre and the south. In the spring of 2004, 97% of respondents in the north said that Coalition forces were liberators and only 1% described them as occupiers, and virtually all of them claimed to have held the same views at the time of the invasion.[158] In October 2004, in the north 75% to 77% were in favour of the presence of the MNF and 18% to 22% against, with 65% to 68% saying they would feel less safe, and 13% to 15% safer, if the Coalition forces left.[159] (Throughout this section of the Chapter, any range of percentages indicated represents the range of opinion across various cities in a region, not an indication of a range of uncertainty in polling results.) US forces have generally engaged in well-received consent-based peacekeeping rather than combat duties in the north, which is in most respects run by a separate *de facto* state divided between KDP- and PUK-controlled sectors. The drastically different context and experiences of the rest of Iraq compared with the north explain why the Coalition, far from gradually winning Arab Iraqi hearts and minds, never had them on its side, and their views have became only more negative.

From the very outset, Coalition forces have been seen throughout the centre and south more as occupiers than liberators, with the initial differences between the centre and south disappearing. As early as August 2003, a poll in Basra, Ramadi, Mosul and Kirkuk showed that 49% saw attacks on US forces as 'resistance operations'.[160] In the autumn of 2003, 35% of respondents in Baghdad described attacks on US forces as justified.[161] Among people in the centre, 64% said that at the time of the invasion they had thought of Coalition forces as occupiers and 25% said that they had thought of them as liberators.[162] The figures for the south were 47% and 35%, and for ethnically mixed Baghdad 40% and 41% respectively. Centre-south differences were effectively eliminated by late March and early April 2004, with only 10% in the centre and 7% in the south saying that they viewed Coalition forces as liberators: 80% in both areas regarded them as occupiers. In Baghdad, a mere 4% saw them as liberators and 82% as occupiers.[163]

Taking any personal hardship into account, 28% in the centre, 74% in the south and 57% in Baghdad thought that the ousting of Saddam Hussein was worth it.[164] The Coalition took great comfort from this as compensation for being seem as occupiers. However, 67% in the centre said that Coalition forces had behaved badly, that being the view of 61% in mainly Shi'a areas and 81% in Baghdad. As the greatest hostility to the Coalition has been in Baghdad which is mixed Sunni and Shi'a, the major factor in hostility to the occupation is direct experience of it rather than sectarian difference. Nor could the Coalition argue that, while people did not like being ruled by an occupier, they thought that it was an unpleasant necessity in the face of the insurgency. Those wanting the Coalition forces to leave within a few months amounted to 65% in the centre, 61% in the south and 75% in Baghdad. 52% said that attacks on Coalition forces were justified, thus showing that the Coalition had failed to establish its legitimacy amongst those Iraqis.[165]

The Abu Ghraib scandal and the US offensives in April 2004 were followed by an even greater deepening of the unpopularity of the Coalition and some shows of Sunni-Shi'a unity. In May 2004, 55% in the centre and south said they would feel safer if Coalition forces left immediately. 92% of respondents now said that Coalition forces were occupiers, and only 2% saw them as liberators.[166] 41% wanted to see Coalition troops withdraw immediately, and a further 45% preferred them to leave after the installation of a permanent Iraqi government.

The reasons given for wanting Coalition forces to leave were principally that they were occupiers, then that 'they brought only death and destruction', that Iraqis could administer Iraq better, and that the Coalition forces wanted Iraq's oil and resources, were 'facilitating Zionist domination of Iraq', did not respect Iraq's religions and cultures, and abused Iraqis.[167] 54% said they thought all US soldiers behaved in the same way as the Abu Ghraib torturers.[168] The Coalition narrative that the insurgent violence was an effort to re-establish the old regime was agreed with by only 27% of Iraqis — 60% disagreed. 79% agreed that the violence had increased because people had lost faith in the Coalition forces and a mere 9% disagreed. In sum, the polls indicated that most Iraqi Arabs had never welcomed the Coalition and wanted them to leave, as they were seen to be making things worse.

While Sunni and Shi'a Arab sectarianism increased later in 2004, this did not translate into a belief among the public that Coalition forces were necessary for security and specifically for the prevention of civil war.[169] By October 2004, across the centre and south, 70% to 95% opposed the presence of Coalition forces, only 5% to 23% were in favour of their presence and only 2% to 15% had confidence in Coalition forces to improve the situation in Iraq. 42% to 84% thought they would feel safer if Coalition forces left immediately, with a much smaller proportion — 13% to 35% — expecting that they would feel less safe.[170] 38% to 76% wanted them to leave immediately, and 7% to 51% wanted them to leave after a 'permanent' government was elected. Very few — 2%

to 20% — wanted Coalition forces to stay as long as was necessary to stabilise Iraq, which was the view of the Coalition and the Iraqi Government. The most unfavourable views of Coalition forces were in the centre, but the south was very hostile too. For example, in the south 70% opposed and 20% supported their presence, and 60% said they would feel more safe and 25% less safe if they left immediately. Although those in the centre tended to want them to leave immediately and those in the south tended to want this to happen after the election of a permanent Iraqi government, it was only a difference of emphasis rather than a sharp divide.[171] In early summer 2005, a Coalition poll had indicated that 45% of the population supported attacks by the insurgents whereas a mere 15% strongly backed the Coalition.[172]

The unpopularity of Coalition forces among Iraqi Arabs was confirmed a week before the 30 January 2005 elections, but with a widening of differences between Shi'a and Sunni Arabs. 30% of Shi'a and 74% of Sunni Arabs wanted an immediate US withdrawal, 39% and 8% respectively wanted a US withdrawal after an elected government was in place, and a mere 19% and 6% wanted US forces to stay until 'safety and security are restored, no matter how long it takes'.[173] The trend towards sectarianism was underlined most strongly in a move towards polarised views of the insurgency. 32% of Shi'a Arabs and 51% of Sunni Kurds as against 3% of Sunni Arabs saw insurgent attacks as being carried out by Saddam Hussein loyalists. Only 7% of Shi'a Arabs and 8% of Sunni Kurds, in comparison with 53% of Sunni Arabs, saw them as legitimate resistance operations.[174] A poll conducted on behalf of the British military discovered that by August 2005 the gap between Sunni Arabs and Shi'a had on this issue closed, with 65% in Maysan province and 25% in Basra (both areas of British force deployment) seeing attacks on Coalition forces as justified.[175] Across Iraq, 45% saw attacks on Coalition forces as justified, 82% were 'strongly opposed' to the presence of Coalition forces and fewer than 1% felt more secure because of the presence of Coalition forces.

The one set of Coalition-created institutions which has been consistently popular is Iraq's new security forces, even though they are weak and, more importantly for the Coalition's state-building efforts, have loyalties that diverge from those of the Coalition-sponsored project. In November 2003, 71% of those polled said they had confidence in the new Iraqi security forces. By May 2004 this had fallen, but only to 62%. The Iraqi police had the confidence of 84% of respondents in November 2003, dropping only slightly to 76% in May 2004.[176] In central and southern Iraq, both the Iraqi army (which had only just been re-established) and especially the police were most strongly endorsed by the public in October 2004: 36% to 90% and 51% to 89% respectively expressed confidence that they were able to improve matters.[177] Endorsement of them in opinion polls suggests that they symbolise national pride and a desire for sovereignty and security: it cannot be a result of their performance.

There are, therefore, areas of significant agreement between Iraq's Sunni Arab and Shi'a populations. There are also significant disagreements within each group, and so perceiving Iraqi politics solely through this sectarian prism is fundamentally misleading. For example, in a January 2006 poll, 88% of Sunni Arabs, 41% of Shi'a Arabs and 16% of Kurds supported attacks on US-led forces.[178] Such figures show that support for the insurgency cannot usefully be labelled solely as 'Sunni Arab', as it so often is. Sunni and Shi'a Arabs tend to agree that violence in general and inter-ethnic violence in particular would decline, as would the presence of foreign fighters, if US-led forces withdrew within six months, whereas Kurds tend to think that all three would increase.[179] On most of these points, around a quarter to a third disagree with the views of their sectarian majority.

Furthermore, despite the deadlock at elite level in attempts to form a government in the first half of 2006, there is a striking degree of consensus across Kurds, Shi'a and Sunni Arabs about the way forward. Iraqis see the efforts of the Arab League to promote Iraqi national reconciliation as valuable, and endorse its positions that all groups should participate in the political process, that terrorism should be rejected and that there should be a timetable for the withdrawal of US-led forces. There is very little support for attacks on Iraqi government security forces and almost none for attacks on civilians. Iraqis think that Sunni Arab support for US non-military assistance would increase if the US accepted a withdrawal timetable, and that day-to-day security would improve. They want the government to decide on a timetable for US withdrawal but think that the US would not withdraw its forces even if the Iraqi Government asked it to do so. Despite US public statements to the contrary, a large majority of Iraqis — Kurds, Sunni Arabs and Shi'a — think that the US intends to retain permanent bases and station forces in Iraq.[180] Most Iraqis, albeit by smaller margins, want the UN to take the lead on economic reconstruction and want an international conference to help coordinate assistance to Iraq. They also think that help is needed from the military forces of other countries to provide security.

The opinion polling data make it clear that the centrality of the US in the state-building process is a crucial element undermining its legitimacy. Iraq's Sunni Arabs have not accepted the legitimacy of the US role and the state that is being formed as a result of it. Moreover, through the insurgency which has sustained itself in the Sunni Arab community, they have demonstrated that they have a *de facto* veto on its success. Popular attitudes demonstrate significant common ground within Iraq for a reoriented state-building process which is regionalised and internationalised rather than US-dominated, but also a shared suspicion that the US could prevent such an outcome from occurring.

CONCLUSION – THE DOWNWARD SPIRAL

The core mission of counter-insurgency is the building of a viable central state. Ideally, it would be popular, but failing that, it would be one where popular indifference or hostility would be contained. This is the declaratory centrepiece of the Coalition's counter-insurgency strategy.

One would therefore expect that the strategy would work against Iraq's fragmentation in both conception and execution. However, the opposite has been the case. Instead of a clear and feasible goal being established and then adapted in a way in which retention of the initiative was prioritised, US policy on Iraq has lurched between extremes in a reactive manner. The viable state that it expected to take over intact was actually one in which the formal institutions of power had been distorted to the brink of collapse under the Ba'th regime. When the invasion and the failure to provide order ensured that those weak formal institutions collapsed completely, the state-building challenge the US faced was massive. The fundamental flaws in the United States' overall state-building project, combined with the vigorous efforts of the insurgency to wreck that project, drove the US counter-insurgency policy in the direction of coercion rather than legitimation. Furthermore, an approach to counter-insurgency dominated by coercion has widened the gap between the state and much of society and has fuelled the insurgency.

The emergence of the insurgency, with its deliberate targeting of the Coalition's state-building enterprise, resulted in the *ad hoc* adoption, by actors at all levels, of measures perceived to be expedient in coping with the insurgency, rather than measures fitting in with a strategic re-adjustment to ensure momentum in state-building. The US military has, contrary to the frequent pronouncements of its leading officials, ended up treating the use of force as sufficient to win a war, thus marginalising concerns about securing the population's support as a mechanism of state-building. Brigadier Nigel Aylwin-Foster, who had been second in command of training Iraqi security forces, commented that US army personnel 'were too inclined to consider offensive operations and destruction of the insurgent as the key to a given situation, and conversely failed to understand its downside', and instead assumed that 'a reluctance to use force merely bolstered the insurgents' courage and resilience, whilst demonstrating Coalition lack of resolve to the domestic population, thus prolonging the conflict'.[181] In this Chapter, we have shown how this downside to the use of military force has actually been a key factor in alienating the population. This has been most apparent in the way establishing the rule of law and a system of accountability has been sacrificed to supposed expedients of intelligence-gathering and freedom of action against suspected insurgents.

The population is not merely threatened by the insurgents; it is also threatened in the many ways by the US forces' attempts to secure victory through an indiscriminate and repressive approach to counter-insurgency. Moreover, the alternative US strategy to securing this victory, through the use of Iraqi security forces, has also suffered as those forces have become thoroughly penetrated by insurgents. One of the quickest ways to get money, transport, uniforms, weapons, training and especially intelligence on the Coalition and those collaborating with it is to become an embedded insurgent. As the Coalition has made little progress in creating security forces loyal to the Iraqi state, it has fallen back on reliance on anyone who will fight. This means cooperating with militias and semi-official paramilitaries which may be working with the Coalition and the Iraqi state only in alliances of convenience — and such cooperation institutionalises the fragmentation of the capability to use armed force.

The policy of securing popular acquiescence by killing 'the bad guys' has been at the expense of state-building rather than being a means of achieving it. Nearly a year into the conflict, US counter-insurgency expert Nagl, wrestling with the realities of the insurgency in al-Anbar, said:

I'm not really all that concerned about their hearts right now … We're into the behavior-modification phase. I want their minds right now. Maybe we'll get their hearts later, as we spend $100,000 on their schools and health clinics this week and another $100,000 on their schools and health clinics next week and $100,000 on their schools and health clinics the week after that. Over time I'll start winning some hearts. Right now I just want them to stop shooting at us, stop planting I.E.D.'s [Improvised Explosive Devices]. If they're not involved in these activities, they should start turning in the people who are. Whatever techniques that are legal and moral that I have to use to accomplish that, I will. Counterinsurgency is not always a pretty thing.[182]

Saying that people should turn in insurgents is not a strategy for ensuring that they will, and there is no reason to believe that giving money for local projects will override the reasons that most Iraqi Arabs articulate for opposing the US strategy in Iraq. In the centre and south in late 2004, perceptions of destroyed infrastructure and a bad economic situation were regarded by almost no-one as priority considerations (2% and 1% respectively). While action to repair the infrastructure, especially electricity, would obviously have been welcomed, only 1% to 13% saw it as the most important issue facing them.[183]

Opinion polls show the unpopularity of the occupation in the centre and south from the outset (aside from gratitude in the south for the overthrow of Saddam Hussein), with that unpopularity deepening as a consequence of the way the occupation has been conducted. Bursts of·initial optimism about Coalition-created institutions have quickly faded away, while the people have found no individual or political party as inspiring widespread national confidence to lead the state. The Coalition and the Iraqi Government speak of Coalition forces staying as long as necessary until Iraqi security forces can handle the insurgency. However, the population in the centre and south mostly considers that the insurgency and their support for it is driven by the presence and conduct of Coalition forces, and wants those forces to leave. If they did leave, it is entirely possible that fighting would continue or escalate among Iraqi Arabs and perhaps the Kurds, and even draw in neighbouring states, as they jockeyed for power. But that is a risk most Iraqis in the centre and south have claimed to be willing to take - though they might change their minds if it came to the crunch. The fact that they have indicated their willingness to take this risk is a measure of the distance between the Coalition and the current Iraqi political elite on the one hand and most Iraqi Arabs on the other. In this context, as we show in the next Chapter, the economic dimensions of state-building, including the reintegration of Iraq into the global economy, have faced severe challenges.

5

CAPITAL

The acquisition and investment of capital are central to the dynamics of state building and state formation. The Coalition narrative on this issue is that Iraqi capital from oil exports is being combined with a large donation of US capital, a smaller donation of other international capital and a reduction of Iraq's debt to manageable proportions as part of a new integration of the Iraqi state, society and economy into the global economic system. An effective Iraqi state operating within global institutions is represented as being created to provide the regulatory context for economic progress which serves the welfare of the Iraqi population. Success in this venture is seen by the Coalition as requiring the defeat or at least marginalisation of the insurgency and criminality. In this narrative, everyone — except the insurgents and criminals of course — is a winner.

In contrast, we argue in this Chapter that an insurgent-driven and profit-driven informal economy is combining with US-led processes of globalisation to fragment the Iraqi state so that its elements serve the interests of those driving these processes rather than the interests of the Iraqi population generally. The formation of an effective state requires the accumulation of capital within that country and its investment in production, and where capital is not directly concentrated in the state's hands, the state must be able to regulate it: this is not what is occurring in Iraq. This is a vastly bigger issue than the transfer (or non-transfer) of *de jure* and *de facto* sovereignty to the Iraqi state by the occupying powers. The US as a state and US capital are leading the way in seeking to install in Iraq practices which are international (that is, involving multiple states) and transnational (that is, involving non-state actors which operate across states). These practices are aimed at ensuring that the post-invasion Iraqi economy serves primarily US political and economic interests within the global economy. Capital extends and intensifies the monetisation of relations for the purpose of private profit, and state practices provide the societal regulation which permits capital to operate. This process is highly uneven and is as much about establishing, relocating and policing hierarchies and borders as about removing them. The US Government and US-based capital are not operating on their own, but through and in the context of the effects of the institutions of global liberal governance.

The question then shifts from the narrow one of 'How sovereign is the Iraq state in relation to the economy?' to 'How is the Iraqi state being formed and transformed in relation to capital?' Owing to smuggling and the UN Oil For Food (OFF) programme (through which Iraq could from 1996 sell some oil to buy goods under UN supervision), the long period of comprehensive and devastating UN economic sanctions was not one of complete isolation of Iraq from the global economy. However, the rearticulation of Iraq to the global economy has accelerated rapidly in the post-invasion period. Although the insurgents have made it very difficult for the institutions of global liberal governance to operate on the ground in Iraq, the country is still being steadily reintegrated into those institutions, in some respects at arm's length.

The US state and US-based capital are very much in a dominant role in this attempted rearticulation, but broader forces are increasingly significant. In this Chapter we indicate how these actors and social forces relate to each other in this dynamic process. We show that a major challenge to the Iraqi state, and to the actors which are reshaping it and reintegrating it into the formal global economy, is the country's burgeoning transnational informal economy. We then map out the US-dominated network of decision-making institutions in relation to the Iraqi economy. We argue that this network is not merely a temporary expedient: it is establishing a pattern of relations in which the Iraqi state is to function effectively as an extension of US-led global liberal governance. In the following section we explain how these institutions are being used to open up the Iraqi economy despite Iraqi public hostility to such actions, so that the gap between the Iraqi state and business elite on the one hand, and the Iraqi population more generally on the other, is widening. This process is being carried out in a way that permits a significant role for non-US capital while still leaving US capital in pole position. After that, we show that the Bush administration has ensured that US-based transnational corporations have been at the top of the contracting hierarchy in management as well as financial terms. We detail how the opening up of the economy has not been accompanied by effective investment in reconstruction, owing to security problems, corruption and the unwillingness of the US administration to take the actions necessary to ensure proper use of the funds available. We indicate the important disciplining role played by Iraq's enormous debt (including compensation for the invasion of Kuwait). The Iraqi state is functioning to enforce a burden of debt which will have to be paid for by the Iraqi people. We conclude the Chapter with a discussion of how the fragmented Iraqi state is failing to deliver for its population, while being transformed through its integration into the structures and processes of US-led globalisation.

THE TRANSNATIONAL INFORMAL ECONOMY

Iraq's transnational informal economy is massive, diversifying and contributing significantly to the fragmentation of Iraq, as overlapping networks outside state regulation assert their power.[1] Although much of the informal economy is primarily regional, it has many global connections. The term 'informal economy' covers all economic activities for which state regulations exist but are not applied; it is more useful than 'illegal economy' because goods can be produced without violence or illegality but traded in an illegal fashion, and because those operating informally are sometimes not trying to evade regulation — with the feebleness of the Iraqi state, the effort to regulate economic activity is distinctly limited. However, some aspects of the informal economy, such as the theft of goods or funds, are straightforwardly criminal and corrupt. The informal economy can be evidence of the early stages of liberal market economic revival which can be gradually brought under state and international regulation. It can also be effective as an alternative economy outside the control of the state.[2] In the case of Iraq, it is in some respects effectively a serious challenge to neoliberal globalisation from above. This is most obviously the case where it is serving insurgents who are overtly aiming to disrupt that process. Economic activity is being fragmented as a host of regional and global networks take control of, and expand, various sources of income.

Of all the many elements of Iraq's informal economy, oil is the most important and is decentred (in not being under the predominant control of a single actor) and transnational in character. Non-state actors have had a significant role both in determining the potential for the state to export its oil officially, through sabotage, and in selling off the oil extracted, through smuggling. The result has been that the state's role in oil sales has been considerably smaller than predicted, as far as can be determined (Iraq's oil production is not metered fully or reliably). In 1990, Iraq was pumping 3.5 million barrels per day (mbd). In 2000, the highest production level during the OFF programme, Iraq produced 2.6mbd, of which 1.9mbd were exported through the programme and 0.3mbd were available for smuggling.[3] Before the invasion, analysts were predicting that under US auspices Iraqi production could reach 4.5mbd by 2008. In contrast, between the invasion and 2006, average weekly production remained stuck around 2mbd, with official exports falling as low as 1.1mbd in January 2006.[4]

Highly effective sabotage of oil pipelines by insurgents has had a significant role in reducing Iraq's export abilities. The northern pipeline, running from Kirkuk to Ceyhan in Turkey, has been continually sabotaged. Although it operated through most of 2004, it was shut down in December 2004, and had resumed only intermittent operation by 2006. The government has paid monthly fees to tribes and other groups to provide guards to supplement the state's Oil Pipeline Protection Force, but there have been frequent allegations that many of these groups have attacked the pipelines themselves to justify the fee paid for protecting them, leading to the indictment of one leading Sunni Arab politician in 2006 who was alleged to have organised this practice.[5]

The attacks on the northern pipeline have left only exports through the southern terminals. These have themselves been attacked, as in April 2004, when an attack by three boats forced the cessation of exports for two days.[6] However, in general, sabotage here has been relatively rare, not least because smugglers predominate over insurgents. In October 2003 the US and British navies intercepted large numbers of road vehicles and small ships smuggling out about 2,000 tons of Iraqi oil — 10% of Iraq's output at the time — to be sold on the black market by Iraqi oil company employees. The smuggling rings tend to be composed of Iraqis living in the United Arab Emirates (UAE), using thousands of tanker lorries or ships crewed by Ethiopians, Iranians, Somalis and Syrians.[7] The British military calculated that the amount of oil being smuggled out of Iraq each week to Kuwait and the UAE had risen to about 3,000 tons per week in December 2003.[8] Iraqi officials put the illegal export of Iraqi refined oil products at up to 25% of output in January 2004.[9] Estimates of oil smuggling went as high as 60% of output in 2004.[10]

Although seizures continue, smuggling and sabotage were calculated as costing Iraq $8 billion per year when fuel imports and lost exports are combined.[11] Basra police shut down 24 illegal terminals and confiscated dozens of vessels, but indicated that they were unable to stop the smuggling: this is hardly surprising as police are often involved in the smuggling themselves.[12] The prosecution of smugglers is rare. In April 2005, the Iraqi State Oil Marketing Organisation estimated that smuggling had been cut to 10% of output: this may have indicated progress, but it may just have been a low estimate, as 'Abd al-Karim Li'aibi, the Oil Ministry's fuel distribution project manager calculated that 40% of the trucks carrying fuel products were attacked or hijacked.[13] Smuggling blends into large-scale corruption in which bribes are demanded and fuel stolen for sale within Iraq. During UN sanctions, oil was smuggled out via Syria, Jordan, Turkey and the Persian Gulf, and there was tacit UN approval of the barter of Iraqi oil for Jordanian goods outside the UN OFF programme.[14] Whereas the profits tended to go to the Ba'th regime in the past (with some officials at all levels managing to skim money off for themselves), they now go to the smugglers and their allies. Coalition military commanders assume that they will never have the resources to catch most of the smugglers, and the US is unwilling to push hard on an issue which would probably implicate some of its Gulf allies. The extent of oil theft indicates that smuggling receives substantial assistance from state officials. In April 2005, the Oil Ministry sacked 450 employees it believed to have been involved in oil theft, but it expected many other employees to turn to corruption to replace them.[15]

Before the invasion, petrol, diesel and heating oil were subsidised to the point that their cost was almost negligible, and those subsidies have been continued for fear of the political cost of charging real prices. Subsidies cost around $8 billion per year, and Iraq imports between $200 and $250 million worth of fuel per month, with one third or more being immediately stolen and re-exported.[16] In addition to oil being smuggled out in tanker trucks stolen from the Ministry of Oil's huge fleet, individuals with cars adapted to be moving petrol tanks fill up with subsidised Iraqi petrol for resale in neighbouring countries at ten times the price for which they bought it.[17]

Many other elements of the decentred transnational informal economy are not only present but appear to be growing in significance. With imports into Iraq, this is a form of economic power that originated with US attempts to create a consumer boom and has resulted from the high salaries paid. But the import routes are now managed by the paramilitaries of al-Anbar province, who take goods and resources from traders in return for allowing those routes to function. With oil exports, the productive power originates with the US orienting its technological assistance and planning to the oil sector, but it thus funds those smuggling the oil out, who ally with insurgents to obtain and protect their resources.[18]

In the early days of the occupation, the significance of looting was played down by Coalition officials, in the expectation that it would cease quickly. However, it soon became apparent that the looting had merged with smuggling, and was being carried out by insurgents as well as criminals. A common practice in the earlier part of the occupation was the theft and melting down into bars of high-tension copper electrical cables, which has been a major obstacle to improvements in electricity supply.[19] In April 2004, the CPA published rules for licensing the export of scrap metal and penalties for violating those rules, but hundreds of flatbed trucks and semi-trailers leave Iraq each day loaded with new components imported for the reconstruction, old military vehicles, scrap of all kinds and even entire dismantled building complexes from former military-industrial sites.[20]

Iraq is being integrated more deeply into world informal trading in weapons, pornography and illegal drugs, including heroin, hashish, cocaine, tranquillisers, anti-depressants and other medications, with drugs looted and stolen from hospitals and pharmacies or entering via Iran, Afghanistan, Saudi Arabia and Syria and being sold openly.[21] It is increasingly used as a transit site for hashish and heroin from Afghanistan (which produces 90% of the world's opium, from which heroin is derived) smuggled through Iran and then Iraq to Jordan.[22] Smuggling of ancient Iraqi artefacts is another widespread practice, to service the global art market centred around Geneva, Tokyo, New York and London.[23] Iraq is also being integrated into the global sex industry. Iraqi and Egyptian human traffickers kidnap and sell Iraqi women into prostitution slavery, sometimes moving them overland to Syria and flying them to brothels in Yemen.[24] Among the 700,000 or so Iraqi refugees in Syria, some women are turning to sex work.[25] Iraq's sex workers now have a major client base in the form of hundreds of thousands of dollar-rich foreign civilian and military personnel. Prostitution is now effectively legal in Iraq in the form of the revival of the ancient practice of 'pleasure marriages', which can be arranged to last from one hour to ten years for a fee.[26] These were banned under the *ancien régime* but now, with the approval of Sistani himself, Shi'a clerics are issuing licences for what can be prostitution or a way of securing freedom to engage in sexual activity outside marriage that would otherwise be dangerous amidst the intolerance and widespread organisation of self-appointed moral police vigilantes.[27] The economies that result from drug and artefact smuggling and sex work complement those of oil smuggling in linking Iraq closely into global networks that have considerable power in reordering the form of aspects of Iraqi society, and thus have a high degree of tenacity.

Overall, it can be seen that Iraq's informal economy has regional and global dimensions. Some of its aspects provide challenges to the transformation of the Iraqi state, some of them operate alongside that transformation and some of them even reinforce it. Aided by the non-transparent nature of much of the formal economy, the capital derived from the informal economy can be hidden within the global financial system or laundered, that is, recycled back into the formal economy through reinvestment in enterprises within it. This allows the penetration of Iraqi society by global criminal networks, and Iraqi oil can be channelled into the global oil market by the back door, while corruption (that is, the use by state officials of their office for personal gain) ensures that the informal economy is able to feed off efforts to create a new state and a reshaped formal economy.

THE US-DOMINATED NETWORK OF
RECONSTRUCTION INSTITUTIONS

Although the informal economy is by definition not under US control, the US has been able, to a substantial extent, to direct a form of globalisation in spheres of Iraq's formal economic activity through its control of the network of institutions reshaping Iraq's economy. This is the core feature of the process it refers to as Iraq's 'reconstruction'. The building of a sovereign liberal state requires the development of legal and effective national decision-making capacity over the allocation of the state's funds and over the rules governing the operation of international official assistance and private capital. From this perspective, US-led decision-making has been a temporary expedient until Iraqi state institutions can take over in the case of Iraqi funds and can operate in voluntary partnership with regard to US and international capital contributions. The handover and partnership are seen as having been hindered by the insurgency and the difficulties of reforming Iraqi institutions, but as essentially moving towards the establishment of that sovereign national capacity.

Instead, we argue that decision-making over the operation of this capital in Iraq since the invasion has become simultaneously internationalised and transnationalised. Iraqi decision-making is not being restored through the return of sovereignty, nor is it being subordinated by a denial of effective sovereignty. It is being transformed into an integral part of the norms and structures of the contemporary form of capitalist globalisation, with the blurring of lines between corporate and public decision-making and between the national, international and transnational. This is not a stable process, as the actors involved are defending and promoting their own sectional interests within it, the insurgents are seeking to disrupt the process, and the rapidly evolving networks of patronage and corruption within and beyond Iraq are seeking ways of accommodating and exploiting this dynamic situation.

The networks into which decision-making on the operation of capital in Iraq has been integrated have simultaneously lacked a clear organisational hierarchy, while still being dominated by US political and corporate actors. In May 2003, project coordination passed from the ORHA to the CPA. Formally, the prioritisation and coordination of all international (including US) assistance as well as Iraq's own funds during and since the formal occupation have been led by Iraqis via the Iraqi Strategic Review Board, the Iraqi Ministry of Planning and Development Cooperation and the Council for International Coordination.[28] The Council for International Coordination is chaired by the Minister of Planning and Development Cooperation — Barham Salih since April 2005 — and has members from over 23 countries involved in Iraq's reconstruction. US dominance and international tensions over the invasion are reflected in the fact that, although this is the main point of contact between US representatives in Iraq and other international donors, it is an information-sharing rather than a decision-making body. Also chaired by the Minister of Planning and Development Cooperation, the Iraqi Strategic Review Board was composed before July 2004 of Iraqi ministry officials, two representatives of the Governing Council and one CPA representative. This made it primarily an Iraqi body, but of course all of the Iraqi members were US-appointed and all Iraqi ministries operated with US advisers. The Ministry of Planning and Development Coordination was responsible for coordinating with the CPA's Programme Management Office (PMO).

Within the PMO, the Project Review Board (PRB) duplicated the responsibilities of the Iraqi Strategic Review Board in being responsible for reviewing requirements for the 'relief and recovery' of Iraq, prioritising these requirements and recommending allocations of US and Iraqi funds.[29] It met twice weekly and its voting membership consisted of a CPA chair; the Directors of CPA economic policy, civil affairs policy, operations and security policy; and the Director of USAID Iraq. Additional voting *ex officio* members included representatives of the Commander of Coalition Forces; the US Departments of the Treasury, Defence and State; the United Kingdom; Australia; the Chairman of the International Coordination Council; and the Iraqi Ministry of Finance. The PRB also involved the CPA Comptroller; CPA General Counsel; the Programme Coordinator of the Board; and representatives of the US Office of Management and Budget, the US Office of the Secretary of Defence, the IMF and the World Bank as non-voting members. The Special Representative for Iraq of the UN Secretary-General and a representative of the International Advisory and Monitoring Board (IAMB) — discussed later in this chapter — were permitted to attend as observers. Hence the total Iraqi voting membership was one US-appointed person from the Ministry of Finance. To underline who was in charge, approval for all funding plans had to be given by CPA Administrator Bremer.[30]

When the formal transfer of sovereignty occurred, the PRB and its PMO were replaced respectively by the Iraq Reconstruction and Management Office (IRMO) and its Project and Contracting Office (PCO). Although these bodies are located in the US Embassy in Baghdad (a Department of State entity), they reported primarily to the Pentagon and the Department of the Army until December 2005, when responsibilities were transferred to the State Department.[31] The IIG took responsibility for the allocation of Iraqi funds that had been controlled previously by the PMO and PRB. The IRMO and its PCO are directly responsible only for controlling US funds. The IRMO interacts with the Iraqi Government through the senior IRMO consultants assigned to each Iraqi ministry and weekly meetings held between the Iraqi Deputy Prime Minister and the IRMO Director.[32] The picture is complicated further because any allocation of US appropriations within Iraq is subject to approval by the Appropriations Committees of both the Senate and the House of Representatives.[33] This was the case with the IRMO recommendation in September 2004 which proposed a change in emphasis from basic services to the security sector and job creation.[34]

The IRMO is meant to coordinate the activities of at least twelve other US agencies, but the US Special Inspector General for Iraq Reconstruction (SIGIR), Stuart W. Bowen, Jr., whose job it is to provide oversight of US spending (previously as the CPA Inspector General), reported in April 2005 that this coordination was not being done in any systematic way. The lines of responsibility and organisational relationships were so unclear that the SIGIR was unable to identify them with confidence. He also noted that, while quantitative data were available on completed projects and outputs, what was lacking was evidence that each project was designed to achieve a strategic goal, or that completed projects had actually advanced US strategic goals.[35] This lack of clarity, coordination and strategy means that elements of the Iraqi state are being shaped by organisational and financial relationships which are pulling them away from the Iraqi centre rather than binding them to it.

US descriptions of this system as 'Iraqi led' ignore the fact that all of the Iraqis involved were initially Coalition appointees, and also ignore the subordinate role played by these appointees in decision-making during the period of formal occupation in particular. Larry Crandall, who served as Deputy Head of the US reconstruction programme until the June 2004 handover, explained:

I know it is still true that the reconstruction program out there has very little Iraqi participation. You hardly ever hear members of the Iraqi government talk about it, be it in terms of their support for it, their concern about it, their participation in it, and it's simply because they don't understand it very well. Therefore, they don't know what to say about it and they have very little opportunity to participate in it, because it's basically implemented through American contractors who have little, if any, contact with significant members of the Allawi administration out there or the previous interim government administration.[36]

Nevertheless, it is important not to see the involvement of Iraqis solely as window-dressing: their function is also to institutionalise the norms and policies of the US and global neoliberal governance into the Iraqi state. Iraqis are capable of dressing up in neoliberal talk the games of state subsidy, corruption and neopatrimonialism, adapted to the new circumstances. However, the forces determined to open up the Iraqi economy have pressed hard and have made substantial progress.

THE US-LED DRIVE TO OPEN UP THE IRAQI ECONOMY

US-led plans to open up the Iraqi economy have been aimed at transforming it and locking it into the US version of the neoliberal model, rather than getting it back on its feet for handing back to a popularly elected sovereign Iraqi government which could make its own choices about the economy's future direction. The CPA's initial economic focus was to end the Iraqi state's protectionism and domination of the economy. Bremer stated in September 2003 that subsidy elimination was 'much more important than privatization' because 'liberalizing prices is a necessary measure on the way to marketization'.[37] CPA-imposed cuts in subsidies for fertilisers and pesticides reinforced Iraq's dependency on food imports and aggravated unemployment and poverty.[38] As they did before the invasion, Iraqis receive a monthly 'food basket' of wheat flour, rice, vegetable ghee, pulses, sugar, tea, salt, milk, infant formula, weaning cereal, soap and detergent. The food rationing system costs about $5 billion per year — about 25% of Iraqi government revenue. It also undermines incentives for local food production, but the ration is the primary source of nutrition for 60% of the population, and 10% of the population need food supplies in addition to the ration. While there is consensus on the need to move away from a state-funded food rationing system, how to move away from it, what constitutes proper access to food for the poorer segments of society, and how or whether this can be ensured, are questions that have not been resolved.

Initial plans by the CPA to replace the food ration with cash payments by June 2004 proved unfeasible, due to concerns over the lack of a supportive private sector and the inadequate regulatory framework.[39] With regard to the fuel subsidy, many Iraqis are concerned that they might be hit hard by a reduction in it, and many believe that they are entitled to heavily subsidised fuel as citizens of an oil-rich country. As a result, the subsidy continues for the moment despite its cost and associated problems such as smuggling.

At the time of the invasion, Iraq had some 200 state-owned firms making a wide range of products. The state employed around half of Iraq's 6.5 million work force then, and now 500,000 state employees are still being paid even though the firms in which they worked are no longer operational and the Government estimates that its Ministries have 40% to 60% more employees than they need.[40] If alternative employment is not provided, any move to sack state employees could fuel the insurgency further. Since state employment also represents a large patronage asset, there is an additional barrier to reform. However, the Iraqi Government is under pressure to find a way forward: it points out that reductions in public spending are a requirement of its IMF debt reduction plans.

The CPA never produced a coherent or practical overall policy regarding state-owned enterprises.[41] The CPA announced plans to privatise around 150 enterprises such as those producing pharmaceuticals, tyres and fertiliser and those mining sulphur and phosphates.[42] However, these announcements did not go further, not least because many of these enterprises had been destroyed by looters, were completely inactive and showed little commercial potential. When the CPA found privatisation to be impractical, it devised a plan to lease 35 companies with an option to buy but with conditions requiring use of Iraqi labour and preventing fundamental switches in commodities produced.[43] The leases were to run for a minimum of 25 years.[44] MerchantBridge, a merchant banking firm with offices in London, Bahrain and Baghdad, was appointed lead adviser for the leasing programme.[45] The scheme collapsed for lack of commercial interest and the Iraqi Ministry of Industry and Materials withdrew the invitation to tender.[46]

There has been no consensus among US oil companies, US governmental institutions and Iraqi officials over how or even whether Iraqi oil should be privatised. Before the invasion, the State Department in consultation with the US oil industry and Iraqi exiles developed options for the Iraqi oil industry, all of which involved continuing Iraqi state ownership of the industry, at least for the first few years.[47] A much faster and more ambitious plan, outlined in a confidential 101-page US contracting document entitled *Moving the Iraqi Economy from Recovery to Sustainable Growth,* was drafted by the Treasury Department and US-AID.[48] This plan, supported by neoconservatives such as then Deputy Secretary of Defense Paul Wolfowitz (as well as by Fadhil Chalabi, cousin of Ahmad Chalabi and a former Iraqi Petroleum Ministry official), favoured mass privatisation of state-owned industries, including oil, to be carried out one year after the invasion, with US contractors carrying out the majority of the reforms.

One benefit the neoconservatives hoped for was that privatisation would weaken the political influence of the Organisation of Petroleum Exporting Countries (OPEC) and bring down oil prices if privatised Iraqi oil refused to cooperate with the OPEC production quotas which help sustain prices. However, the shareholders of US oil companies benefit from OPEC-promoted high oil prices and any potential gains from involvement in Iraqi privatisation have to be balanced by them against potential falls in oil prices from increased output. Philip Carroll, the former Chief Executive Officer (CEO) of Shell Oil USA appointed in May 2003 by the US Government to run Iraq's oil production, made it clear that he was not interested in carrying out the privatisation of Iraqi oil. This lack of US corporate interest, the insurgency and anticipated public opposition in Iraq and beyond meant that the idea of privatising Iraq's oil had to be rethought.[49] In September 2003, CPA Order 39 signalled acceptance of this by ruling against foreign ownership of Iraq's natural resources, including oil.[50]

Revenue from oil exports, which constitutes up to 95% of the Iraqi Government's income, has been insufficient to meet reconstruction needs or even cover government spending, with an anticipated budget shortfall of $5 billion for 2005.[51] In an effort to increase oil revenue, the Iraqi authorities and the Coalition are engaging in what they call a 'strategic partnership' between the Iraqi Government and private oil companies.[52] This is effectively privatisation by the back door, as transnational oil companies are being contracted to engage in the development, rehabilitation, production and distribution work that would previously have been done by the Iraqi national oil company.[53] One such contract was awarded on a no-bid basis to the Halliburton subsidiary Kellogg Brown and Root (KBR) even before the invasion took place.[54] Iraq signed contracts in May 2005 with Hydrocarbon Supply of Texas and Prokop of the Czech Republic to modernise and increase the capacity of the Doura plant, the third largest oil refining plant in Iraq, and has also announced its intention to construct a new oil refinery in Basra, a contract for which eight companies are competing.[55] Approximately thirty Memoranda of Understanding (MOUs) have been signed between Iraq and assorted foreign companies to engage in training of Iraqi staff, consulting and studies of oil fields.[56] As an indication of the fragmentation of political authority, the Norwegian company DNO is conducting oil exploration on the basis of a deal signed in July 2004 with the KRG without the agreement of the government in Baghdad.[57] In June 2005 the new Iraq Oil Minister, Ibrahim Muhammad Bahr al-'Ulum, announced that a committee would be formed to review multi-billion dollar oil contracts signed before 2003 with oil companies from China, France and Russia, including a $3.7 billion deal with Russia's Lukoil to develop the West Qurna oil field and a $1.3 billion contract with China's National Petroleum Company to develop the al-Ahdab oil field.[58] It is a distinct possibility that these contracts will be reallocated to US companies or US-led consortia to reflect the new political situation.

Although the existence of these contracts shows that the transnational privatisation of some aspects of Iraq's oil industry is not entirely new, the trend is accelerating.[59] Nevertheless, the limitations on corporate involvement in Iraq's economic transformation are significant. In addition to concerns over security, foreign companies have an incentive to wait until the form of Iraq's government has stabilised to avoid any international legal challenges and due to fear of a possible re-nationalisation of the oil industry similar to what occurred in Russia.[60] Instead, companies such as Shell have favoured production sharing agreements whereby Iraq signs a long-term contract with a company to manage production rather than permanently signing over development rights.[61] In the meantime, the US has played a major role in establishing a regulatory framework conducive to future privatisation by US and global capital.

By passing a raft of decrees and embodying them in many practices and networks, the CPA sought to set the parameters of choice for any sovereign Iraqi government, which would have the effect of advantaging those seeking office on the basis of working within rather than challenging the status quo. The aim was that new values would be internalised so as to avoid a perception that policies were being imposed by the US. In October 2003 Thomas Foley, director of private sector development for the CPA, said that the goal was to change Iraq's state-led economy into a 'fully thriving capitalist economy' characterised by low taxes, low import duties and access and high mobility for international investors. CPA Order Number 37 of September 2003 exempted from taxation the CPA, Coalition forces and Coalition contractors and sub-contractors and all organisations providing humanitarian assistance; suspended nearly all taxes for the remainder of 2003; and limited taxes on individuals and corporations to a maximum of 15% not just for 2004 but also for 'subsequent years'.[62] The flat tax was a policy which conservatives had failed to have adopted in the US but which they were able to institute in Iraq by decree.[63] CPA Order Number 38 imposed a 5% levy for 2004 and 2005 on non-humanitarian goods imported into Iraq, with all those organisations involved in the occupation and reconstruction again exempt.[64]

Simultaneously, CPA Order Number 39 permitted 100% foreign ownership of all businesses in Iraq except those engaged in extraction and initial processing of natural resources and those in the banking and insurance sectors, and allowed the transfer abroad of all profits.[65] It also ordered that, while foreign investors could be treated no less favourably than Iraqi investors, foreign investors could be favoured over Iraqi ones. CPA Order Number 40 permitted the opening of up to six foreign banks until the end of 2008 and decreed that there should be no limit to the number thereafter, thus indicating the presumption of a right to tie the hands of a 'sovereign' Iraqi government in 2009 and beyond.[66] It also permitted foreigners to have up to and including 50% ownership of Iraqi banks. The restrictions on the number of foreign banks permitted and on the degree of foreign ownership of Iraqi banks were summarily abolished completely in CPA Order Number 94 in June 2004, rushed through in the days before the formal transfer of sovereignty.[67]

The preambles to many of the CPA Orders on the economy portrayed the agenda of opening up Iraq's economy as one arrived at in a consensual and hence legitimate fashion. They asserted that these CPA Orders were consistent with UN SCR 1483 and UN Secretary-General Kofi Annan's report to the Security Council of 17 July 2003. They claim that they were produced in 'close consultation' and 'coordination' with the IGC and in coordination with the international financial institutions, notably the International Monetary Fund (IMF) and the World Bank. The CPA's transformative denationalisation agenda was indeed endorsed in the report by Annan.[68] That report referred to the need for 'transition from a centrally planned economy to a market economy'. It argued that Iraq needed 'a market-oriented environment that promotes integration with the global marketplace' as the only feasible route to sustainable economic growth in Iraq. It anticipated that 'Such a profound transformation of the economy will have far-reaching social implications' and that its success would require broad-based Iraqi involvement and political support.[69] There was a positive reference to weekly meetings held by the CPA with Iraqi business people, economists, government civil servants, bankers, political groups, the UNDP and international financial institutions, focused mainly on job creation, banking and foreign direct investment.[70] However, there is no indication that those Iraqis invited were given a significant decision-making role or included those who objected to the changes or the way they were being carried out.

Despite UN endorsement of the transition to a more open economy, the consensus claimed by the CPA did not exist. Hostility to those who might challenge the agenda being set was evident in the Coalition's treatment of Iraq's trade unions. Coalition forces raided the offices of the Iraqi Federation of Trade Unions and arrested some of its officials. The CPA endorsed the Ba'thist law from 1987 which banned unions from public enterprises, it did not consult them while drafting Iraq's new labour laws, and it cold-shouldered the Union of Unemployed in Iraq.[71] The IGC was also marginal in the processes of policy formulation, choice and implementation. Although all IGC members were US appointees, the moves towards privatisation and the investment decree were denounced by some of them.[72]

Further concerns about the CPA's privatisation programme came from within the US political and corporate circles more broadly. Jeffrey Sachs, who had been a key figure in Poland's crash post-Communist marketisation, described CPA plans for privatisation as 'reckless' because they would fuel the insurgency on account of their perceived illegitimacy, have a destructive effect on employment, and be illegal.[73] Potential buyers and investors have been worried about the legality of privatisation, especially in relation to the extent of changes occupying powers are allowed to make under the provisions of the 1907 Hague Regulations and the 1949 Geneva Conventions.[74] This concern was allayed substantially by the formal transfer of sovereignty to the IIG and subsequent elected Iraqi governments, as it could then be argued that earlier changes had been tacitly or explicitly endorsed by a sovereign government. Buyers and investors have also been concerned that a new Iraqi government might renationalise enterprises or challenge the deals made. Global capital was not persuaded that the new Iraqi state had been internationalised in the desired fashion with sufficient reliability.

In order to provide reassurance, the US Overseas Private Investment Corporation (OPIC) as well as the US Export-Import Bank underwrote US corporate activity in Iraq in relation to currency inconvertibility, expropriation and political violence, with the explicit aim of serving US foreign policy goals as well as US businesses and US citizens.[75] Although OPIC is a US federal agency, it provides its services at commercial rates, and is not subsidised by the US taxpayer. By July 2005, OPIC had committed over $144 million for seven projects in Iraq. This was dominated by a deal in which OPIC guaranteed $93 million of lending by Citigroup linked to a $23 million CPA grant and a further $15 million of separate bank lending from a syndicate of Citigroup, the Dallas-based global investment firm HBK and the Paris-based global lender BNP Paribas to Iraqi financial institutions, which in turn lend to small and medium-sized businesses operating in Iraq.

The overall picture of Iraq's activities through the state-owned Trade Bank of Iraq (TBI), established in November 2003, is distinctly globalised rather than US-centric.[76] Audited by Ernst & Young, the TBI had established $6.5 billion worth of letters of credit by September 2005, backed by cash from Iraq's oil sales. Because of the TBI's lack of capacity, they are issued on its behalf by an operating consortium of JP Morgan Chase, Standard Chartered Bank, Australia and New Zealand Bank, Bank Millennium SA and National Bank of Kuwait. They enable

Iraqi government ministries, state-owned enterprises and in rare cases the private sector to purchase goods and services abroad. 51% were with companies in Asian countries, 40% in Europe and only 6% in the Americas. In December 2003, the TBI managed to secure over $2.4 billion in export credit guarantees worldwide from over fifteen states, in which the governments of foreign countries promise to reimburse their companies should Iraq default on payments for goods received.[77] In addition, fifteen banks from Japan, France, Germany, Italy, the Netherlands, Portugal, Russia, Turkey, Canada, South Africa, India, South Korea, Japan, China and Singapore are 'participating banks' for the TBI to help it engage with export credit agencies worldwide and eventually secure credit. It secured its first line of trade-related credit not fully backed by cash in July 2005 — $150 million from OPIC and Citibank. This package is characteristic of the developing pattern of Iraq's capital relations — the US state and US capital setting the context of engagement, capital from other countries playing a major contributory role, and Iraqi institutions acting as executors of that essentially externally-derived but increasingly internalised set of priorities.

The more the Iraqi state internalises the neoliberal economic model that is a constituent element of US-led globalisation, the less necessary external impositions become to ensure that it operates the policies related to that model. The IIG endorsed the fundamental socio-economic approach required of it in its Letter of Intent and Memorandum of Economic and Financial Policies to the IMF in September 2004. This made it clear that its policies in 2004-5 would be aimed at public welfare, political and social stability and debt sustainability, to be achieved by means of a 'more market-oriented economy' so that Iraq could 'reintegrate into the world economy'.[78] It also fully endorsed the 'liberal and open' banking, trade, tax and foreign investment liberalisation measures decreed by the CPA, such as the very low flat rate 5% import levy and 15% flat rates of personal and corporate tax. Aside from potential progressive taxation in relation to increasing personal income tax allowances, all of the other taxation measures that the IIG indicated it was considering were forms of flat tax (such as a sales tax of 10%). This key document made reference to debt only in terms of achieving debt sustainability, and hence contained no challenge in principle to any of the debt.

The IIG anticipated (very over-optimistically) that plans for restructuring state-owned enterprises would be completed by the end of 2005 and in the meantime intended to continue subsidising them, although at what level was unclear.[79] While committed to monetisation of the food basket, it attached no timescale to the achievement of this objective.[80] The IIG prepared a draft interim national development strategy for discussion at a subsequent international donors' conference and in the Iraqi National Assembly, and Iraq was given observer status at the World Trade Organisation (WTO) in anticipation of full membership in due course.[81] The hollowness of any opposition within the IIG to neoliberal globalisation was displayed in this report of an interview with Ibrahim Bahr al-'Ulum, the Minister for Oil from September 2003 to June 2004:

[Bahr al-'Ulum] thought the policies of the interim government are similar to those the IMF would recommend, however he still rejected [IMF] conditionality because of the limitation on Iraq's freedom: 'We are Iraq! We were the cradle of civilisation and I don't want to see anyone controlling our economy by any means.'[82]

The defiance in this statement was wholly undermined by being combined with a commitment to following IMF policies. The agricultural sector provides a sharp illustration of the path being followed. No mention was made in the IIG's Letter of Intent of the deleterious effects on Iraqi agricultural production caused by Iraq's imports of agricultural products, such as some three million tonnes of wheat per year. Instead it asserted blandly that 'there appears to be a revival of agricultural activity'.

Fundamental attitudes to the relationship between the state and the economy formed a significant part of the negotiations over the new Iraqi constitution in the summer of 2005, in which Khalilzad — a former UNOCAL oil company risk analyst as well as being US Ambassador to Iraq and a PNAC member — played a major role.[83] Very little attention has been paid to this aspect of the negotiations. Most public and specialist attention was focused on disputes over federalism, the role of Islam in relation to law-making and regional control of oil income, with Kurds and Shi'i pushing through their preferences on these issues over the objections of Sunni Arab negotiators.[84] However, the Center for International Private Enterprise (CIPE), an affiliate of the US Chamber of Commerce with a major outreach programme to the private sector in Iraq, understands the stakes and has stated: 'the economic dimensions of constitutions are often overlooked, though extremely important'.[85]

During the negotiations on the constitution, CIPE interviewed Noah Feldman, New York University School of Law Professor, former CPA constitutional adviser and, as CIPE puts it, 'adviser to Iraqis involved in the constitutional process'. Feldman made clear the brute power realities and the need to obscure them:

Iraq is now in need of international assistance and the international institutions like the IMF or in the World Bank are in a position to impose certain conditions as a prerequisite for aid … From the point of view of the Iraqis, it would be better if they could come to that conclusion themselves. We've seen this throughout the world, that various decisions that the government needs to take tend to have more buy-in from the public if they're perceived as having been made domestically rather than imposed by the international organizations that control inflows of capital.[86]

Iraq needs capital, and Iraqi politicians need to sell to the Iraqi public the conditions being required of them as being ones they endorse voluntarily, and indeed they need to learn to endorse them voluntarily. Having quizzed Feldman on the likely constitutional outcome on social welfare provisions, employment rights and private property rights, land ownership and other investment rules, CIPE declared itself to be hopeful.

Nevertheless, Iraqi public support has not been secured for the programme of economic liberalisation, and so economic policy could be susceptible to radical revision if the state were to move out of the sphere of direct US influence. An opinion poll in Iraq in November-December 2004 by the International Republican Institute showed that 65% preferred a large role for the state in the economy and only 5% a smaller economic role for the state.[87] This was the only attempt made to assess Iraqi public opinion on this issue, and it indicated a fundamental rejection of what the US and US-backed Iraqi politicians were trying to do. This was underlined when respondents indicated their economic policy priorities in considering who to vote for in the January 2005 National Assembly elections. 30% said that the most important part of an entity's approach to the economy was increasing employment, followed by 27% for improved wages and salaries and 19% for improving the agriculture sector, 10% for increased benefits for pensioners, 10% for improving the industrial and oil sectors, 3% for increased subsidies for basic goods, 3% for increased benefits for the unemployed and 2% for promoting foreign investment.[88]

A poll conducted among business people in Baghdad, Irbil and Hilla by Zogby International at roughly the same time — between October and December 2004 — on behalf of CIPE showed strikingly contrasting results to the views of the general public, with little geographical, ethnic or religious variation.[89] 68% believed that the new laws and regulations being implemented would help their business and only 4% believed that they would hurt. Similarly, 86% of those surveyed believed that opening Iraq's economy internationally would improve their business, with 50% believing that it would improve it substantially and only 3% thinking it would hurt it. The IIG was seen as an effective mechanism for connecting Iraq to international trade by 47%, with only 14% thinking it was ineffective. Again, to some extent this is to be expected — the lifting of UN sanctions was generally going to be good for business — but there was no sense that Iraqi entrepreneurs felt that they were losing out to foreign capital. A substantial minority of business people felt the need for clearer and more easily available commerce laws and regulations and for more transparency in the award of government contracts, and most felt the need for more business laws and regulations as a bigger priority than more effective enforcement of existing ones.

Aside from insecurity, the factors seen to be inhibiting growth were lack of regulatory enforcement and business information, high taxation, poor communications, shortage of credit, unclear property rights and lack of international partners. Almost no-one saw shortages of raw materials or electricity as significant. 69% were optimistic about Iraq's economic future (only 10% were pessimistic). This optimism applied to anticipated growth rates, employment levels and government policy towards business. Sunni Arab business people shared in the general optimism, thus suggesting that they did not feel that the loss of what is usually represented as Sunni Arab political dominance would cost them in business terms: 44% felt that the business environment had improved for them since the fall of Saddam Hussein, as against 21% who felt that it had worsened. Considering the very low baseline, including the desperate state of the economy produced by the period of economic sanctions, repeated wars and Saddam Hussein's corruption and mismanagement, some optimism is not greatly surprising. What matters here is that Iraqi business people fairly uniformly anticipated that they would benefit from the opening up of the Iraqi economy.

Despite all its advantages, including preferential treatment for US-based transnationals, the US had by late 2004 not managed to establish itself as the natural ally of the Iraqi business class or promote a pro-US Iraqi political party attracting that class. In the Zogby International poll of business people, only 17% felt that the Coalition was the best partner for the IIG to provide security conducive to their business: 34%

preferred the help of the UN, 22% preferred doing without outside help and 13% felt that other Arab states would be of greatest assistance. Iraqi capital did not see the Coalition as its preferred partners or enforcers. Nor had the Coalition managed to assist the rise of a natural party of business in the centre and south. In the centre (Baghdad) 78% and in the south (Hilla) 55% did not think that any particular political party stood out as representing the views of business, or thought that no political party did so. The most support for any party was a mere 10% for al-Da'wa, with SCIRI next at 7%. The exception was in Irbil, where the PUK was endorsed by 57% and the KDP by 21%.

Nor were Iraqi business people focused on the US as the main source of their future business partners — instead, Arab countries and Europe dominated. Those in Baghdad mainly looked to the UAE (32%), Europe (12%), Lebanon and Jordan (both 11%) and only then the US (9%). Those in Hilla focused on the UAE (32%), followed by the US (21%), Lebanon (10%) and Europe (9%). Those in Irbil expected to expand their business links mostly with Europe (40%), then the UAE (20%), Lebanon (10%) and the US (8%). Turkey only scored 4%. Nearly all of the other countries mentioned were Middle Eastern (Jordan, Egypt, Saudi Arabia, Kuwait and Syria). Despite the Bush administration's claims of undue Iranian influence in Iraq, no Iraqi business people nominated Iran as a future partner, even in the South. This suggests that, despite concerns expressed by the US regarding talks between Iran and Iraq in mid-2005 on an oil export pipeline from Basra to the Iranian port of Abadan, the Iraqi business class is principally looking elsewhere.

The US is better placed in business terms than these opinion poll figures suggest. Business partners in the UAE could easily be regional offices of US-based transnational capital or UAE-US joint ventures. For example, Halliburton, KBR and Parsons have sub-offices in the UAE. Middle Eastern banks (including those of Israel) accounted for a mere 2.7% of global capital in 2003 and are therefore in no position to compete seriously with US-based finance houses such as Citigroup, which also has a sub-office in the UAE.[90] Furthermore, the extensive role of US finance in devising and implementing the reconstruction programmes from 2003 meant that US-based transnational corporations would be able to take the leading role in international involvement in the Iraqi economy.

THE LEADING ROLE OF US-BASED
TRANSNATIONAL CORPORATIONS

US-based transnational corporations are central actors in the shaping and implementation of economic programmes in Iraq, and the US Government has worked hard to ensure that that is the case. The Department of Commerce runs an Iraq Investment and Reconstruction Task Force to assist US-based companies seeking reconstruction and other contracts in Iraq.[91] In December 2003, the Pentagon issued an order signed by the then Deputy Secretary of Defence Paul Wolfowitz (who went on to become President of the World Bank in June 2005) which denied countries that had not been part of the Coalition the right to bid to become prime contractors in the award of US-funded contracts.[92] However, the order was rescinded in the summer of 2004 and never prevented Coalition prime contractors from using non-US and non-Coalition foreign subcontractors. According to the PCO website, the top layer of US-funded reconstruction management is 'ownership' by 'the people of the United States', a symbolic rather than operational status.[93] The next layer is the PCO with a support office provided by AECOM based in Los Angeles. The third layer involves sectoral programme management, in oil, public works and water, security and justice, transportation and communications, electricity, buildings, and education and health, each headed by a US citizen. The bottom layer involves the sectoral prime contractor or contractors, again with head offices often located in the US.[94] For example, the initial contractors for each sector included Parsons Delaware of California for buildings, education, health, security and justice; KBR of Texas for oil; a joint venture led by Contrack International of Virginia for transport; Lucent Technologies of New Jersey for communications; Washington Group International of Idaho for electricity and water; and Perini of Massachusetts for electricity. US corporate actors are so deeply involved with the process that they cannot be regarded as simply subordinate to US governmental ones - the PCO itself describes the system as a 'hybrid public-private model'.[95]

Out of 59 prime contracts awarded from US appropriations in the 2004 financial year up to November 2004, 48 went to US companies.[96] Several of the remaining eleven contracts were with firms in which US capital had a significant stake, including three with FluorAMEC, a US/UK joint venture, and one with ANHAM, a US/Jordanian joint venture. The remaining prime contracts were allocated to Italian, Israeli, Jordanian, Australian, British and Iraqi companies. Although Parsons operates in 46 US states, it also does business in 37 countries other than the US.[97] Contrack is more transnational in being 45% owned by Egypt-based Orascom Construction Industries, and the other leading companies in the transport joint venture were the Swiss-based firm Archirodon and American International Contractors.[98] Hence it can be seen that the degree to which US-based prime contractors have been transnational has varied widely, but the underlying pattern is one of US control.

US-led transnational capital emphasises its commitment to subcontracting to Iraqi firms and using Iraqi employees wherever possible, but the scale of that employment is small and it has been hierarchical in a way which tended to put Iraqis at the bottom. Parsons has on its team three British companies and a commitment to using at least 80% Iraqi labour, purchasing Iraqi materials and equipment where possible and training at least 400 Iraqis for professional and management positions. Its infrastructure project is headed by Bechtel of California, supported by Horne Engineering Services of Virginia and coordinated with US-AID. Bechtel, which oversees a $1.8 billion construction project, has an outreach programme to Iraqi subcontractors, with simplified documentation, presentations to Iraqi business associations and translation into Arabic of necessary documentation. It waives insurance requirements, advances interest-free capital and provides banking services and professional training (including a joint training programme with Baghdad University).[99] By August 2005, Bechtel had identified more than 1,000 qualified Iraqi contractors, had awarded 253 out of 393 subcontracts to Iraqi companies, and expected to employ more than 40,000 Iraqis. It also had registered on its supplier and contractor portal over 10,000 companies from 100 countries.[100]

Parsons drew attention to its $33.8 million Taji Military Base reconstruction project near Baghdad, which used 98% Iraqi labour (2,500 people).[101] This does not mean that 98% of those who worked on the project were Iraqi, as it takes more than labourers to deliver a construction project. In June 2005, Perini reported that 5% of its employees in Iraq (mainly in senior management positions) were from the US or Britain, 40% were third country nationals, and the remaining 55% were Iraqi (working as subcontractors or tradeworkers).[102] This still exaggerates the proportion of Iraqis on Perini's Iraq projects, as very few Iraqis were likely to have been among those working on those projects outside Iraq. There is a hierarchy of reconstruction employees with those from the global North (especially the US) at the top, then those from the global South, then Iraqis in terms of position held within the project and pay levels.[103]

According to the NGO Iraq Revenue Watch:

the CPA awarded U.S. firms 74 percent of the value of the total $1.5 billion in contracts paid from Iraqi funds. When British firms are added to the equation, U.S. and U.K. companies wind up receiving 85 percent of the value of contracts paid for from Iraqi funds.[104]

Owing to security problems, foreign contractors have withdrawn or grown more willing to sub-contract to Iraqi companies. As tasks such as mending roads obviously meant it could not be site based, 60% of Contrack's costs were on security alone, and it struggled to get raw materials as suppliers were warned off by insurgents. In the end Contrack withdrew from its $325 million contract, having received only $30 million in eight months, mainly for assessment and design work.[105] In response, the PCO decided to manage Contrack's eighteen subcontractors directly. In August 2005, the PCO reported having only 44,315 Iraqis working on projects funded by US appropriations.[106] 40% of new contracts issued in the first quarter of 2005 from all funding sources were awarded to Iraqi companies, employing about 158,000 Iraqis.[107] The US Government announced a policy of allowing Iraqi ministries 'with a proven track record' to award contracts funded by US appropriations, to lower security costs and 'lessen the expatriate footprint'.[108] However, the sums involved have been small, such as the $50 million allocated in February 2005 to the Housing and Construction Ministry.

If the US is to keep other states and non-US capital on board with a system in which the US is dominant, those others need to gain substantially from it. However, this has led to US corporations losing out in profitable sectors. Dan Amstutz, the senior US adviser to the Iraqi Ministry of Agriculture, had previously been an executive of the world's biggest grain exporter, the US company Cargill, as well as a US Department of Agriculture Undersecretary and the United States' chief negotiator in the Uruguay round of the General Agreement on Tariffs and Trade (GATT) negotiations on agriculture and other matters.[109] Despite Amstutz's role, in October 2004 Australian monopoly wheat exporter AWB secured a deal with the IIG to export one million tonnes of wheat to Iraq over the following six months. A further set of disagreements over price in the talks between the IIG and Cargill led to the Iraqi Government cancelling orders with Cargill and moving to AWB as its primary supplier.[110] Hence, despite the fact of the US military presence and the role of senior advisers, the United States has not always been able to privilege its own companies in contract negotiations.

The operation of the CPA more generally in the agriculture sector reflected a pattern of promoting US-led but still global capital. Seed saving and sale is routine for virtually every Iraqi farmer, but CPA Order Number 81 of April 2004 explicitly bans farmers from saving genetically modified seeds from one year to use the following year or selling them on without the patent holders' permission.[111] Iraqi farmers do not have to buy genetically modified seeds but the huge promotional resources of multinationals will mean that these are strongly placed to dominate the market. Monsanto, Syngenta, Bayer, Dow Chemical and others are being allowed to claim sole credit for developing 'new' varieties of plant, as if thousands of years of farmers' plant breeding (in Iraq among other countries) count for nothing.[112] The US is at the forefront of pressure worldwide for such patenting via the WTO, and promotes it within the framework of the Union for the Protection of New Plant Varieties in Geneva which has 48 member states.[113] Iraq's National Development Strategy in June 2005 referred to the importance of rebuilding Iraq's national seed gene bank (destroyed in the early days of the occupation by looters) and its national seed production, which suggested some resistance to domination by global capital in this area. However, it also noted that there was a shortage of seeds of all kinds, which meant that any initial revival of Iraqi agriculture would have to be based on imported seeds.[114] In this context, national self-reliance regarding seeds is limited to an aspiration and the underlying trend is towards a new reliance on the US-dominated global seed market.

The US-led drive to open up the Iraqi economy is being conducted in a way that gives it overall control of the process while engaging other international and transnational actors in a subordinate role and in a way that is generally impeding the emergence of a strong Iraqi state. This can be seen in more depth by an examination of the management of the three main categories of capital used in security and the economy — Iraqi revenue, US appropriations and other international funds.

LARGE AMOUNTS OF CAPITAL, LITTLE SPENT ON RECONSTRUCTION

Since the invasion and then the lifting of UN economic sanctions, Iraqi revenue has come in a number of forms — oil exports income (including leftover funds from the UN Oil For Food programme, raised by Iraqi oil exports in the period of sanctions), repatriated funds from previously frozen Iraqi accounts in at least ten countries or held by the Bank for International Settlements, taxes and income from state-owned enterprises.[115] These funds have generally been deposited in the Development Fund for Iraq (DFI) established by SCR 1483 in May 2003.[116] DFI funds had totalled $20.7 billion by the time of the formal handover of sovereignty, at which point, as required by SCR 1546, formal control of the fund shifted to the IIG.[117] However, funds are parcelled out to the Iraqi Central Bank by the Federal Reserve Bank of New York and contracts for which DFI funds had already been allocated were to continue to be managed by the US. On the latter point, delegation of this responsibility by the Minister of Finance to the US Mission was gradually extended to 31 December 2005, by which point almost all these funds had been spent.[118]

The name 'Development Fund for Iraq' has proven to be misleading. US Government auditors concluded that, of the $37.1 billion of Iraqi funds up to March 2005, '[o]nly a small portion was used for reconstruction': it was used mainly for wages, fuel subsidies, food rations and the other running costs of the government.[119] Furthermore, 5% of the revenue has also gone to the UN Compensation Fund in accordance with SCR 687 (1991) and SCR 1483 (2003) for those individuals, multilateral institutions, corporations and governments which were deemed by the United Nations to have incurred losses as a result of Iraq's invasion of Kuwait in 1991.

In violation of SCR 1483, the DFI has not been spent, as the resolution phrases it, 'in a transparent manner to meet the humanitarian needs of the Iraqi people'. In order to provide audit oversight of the DFI, SCR 1483 mandated the creation of the IAMB, with representatives from the UN, the World Bank, the IMF and the Arab Fund for Economic and Social Development and then additional representatives of the Iraqi Government. However, the CPA showed little interest in setting up a body which would audit its use of Iraqi money.[120] Eventually, international criticism led to the establishment of the IAMB in December 2003. Further CPA foot-dragging ensured that a full audit of DFI activity was not published until 15 July 2004, over a year after the DFI was established and two weeks after the CPA had been dissolved.[121] In other words, throughout its existence the CPA and its contractors had a free hand with Iraq's revenue and tended to spend these funds first, thus avoiding many of the procedures and controls that are meant to apply to spending of US funds.[122] The CPA also often used a mix of Iraqi and US funds, with Iraqi funds predominating. For example, $1.6 billion of the $2.5 billion paid to Halliburton for the Restore Iraq's Oil (RIO) contract came from DFI funds.[123] Such contracts have been investigated using US audit procedures, and we consider the RIO contract in more detail below.

Audits found increasing evidence that around half of Iraq's revenue was not being controlled properly by the US and Iraqi ministers. The first audit was conducted on behalf of the IAMB by the international accounting firm KPMG for the period up to the end of 2003. Oil production was not metered properly, so that it was not possible to know how much oil was produced and therefore how much had been stolen. The CPA and Iraqi ministries had failed to track Iraq's oil money to a degree that the IAMB could be confident that the money was being spent as intended, although it found no proof of fraud.[124] Decision-making was not transparent: PRB minutes were not a clear record of decisions and reasons for them, the PRB often took decisions when not quorate, and the relevant Iraqi official only attended two of the PRB's 43 meetings up to the end of 2003. There were many procedural irregularities in the contracting process, such as extremely short timescales for bids which undermined effective competition, lack of clear documentation of award of contracts on a non-competitive basis, frequent use of hand-written records, and award of funds to contractors without adequate monitoring of performance.[125]

The second KPMG audit for the first half of 2004 was much more damning — there were contracts with no public tenders, contracts with no records of bidding or of justification for sole-source supply, absence of evidence of goods or services being provided, use of funds for activities specifically prohibited by regulations, huge discrepancies in records and straightforward theft.[126] The sums involved were often in tens of millions of dollars. Around half of the $5 billion of DFI funds disbursed could not be accounted for adequately. In the most extreme case, $1.4 billion in cash was given in April 2004 by the CPA to the KRG in Irbil for humanitarian projects, but the KRG denied KPMG access to its accounting records. KPMG was unable to obtain any further information beyond being told that by the KRG that none of the money had been disbursed. It is possible that the money was spent eventually as it should have been, but there is no way of knowing. In June 2004 alone the CPA flew into Iraq the enormous sum of $2.4 billion in DFI cash to disburse in the weeks before the formal handover of sovereignty, with no indication that proper records were kept.[127] The SIGIR found that 'The CPA provided less than adequate controls for $8.8 billion' of DFI funds, an astonishing sum, nearly half the total.[128]

Matters did not improve with the transfer of formal sovereignty to the IIG, as was shown by the third KPMG audit, covering the second half of 2004.[129] Among payments totalling $1.9 billion in DFI funds, it found that contracts often worth tens of millions of dollars were award-

ed with insufficient justification for their non-competitive basis, fewer
than the required three bidders, insufficient monitoring, absence of
supporting documentation to show the provision of goods and services
(one case involved a contract worth $47 million), inaccurate record
keeping, no formal funding approval, and breaches of awarding procedures through insufficient notice time provided to bidders or insufficient advance notice provided to selected companies. Contracts were
awarded for proposals submitted after the due date, with insufficient
justification (including a contract managed by the Ministry of Electricity for $229 million), without any public tender or with no justification
provided for preferring a company which charged twice the lowest bid.
As with the previous audit, access was not granted to KPMG to view
the accounting records meant to be maintained by the KRG for receipt
of a further $798 million, despite that government's refusal to account
for the $1.4 billion it had received previously. Regarding $3 billion
in outstanding contract payments previously arranged by the CPA and
then to be managed by the ITG, KPMG discovered turnover of incomplete files and modification of contracts by US agency representatives
without authorisation from the ITG. Abuses of the DFI included the
funding of a $2 million contract entirely by that Fund, although, ac-
cording to the contract, 50% was to be covered from non-DFI funds;
the extension without justification of a contract granted on the 28 June
2004 with an increase in price from $22 million to $52 million, though
services only increased by 50%; and a $96 million contract awarded by
the US without bidding or awarding documentation, which was meant
to be paid for from US funds but was in the end financed from the
DFI.[130] In July 2005, the office of the SIGIR reported that, of the 69
contracts issued after 28 June 2004 that it reviewed, for 21 contracts
files could not be located by officials responsible and the remaining 48
contracts examined contained errors.[131]

In such lax circumstances, profiteering and other large-scale abuses
could and did flourish, and continue to do so.[132] For example, the

US-based company Custer Battles charged $20 million to provide se-
curity guards but subcontracted to an Iraqi Kurdish company for the
work and pocketed as profit the difference of approximately 95% of
the value of the contract.[133] In this case, US government auditors disputed two-thirds and withheld $5 million of the $20 million.[134] There
was no reason to believe that transfer of control of funds to the Iraqi
Government would improve matters, as what had been disappearing
into the pockets of US corporations could vanish into the pockets of
corrupt Iraqi officials and their domestic and foreign criminal allies, or
disappear in careless deals with fraudsters. Indeed, the abuses became
more extensive and flagrant. Four members of the IIG including Prime
Minister 'Allawi and Defence Minister Hazim al-Sha'lan were alleged
to have secretly diverted $500 million in cash from the Central Bank
in January 2005 and flown it to Lebanon to pay for armoured personnel carriers, tanks and Humvees made in Poland, the Czech Republic,
Turkey, Ukraine and the US. Muwafaq al-Rubiy'i, the Iraqi National
Security Adviser at the time, claimed to have been unaware of the deal
and stated: 'I am sorry to say that corruption here is worse now than
in the Saddam Hussein era'.[135] No evidence has been provided publicly
that the money was actually spent on weapons, or that any weapons
have been or will be delivered.

Iraq's Commission on Public Integrity, established at the time of the
formal transfer of sovereignty, has begun investigations of hundreds of
suspected cases of corruption, such as overcharging, awarding of contracts to relatives, kickbacks for award of contracts, and taking money
for facilities that are never built. Some of those being investigated include the former Labour and Transport ministers in 'Allawi's IIG as
well as provincial and city administrations, although counter-allegations
have been made that the investigations indicate bias by Shi'a officials
against Sunni Arabs and Kurds.[136] In June 2005, Deputy Parliament
Speaker Husayn al-Shahristani described corruption in the ITG as being
of 'disastrous proportions', with inspectors general who are meant to

be preventing criminal diversion of funds and goods participating in it.[137] The Iraqi Board of Supreme Audit reported in August 2005 that, in the first eight months after the formal transfer of sovereignty, half or more of $1.3 billion of Iraqi money spent on military procurement had been stolen or wasted on useless and vastly overpriced equipment. Throughout the period, twenty US officials worked in the Defence Ministry. Some Iraqi officials were charged, such as the US-appointed former ITG Minister of Defence Sha'lan who was in Jordan, but the money had gone. The auditors estimate that $500 million to $600 million more had disappeared from the Electricity, Transport, Interior and other ministries.[138]

There has been a tighter rein on US funds, but that has not prevented major scandals. The management of capital from US foreign aid appropriations — involving the control of around $30 billion for reconstruction and security assistance, excluding the many billions spent on US military operations — has given the US major advantages in its attempts to shape the Iraqi state towards US priorities, US-led capital and pro-US actors.[139] In April 2003 in the immediate aftermath of the invasion, the United States established the Iraq Relief and Reconstruction Fund (IRRF) with $2.48 billion for water, sanitation, food, electricity, education and the rule of law.[140] It had assumed that Iraqi oil revenues would pay for the reconstruction and that there would be no insurgency.[141] As these revenues materialised slowly and the insurgency materialised quickly, a second bill for $18.4 billion was passed in November 2004, intended for infrastructure reconstruction ($10.1 billion); security ($4.9 billion); and agriculture, training and government ($3.4 billion).[142] As of 28 December 2005, $15.2 billion (83%) of this sum had been obligated (that is, committed to particular projects) and $10.1 billion (54.9%) disbursed. Of the sum disbursed, $4.4 billion was spent on the security sector (including prisons and protection of facilities). $3.5 billion was officially spent on the electricity, oil, water, transport and construction sectors, but security accounts for between 16% and 22% of such civilian project costs.[143] As part of a very belated effort to reverse its failure to develop reliable Iraqi security forces, the US allocated a further $5.7 billion to a new Iraq Security Forces Fund (ISFF) in May 2005.[144] The Bush administration requested that Congress approve a separate $414 million for reconstruction and anti-terrorism, anti-narcotics and military training for 2006.[145] In sum, security spending in all its forms predominates and spending on substantial reconstruction projects using US appropriations has been relatively small.

The US Embassy described US appropriations as 'a gift … from the American people to the people of Iraq'.[146] However, the decision-makers on what to do with that gift have mostly been from the US, even after the formal transfer of sovereignty. Control had shifted from the Defence Department to the State Department through the US Embassy, while a number of other US agencies continued to be involved. Furthermore, the principal beneficiaries have been US-based multinational corporations. Despite the handover of the PCO to the State Department, the Pentagon continued to manage funds allocated through the military command structure and the $5.7 billion in the ISFF for training Iraqi security forces. US reconstruction efforts and the allocation of contracts and their management are overseen by the office of the SIGIR, which had its authority extended to continue ten months beyond the date of obligation of 80% of the IRRF.[147] SIGIR representatives also sit on the Iraq Inspectors General Council (IIGC) in Arlington, Virginia, and on the Iraq Accountability Working Group (IAWG) in Baghdad. There are no representatives from the Iraqi Government on these oversight bodies.

US auditors have uncovered extensive problems with the control of projects involving US appropriations alone and US appropriations combined with Iraqi funds, including the mismanagement by the PCO of 37 files for contracts worth $184 million and lack of sufficient oversight for a $293 million contract with the British-based Aegis Defence

Services corporation for reconstruction security.[148] Further ongoing investigations as of July 2005 included 49 into possible procurement fraud, theft, cost mischarging, product substitution, bribery, kickbacks, gratuities, bid rigging, conflicts of interest, public corruption, computer crime, embezzlement, and false claims.[149] The Pentagon has 149 US-funded and Iraq-related prime contracts worth $42.1 billion with 77 contractors. Most of the contract value — 52% — is with one company, Halliburton, and its subsidiary KBR, and according to the US Defence Contract Audit Agency (DCAA) this is the contractor with which there have been the greatest problems.[150]

The Logistics Civil Augmentation Program (LOGCAP) contract for troop support in Iraq was awarded without competitive bidding to KBR in November 2002.[151] The contract value, originally estimated at over $4 billion for Iraq alone, soon increased to over $8 billion, and could possibly reach $18 billion. When audited by the DCAA, KBR's LOGCAP contract was found to contain $813 million in questioned costs (that is, costs which an audit has shown are unreasonable on account of breaching contractual terms, not being incurred specifically for the contract, or representing excessive charges). Previously, the auditors had discovered that KBR had billed the Army $200 million for meals never served to soldiers in Iraq.[152] An additional $382 million in unsupported costs (that is, costs which were not supported by sufficient documentation to allow an audit to conclude whether or not they were reasonable) was also detected. KBR inflated estimates (its estimate for a Baghdad International Airport contract was $12.8 million when the US government estimated $1.9 million), charged excessively (for soft drinks, film rentals, tailoring services, laundry services, personnel and heavy equipment to a sum total of over $4 million) and issued duplicated bills (such as charging for freight costs worth over $2.6 million twice). According to the auditors, the Pentagon took a permissive attitude despite repeated warnings.[153]

Halliburton's five-year Restore Iraq's Oil (RIO) contract to rebuild Iraq's oil infrastructure and import fuel into Iraq was also awarded secretly and without competitive bidding in March 2003. Bunnatine Greenhouse, the Principal Assistant Responsible for Contracting with the Army Corps of Engineers, argued that a conflict of interest occurred when Halliburton employees were involved in the preparation of the RIO contract.[154] Moreover, in its examination of an $875 million contract for the provision of fuel, the DCAA found over $108 million in questioned costs and $1.3 million in unsupported costs.[155] This included $171 million spent on fuel imported from Kuwaiti and Turkish suppliers at a price that could not be justified.[156] As the RIO contract was paid for from a mix of Iraqi and US funds, the IAMB was entitled to relevant documentation to ensure that those Iraqi funds were being used transparently for the needs of the Iraqi people. $1.6 billion of Halliburton's total RIO fee of $2.5 billion came from Iraqi money in the DFI. However, at Halliburton's request, the Pentagon 'redacted' (censored) all references to questioned and unsupported costs, so that in December 2004 the chair of the IAMB reported himself unable to assess the scale of the problem.[157]

In January 2004, the RIO contract was replaced with a competitively bid RIO 2 contract for southern Iraq worth up to $1.2 billion.[158] RIO 2 was awarded to KBR for the southern part of Iraq despite all the problems with RIO 1, while the US-based Parsons Corp. and Worley Group Ltd from Australia were awarded an $800 million contract for the north of the country. With full auditing still to be carried out on RIO 2, US Air Force Major Mike Waggle, the contracting officer in charge of the contract, reported $436 million in cost overruns.[159]

All three contracts were issued using a system known as cost-plus, with a guaranteed percentage fee on top of costs. Halliburton receives a fee of up 3% of its LOGCAP costs and up to 7% of its RIO costs (including a guaranteed base fee 1% for LOGCAP and 2% for RIO of its costs). The fee associated with RIO 2 has not been made public.[160]

Cost-plus creates an incentive to inflate costs. Performance fees potentially work to counteract this in possibly rewarding cost efficiency, but that has not been how it has worked out. For LOGCAP the performance fee is 2% and for RIO it is 5%. The extent of performance fees awarded for specific tasks despite the overall poor performance is unclear, but they include $72 million in May 2005 from the US Army to Halliburton under LOGCAP.[161] Many other official US audits reached similar conclusions about problems with Halliburton and KBR, but the Bush administration, the Pentagon and the Department of the Army have shown only very limited willingness to penalise Halliburton or require it to improve its performance, and instead have given it the preferential treatment outlined above.[162]

Since only small amounts of international (by which we mean, in this context, non-Iraqi and non-US) reconstruction funding have been forthcoming, there has been little challenge to US influence by this route, even though institutional structures to allow for more influence have been put in place.[163] Regular international donors' conferences are held to try to raise funds and agree priorities based principally on the October 2003 UN-World Bank Needs Assessment which was produced with Iraqi involvement.[164] Over 60 countries and international organisations are represented at the Expanded Donor Committee meetings, of which 17 are granted member status and the right to attend the Donor Committee meetings by contributing at least $10 million.[165] By January 2006, not including US funds, $8 billion in grants and $5.5 billion in loans have been promised for 2004-2007. These pledges were mainly bilateral (especially from Japan), and also multilateral (from the World Bank, the IMF and the European Commission). Only $3.2 billion of this total of $13.5 billion had been disbursed by the end of 2005.[166] The wide gap between promises of funding and what is actually provided is typical of what happens at donor conferences, and this tendency to fail to deliver on promises was reinforced by scepticism about whether security and other problems could be overcome to ensure effective use of any funding. These grants and loans are supplemented by the International Reconstruction Fund Facility for Iraq (IRFFI), which is made up of the World Bank Iraq Trust Fund (focused on economic transition, governance, public sector reform, and poverty and safety net issues), and the UN Development Group Iraq Trust Fund (focused on basic services, infrastructure, capacity building, employment generation and community-level rehabilitation).

These bodies liaise with the Iraqi Strategic Review Board, the Ministry of Planning and Development Cooperation, and the CIC Assembly, which in turn liaise with bilateral contributors and the Ministry of Finance in relation to the national budget. All of these bodies liaise with recipients and executing agencies (UN agencies, international financial institutions, NGOs, ministries, governorates, municipalities, other elements of the public sector and the private sector) to allocate IRFFI funds in accordance with the priorities in the UN-WB Strategic Transitional Programmes (which were based on the Needs Assessment). This elephantine decision-making structure has been in prolonged labour and brought forth the tiniest of financial mice. As of January 2006, $1.33 billion had been deposited in the IRRFI, nearly all of which had been obligated on paper to various projects, but by the end of 2005 only $402 million had actually been spent.[167]

Despite the elaborate organisational arrangements put in place, there is no centralised tracking of IRRFI and other international funding or its coordination with Iraqi-funded and US-funded activities.[168] Furthermore, in July 2005 the IMF highlighted 'the fragmentation of Iraq's fiscal accounts' into the Iraqi government's official budget (with the northern governorates spending autonomously and providing only limited information to central government), US spending from the DFI, expenditure by international donors, and operations of oil-related state-owned enterprises (such as proceeds from domestic sales) which do not feature in the official budget.[169] In these circumstances, the 'sovereign' Iraqi state either is excluded from decision-making or participates in a subordinate or incoherent way. This is particularly the case with regard to Iraq's enormous debt obligations. Where the debt is concerned, for once, many actors other than the US are crucial, and the Iraqi state has been disciplined very effectively into acting as an enforcer of debt obligations upon the people of Iraq.

DISCIPLINED BY DEBT

While capital flows out of, as well as into, Iraq via the formal economy through being absorbed by foreign state and corporate actors for goods and services, it also flows out in relation to debts. In 2003, Iraq's combined multilateral and bilateral debt inherited from the Saddam Hussein era was estimated to be as much as $136 billion.[170] This figure did not take into account unpaid interest (which could have more than doubled the total) or reparations for damage related to the invasion of Kuwait in 1990, awarded by the UN Compensation Commission (UNCC).[171]

Also excluded from this figure were potential (although less substantiated) claims not considered by the UNCC. These involve a $97 billion claim by the Iranian government and up to $100 billion of claims by individual Iraqi-Jewish claimants from among the 600,000 who left, voluntarily or otherwise, following the establishment of the state of Israel in 1948.[172] The Iranian claim seeks compensation for the cost of non-military damage during the Iran-Iraq war and is based on an estimation of damage by the then UN Secretary-General, Javier Pérez de Cuellar, who visited Iran in 1990.[173] In May 2003 Annan informed Iran that it should seek compensation bilaterally, and in October 2004 the Iranian Foreign Minister Kamal Kharrazi stated that Iran would continue to seek reparations once an Iraqi government was elected. Kharrazi called upon the UN to assess the full damage due to the war and to formally identify Iraq as the aggressor in the conflict, highlighting the UN's failure to respond officially to Pérez de Cuellar's report.[174] The call for reparations was repeated in May 2005, and to the annoyance

of both the Sunni community in Iraq and many of the Shi'a population, some senior Iraqi Shi'a officials seemed to support Iranian claims
for compensation.[175] At a press conference in October 2003 the SCIRI
leader 'Abd al-'Aziz al-Hakim, then President of the IGC, sent a confused message when he stated: 'According to the U.N., Iran deserves
reparations. She must be satisfied. ... Whether we will pay or not is
something which we need to discuss further.'[176] In July 2005, Iraq's
Defence Minister Sa'dun al-Dulaymi publicly adopted the position that
Iraq was the aggressor state in the Iran-Iraq War and apologised for war
crimes committed by Iraq. During a visit to Iran, Dulaymi declared,
'I have come to Iran to ask forgiveness for what Saddam Hussein has
done'.[177] The significance of this episode for our central theme is that
key state officials are perceived by some not to be representing the
views and interests of Iraq to a foreign power, but the reverse. However, in response to these statements, Iran pledged $1 billion for Iraq's
reconstruction, mainly for infrastructural projects.[178]

Even when the Iraqi state acts coherently, it is not necessarily as
a representative of Iraqi interests. It functions to enforce compensation demands on Iraqi society for Iraq's invasion of Kuwait. The US
was a key player in the passage of UN SCRs requiring reparations and
the assessment via the UNCC of claims by individuals, governments,
international organisations and companies. The UNCC is a subsidiary
organ of the UN Security Council, and its membership mirrors that of
the Security Council.[179] Out of $354 billion in claims received by the
UNCC, $52 billion was awarded and as of June 2005, Iraq had paid
$19 billion.[180] The majority of the remaining $33 billion debt is owed
to Kuwait, which has filed over 24,000 claims.[181] In June 2005, the
ITG announced that it was keen to deal with outstanding claims bilaterally, arguing that the funding of reparations through oil revenue was
crippling the country's economy and resulting in unnecessary suffering
amongst the Iraqi population. Creditors (most notably Kuwait) insisted
on a continuation of the existing system, and the Iraqi Government did

not demur further.[182] Payments such as $8 million to Israeli farmers for fruit and flowers unpicked due to emergency restrictions on movement, and $15 million to Israeli hoteliers and travel firms rankle, partly because they are payments to Israel and also because payments which are seen as relatively frivolous are being made at a time of desperate need in Iraq.[183] Iraq has been allowed to make only very limited representations to the UNCC. Without an advocate in that forum, it has had to rely on the UN's auditors to protect its interests. Early audits highlighted comparatively minor overpayments, but the most damaging audit was published in December 2004, suggesting that $2.2 billion was overpaid through claims being calculated on the basis of inaccurate exchange rates and concluding that a further $1.27 billion would be overpaid if changes in procedures were not made.[184] The chances of repayment are slim. In the end, the Iraqi state is the executor of the will of other actors in relation to war compensation, and essentially the same is true of the rest of its debt burden.

The Iraqi state's approach to its debt burden is based on acceptance that the key criterion is sustainability, that is, an assessment of how much of a reduction is necessary to ensure that Iraq can generate the maximum return for its creditors. Rhetoric about the immorality of making Iraqis pay Saddam Hussein's debts is deployed occasionally by the Iraqi Government, but the payments are made nevertheless. Generally speaking, Iraq's debt is to governments, either for money loaned by them directly to Iraq or for sums paid out by those governments to their companies in export credit guarantees (where the government stepped in for Iraq refusing to pay its bills), though some of it is to companies and multilateral institutions.[185] In September 2004, Iraq paid arrears to the IMF of $81 million in order to trigger approval by the IMF of a loan of $436 million in emergency 'post-conflict assistance'. The purpose of the loan was to improve Iraq's fiscal administrative capacity, with the explicit expectation that the increased capacity would be directed towards preparing Iraq for debt management and marketisation.[186] In other words, the Iraqi state has borrowed money which it is going to use to reshape itself into the mould desired by the IMF, so that it can repay that and other money, and borrow more.

Securing the loan was instrumental in the November 2004 decision by the Paris Club of creditor states to write off up to 80% of Iraq's debt to them in three stages by 2008 — a total debt cancellation of $30 billion, leaving $7.4 billion to pay over the next twenty-three years.[187] An immediate 30% reduction was made by the Paris Club with a planned further 30% reduction once the IMF approved a stand-by arrangement for credit, a final 20% reduction after the stand-by arrangement had been in operation for three years, and efforts by the Iraqi Government to secure an equivalent deal with other creditors. The huge debt cancellation by the Paris Club was surpassed in percentage but not absolute terms by the US, which in December 2004 cancelled 100% of the debt owed to it by Iraq — a total of $4 billion.[188] Assuming that all stages of the debt reduction go ahead as planned and no new borrowing is taken on, the IMF anticipates that Iraq's debt will be $34 billion in 2010, after which it is expected to commence paying interest and repaying principal.[189] In fact, Iraq is securing new credit from other institutions such as the Islamic Development Bank, which agreed to lend Iraq $500 million for infrastructural and humanitarian projects.[190] According to the IMF, Iraq's debt is 'unsustainable' without the implementation of all of the stages of the Paris Club plan, including a matching 80% reduction in Iraq's debt to other creditors.[191]

The US regularly urges Iraq's creditors to at least match the Paris Club's terms and preferably cancel Iraq's debt.[192] In June 2004, the 56 member states of the Organisation of the Islamic Conference (OIC) endorsed this view.[193] OIC member Jordan said it would offer full support to 'rebuild Iraq's national institutions and ease its debt burden', but a year later had failed to offer a firm commitment to cancel the $1.3 billion debt owed to it by Iraq.[194] Kuwait, Saudi Arabia, Qatar and the UAE are owed a total of around $51 billion: also OIC members, they have been reluctant to make any debt relief concessions.[195] However, international pressure increased through 2005. The Iraq International Conference (hosted by the US and the EU in June 2005) reiterated the call for debt reductions in line with those of the Paris Club.[196] Immediately afterwards, Saudi Arabia (owed around $28 billion) promised $1 billion in reconstruction assistance and declared itself willing to consider debt reduction, though without making any specific concessions.[197] With the Paris Club deal in place, a crucial factor (in addition to oil prices) in Iraq achieving debt sustainability will be the attitude of the big creditor states in the Arab world. Iraq can exercise only very limited influence on this outcome. Other states with relatively small amounts owed to them have adopted a mix of positions on the cancellation of debt, with a general trend towards concessions. For example, Romania, which had been insisting on payment in full, agreed in August 2005 to cancel 80% of the $2.5 billion owed to it.[198]

The IMF reported that 'there was a considerable convergence of views on many issues' between itself and the ITG: the discipline of debt is operating to inculcate in the Iraqi state aspects of the attitude required of it, even while corruption and fragmentation run rampant.[199] The economic problems facing Iraq tie it ever more strongly to the dollar-dominated international financial system, as Iraq must satisfy the demands placed upon it to deal with its budget deficit and enormous debt. The dollarisation of the Iraqi domestic economy is, according to the IMF, 'extensive', partly as a legacy of the sanctions era but also because of the policy followed by the US and others of making payments to contractors in Iraq in cash and in dollars rather than dinars.[200] The US government and US-led institutions, most obviously the IMF and the World Bank, set the international financial rules, while other actors such as Iraq's Arab creditor states take very important decisions within them. Weaker actors, including the Government of Iraq, sovereign or not, have to abide by those rules in order to participate in the global economy, and have major incentives to internalise those rules as their own 'natural' preferred mode of operation, with that mode appearing to provide the only parameters for effective policy choice.

CONCLUSION – GLOBALISATION AND THE TRANSFORMATION OF THE IRAQI STATE

Far from accumulating capital and concentrating it in its hands in order to build a strong state, Iraq's fragmented state is haemorrhaging capital while being reshaped by US-led globalisation. The informal economy, corruption in government ministries, lax controls over contractors, preferential treatment for US-based transnationals, the insurgency, compensation and debt are combining in crippling fashion. In the three years and more since the invasion, little has been spent on actual economic reconstruction, and insurgents are often able to destroy what does not fall apart through lack of maintenance. According to the IMF, the US managed to disburse only $2.2 billion in US funds for Iraq-related civilian projects in 2004. Only two-thirds of this was spent in Iraq, and up to half was spent on security.[201] This works out at only $0.7 billion of US appropriations spent on civilian programmes inside Iraq in that year — about $28 per person. As of January 2006, out of $2.1 billion allocated by the US to the water and sanitation sector for that purpose, only $688 million had been disbursed and $52 million worth of those projects were not operating as intended.[202] While a great deal of information is available on money spent and projects completed, there is very little data gathering on the impact of those projects, and the evidence that is available is not very positive. Furthermore, according to James Jeffrey, a senior State Department adviser on Iraq, 'We have scaled back our projects in many areas … We do not have the money', and US appropriations are being redirected away from reconstruction towards running facilities that the Iraqi Government can no longer afford to fund.[203]

In the meantime, where it has not been hijacked by the informal economy, waste, neopatrimonialism and corruption, what little central capacity exists in the Iraqi state has sought to adapt itself to the external demands being made upon it. Indeed, Iraq is becoming an integral and subordinate part of the internationalisation and transnationalisation of states within US-led global governance. In this sense, the Iraqi state is not representing Iraq in a globalising world: it is representing the globalising world in Iraq. It is not that there is an Iraqi government that somehow stands outside globalising forces which act as limitations upon that government's actions. Instead, globalising forces have largely shaped the preferences of the Iraqi Government, its mode of assessing the methods to realise those preferences, its mechanisms for implementing those methods, its choices of which preferences to prioritise, and its ways of assessing whether those preferences have been realised. These forces do not simply remain by permission of the Iraqi Government, but are, with varying degrees of success, embedding themselves into and reshaping Iraq's state, society and economy.

The fact that the US physically occupied Iraq, installed a government and passed substantial amounts of economic legislation by decree might suggest almost total US dominance over broader globalising forces, and thus that the Iraqi state is almost solely an instrument of US interests. Certainly, Iraq's globalisation from above is not primarily decentred in terms of the actors involved or the interests served: US actors and interests have been at the forefront. However, the actions of US actors have tended to advantage US political power and the US-based fraction of capital less than the fact of occupation would suggest: actions by the US are not necessarily actions narrowly on behalf of the US. Furthermore, this advantage has declined over time. The US has experienced considerable tension between trying to retain freedom of manoeuvre through retaining control over decision-making and seeking to consolidate its position through the establishment of effective co-opted Iraqi decision-making and the involvement of other international and transnational actors. It has sought to square this circle by a gradual shift to emphasis on the second approach, dangling the prospect of more access to contracting and subcontracting in the hope of attracting more political and military support, and permitting Iraqis more decisions over the allocation of Iraqi resources. Other states have positioned themselves to maximise their corporate penetration of Iraq and the debt and compensation repayments to them, while letting the US bear the costs of facing the insurgency.

The workings of the transborder informal economy — globalisation from below — reinforce the decentred aspects of globalisation in Iraq, and this globalisation from below demonstrates that actors in Iraq are not solely the passive objects of globalisation from above, even if they are mostly on the receiving end of events. Many but not all of the activities of this informal economy are closely related to the insurgency. Capital is in the business of protecting and extending profit, and more profit could be made if Iraq resembled the prosperous industrial global North rather than the marginalised, impoverished and policed global South. However, capital does not act as a whole, but in particular fractions such as companies, states, multilateral institutions and entities within them, and the outcome thus far of their actions and interactions with the insurgency is that most of Iraq is firmly at the bottom of the heap along with the rest of the global South.

The globalisation of Iraq from above and from below is proceeding in a highly dynamic fashion, due to, and resulting in, a considerable level of unpredictability. For example, the US has been forced to change its plans for Iraq repeatedly, and international actors such as the UN, World Bank and IMF have been forced to operate mostly at arm's length from outside Iraqi territory. The interaction of all these forces is generating sometimes competing and sometimes mutually reinforcing effects, and those effects are highly contingent. Further major changes of direction and reversals are easy to imagine as the contest over Iraq is played out.

6

CONCLUSION – THE OCCUPATION AND ITS LEGACY

The project to transform Iraq from an impoverished dictatorship to a prosperous, functioning, multi-ethnic liberal democracy with an open economy that would act as an ally of the US and a role model for the other states of the Arab Middle East, has been an extremely ambitious one. That project has run into profound difficulties not simply because of mistakes and the commitment of insufficient resources to the task, although there have been mistakes and shortages of human, material and financial resources. Our central argument is that the US has subordinated or distorted the state building process to its attempts to shape its outcome in the particular direction it desired, so that what is being formed is a fragmented state rather than a coherent one. There is fundamental doubt over whether most Iraqis would ever have accepted US control of the construction of a post-Ba'th state. Many commentators have observed that there seemed to be a window of goodwill for the US presence in Iraq that lasted only a few months. Our review of the opinion poll evidence shows that there was a great deal of suspicion amongst Iraqi Arabs from the outset, and the mere fact, and the conduct, of the occupation rapidly turned the suspicion to hostility among most of them. The dominant view among Kurds and Shi'i has been satisfaction at seeing the removal of Saddam Hussein but opposition to the continuation of a substantial US presence after-

260

wards, while there has been strong disapproval of that presence from most Sunni Arabs, largely untempered by any approval of the original ousting of the Ba'th regime.

At first Washington expected to be able to transfer power quickly to the exiles it had cultivated before the invasion to transform Iraq in the desired direction. When it became clear that those exiles lacked support within Iraqi society or the ability to develop it, the US was faced with a fateful choice. It could have decided to go ahead with a rapid transfer of power anyway, leaving the precise dimensions of that process to Iraqis to decide, without any clear indication of who would be likely to take control or in which political direction they would take Iraq. After the ravages of multiple wars, economic sanctions and Saddam Hussein's distortion of the institutions of the state, Iraqis would certainly have had a major task on their hands to rebuild their state. Furthermore, as the steps by which Iraqis could take control of state building were so fraught with potential dispute, such a choice could have turned out disastrously. However, such an outcome was not inevitable and the risk of it was not the reason for that path rejected being by the US. Instead, the US decided to try to carry out the state building process itself over an extended period, in order to lock in its preferred outcome. This was presented in terms of Iraqis not being ready to take over. However, we have documented extensively actions by the US — such as appointing local leaders who were independent of its appointees in Baghdad — geared towards containing Iraqi political energies and incentives, and diverting them from generating a national political process that might challenge US priorities. When direct US control also became unsustainable, the US was forced to transfer formal sovereignty in June 2004 to actors, and a national political process, that were increasingly beyond its ability to direct. Since relinquishing formal sovereignty, it has still sought, with rather variable but generally limited success, to play a guiding role in all spheres from counter-insurgency to local government to the economy.

Our goal in this concluding Chapter is to provide a thematic analysis of the legacy of the occupation for the Iraqi state. The central framing by the US and UK governments, as well as by the supporters of their overall strategy in Iraq, has been democratisation. This is envisaged as a struggle to create a democratic and constitutionally bound government which achieves legitimacy primarily through popular elections. Within this framing, opponents of the official political process are portrayed as anti-democratic.[1] Those who envisage Iraq's transformation in this way assume that the elections that have taken place have changed the relationship of the people to the state in a decisive way. However, in terms of what a state can actually do to impact upon the lives of its citizens, the form of government matters only insofar as there are state institutions for a government to act through. Popular self-rule can only take place through governing institutions, which are created through the process of state building. For the Coalition and its supporters, state building in Iraq is heading in basically the right direction, with the US playing a necessary role in gradually developing the capacities of the Iraqi state, though progress has been slower than anticipated (and potentially reversible).[2] In contrast, we argue that the state building process has been fundamentally flawed and is causing the formation of a fragmented state. Many of the occupation's critics have concluded that Iraq is already a failed or collapsed state. For example, Juan Cole argued in May 2005 that 'Iraq is a failed state' because the US military does not control the capital.[3] As we explain further below, we provide a multi-themed analysis of the Iraqi state focused on the notion of fragmentation rather than that of failure.

A THEMATIC ANALYSIS OF THE LEGACY
OF THE OCCUPATION

The legacy of the occupation for the Iraqi state can usefully be understood in relation to the following five themes: functional scope, institutional capacity, domestic and international autonomy, state identity and coherence. We discussed these briefly in Chapter One and drew on them in the subsequent Chapters. Here we elaborate upon them and then use them to draw conclusions about the nature of the Iraqi state.

By scope, we mean the range of functions that the state is formally committed to carrying out such as defence, law and order, poverty reduction, macroeconomic management, public health, education, environmental protection, utility and business regulation, redistributive pensions, family allowances and unemployment insurance, operation of nationalised industries and redistribution of wealth. States vary widely in the scope of functions they take on, from minimalist ones in which, for example, economic activity is primarily private and deregulated to maximalist ones in which economic activity is carried out mainly by the state.[4] Where the state, either through choice or through incapacity, does not ensure the fulfilment of the basic needs of its population, for such things as food, health and physical security, it is a failed state. To label such a state a failed state is to emphasise that it is failing its population. State failure encompasses phenomena such as civil war and famine, and may be confined to particular sectors of the state's social welfare activities or apply across the range of functions. In so far as the notion is used in portrayals of state failure as deriving from internal causes alone, neglecting serious consideration of external factors including those emanating from the West and the patterns of world politics more generally, it is usually an ideological one justifying Western and overtly imperial intervention.[5] State failure is, in the modern world, inextricably bound up with international and transnational factors.

The second dimension of the state is its capacity, which we define as the ability of state institutions to formulate and enforce policy. The functional account of failure is therefore distinct from the extreme case of weak institutions, which is that of state collapse, when there is no meaningful institutional capacity.[6] As we conceive it, strength, weakness or even collapse may be measured against the capacity of particular institutions or across the range of the state's activities. A strong state is one with effective capacity across its key institutions. In our terms, it is possible to have a strong state that is also a failed state — that is, one with effective institutions which do not serve the needs of its population.[7] Such a state might act capably to preserve the ruling regime by repressing its citizens while extracting natural resources and fighting wars with its neighbours.

The third dimension is that of the state's autonomy, which subdivides into the domestic and the international. A state has domestic autonomy when it can act without institutionalised negotiation with its society.[8] This often happens when the state's power comes from outside that society, either from natural resource wealth or from external sponsorship. Indeed, domestic autonomy may be made possible by international dependence (as when the ruling elite remains in place only with the support of foreign troops), internationalisation (when the state's functions are integrated into those of other states) or transnationalisation (when the state's functions are integrated into those of non-state actors such as international organisations, business corporations or criminal networks). A state that is wholly autonomous from society can be said to be external to it, and in such circumstances may become predatory upon society owing to the lack of domestic constraints upon it.

The fourth dimension, state identity, derives from the nature of the state as a conceptual abstraction or fiction that is accepted by both rulers and ruled.[9] Taking the state as a site of authority, institutionally represented by but not identical with a set of rulers (the government), state identity is measured by the extent to which the state's authority is accepted by those who act through it or are acted upon by it. If a party, a sect, a private corporation, an international institution or another state actor successfully persuades followers to accept that it rather than the existing state has political authority within a particular territory, this is evidence of weak state identity. As state identity is an ideational construct, it can exist even if a state is failing to function in relation to the welfare of its population, if the institutions of the state have collapsed, if the state is external to society and dependent on another state, or if political authority has fragmented. However, such conditions could undermine state identity in the perceptions of the ruled. They may reject the notion of the state as such as the locus of political authority, or they may transfer their allegiance to a neighbouring state or a new state based on part of the territory of the previous one.

The fifth dimension is that of state coherence, that is, the degree to which state institutions have recognised spheres of authority, and, in cases of overlapping spheres of authority between different institutions, there are agreed procedures for resolving differences in a predictable and orderly way. The US — often held up as a model of a state with competing bureaucracies, each with its own interests and approaches[10] — has a high degree of coherence, as there are entrenched constitutional procedures for establishing the role of each institution, so that the outcomes of disputes between them are usually clear. In cases where it remains persistently unclear which state institutions have authority in particular spheres, with each claiming to act in the name of the state but in conflicting ways, one can speak of a fragmented state. Typical cases of fragmentation would be where local and national governments or different government ministries each assert that they hold legitimate authority in a particular sphere, and there are no procedures that each accepts for resolving the dispute. The result is often a protracted struggle with each state institution seeking to assert its power against the other, and perhaps sending its personnel to carry out functions that other institutions claim as their responsibility. Each of these institutions can itself have a high degree of capacity, and to some extent be successful in distributing benefits to the population, so that a fragmented state is not necessarily a failed state and is not a collapsed state.

The set of concepts laid out above provides us with the tools necessary for assessing the legacy of the occupation. When the US invaded

Iraq, the scope of state functions there was very extensive, and one of the central goals of the occupation has been to reduce the scope of those state functions, particularly with regard to state ownership of industry. The Iraqi state is formally committed to reducing its scope, but doing that in any managed way has proved very difficult. For example, the state's ownership of its nearly inoperative industries continues. The domestic externality of the Iraqi state from most of society is indicated by the opinion poll evidence, reviewed in Chapter Five, which shows strong societal opposition (outside the business elite) to such a reduction in the state's scope.

Besides seeking such a reduction, the US has sought to increase the state's institutional capacity, as have international organisations and transnational corporations. There is a widespread perception in the US and Iraqi Governments that they are faced with a conundrum: economic reconstruction is not possible without security, but security is not possible without economic reconstruction. In other words, the institutional capacity of the state in these two functional sectors is seen as highly interdependent. The two Governments' response to this perceived conundrum has been twofold. They sometimes try to create virtuous circles of small gains in either sector, providing an opportunity for small gains in the other sector which then feed back into the first; this has had very limited success. In addition, they have prioritised the pursuit of security through coercion, even at severe cost to economic reconstruction. However, the problem is essentially political: as long as state building is in the hands of US-sponsored actors and as long as the Iraqi Government remains unresponsive to the majority of the population on many issues, and to the views of Sunni Arabs in particular, insecurity will be rife and economic reconstruction hobbled. These problems cannot be resolved by military offensives, technocratic reconstruction projects or the political procedures of elections and referendums.

The PCO has mapped out five levels of capacity development — policy, law and regulations, public and private inter-organizational systems, Iraqi ministry systems, and infrastructure at the plant or facility level.[11] It also manages a database to track the extent to which contractors are meeting commitments to capacity building. In terms of capacity focusing on meeting the basic needs of the population, we have shown that this is low but not negligible, with much variability both regionally and sectorally. A US State Department report in January 2006 described the situation in al-Anbar province as 'critical', with a non-functioning form of government and a security situation marked by high levels of insurgent activity, and six other provinces, including Baghdad and Basra, as 'serious', with the government incapable of addressing needs or preventing routine insurgency activity. It also found that governance was functional, albeit with areas of concern, in eight governorates and was fully functional in the three governorates that make up the KAR.[12] However, within each region there was little consistency between the effectiveness of institutions in different sectors. For example, Basra governorate has had a moderate level of electricity provision for most of the period since 2003, coupled with a high level of physical insecurity.

Families across Iraq still receive a monthly ration and highly subsidised fuel, but chronic malnutrition occurs among a large minority of the population and there are difficulties in acquiring the subsidised fuel. Educational and health centres have kept running throughout Iraq, although the endemic violence in some regions, particularly manifest in the rate of kidnappings, has meant that significant numbers of people have great difficulty in accessing these services. Finally, the wages paid by state institutions constitute a major source of income for Iraqi society. In short, it is an exaggeration to label Iraq as a failed state, although in some of its institutions, and in some areas of the country, it is failing.

Iraq cannot be called a collapsed state, because its institutions have been revived to some extent, even if some are still highly fragile. As well as those institutions which are managing to address in part some of the basic needs of the Iraqi population (such as providing food rations), other bureaucracies such as those of the Ministries of Finance and Foreign Affairs have been operating, especially since 2004. They have done so primarily under foreign guidance, especially that of the US but also that of organisations such as the IMF. The capacity of state institutions has been extensively hijacked through corruption and the informal economy, but some of the bureaucracy broadly operates as it should.

Even those institutions that are not providing substantive benefits for much of the population — and indeed sometimes inflict hardship on them — have demonstrated significant capacity. Here, the police forces throughout much of Iraq offer an illustration. Mass resignations from the police force and army have occurred frequently in particular places, notably in disputes over pay and US-led counter-insurgency operations. Furthermore, the police have been shown to be often corrupt and brutal. Police forces have been a regular site of confrontation between opposing political groupings. As a local prize, they have sometimes been as important as mayoral offices, if not more so. However, with only a few exceptions, police forces have not disintegrated as a result of that competition: in fact, they have been a site of contestation precisely because they are fairly well resourced, in terms of money and weapons. Often they have not succeeded in assuring people of their physical security or in curtailing criminality, but in general political groupings have not sought to gain control of police stations for those purposes. Instead, police forces can be considered strong institutions of the Iraqi state because they have been a primary mechanism for political groupings to augment their local power, to impose a particular version of social morality upon the population, and to secure funds and weapons for supporters. If the institutions of the Iraqi state had collapsed, political actors would not have sought to achieve these purposes through taking over state institutions, but clearly they have done so.

Nevertheless, even with the control of the police across southern and central Iraq residing in the hands of one party, the Interior Ministry could not transmit its authority to the local level, and political parties have not sought to attain local power only through the institutions of the state, at either local or national level. This point can be generalised: although the institutions have not collapsed, they have not functioned in a unified way or without non-state challengers to their authority that have often predominated in particular regions. Therefore, whilst state institutions have re-established substantial capacity, they have not been decisively strong in general. These are points which relate to fragmentation and state identity respectively, to which we will now turn.

A consistent theme in our account of the Iraqi state has been the extent to which parties and other political actors have captured and operated through state institutions, and have used those institutions for particularist gains. Furthermore, there has been no reliable way of resolving disputes between those institutions. For example, the de-Ba'thification Commission has sought to exclude actors from the political realm and state institutions, and has at various times been opposed by other state institutions — the Prime Minister's office, the Interior and Justice Ministries and the Electoral Commission — in those attempts. Its successes or failures have not been due to its place within the constitutional order, but to its ability to marshal political forces from inside and outside Iraq for its causes, and its willingness to face down its opponents. The Justice and Interior Ministries and the Electricity and Oil Ministries have been locked into a series of disputes with each other that have at times paralysed or thwarted their work, again with no rational or predictable mechanism of resolution. This has been in part the result of Coalition strategies of attempting to balance competing Iraqi political parties against each other, to prevent any one grouping from becoming dominant internally and thus able to dispense with coordination with Coalition actors. Furthermore, foreign contractors have had an extensive role in managing large spheres of Iraq's infrastructure, economy and security, and they have acted in a highly unclear regulatory environment and with little oversight from the institutions of the Iraqi state. This has meant that coordination has often been poor, and the two sets of agencies — official and corporate — have undertaken projects in the same areas amidst high degrees of uncertainty over which agency has ultimate decision-making authority.

In addition to this sectoral fragmentation, there has been geographical fragmentation, not into neat parcels of Sunni Arab, Shi'a and Kurdish areas, but instead in cross-cutting, interpenetrated ways. Neighbourhoods, towns, governorates and regions have all asserted primacy as state actors, often adopting a discourse of decentralisation or federalisation to justify their power, but actually securing it through extra-constitutional mechanisms. Within individual political parties, the limitations of centralised control have been shown with examples of the way party officials in Basra and Karbala' implemented policy that served local interests but was against the decisions of their party's central officials. Iraq, in this respect, has demonstrated strong centrifugal tendencies. These tendencies come principally not from sectarian loyalties among the general population, but from the political and economic benefits available to officials and elites at the local level, whose access to such benefits would be disrupted by the intrusion of the central state.

We have also argued that there have been strong challenges to the state, not just from those who seek to overturn the form of governance in place since 2003, but also from those seeking to replace the state as a site of authority, conferring that authority instead upon subnational and transnational groupings such as those based on ethnic (Kurdish) nationalism or sectarian affiliation. These groupings do not seek to gain control of the Iraqi state as a primary goal, and do not claim to speak in its name, but instead attempt to capture political authority for themselves. The position of Sistani is emblematic in this respect: an actor who disavows any direct engagement for himself with state power is seen by many as the political lynchpin of contemporary Iraq. This view of the political dynamics of post-invasion Iraq sits well with a perspective articulated frequently in post-colonial studies: that the Southern state is made up of competing locations of authority, each weaker in coercive terms than the state but stronger than it in terms of political legitimacy.[13] From this perspective, the state may be able to make alliances with non-state sites of legitimacy, and attempt to build its authority through them, but is unable to supplant them. The result is that the state is marginalised as an authoritative body.

While patrimonialism is a significant force in post-invasion Iraq — involving, for example, a higher degree of moral authority for religious leaders in southern and central Iraq — it would be an oversimplification to conceive Iraqi politics primarily in this way, as it does not represent Iraqi conceptions of the rightful site of political authority. We have shown that throughout the period since 2003, there has been no evidence of rejection by Iraqis of the state, or of an aspiration to live in a form of political community in which the state is not the primary political actor. Rather, all the evidence from opinion polls we have reviewed in preceding chapters indicates that there is a strong sense of obligation to an Iraqi state, and a predominant desire throughout the country for a high degree of centralisation and state power. Innumerable statements from Kurdish political leaders can be adduced indicating an assertion of a Kurdish right to independence, but also the position that Iraqi Kurds' future lies with autonomy within an Iraqi state. This has been endorsed by ordinary Kurds: for example, in late 2004 most of those polled — 52% to 78% (across different cities) — said they would prefer to live in an ethnically mixed Iraq, whereas only 25% to 40% said they preferred an independent Kurdish state.[14] It is likely that any desire for independence is tempered by the fear that attempting to achieve it could be very dangerous. A low degree of success in welfare provision, and low capacity and coherence, may undermine commitment to the idea of Iraqi state identity more widely in Iraqi society. However, so far the low degree to which the state has provided for basic needs has resulted in greater popular support for a strong Iraqi state, not support for an alternative form of political authority.

In the longer term, two further factors may work against Iraqi state identity and political coherence: the state's relative autonomy from society and its lack of autonomy from foreign actors. The Iraqi state under the *ancien régime* was external to society: as it was a rentier state, prior to 1990 in particular, its oil income, as well as international political, economic and military support, gave it an ability to act in a relatively unhindered way in its relations with Iraqi social movements. It also had a considerable degree of autonomy from other states, international organisations and transnational actors due to its oil wealth, military capabilities and diplomatic ability to play those actors off against each other. This high dual autonomy continued under UN sanctions: the state's internal autonomy was enhanced against an impoverished society, and the mechanisms of UN oversight and enforcement by member states were limited enough to permit the Iraqi Government considerable latitude of decision.

Since the invasion, the Iraqi state has retained a high degree of domestic autonomy for three main reasons. Firstly, one of the key successes of the insurgency has been that the personnel and institutions of the state have been limited severely in their ability to engage with the citizenry. Secondly, the electoral processes have not generated significantly greater responsiveness among politicians to the populace. This is because the list-based electoral system encourages primary emphasis on strategies of making deals at the centre rather than mobilising constituencies. Thirdly, the Iraqi state has relied on foreign, overwhelmingly US, sponsorship. At the most basic level, successive governments have known that their hold on power has existed solely by virtue of the US military presence in the country. As a result, the personnel of the state have accepted the integration of Coalition personnel into decision-making roles in all spheres of government activity, and their priorities and purposes have only occasionally been in conformity with Iraqi popular wishes.

This third factor, the integration of the Iraqi state into the activities of foreign actors, has dimensions which are both international (involving states) and transnational (involving non-state actors). SCR 1546 (2004) gave the lead role to the Coalition in dealing with challenges to the security and stability of Iraq, and the US has interpreted this provision permissively in relation to its own freedom of action. As we have argued, the armed conflict in Iraq from 2003 onwards has been primarily one in which the US has attempted to bring Iraq under the rule of a central government and the insurgents have concentrated their attacks on Coalition personnel. Although inter-sectarian violence has grown considerably in Iraq since 2005, this has remained on a smaller scale than violence between the Coalition and insurgents. Hence representations of the armed conflict as being primarily a civil war are — thus far — misleading. This could change rapidly and decisively if the kind of fighting that broke out in April 2006 in the mainly Sunni Arab al-Adhamiyya district of Baghdad escalated and the US decided to stand aside rather than back the Shi'a forces as it has done so far. In response to sectarian attacks, many informal neighbourhood self-defence militias have sprung up. Many of the Sunni Arab militias have not been part of the anti-occupation insurgency: while they tolerate US forces, they open fire on the Shi'a dominated police and Ministry of Interior forces, making these districts no-go areas for the state.[15] Khalilzad stated that 'More Iraqis are dying from the militia violence than from the terrorists' and called for them to be reined in by the Iraqi Government.[16] Such local self-defence militias could link up and coalesce into much larger sectarian armed formations with potentially catastrophic consequences. However, the US has continued to work with them as its counter-insurgent allies, thus demonstrating practically the extent to which the counter-insurgency campaign has been prioritised by the US.

The high degree of US involvement in the functioning of the Iraqi state lends itself to accounts of the Iraqi state in terms of US imperialism. This view resonates with those within US policy-circles who take direct or indirect US rule of another country as both necessary for US interests and also benign for the people of that country. Early in the occupation, Iraqis soon found that the task of state building was being kept out of their hands by the US, which was determined only to hand it over to those it felt would proceed in a direction acceptable to Washington. The US goal was to try to lock in a state with the kind of economy, politics and foreign policy it favoured, but it saw no distinction between that and the desires of what it regarded as genuine and freedom-loving Iraqis (going so far as labelling those who opposed it 'anti-Iraqi forces'). Before and after the period of formal occupation, the US, international organisations and transnational corporations have had a high degree of involvement in the functioning of the Iraqi state, in conducting counter-insurgency operations, in opening up Iraq's economy to foreign capital and many other activities. In other words, the Iraqi state has been and continues to be integrated into international and transnational constructions of the identity and practical meaning of its statehood. To the extent that this is hierarchical, or not reflective of the wishes of the Iraqi population, or primarily serves the interests of those foreign actors, it is not a benign imperialism. We have provided extensive evidence of hierarchical relations running counter to expressed Iraqi preferences and concentrated on serving the interests of foreign actors.

Nevertheless, we have also demonstrated the impact of divisions and competition within the US administration over its project within Iraq. One contributory factor in the failure of the reconstruction project was the competition between the Pentagon, State Department and Congress for control over its direction. Iraq has been subjected to an intense process of US-led internationalisation and transnationalisation since 2003, but the hierarchies organising and constituting that process have been neither stable over time nor uniform across different spheres. This has left room for Iraqi forces to form pragmatic alliances with individual US agencies, to play them off against each other, or to exploit the consequent US ineffectiveness by allying themselves with non-Coalition forces in attempts to assert their own power. Even those Iraqi political parties which had coordinated closely with the US prior to the invasion have not been fully responsive to US urging. This was demonstrated by the overt rejection of US interference in Iraq's political processes in early 2006. The INA refused to accept the Ja'fari-led national unity government, initially promoted by the US, and al-Da'wa then refused to give up the UIA's authority to nominate the Prime Minister and Interior and Defence Ministers, despite Khalilzad making it clear that the US no longer saw Ja'fari as a suitable candidate for the first position and wanted to see non-sectarian candidates in the latter two positions. In those cases, it was only after protracted bargaining that compromises were reached, as we discussed in Chapter One. The US thus has often been unsuccessful in converting its Iraqi allies into its agents.

By mid-2006, what remained of the broader US state-building programme was fitful at best. The US has increasingly emphasised investment in Iraq's security forces and military infrastructure as a way to extract its own personnel, and especially ground troops, from the arenas of combat. The Bush administration had made it clear by the start of the year that it would seek no more funds from Congress for other aspects of Iraq's reconstruction, and USAID, while seeking bids from contractors for $1.3 billion to stabilise Iraq's main cities via job creation and infrastructure projects, acknowledged that its assistance would offer 'little in the way of conflict mitigation' in relation to large parts of the insurgency.[17] At the same time, after almost a year of planning, the US had been able to deploy only three out of eighteen of its planned Provincial Reconstruction Teams aimed at reviving Iraqi local government, the Pentagon being unwilling to provide troops for the State Department staff originally planned to run them, and the State Department unable to recruit the necessary personnel.[18] The Bush administration was reduced to speculating that perhaps Iraqis or internationals might take over most of these teams, but with no indication that this would actually take place.

Struggles over the fundamentals of political authority ensure that carrying out the formal functions of state institutions has come second to servicing the interests of the actors who run them. In such circumstances, the technocratic capacity building programmes of foreign actors such as the US, the IMF and transnational corporations are carried out only to the extent to which they are perceived to be in the interests of the sponsors. In some cases of state building, it is an immediate priority of the state builders that the capacity of national institutions should be high. However, the case of post-invasion Iraq demonstrates what happens when the range of political, financial, military and strategic priorities of the sponsor diverges markedly from the requirements of a comprehensive state building programme. The result has been a form of fragmentation in which private actors, operating either through state institutions or through non-state organisations, and organised either sectorally or geographically, have been able to commandeer considerable financial and military resources to solidify their positions. In Iraq, therefore, the fragments have more power than the central authorities.

How long this situation will continue remains to be seen. Iraqi political actors remain locked into a struggle to strengthen their positions against their rivals, not only from different sectarian or ethnic groups, but also from within their own groups. These struggles have not been successfully mediated through the institutions of the Iraqi state, and the United States' ability to constrain that conflict when it has been in its interests to do so has receded as those actors have gained in power. But the scale of material resources at the disposal of the Iraqi state is still potentially high, primarily because of its continued ownership of Iraq's petroleum resources.

This creates a major incentive for the fragments to continue to vie for control of state institutions, and to seek support from international and transnational forces to strengthen their positions while doing so. As the state does not provide a framework to regulate that contest, and as Iraqi political groupings retain a high degree of autonomy from society and are thus relatively unconstrained by its needs, the potential for violent escalation is high. One thing is clear: the fragmentation of political authority that is the central legacy of the occupation is an additional burden that the long-suffering people of Iraq could have done without.

NOTES

1. INTRODUCTION

1.   Ivo H. Daalder and James M. Lindsay, *America Unbound: The Bush Revolution in Foreign Policy*, Washington, DC: Brookings Institution Press, 2003, pp. 46-7; also, Stefan Halper and Jonathan Clarke, *America Alone: The Neo-Conservatives and the Global Order*, Cambridge University Press, 2004, pp. 9-15, 76-81. Since the invasion, a number of neoconservatives have left the Bush administration and, in the case of Francis Fukuyama, renounced neoconservatism. See Francis Fukuyama, *After the Neocons: America at the Crossroads*, London: Profile Books, 2006.

2.   Public Broadcasting Service, 'Excerpts from 1992 draft "Defense Policy Guidance"', Frontline, <http://www.pbs.org/wgbh/pages/frontline/shows/iraq/etc/wolf.html>. Background is provided by James Mann, *Rise of the Vulcans: The History of Bush's War Cabinet*, London: Penguin, 2004, pp. 198-215.

3.   White House, *The National Security Strategy of the United States of America*, 17 September 2002, <http://www.whitehouse.gov/nsc/nss.pdf>. Context is provided by Mann, *Rise*, pp. 311-31.

4.   Key elements of these ideas are contained in Institute for Advanced Strategic and Political Studies, 'A clean break: a new strategy for securing the realm', 8 July 1996, at <http://www.israeleconomy.org/strat1.htm>. This paper was written for Israeli Prime Minister Binyamin Netanyahu, and was by a study group led by Perle and including Feith. See also Paul Wolfowitz, 'Rebuilding the anti-Saddam coalition', *Wall Street Journal*, 18 November 1997; and Zalmay Khalilzad and Paul Wolfowitz, 'Overthrow him', *Weekly Standard*, 1 December 1997.

5.   Project for the New American Century, *Rebuilding America's Defenses: Strategy, Forces and Resources for a New Century*, September 2000, pp. 14, 17,

<http://www.newamericancentury.org/RebuildingAmericasDefenses. pdf>.

6. 'Iraq Liberation Act of 1998', H.R. 4655, Public Law 105-388, 105th Congress, 31 October 1998; Office of the Press Secretary, White House, 'The Iraq Liberation Act – Statement by the President', 31 October 1998, <http://www.library.cornell.edu/colldev/mideast/libera.htm>.

7. Michael Ledeen, 'The War on Terror won't end in Baghdad', *Wall Street Journal*, 4 September 2002.

8. 'Vice President speaks at the VFW 103rd National Convention', 26 August 2002, <http://www.whitehouse.gov/news/releases/2002/08/ 20020826.html>.

9. State of the Union address, 29 January 2002, <http://www.whitehouse. gov/news/releases/2002/01/20020129-11.html>.

10. For an overview see US Department of State, *Duty to the Future: Free Iraqis Plan for New Iraq*, April 2003, <http://usinfo.state.gov/products/pubs/ archive/dutyiraq/> and David L. Phillips, *Losing Iraq: Inside the Postwar Reconstruction Fiasco*, London: Westview Press, 2005. Reports from twelve of the seventeen working groups are available at <http://www. thememoryhole.org/state/future_of_iraq/>.

11. Prepared statement of Douglas J. Feith, in Senate Committee on Foreign Relations, 'The Future of Iraq', Senate Hearing 108-43, pp. 20-1, 23-4.

12. Comments by former CPA Regional Coordinator, February 2006.

13. Paul Wolfowitz, 'Prepared statement for the Senate Armed Services Committee: the future of NATO and Iraq', 10 April 2003; also National Security Adviser Condoleezza Rice, press briefing, 4 April 2003.

14. NBC 'Meet the Press', 13 April 2003; also Colin Powell's interview on NBC News, 11 April 2003.

15. Toby Harnden, 'US names its choice to succeed Saddam', *Daily Telegraph*, 12 February 2003; Wolfowitz, 'Prepared statement'; Rice, press briefing.

16. Christopher Dickey and Mark Hosenball, 'Banker, schmoozer, spy', *Newsweek*, 12 May 2003; John Dizard, 'The implosion of Chalabi's Petra Bank', Salon.com, 4 May 2004.

17. Douglas McCollam, 'How Chalabi Played the Press', *Columbia Journalism Review*, July/August 2004; John Dizard, 'How Ahmed Chalabi conned the neocons', Salon.com, 4 May 2004.

18. Jeffrey Goldberg, 'A Little Learning: what Douglas Feith Knew and

When he knew it', *New Yorker*, 9 May 2005; Milan Rai, *Regime Unchanged*, London: Pluto Press, 2003.

19. Ahmed S. Hashim, 'The Sunni Insurgency in Iraq', *Middle East International Perspective*, 15 August 2003, <http://www.mideasti.org/articles/doc89.html>. Also Ahmed S. Hashim, 'The Insurgency in Iraq', *Small Wars and Insurgencies*, 14:3 (Autumn 2003), pp. 1-22; Thom Shanker, 'Rumsfeld doubles estimate for cost of troops in Iraq', *New York Times*, 10 July 2003; John Diamond, 'Prewar intelligence predicted Iraqi insurgency', *USA Today*, 24 October 2004.

20. Interview with Lt-Gen. Jay Garner for PBS Frontline, Director of ORHA, 17 July 2003, <http://www.pbs.org/wgbh/pages/frontline/shows/truth/interviews/garner.html>.

21. John Sawers, UK Prime Minister's Special Representative for Iraq, 'Iraq: what's going wrong', confidential memo from 11 May 2003, available via <http://www.guardian.co.uk/>.

22. Edward Chaplin, 'Iraq's new constitution: recipe for stability or chaos?', presented at Cambridge University, UK, 1 November 2005.

23. The CPA's creation was proclaimed in its Regulation No.1, officially dated 16 May 2003. However, this regulation seems to have been written at least six days after that date, as it makes two references to Security Council Resolution 1483, passed only on 22 May 2003. Our CPA contacts were unable to explain this anachronism, which they admitted was a reflection of the highly charged circumstances in which the CPA was created.

24. International Crisis Group (ICG), *Governing Iraq*, 25 August 2003, pp. 10-12.

25. Nicholas Blanford, 'The specter of sectarian and ethnic unrest in Iraq', *Middle East Report Online*, Middle East Research and Information Project (MERIP), 7 January 2004; Glen Rangwala, 'Iraq's Governing Council', <http://middleeastreference.org.uk/iraqgc.html>.

26. Michael O'Hanlon and Adriana Lins de Albuquerque, *Iraq Index*, Brookings Institution, Washington, 21 June 2004, p. 3, <http://www.brookings.edu/iraqindex>.

27. Gen. John Abizaid, Department of Defense (DoD) news briefing, 16 July 2003.

28. Statement by Ayatollah Sistani, quoted in *al-Zaman*, 1 July 2003, and quoted at <http://www.juancole.com/2003/07/grand-ayatollah-ali-sistani-has.html>.

29.   O'Hanlon and de Albuquerque, *Iraq Index*, p. 8.

30.   Independent Panel on the Safety and Security of UN Personnel in Iraq, *Report*, 20 October 2003.

31.   O'Hanlon and de Albuquerque, *Iraq Index*, p. 9.

32.   John Banusiewicz, American Forces Press Service, 'AF supports Operation Iron Hammer', 13 November 2003, <http://www.af.mil/news/story.asp?storyID=123006005>; John Banusiewicz, American Forces Press Service, 'Army launches "Ivy Cyclone II" to target insurgents', 16 November 2003, <http://www.defenselink.mil/news/Nov2003/n11162003_200311162.html>.

33.   He was put on trial in Baghdad in October 2005: as of June 2006 that trial had not concluded and had been rather marginal to Iraqi politics.

34.   Major William S. McCallister, 'Iraqi Insurgency Model', 14 January 2004, p. 23. McCallister was also co-author with Chris Alexander and Charles Kyle of an earlier paper 'The Iraqi Insurgency Movement', dated 14 November 2003.

35.   McCallister, 'Iraqi Insurgency Model', p. 25.

36.   Such concerns had been expressed in an earlier paper by CPA adviser Ahmed Hashim, as we discuss in Chapter Four.

37.   IGC and CPA, 'Agreement on Political Process', 15 November 2003.

38.   Statement, Office of His Eminence Ayatullah Sayyid Seestani, Najaf, 28 November 2003. <http://www.najaf.org/English/statements/mee4.htm>; Edward Wong, 'Direct election of Iraq assembly pushed by cleric', *New York Times*, 21 January 2004.

39.   'The political transition in Iraq: report of the fact-finding mission', 23 February 2003, esp. pp. 19-23.

40.   'Law of Administration for the State of Iraq for the Transitional Period', 8 March 2004.

41.   David McDowall, *A Modern History of the Kurds*, London: I.B. Tauris, revd edn, 1997, pp. 332, 339-40; ICG, *Iraq's Kurds: Towards a Historic Compromise?* 8 April 2004.

42.   Human Rights Watch (HRW), *Claims in Conflict: Reversing Ethnic Cleansing in Northern Iraq*, HRW Index No. E1604, 3 August 2004, pp. 57-8, <http://hrw.org/reports/2004/iraq0804/>.

43.   Phillips, *Losing Iraq*, especially pp. 165-7.

44.   PR Newswire, 'Kirkuk Foundation looking to build socioeconomic reform', 28 July 2004, <http://www.iraqprocurement.com/docs/

new379.htm>.

45.   HRW, *Claims in Conflict*, pp. 17, 46-50, ICG, *Iraq's Kurds*, p. 17.

46.   HRW, *Claims in Conflict*, pp. 43-45, 58-63.

47.   HRW, *Claims in Conflict*, pp. 70-77; ICG, *Iraq's Kurds*, p. 11.

48.   AP, 'Cracks in Iraq Shia-Kurd coalition', 2 October 2005; Steven Fainaru, 'Kurds reclaiming prized territory in Northern Iraq', *Washington Post*, 30 October 2005.

49.   Iraqi Constitution, October 2005, articles 109, 110 and 149.

50.   HRW, *Claims in Conflict*, pp. 69-70; ICG, *Iraq's Kurds*, pp. 12-14.

51.   Jonathan Steele, 'Oil town looks to property tribunal for justice', *Guardian*, 8 July 2004; K. Gajendra Singh, 'Turkey snaps over US bombing of its brethren', *Asia Times*, 18 September 2004.

52.   Charles Glass, 'Diary', *London Review of Books*, 16 December 2004, pp. 34-5; Michael Howard, 'Insurgents step up the battle for Mosul', *Guardian*, 25 November 2004.

53.   Inur Ievik, 'Talabani: visit of Barzani to White House is recognition of identity of Iraqi Kurdistan', *New Anatolian*, 30 October 2005.

54.   Nicholas Birch, 'Kurds' disconnect bigger than phones', *Washington Times*, 7 November 2005.

55.   'Kurdish Regional Government Unification Agreement', 21 January 2006; also, Kathleen Ridolfo, 'Kurds to agree to unify administrations', Radio Free Europe/Radio Liberty (RFE/RL), 12 January 2006.

56.   O'Hanlon and de Albuquerque, *Iraq Index*, pp. 3, 11.

57.   Lt-Gen. Ricardo Sanchez, speaking at a CENTCOM Operational Update Briefing, 12 April 2004.

58.   Interview with senior Coalition military officer, February 2005.

59.   Jonathan Steele, 'Marooned and bewildered, Polish troops watch militia take control', *Guardian*, 9 April 2004.

60.   Ann Scott Tyson, 'Sadr's militia regrouping, rearming', *Christian Science Monitor*, 15 July 2004.

61.   Rory McCarthy, 'Iraqi politicians secure deal to end Najaf crisis', *Guardian*, 28 May 2004.

62.   Edmund Sanders, 'Battles take daily toll in Sadr City', *Los Angeles Times*, 7 June 2004.

63.   Tony Blair, 'Why we must never abandon this historic struggle in Iraq', *Observer*, 11 April 2004.

64.   Quoted in Cole, 'Portrait of a Rebellion'.

65.   Interviews with two Coalition military officers, one senior, May 2004; also, leaked memo from Michael Rubin, a prominent DoD official seconded to Baghdad, written in March 2004: <http://aan.org/gyrobase/Aan/view Article?oid=oid:134346>.

66.   Bing West, *No True Glory: A Frontline Account of the Battle for Fallujah*, New York: Bantam Books, 2005, pp. 58-62; interview with a Coalition military intelligence officer, May 2004; Patrick J. McDonnell, 'Outgoing marine general faults Fallouja strategy', *Los Angeles Times*, 13 September 2004; Alissa J. Rubin and Doyle McManus, 'Why America has waged a losing battle on Fallouja', *Los Angeles Times*, 24 October 2004.

67.   Kimmitt, DoD news briefing, 'Coalition forces will pacify Fallujah', 1 April 2004.

68.   Kimmit, 'Coalition forces'. In fact, armed opposition continued in both Samarra' and Ba'qubah and to a lesser extent in Tikrit (which showed no sign of accepting the legitimacy of the US presence or its appointees).

69.   Patrick Wintour, 'Defeat would be victory for fanatics, says Blair', *Guardian*, 12 April 2004.

70.   Lt-Gen. Ricardo Sanchez, CPA briefing, 8 April 2004.

71.   Jonathan Steele, 'Shells and rockets were falling like rain', *Guardian*, 12 April 2004; Laura King, 'Insurgents and Islam now rulers of Fallouja', *Los Angeles Times*, 13 June 2004.

72.   HRW, 'Violent Response: The US Army in al-Falluja, 2003', <http://www.hrw.org/reports/2003/iraqfalluja/>.

73.   Jonathan Steele, 'Iraq council was regarded with scorn - but now it has found its voice', *Guardian*, 12 April 2004.

74.   Larry Diamond, 'Transition to what in Iraq?', Stanford Institute for International Studies, 11 May 2004, p. 10, <http://iis-db.stanford.edu/evnts/3864/IraqDiamond504.pdf>.

75.   King, 'Rulers of Fallouja'.

76.   Quoted in Jack Fairweather, 'Biggest threat to Iraq is from outside, says US General', *Daily Telegraph*, 3 July 2004.

77.   Bradley Graham, 'Marine commander admits Iraqi unit has been erratic', *Washington Post*, 19 June 2004.

78.   Toby Dodge, *Iraq's Future: The Aftermath of Regime Change*, London: International Institute for Strategic Studies, March 2005, p. 36.

79.   Letter from US Secretary of State Colin Powell to the President of the Security Council, 5 June 2004, annexed to Security Council Resolution

1546 (8 June 2004).

80.   Peter Baker and Roger Wright, 'In Iraq, Bush pushed for deadline democracy', *Washington Post*, 11 December 2005.

81.   Rory McCarthy, Suzanne Goldenberg and Nicholas Watt, 'Amnesty for Iraqi insurgents', *Guardian*, 5 July 2004; Rory McCarthy, 'Straw endorses Iraqi amnesty', *Guardian*, 6 July 2004.

82.   BBC NewsOnline, 'Iraq amnesty "excluded killers"', 17 July 2004; Mariam Fam, 'Iraq amnesty plan won't cover killers', Associated Press, 4 August 2004.

83.   'Text: Iraqi security law', *Washington Post*, 7 July 2004; Jonathan Steele, 'Iraq PM given sweeping powers', *Guardian*, 8 July 2004.

84.   UN Assistance Mission for Iraq, 'Iraq: reimposition of the death penalty is a step backwards', 11 August 2004, <http://www.uniraq.org/newsroom/story.asp?ID=1117>.

85.   AFP (Agence France Presse)/Reuters, 'US troops surround Sadr's Najaf home', 2 August 2004; Xinhuanet, 'Clashes in Najaf, Baghdad kill 43 in 24 hours', 8 August 2004.

86.   AFP, 'Sadr surrender in Najaf: Iraqi police', 7 August 2004.

87.   BBC NewsOnline, 'Poland yields to US in Iraq Zone', 9 August 2004.

88.   The different stages in the process can traced via Scott Baldauf, 'Standoff bolstered Sadr's support', *Christian Science Monitor*, 30 August 2004; Dexter Filkins, 'Militant cleric considers entry into Iraqi politics', *New York Times*, 3 October 2004; and Anthony Shadid, 'Sadr's disciples rise again to play pivotal role in Iraq', *Washington Post*, 30 August 2005.

89.   For an account from the perspective of the US military, see West, *No True Glory*, pp. 255-316.

90.   Lt-Gen. John Sattler, DoD news briefing, 18 November 2004.

91.   Patrick Cockburn and Andrew Buncome, 'Fallujah did not break the back of the insurgency', *The Independent*, 8 December 2004.

92.   Richard Sale, 'Analysis: Iraq's new war', UPI, 24 December 2004.

93.   The UN Electoral Assistance Division recorded that 14,270,000 people registered to vote in January 2005, of whom 265,000 registered to vote abroad: 'Electoral fact sheet' (undated), at: <http://www.un.org/news/dh/infocus/iraq/iraq-elect-fact-sht.pdf>. This makes a total of 14,005,000 Iraqis who were registered to vote within Iraq, of whom 8,193,000 voted. Iraqis were not able to vote abroad for the October referendum, and 15,570,000 registered in Iraq to vote. Assuming the full

eligible population registered for the October referendum, and that the number of returning Iraqis (who, by most accounts, were relative few in number) and the population growth were negligible between January and October, this would mean that 52.6% of the eligible population within Iraq voted in the January election.

94.   SCIRI won the governorate elections by itself in Baghdad, Karbala', Najaf, al-Qadisiyya and al-Muthanna. It formed alliances with other parties, including al-Da'wa, that came out as the leading coalition in Diyala, Babil, Wasit and Basra. The three governorate councils in which neither SCIRI nor the Kurdish parties formed the leading bloc were al-Anbar (won by the Iraqi Islamic Party), Dhi Qar (won by the Fadila Party) and Maysan (won by the Husayni Thought Forum), with SCIRI forming the second largest bloc in the latter two governorates.

95.   Coalitions in which both the KDP and PUK participated became the leading bloc of local government in Salah al-Din, al-Ta'mim and Ninawa, extending their leadership beyond the heartland governorates of Irbil, Sulaymaniyya and Dahuk.

96.   Jonathan Steele, 'Radical MPs call for troop withdrawal', *Guardian*, 5 February 2005; BBC NewsOnline, 'New Iraqi government ministers', 8 May 2005.

97.   Jack Fairweather and Anton La Guardia, 'Shia parties triumph in Iraq election', *Daily Telegraph*, 14 February 2005; Robin Wright and Peter Baker, 'Iraq, Jordan see threat to election from Iran', *Washington Post*, 8 December 2004; Robert Gibbons, 'Saudi says U.S. policy handing Iraq over to Iran', Reuters, 21 September 2005; Juan Cole in Middle East Policy Council, 'A Shia crescent: what fallout for the U.S.?', 14 October 2005, <http://www.mepc.org/public_asp/forums_chcs/41.asp>.

98.   Michael O'Hanlon and Nina Kamp, *Iraq Index,* 23 March 2006, p. 22.

99.   Eric Schmitt, 'New U.S. commander sees shift in military role in Iraq', *New York Times*, 16 January 2005; Eric Schmitt, 'General seeking faster training of Iraq soldiers', *New York Times*, 23 January 2005; Robin Wright and Josh White, 'U.S. plans new tack after Iraq elections', *Washington Post*, 23 January 2005.

100.   For example, the attack on Karabila on the Iraqi-Syrian border in June 2005. See Rory Carroll and Richard Norton-Taylor, 'RAF joins US forces in Iraq assault', *Guardian*, 20 June 2005.

101.   Kathleen Ridolfo, 'Constitutional deal spells opportunity for broader

Sunni views', RFE/RL, 17 June 2005.

102. Interview with Baghdad-based UN official engaged in Iraq's constitutional process, September 2005.

103. We draw upon the Arabic-language text of the draft constitution, as placed on the Iraqi Government website <http://www.iraqigovernment.org>; the translations are our own.

104. Ali Merza, 'Reconstruction under uncertainty' (October 2005), unpublished paper, p. 27.

105. The official results by governorate were posted at <http://www.ieciraq. org/final cand/Certified Referendum Results Arabic.pdf>.

106. MNF-I briefing by Maj.-Gen. Rick Lynch of 10 November 2005; O'Hanlon and Kamp, *Iraq Index*, p.22. Insurgent attacks averaged 92 per day a month after the referendum, in contrast to an average of 70 per day for May, June, July and August before it. They fell again to an average of 75 per day in December 2005 and January 2006. The number of daily attacks has climbed steadily each year from 2003 onwards.

107. MNF-I briefing by Maj.-Gen. Rick Lynch of 10 November 2005; Edward Wong, 'U.S. goals for Iraqi forces meet success and challenges in Najaf', *New York Times*, 3 December 2005.

108. Testimony of US Secretary of State Condoleezza Rice to the Senate Committee on Foreign Relations, 19 October 2005.

109. Lt-Gen. David Petraeus, commander of the MNSTC-I, comments to press briefing, 5 October 2005, at <http://www.dod.gov/transcripts/2005/ tr20051005-4021.html>; remarks to the Center for Strategic and International Studies, 7 November 2005, at <http://www.csis.org/ media/csis/events/051107_petraeus_transcript.pdf>, pp.19-20.

110. Seymour Hersh, 'Up in the air', *New Yorker*, 5 December 2005; Sarah Baxter, Ali Rifat and Peter Almond, 'US forces step up Iraq airstrikes', *Sunday Times*, 1 January 2006; 'Daily Airpower Summary', <http:// www.af.mil/news/>.

111. 'Paper by Secretary of State', undated (probably early June 2005), confidential, but posted at: <http://www.dailymail.co.uk/pages/live/ articles/news/news.html?in_article_id=355251&in_page_id=1770>; also L. Paul Bremer with Malcolm McConnell, *My Year in Iraq*, New York: Simon & Schuster, 2006, pp. 155, 162.

112. Press Association, 'Five groups denounce Iraq elections', 12 December 2005; al-Jazeera.Net, 'al-Qaida rejects Iraq polls', 12 December 2005;

Juan Cole, 'What the Sunni Arab Vote Really Means', *Informed Comment*, 16 December 2005.

113.   'Sistani urges pro-religious vote', Reuters, 3 December 2005; Ashraf Khalil, 'Iraqi mosques flex election muscle', *Los Angeles Times*, 3 December 2005.

114.   Full results via <http://www.ieciraq.org/Arabic/result_of_election_part3.php>.

115.   Paul Garwood, 'Bombs target four churches; 3 dead', Associated Press, 29 January 2006; Zalmay Khalilzad, 'A political blueprint for Iraq', *Los Angeles Times*, 12 February 2006; Jonathan Steele, 'I will not be forced out by US and Britain – Iraqi PM', *Guardian*, 5 April 2006.

116.   In a valuable essay, Charles Tripp explores the incoherence of the US project in Iraq in terms of it being ambivalent about whether it was trying to establish a transformed liberal democratic secular market-based state, a centralised security state or a decentralised state dominated by local communal politics. Charles Tripp, 'The United States and State-building in Iraq', *Review of International Studies*, vol. 30 (2004), pp. 545-58.

2. THE STATE – FRAGMENTING POLITICAL AUTHORITY

1.   We borrow this distinction from Bruce Berman and John Lonsdale, *Unhappy Valley: Conflict in Kenya and Africa*, London: James Currey, 1992, esp. pp. 5, 13-44. It has been profitably employed by Béatrice Hibou, ed., *Privatising the State*, London: C. Hurst & Co., 2004, pp. viii, 1-46. This distinction is not to be confused with Charles Tilly's discussion of 'statemaking' and 'state formation', neither of which is connected with the agents' intent: Tilly, *Coercion, Capital, and European States, AD 990-1992*, Oxford: Blackwell, 1992, esp. pp. 20-8, 96-9.

2.   Illustrated in Francis Fukuyama, *State-Building: Governance and World Order in the Twenty-First Century*, London: Profile Books, 2004, esp. pp. ix, 124-60.

3.   Tilly, *Coercion*; in shortened form, Charles Tilly, 'War Making and State Making as Organized Crime', in Peter B. Evans, Dietrich Rueschemeyer and Theda Skocpol, eds, *Bringing the State Back In*, Cambridge University Press, 1985, pp. 169-191.

4.   Sami Zubaida, 'The Nation State in the Middle East', in *Islam, People and the State: Essays on Political Ideas and Movements in the Middle East*, London: Routledge, 1988, pp. 121-82, at p. 126.

5.   Abbas Alnasrawi, *The Economy of Iraq: Oil, Wars, Destruction of Development and Prospects, 1950-2010*, Westport, CT: Greenwood Press, 1994, pp. 62-75, 133-45; Charles Tripp, *A History of Iraq*, 2nd edition, Cambridge University Press, 2002, pp. 205-10; Nazih Ayubi, *Over-Stating the Arab State: Politics and Society in the Middle East*, London: I.B. Tauris, 1995, pp. 362-6.

6.   Hazem Beblawi, 'The Rentier State in the Arab World', in Hazem Beblawi and Giacomo Luciani, eds, *The Rentier State*, London: Croom Helm, 1987.

7.   As formulated by Hannu Batatu, 'Iraq's Underground Shi'i Movements', MERIP reports, no. 102 (January 1982), p. 7.

8.   This point is made with regard to an earlier era in 'Isam al-Khafaji, 'The Parasitic Base of the Ba'thist Regime', in CARDRI, *Saddam's Iraq: Revolution or Reaction*, London: Zed Press, 1986, pp. 73-88.

9.   In *Revue du Monde Musulman* XIV: 5, May 1911, p. 255.

10.   Most notably by Bremer: Bremer and McConnell, *My Year in Iraq*, pp. 10, 356-7; and as quoted in Robin Wright and Thomas E. Ricks, 'Bremer criticizes troop levels', *Washington Post*, 5 October 2004. Also, Feith quoted in Ann Scott Tyson, 'Official admits errors in Iraq', *Washington Post*, 13 July 2005. A number of other commentators are cited in Michael R. Gordon, 'The strategy to secure Iraq did not foresee a 2nd war', *New York Times*, 19 October 2004.

11.   James Dobbins *et al., America's Role in Nation-Building: From Germany to Iraq*, Santa Monica, CA: RAND, 2003, pp. 197-8. More critically, Larry Diamond, *Squandered Victory: The American Occupation and the Bungled Effort to Bring Democracy to Iraq*, New York: Times Books, 2005, pp. 282-7.

12.   Steven R. Weisman, 'U.S. to let Kurds keep autonomy', *New York Times*, 5 January 2004; ICG, *Iraq's Kurds*, esp. pp. 17-22; Transitional Administrative Law, 8 March 2004, articles 53 and 54; Constitution of Iraq, 15 October 2005, article 113(1).

13.   Diamond, *Squandered Victory*, pp. 114-7; Tripp, 'The United States and State-building in Iraq', p. 548; interviews with senior Coalition political official, February 2004, and Coalition military official, May 2004.

14.   Nancy A. Youssef, '7 U.S. marines killed in attack near Fallujah', Knight Ridder Newspapers, 6 September 2004; 'Iraq: is it getting safer?', *The Economist*, 9 September 2004.

15.   Nir Rosen, 'Home Rule', *New Yorker*, 5 July 2004; Christoph Wilcke,

'Castles Built of Sand: US Governance and Exit Strategies in Iraq', *Middle East Report*, no. 232 (Fall 2004).

16.   Ali Hamdani and James Hider, 'US troops poised to move against desert town spared by war', *The Times*, 14 October 2004; interview with Coalition commanding officer, November 2004.

17.   Louise Roug, 'Islamic law controls the streets of Basra', *Los Angeles Times*, 27 June 2005; Edward Wong, 'Shiite theocracy takes hold in Iraqi oil city', *New York Times*, 8 July 2005; Oliver Poole, 'British keep out of Basra's lethal Islamic take-over', *Daily Telegraph*, 15 July 2005.

18.   al-Zaman, cited in Juan Cole, *Informed Comment*, 19 February 2004.

19.   Juan Cole, 'The United States and Shi'ite Religious Factions in Post-Ba'thist Iraq', *Middle East Journal*, vol. 57, no. 4 (Autumn 2003), p. 560; Nir Rosen, 'Muqtada's powerful push for prominence', *Asia Times*, 18 March 2004; Tom Lasseter, 'Cleric's army quietly takes control', Knight Ridder Newspapers, 14 July 2004.

20.   Spencer Ackerman, 'Badr to worse: the U.S. failure to disarm Iraq's militias', *The New Republic*, 11 July 2005.

21.   Press briefings, 2 September 2003 and 6 September 2003.

22.   Tarek al-Issawi, 'Previously banned militia patrols Iraqi holy city, with coalition's blessing', Associated Press, 6 September 2003; Kenneth Katzman, 'Iraq: US regime change efforts and post-Saddam governance', Congressional Research Service (CRS) Report for Congress (7 January 2004), p. 12.

23.   Robert Fisk, 'Hooded men executing Saddam officials', *The Independent*, 28 December 2003; Stephen Grey, 'British back Iraqi kidnap police', *Sunday Times*, 24 January 2004; Edward Wong, 'Iraqi militias resisting U.S. pressure to disband', *New York Times*, 9 February 2004; interview with recently retired middle-ranking US official in Iraq, March 2004.

24.   The plan for a 'Najaf Brigade' is recounted in Nicolas Pelham, 'US approaches insurgents to help control Najaf', *Financial Times*, 12 May 2004.

25.   Charles Glass, 'Diary', *London Review of Books*, 16 December 2004, pp. 34-5.

26.   CPA Order no. 91 (7 June 2004), sections 4 and 5; Terrence Kelly (former CPA Director for Transition and Reintegration Programs), 'Militia transition and integration', 31 January 2005, at <http://www.dean.usma.edu/sosh/Academic   Program/Courses/SS490B/Kelly   4.ppt>,

slide 10; Tom Lasseter, 'U.S. knew Shiite militias were a threat but took no action because they were focused on Sunni insurgency', Knight Ridder Newspapers, 17 April 2006.

27. Edward Wong, 'Leaders of Iraq praise Iranian-trained militia', *New York Times*, 9 June 2005.

28. This formulation draws upon Berman and Lonsdale, *Unhappy Valley*, p. 31.

29. Zainy is quoted in Oliver Morgan, 'Fields of dreams turned to ashes', *Observer*, 21 September 2003; and in Dean Calbreath, 'A blueprint for a nation', *San Diego Union-Tribune*, 4 July 2004. Other IRDC members who commented critically include Farouk Darweesh and Isam al-Khafaji: see Warren Vieth, 'Iraq exiles push for bigger role', *Los Angeles Times*, 11 August 2003; Omayma Abdel-Latif, 'Broken promises', *al-Ahram Weekly*, 7-13 August 2003; Isam al-Khafaji, 'I did not want to be a collaborator', *Guardian*, 28 July 2003; and broadcast interviews with Khafaji on 'Amsterdam Forum', Radio Netherlands, 12 September 2003; 'The Choice', BBC Radio 4, 18 November 2003; and BBC Hardtalk, 11 February 2004. More generally on the personnel of the IRDC, see Glen Rangwala, <http://middleeastreference.org.uk/irdc.html>.

30. This section draws upon interviews with Coalition personnel in Baghdad conducted over the period 11-25 September 2003, and subsequent correspondence. The theme of the Green Zone 'security bubble' is also discussed briefly in a leaked memo from Michael Rubin, a prominent DoD official seconded to Baghdad, written in March 2004: <http://aan.org/gyrobase/Aan/viewArticle?oid=134346>.

31. Interviews with two Coalition military officers, one senior and one mid-ranking, May 2004. Similar accounts include those by Christopher H. Varhola, a Coalition civil affairs officer, 'American challenges in post-conflict Iraq', 27 May 2004, <http://www.fpri.org/enotes/20040527.americawar.varhola.iraqchallenges.html>; and an interview with Col. Philip J. Dermer, a CPA official responsible for governance in Baghdad, in Iraq from May 2003 to July 2004 (22 August 2004), <http://www.usip.org/library/oh/sops/iraq/gov/dermer.pdf>, p. 15.

32. State Department/USAID, 'Iraq Humanitarian and Reconstruction Assistance Fact Sheets', 16 July 2003 and 6 August 2003.

33. Thom Shanker, 'U.S. team in Baghdad fights a persistent enemy: rumors', *New York Times*, 23 March 2004; interviews and correspondence with

two Coalition military personnel, May 2004 onwards; Stephanie Kelley, 'Rumors in Iraq: a Guide to Winning Hearts and Minds', *Strategic Insights*, vol. 4, no. 2 (2005), note 4.

34. Interview with Coalition military officer, May 2004.

35. Interview with former CPA Governorate Coordinator, May 2005.

36. Walter Pincus, 'An intelligence gap hinders U.S. in Iraq', *Washington Post*, 24 December 2004. In greater detail, Anthony H. Cordesman, 'Strengthening Iraqi Security Forces', CSIS Draft Paper, 17 February 2005, <http://www.csis.org/features/iraq_strengtheningforces.pdf>, p. 81.

37. Larry Diamond, 'An eyewitness to the Iraq botch', *Los Angeles Times*, 10 June 2004. Also, Larry Diamond, 'What Went Wrong in Iraq', *Foreign Affairs*, September/October 2004.

38. Andrew Rathmell, 'Planning Post-conflict Reconstruction in Iraq: What can we Learn?', *International Affairs*, vol. 81 no. 5 (2005), p. 1028 n. 55. The other four pillars, which remained in the strategic plan, were security, essential services, the economy and governance.

39. *USA Today*, 'How Iraqis view the role of the media', 29 April 2004, <http://www.usatoday.com/news/world/iraq/2004-04-29-gallup-poll-media-full.htm>.

40. Dermer, interview, p. 9. SAIC, the US-based contractors who ran *al-Sabah*, claimed a circulation of 60,000: Ben Haddad, 'SAIC and news coverage of the Iraqi Media Network (IMN)', 26 January 2004, <http://www.saic.com/cover-archive/natsec/imn.html>.

41. Tarik Kafala, 'Iraq's media free-for-all', BBC News Online, 27 June 2003, <http://news.bbc.co.uk/1/hi/world/middle_east/3023752.stm>.

42. Yochi J. Dreazen, 'Army orders troops to seize TV Station in northwest Iraq', *Wall Street Journal*, 8 May 2003.

43. Andy Sennitt, 'Mosul TV fights for independence', Radio Netherlands Wereldomreop web site, 14 July 2003, <http://www.rnw.nl/realradio/features/html/mosul030714.html>; more generally, Rohan Jayasekera, 'A Limit to the Demands of Military Security', *Index on Censorship*, 24 July 2003, <http://www.indexonline.org/news/20030727_iraq.shtml>.

44. 'Iraq television viewership poll', Office of Intelligence and Research, State Department, 16 October 2003, <http://www.stanhopecentre.org/iraqmediapoll.shtml>.

45. *USA Today*, 'How Iraqis view', 29 April 2004.

46.   Gordon Robison, who acted as a consultant to the IMN for eight months from October 2003, recorded that staff were paid a flat fee of $120 per month, compared to salaries of $800 per month for cameramen and $1,000 for reporters paid by Western news bureaus: 'Rebuilding Iraqi television: a personal account', October 2004, p. 10, <http://uscpublicdiplomacy.com/pdfs/Robison_Iraqi_Media_Oct04.pdf>.

47.   Interview with Kate Butler, by email, 29 August 2004.

48.   Interview with senior Coalition military officer, February 2005.

49.   *O'Dwyer's PR Daily*, 30 September 2004, via <http://www.odwyerpr.com/>, reporting that Iraqex (later renamed Lincoln Corp) had been contracted to oversee public affairs and advertising for Multinational Corps-Iraq.

50.   Senator John Warner, chairman of the Senate Armed Services Committee, transcript of press conference on Iraqi Media, 2 December 2005, via <http://www.washingtonpost.com>; Mark Mazzetti and Borzou Daragahi, 'U.S. military covertly pays to run stories in Iraqi press', *Los Angeles Times*, 30 November 2005; Josh White and Bradley Graham, 'Military says it paid Iraq papers for news', *Washington Post*, 3 December 2005.

51.   Jeff Gerth, 'Propaganda: military's information war is vast and often secretive', *New York Times*, 11 December 2005.

52.   Rick Jervis and Zaid Sabah, 'Probe into Iraq coverage widens', *USA Today*, 9 December 2005.

53.   e.g., Kenneth Pollack, 'After Saddam: assessing the reconstruction of Iraq' (12 January 2004), accessed via <www.foreignaffairs.org>; Anne Ellen Henderson, 'The Coalition Provisional Authority's experience with economic reconstruction in Iraq: lessons identified', United States Institute of Peace Special Report 138, April 2005.

54.   DoD weekly report, 12 January 2004, p. 11; DoD weekly report, 20 January 2004, p. 11.

55.   CPA, *An Historic Review of CPA Accomplishments*, Iraq: Baghdad, 2004, p. 27; State Department weekly report, 27 October 2004, p. 11. A different estimate is from a UNDP/Ministry of Planning and Development Cooperation (MOPDC) survey, which found that 54% of households received a safe and stable supply of drinking water: *Iraq Living Conditions Survey 2004*, Volume II, Baghdad, 2005, p. 19.

56.   US Government Accountability Office (GAO), 'U.S. water and sanitation

efforts need improved measures for assessing impact and sustained resources for maintaining facilities', Report to Congressional Committees, 7 September 2005, p. 14.

57.   GAO, 'Rebuilding Iraq: enhancing security, measuring program results, and maintaining infrastructure are necessary to make significant and sustainable progress', Testimony to Congressional Committees, 18 October 2005, p. 17.

58.   GAO, 'U.S. water and sanitation efforts', p. 20; GAO, 'Rebuilding Iraq: enhancing security', p. 16.

59.   Ariana Eunjung Cha, 'Iraqi experts tossed with the water', *Washington Post*, 27 February 2004.

60.   State Department, *Quarterly Report to Congress (2207 Report),* July 2005, Appendix I, p. 63.

61.   GAO, 'U.S. water and sanitation efforts', p. 25.

62.   GAO, 'U.S. water and sanitation efforts', p. 26.

63.   Office of Management and Budget, *Quarterly Report to Congress (2207 Report),* April 2004, Appendix I, p. 16; also, Jeremy M. Sharp and Christopher M. Blanchard, 'Post-war Iraq: a table and chronology of foreign contributions', CRS Report for Congress (18 March 2005).

64.   Tom Wheelock and Robyn McGuckin, 'Iraqi power sector: CPA's legacy and lessons', July 2005, unpaginated; partially published in *Middle East Economic Survey*, 18 July 2005. Wheelock was director of the USAID Iraq Infrastructure Reconstruction Program (February 2003 to May 2004); McGuikin was Deputy CPA Senior Adviser for Electricity (July 2003 to June 2004). Also Wheelock, interview <http://www.usip.org/library/oh/sops/iraq/rec/wheelock.pdf>, p. 12.

65.   Wheelock and McGuckin, 'Iraqi power sector'; interview with Leslie Dean, CPA Regional Coordinator for Baghdad from January to September 2004 (28 October 2004), <http://www.usip.org/library/oh/sops/iraq/rec/dean.pdf>, p. 10.

66.   Press conference, 9 October 2003, at <http://www.cpa-iraq.org/transcripts/20031009_Oct-09Bremerpresscon.htm>.

67.   See successive DoD weekly reports. Accounts of the status of electricity generation were relegated in the weekly report from p. 3 to somewhere between pp. 18 and 22 from 4 May 2004.

68.   Commander of the US Army Corps of Engineers Major General Thomas Bostwick, quoted in 'Iraq's power supply sinks to record low', AFP, 12

January 2005.

69.   First used in State Department weekly report, 9 March 2004, p. 4.

70.   The new 'goal' is used, without comment on the change, in State Department weekly report, 22 June 2005, p.10.

71.   Successive State Department weekly reports, up to 18 January 2006.

72.   e.g., Karl Vick, 'The critical battle for Iraq's energy: attacks by saboteurs cripple infrastructure', *Washington Post*, 15 January 2005.

73.   Mark Etherington, *Revolt on the Tigris: The Al-Sadr Uprising and the Governing of Iraq*, London: Hurst & Co., 2005, pp. 222-3.

74.   Jackie Spinner, 'Lights are coming on, slowly, in Iraq', *Washington Post*, 7 February 2004.

75.   Wheelock and McGuckin, 'Iraqi power sector', describe how Siemens and General Electric both took this approach, and how this delayed key generation projects.

76.   Interview with two Coalition officers, both formerly on tour of duty in Maysan, November 2004 and September 2005.

77.   Wheelock and McGuckin, 'Iraqi power sector'.

78.   Interview with senior Coalition military officer, February 2005; Wheelock and McGuckin, 'Iraqi power sector'.

79.   Wheelock and McGuckin, 'Iraqi power sector'.

80.   USAID Office of Inspector General, 'Audit of USAID/Iraq's electrical power sector activities', 29 June 2005, pp. 21, 25; GAO, 'Rebuilding Iraq: enhancing security', pp. 21-22.

81.   Spinner, 'Lights are coming on'; also, Wheelock and McGuckin, 'Iraqi power sector', and an interview with a senior Coalition military officer, May 2004.

82.   DoD weekly report, 16 March 2004, pp. 4-5.

83.   Hilary Synnott, 'State-building in Southern Iraq', *Survival*, vol. 47, no. 2 (Summer 2005), p. 52. It was receiving electricity for only seven hours per day in mid-January 2005: State Department weekly report, 26 January 2005, p. 16.

84.   State Department weekly report, 20 July 2005, p. 11.

85.   Neil Macdonald, 'Basra pulls the plug on Baghdad', *Financial Times*, 14 October 2005.

86.   State Department weekly report, 18 January 2006, p.11; Ambassador Khalilzad to Secretary of State Rice, 'Snapshots from the office: Public Affairs staff show strain of social discord', June 2006, p. 3, leaked to the

Washington Post, at <http://www.washingtonpost.com/wp-srv/opinions/graphics/iraqdocs_061606.pdf>, p.3.

87.   CPA Order no.1 (16 May 2003). Originally laid out by Donald Rumsfeld, Defence Department briefing transcript, 25 April 2003; and testimony of Under Secretary of Defence for Policy Douglas Feith to the House of Representatives Committee on International Relations, 15 May 2003.

88.   Paul Bremer, Defence Department news briefing, 12 June 2003. Ahmad Chalabi gave a figure of 28,000 dismissed in the period up to January 2004: see Hamza Hendawi, 'Iraq details plans to uproot Ba'athists', Associated Press, 11 January 2004.

89.   CPA Order no. 2 (23 May 2003). Walter Slocombe, who was responsible for the disbanding of the Iraqi army, gave his account in 'To build an army', *Washington Post*, 5 November 2003. Detailed critical accounts of the impact of these measures include Jon Lee Anderson, 'Out on the Street', *New Yorker*, 15 November 2004; and Faleh A. Jabar, 'Postconflict Iraq: a Race for Stability, Reconstruction, and Legitimacy', United States Institute of Peace Special Report 120, May 2004.

90.   David Bacon, 'U.S. arrests Iraqi union leaders', Pacific News Service, 10 December 2003; interviews with members of the Iraqi Union of the Unemployed, Baghdad, September 2003.

91.   DoD weekly report, 4 November 2003, p. 20; Etherington, *Revolt*, pp. 44-5.

92.   DoD weekly report, 4 November 2003, p. 20.

93.   DoD weekly report, 16 March 2004, p. 30.

94.   DoD weekly report, 8 December 2004, p. 13; and subsequent weekly reports.

95.   Sue Pleming, 'New approach to Iraq rebuilding bears fruit', Reuters, 15 December 2004; Sue Pleming, 'U.S. reviews rebuilding, gives more power to Iraqis', Reuters, 1 February 2005.

96.   IRI, *Survey of Iraqi Public Opinion, 24 November–5 December 2004*, <http://www.iri.org/pdfs/NovemberSurveyPresentation.ppt>, pp. 7, 17. An earlier IRI survey of 24 September–4 October 2004 had similar results: <http://www.iri.org/pdfs/IraqSept-OctPublicOpinion.ppt>, pp. 7, 24.

97.   UNDP/MOPDC, *ILCS 2004*, Vol. II, p. 120.

98.   UNDP/MOPDC, *ILCS 2004*, Vol. II, pp. 120-1, 126.

99.   UNDP/MOPDC, *ILCS 2004*, Vol. II, p. 133.

100.   Briefing handout by Charles Hess, PCO Director, 7 October 2004, at: <http://www.defenselink.mil/news/Oct2004/d20041007slides.pdf>, p. 2.

101.   Charles A. Krohn, 'A Baghdad Journal', *Columbia Journalism Review*, no. 2 (March/April 2004), and articles cited therein.

102.   Sue Pleming, 'U.S. opens bidding for new Iraq work', Reuters, 7 January 2004.

103.   Synnott, 'State-building', p. 42. Also, Marc Houben (former Netherlands liaison officer to the CPA), 'Operations in Iraq: the new face of international crisis management', *DIAS Analysis*, no. 6 (July 2004), pp. 23-4; and Dean, interview, pp. 12-13.

104.   Deborah Haynes, 'Pentagon awards 1.1 bln dollars in Iraq contracts to US, British firms', AFP, 12 March 2004; Paul Peachey, 'Iraqi businessmen seek US reconstruction cash', AFP, 19 April 2004.

105.   Office of Management and Budget (OMB), *Quarterly Report to Congress (2207 Report)*, 2 July 2004, pp. 17-20; Rajiv Chandrasekaran, 'U.S. funds for Iraq are largely unspent', *Washington Post*, 4 July 2004.

106.   Sue Pleming, 'U.S. hopes to woo wary Iraqis with small projects', Reuters, 24 May 2004. As of 31 March 2006, the figure had leapt to 2,780 PCO projects begun and 2,201 out of 3,108 planned. PCO, *Iraq Reconstruction Update*, 31 March 2006, p. 9.

107.   OMB, *Quarterly Report to Congress (2207 Report)*, 5 April 2004, pp. 11; successive State Department weekly reports from 2005.

108.   ICG, *Reconstructing Iraq*, 2 September 2004.

109.   Ben Brown, 'Iraq contrast: candy and kicks', BBC NewsOnline, 4 February 2004; similarly, Josh White, 'In Samarra, attacks hamper rebuilding', *Washington Post*, 19 December 2004.

110.   Doug Struck, 'U.S. using cash as a defensive weapon', *Washington Post*, 26 July 2004.

111.   Interview with former CPA Governance Coordinator, May 2005.

112.   Eric Bauer, a CPA Governance Officer from October 2003 until April 2004, interview (21 October 2004), <http://www.usip.org/library/oh/sops/iraq/gov/bauer.pdf>, p. 23.

113.   Press release of 5 July 2004, at <http://www.iraqdirectory.com/files/articles/article059.htm>; also DoD weekly report, 25 May 2004, p. 19.

114.   DoD weekly reports of 25 August 2004, pp. 6, 20; 1 September 2004, pp. 4, 21; and 5 January 2005, p. 9.

115.   UNDP/MOPDC, ILCS 2004, Vol. II, pp. 127-8.

116.   State Department, *Quarterly Report to Congress (2207 Report),* 5 October
       2004, p. 78; State Department, *Quarterly Report to Congress (2207 Report),*
       July 2005, p. 20.

117.   State Department weekly report, 4 January 2006, p. 21.

118.   Edward Wong, 'Iraq's lack of fuel stokes fires of anger, resentment', *New
       York Times,* 2 December 2003; Neela Banerjee, 'Shortages of power and
       fuel plague Iraq', *New York Times,* 9 January 2004; Patrick Cockburn, '"I
       started queuing yesterday and I expect petrol tomorrow"', *The Independent,*
       10 December 2004; Rory McCarthy and Osama Mansour, 'Iraq fuel crisis
       adds to chaos', *Guardian,* 13 December 2004; Oliver Poole, 'Petrol
       rationing in a country awash with oil', *Daily Telegraph,* 6 September 2005;
       Kelley, 'Rumors in Iraq', p. 3.

119.   AFP, 'UNICEF sounds Iraq malnutrition alarm', 19 December 2004.

120.   UNDP/MOPDC, *ILCS 2004,* Vol. II, p. 57.

121.   World Food Programme (WFP), 'WFP Food Survey Shows High
       Prevalence of Food Insecurity in Iraq', 28 September 2004, <http://
       www.wfp.org/index.asp?section=2>; UNICEF, 'Food Insecurity in Iraq
       Persists: Children Suffer', 11 May 2006.

122.   Quoted by George Packer, 'Caught in the crossfire: will moderate Iraqis
       embrace democracy - or Islamist radicalism?', *New Yorker,* 17 May 2004.

123.   Steven R. Weisman, 'Sensing Shiites will rule Iraq, U.S. starts to see friends,
       not foes', *New York Times,* 20 November 2003; Rajiv Chandrasekaran and
       Robin Wright, 'U.S. weighs elections for Iraq's provisional government',
       Washington Post, 28 November 2003; Charles Clover and Roula Khalaf,
       'Shia unrest spells trouble for US policy in Iraq', *Financial Times,* 13
       January 2004; Warren P. Strobel and Jonathan S. Landay, 'CIA officers
       warn of Iraq civil war, contradicting Bush's optimism', Knight Ridder
       Newspapers, 22 January 2004.

124.   Patrick E. Tyler, 'Iraqi groups badly divided over how to draft a
       charter', *New York Times,* 30 September 2003; Robin Wright and Rajiv
       Chandrasekaran, 'Alternatives to Iraqi council eyed: inaction of hand-
       picked Baghdad officials frustrates Washington', *Washington Post,* 9
       November 2003; Daniel Williams, 'Iraqi warns of delay on constitution,
       vote', *Washington Post,* 10 November 2003; ICG, *Iraq's Constitutional
       Challenge,* 13 November 2003, pp. 5-7, 22-3.

125.   Diamond's account of this process is particularly thorough: *Squandered*

Victory, pp. 171-8, 183-4, 202-3, 248-9.

126. Letter from Ayatollah Sistani to UN Secretary-General Kofi Annan, quoted in Juan Cole, *Informed Comment*, 8 June 2004; letter from Masoud Barzani and Jalal Talabani to President Bush, 1 June 2004, accessed via <http://web.krg.org/>; Dexter Filkins, 'Kurds threaten to walk away from Iraqi State', *New York Times*, 9 June 2004; Steven R. Weisman, 'Kurds find U.S. alliance is built on shifting sands', *New York Times*, 11 June 2004.

127. e.g., Robin Wright and Rajiv Chandrasekaran, 'Alternatives to Iraqi council eyed', *Washington Post*, 9 November 2003; Rory McCarthy, 'Governing council put in frame as US makes no bones about how situation is unravelling', *Guardian*, 13 November 2003; Robin Wright and Walter Pincus, 'U.S., U.N. seek new leaders for Iraq', *Washington Post*, 24 April 2004.

128. *Al-Qabas* (Kuwait), 19 March 2004; *an-Nahar* (Lebanon), 19 March 2004; Naomi Klein, 'Baghdad Year Zero', *Harper's Magazine*, September 2004; Nicholas Pelham, 'Iraq interior minister resigns as battles rage', *Financial Times*, 8 April 2004.

129. Demetri Sevastopulo, 'US authorities in Iraq probe phone contracts', *Financial Times*, 11 November 2003; Demetri Sevastopulo, Nicolas Pelham and Roula Khalaf, 'US staff in Iraq bribe probe', *Financial Times*, 22 November 2003; Nicolas Pelham, 'Dispute grows over Iraq mobile phone licences', *Financial Times*, 23 November 2003.

130. Nicolas Pelham and Joshua Chaffin, 'Iraqi threat to overturn US broadcasting contract', *Financial Times*, 9 January 2004.

131. Orders 65 and 66 (20 March 2004).

132. Nicolas Pelham and Mark Turner, 'Bremer seeks to cement Iraq measures', *Financial Times*, 25 March 2004.

133. Naomi Klein, 'Freedom fires', 5 April 2004, at: <http://nologo.org/newsite/detail.php?ID=380>.

134. Interview with a senior Coalition military officer, May 2004.

135. Etherington, *Revolt*, pp. 156 and 167.

136. 'Iraqi interior minister resigns', al-Jazeera.net, 8 April 2004.

137. Iyad Allawi, 'Give us back our dignity', *Independent on Sunday*, 27 June 2004; 'Iraqi president discusses amnesty', *RFE/RL Iraq Report*, vol. 7, no. 26, 15 July 2004.

138. 'Daily reports Iraqi president, U.S. ambassador at odds over amnesty', *RFE/RL Iraq Report*, vol. 7, no. 27, 22 July 2004; 'No amnesty for

Iraqis who kill US GIs', al-Jazeera.net, 17 July 2004; 'Limited amnesty announced by Allawi', Knight Ridder Newspapers, 8 August 2004; Dodge, *Iraq's Future*, p. 17.

139.   Zaki Chehab, *Iraq Ablaze: Inside the Insurgency*, London: I.B. Tauris, 2005, p. 92.

140.   Louise Roug, 'U.S. to restrict Iraqi police', *Los Angeles Times*, 30 December 2005; also, Dexter Filkins, 'G.I.'s to increase U.S. supervision of Iraqi police', *New York Times*, 30 December 2005.

141.   Security Council Resolution 1546 (8 June 2004), para.10; the mandate was extended in Security Council Resolution 1637 (8 November 2005), para.1.

142.   Guy Dinmore, 'US "losing its grip" on Baghdad's political process', *Financial Times*, 31 May 2005.

143.   Hanna Batatu, *The Old Social Classes and the Revolutionary Movements of Iraq*, Princeton University Press, 1978, pp. 24-5, 88-92.

144.   Faleh A. Jabar, 'Sheikhs and Ideologues: Deconstruction and Reconstruction of Tribes under Patrimonial Totalitarianism in Iraq, 1968-1998', in Faleh Abdul-Jabar and Hosham Dawod, eds, *Tribes and Power: Nationalism and Ethnicity in the Middle East*, London: Saqi, 2003, pp. 88-96; Amatzia Baram, 'Neo-tribalism in Iraq: Saddam Husayn's Tribal Policies 1991-1996', *International Journal of Middle Eastern Studies*, vol. 29, no.1 (1997), pp. 1-31.

145.   Charles Clover, 'US builds up tribal rule on coke, doughnuts and power', *Financial Times*, 14 July 2003; Yaroslav Trofimov, 'To find peace in Sunni Triangle, talk to the sheiks', *Wall Street Journal*, 5 November 2003; Wheelock and McGuckin, 'Iraqi power sector'; David Axe, 'Tribe, family take priority over the law', *Washington Times*, 27 July 2005; Steven Vincent, 'A power problem in Basra', *National Review*, 2 August 2005; James Glanz, 'Iraq's oil starts flowing once more', *New York Times*, 3 September 2005; interviews with former CPA Governorate Coordinator, May 2005; and Lt. Col Christopher Hughes, interview (29 October 2004), <http://www.usip.org/library/oh/sops/iraq/sec/hughes.pdf>, p. 13.

146.   Mohamad Bazi, 'On their terms: U.S. soldier reaches out to understand Iraqi tribal system', *Newsday*, 21 December 2003; Annia Ciezadlo, 'From better to verse', *Washington Times*, 3 January 2004; Wheelock and McGuckin, 'Iraqi power sector'; Valentinas Mite, 'Tribal influence still strong, but some say its power is waning', RFE/RL, 16 July 2004.

147. e.g., Hughes, interview, pp. 4-5, 20.

148. Interview by email with Lt-Col. Alan King, 17 January 2004.

149. e.g., 'Tribal leaders vow to fight crime, protect transport routes', *RFE/RL Iraq Report*, vol. 7, no. 23, 25 June 2004; George Packer, 'Letter from Basra: testing ground', *New Yorker*, 28 February 2005.

150. ICG, *Can Local Governance Save Central Government?* 27 October 2004, pp. 15, 18; Ivan Stoyanov, 'Local Governance and Democratization in Iraq', unpublished MS, 13 May 2004, pp. 22, 31.

151. Etherington, *Revolt*, p. 103; also, Sheik Hamed quoted in Trofimov, 'To find peace', and Synnott, 'State-building', p. 49.

152. CPA Order no.22 (7 August 2003). One senior Coalition military officer claimed Slocombe made these decisions for 'ideological reasons': interview, May 2004.

153. United States Department of Defence, News Transcript, 17 September 2003.

154. Dermer, interview, p. 22.

155. Barak Salmoni, 'Iraq's unready security forces: an interim assessment', *Meria Journal*, vol. 8, no. 3 (September 2004).

156. Dermer, interview, pp. 22-31; CPA Order 67 (21 March 2004).

157. Figures from Bowman, 'Iraq', p. 5; Gilmore, 'U.S. troops'; and State Department weekly report, 25 January 2006, pp. 7, 24.

158. Anthony H. Cordesman, *Iraqi Armed Forces on the Edge of War*, Washington, D.C.: CSIS, 7 February 2003, pp. 1, 37.

159. Doug Brooks, 'Private warriors', PBS Frontline, 21 June 2005: <http://www.pbs.org/wgbh/pages/frontline/shows/warriors/faqs/>.

160. Amy Belasco, 'The Cost of Operations in Iraq, Afghanistan, and Enhanced Security', CRS Report for Congress (14 March 2005), p. 6.

161. State Department, *Quarterly Report to Congress (2207 Report),* July 2005, p. 18; State Department, *Quarterly Report to Congress (2207 Report),* October 2005, p. 20.

162. State Department, *Quarterly Report to Congress (2207 Report),* April 2004, p. 15.

163. Higher figures are presented in GAO, 'Rebuilding Iraq: enhancing security', p. 5. The GAO incorporates spending on 'democracy promotion' within its calculations of security and justice spending, whereas we have excluded these costs from our calculations.

164. GAO, 'U.S. water and sanitation efforts', pp. 7-10, 25. Also, Christian

Miller, 'Some Iraq projects running out of money, U.S. says', *Los Angeles Times*, 8 September 2005.

165.   GAO, 'Rebuilding Iraq: enhancing security', p. 14.

166.   e.g., Mohammed Ayoob, *The Third World Security Predicament: State Making, Regional Conflict, and the International System*, Boulder, CO: Lynne Rienner, 1995, esp. pp. 15, 191-3; Christopher Clapham, *Third World Politics*, London: Croom Helm, 1985, chapter 4; Crawford Young, *The African Colonial State* in Comparative *Perspective*, New Haven: Yale University Press, 1994, pp. 40-2.

167.   Dana Priest, *The Mission: Waging War and Keeping Peace With America's Military*, New York: W.W. Norton & Co, 2004; Tarak Barkawi, *Globalization and War*, Oxford: Rowman & Littlefield, 2006.

168.   Quoted in Packer, 'Caught in the crossfire'.

169.   e.g., Interview with Larry Crandall, Deputy Head of the CPA Programme Management Office between January and June 2004 (20 September 2004), <http://www.usip.org/library/oh/sops/iraq/rec/crandall.pdf>, p. 10.

170.   e.g., Jen Banbury, 'Inside the Green Zone', Salon.com, 6 February 2004; Salaam Jihad, 'Still walled in', Institute for War and Peace Reporting, 8 March 2004; and from a very different perspective, Michael Rubin, 'A fresh start', *National Review*, 28 January 2005.

171.   Patrick Cockburn, 'US soldiers bulldoze Iraqi crops', *The Independent*, 1 October 2003; Chehab, *Iraq Ablaze*, p. 24.

3. GOVERNANCE – CENTRE AND PERIPHERY

1.   Houben, 'Operations in Iraq', p. 10; Synnott, 'State-building', p. 38; Etherington, *Revolt*, pp. 7-8, 15 *et passim*.

2.   In March 2004, the CPA had 558 US federal personnel and an estimated 1,196 personnel overall, despite having the authorisation for 2,117 positions: see CPA Inspector General, 'Management of personnel assigned to the Coalition Provisional Authority in Baghdad, Iraq', 25 June 2004, pp. 1, 3; L. Elaine Halchin, 'The Coalition Provisional Authority (CPA): origin, characteristics, and institutional authorities', CRS Report for Congress (6 June 2005), pp. 14-15. Estimates of the total number of CPA staff based in its central headquarters vary from 500 to over 1,000: interview with CPA senior policy adviser, Baghdad, September 2003; interview with Col. Mark Yanaway, liaison officer between the IGC and

CJTF-7 (14 July 2004), <http://www.usip.org/library/oh/sops/iraq/gov/yanaway.pdf>, p. 18; Diamond, *Squandered Victory*, p. 76.

3. Etherington, *Revolt*, pp. 7-8, 48, 98-9. The numerical imbalance in the south-east is discussed by Greg Mills, 'Better with the UN? Searching for Peace and Governance in Iraq', *Global Governance*, vol. 10 (2004), p. 284.

4. Major General Charles H. Swannack, Commander of 82nd Airborne Division, news briefing, 18 November 2003; Yaroslav Trofimov, 'To find peace in Sunni Triangle, talk to the sheiks', *Wall Street Journal*, 5 November 2003; Rajiv Chandrasekaran, 'In a hostile land, trying whatever works', *Washington Post*, 23 December 2003.

5. Etherington, *Revolt*, pp. 54-5.

6. Written comments from a senior State Department official, 23 June 2003; interview with CPA senior policy adviser, Baghdad, September 2003; Charles Grinnell, Senior Adviser to Iraq's Commission on Public Integrity, based in Iraq from April 2003 to October 2004 (22 October 2004), <http://www.usip.org/library/oh/sops/iraq/gov/grinnell.pdf>, pp. 22-3.

7. Interview with Robin Raphel, ORHA and CPA Senior Adviser on Trade from April to August 2003 (13 July 2004), <http://www.usip.org/library/oh/sops/iraq/rec/raphel.pdf>, p. 12.

8. Interview with Jay Bachar, civil affairs officer in Baghdad, 20 April 2003 to 1 March 2004 (19 July 2004), <http://www.usip.org/library/oh/sops/iraq/sec/bachar.pdf>, p. 18.

9. David Sanger, 'White House to overhaul Iraq and Afghan missions', *New York Times*, 6 October 2003; Bill Powell and Aparisim Ghosh, 'Paul Bremer's rough ride', *Time Magazine*, 28 June 2004; Caroline Daniel and Guy Dinmore, 'State Department takes over Iraq reconstruction', *Financial Times*, 15 December 2005.

10. Dean, interview, p. 13; Houben, 'Operations in Iraq', pp. 7-9.

11. Interview with former CPA Regional Coordinator, February 2006.

12. Wheelock, interview, p. 18; Bachar, interview, p. 30; interview with Adam Sugar, assistant to the CPA senior advisers on trade and foreign affairs, from July 2003 to April 2004 (1 November 2004), <http://www.usip.org/library/oh/sops/iraq/gov/sugar.pdf>, p. 6; Etherington, *Revolt*, pp. 151-2; Synnott, 'State-building', pp. 37-8; GAO, 'U.S. water and sanitation efforts', pp. 23-4.

13. Houben, 'Operations in Iraq', p. 7; interview with Charles Costello,

Deputy Chief of Party in the Local Governance Support Project, May 2003 to May 2004 (14 October 2004), <http://www.usip.org/library/oh/sops/iraq/gov/costello.pdf>, p. 28; Yanaway, interview, p. 18.

14. Andrew Rathmell, 'Planning Post-conflict Reconstruction in Iraq: what can we Learn?', *International Affairs*, vol. 81 no. 5 (2005), p. 1020. Rathmell served as the CPA's Director of Planning, Policy and Analysis for ten months from August 2003 onwards.

15. Etherington, *Revolt*, pp. 60, 155. More generally, see Rathmell, 'Planning', pp. 1030-1.

16. Etherington, *Revolt*, pp. 20-1, 61, 100.

17. Synnott, 'State-building', pp. 36, 40-1; Costello, interview, pp. 15-16, 21-2; Dermer, interview, p. 20.

18. Interview with senior Coalition military officer, February 2005.

19. Rathmell, 'Planning', p. 1033; Synnott, 'State-building', p. 43; Etherington, *Revolt*, pp. 96, 131, 190-1; interview with Sherri Kraham, Deputy Director of the CPA Office of Management and Budget (5 November 2004), <http://www.usip.org/library/oh/sops/iraq/rec/kraham.pdf>, pp. 5-6.

20. Correspondence with Rory Stewart, Deputy Governance Coordinator of Dhi Qar governorate, 28 April 2004.

21. Etherington, *Revolt*, p. 152.

22. Synnott, 'State-building', p. 42.

23. Etherington, *Revolt*, p. 124-5, 224; Synnott, 'State-building', p. 51; Costello, interview, pp. 18, 28.

24. Rajiv Chandrasekaran, 'Attacks force retreat from wide-ranging plans for Iraq', *Washington Post*, 28 December 2003; Rathmell, 'Planning', p. 1029.

25. Synnott, 'State-building', pp. 47-8.

26. Glen Rangwala, <http://middleeastreference.org.uk/iraqgc.html>.

27. Namely, Ahmad Shya'a al-Barak Al Bu Sultan, Raja' Habib al-Khuza'i, Wa'il 'Abd al-Latif, 'Abd al-Karim Mahmud al-Muhammadawi (Abu Hatim), 'Abd al-Zahra Uthman Muhammad ('Izz al-Din Salim) and Aqila al-Hashimi.

28. Dana Priest and Robin Wright, 'Iraq spy service planned by U.S. to stem attacks', *Washington Post*, 11 December 2003; Edward Wong, 'New Iraq agency to hunt rebels', *New York Times*, 31 January 2004; RFE/RL, 'U.S. civil administrator appoints defense minister, intelligence chief', 5 April

2004; interview with a senior Coalition military officer, May 2004.

29.   Yanaway, interview, pp. 3-4; personal observations and visits in Baghdad, September 2003.

30.   NDI, 'Iraq: reinforcing the democratic middle', undated factsheet, apparently from 2004, at <http://www.accessdemocracy.org/library/1734_iq_infocus_060104.pdf>.

31.   GAO, 'Rebuilding Iraq: U.S. assistance for the January 2005 elections', Report to Congressional Committees, 7 September 2005, p. 6.

32.   Joel Brinkley, 'Some members propose keeping Iraqi council after transition', *New York Times*, 25 November 2003; Chibli Mallat, 'Note to the UN: hands off Iraqi politics', *New York Times*, 19 January 2004; Rajiv Chandrasekaran, 'Council in Iraq resisting Ayatollah', *Washington Post*, 2 December 2003; Dodge, *Iraq's Future*, pp. 35-6; Wilcke, 'Castles built of sand'; Annia Ciezadlo, 'Old Iraqi council clings to key roles', *Christian Science Monitor*, 24 June 2004. Diamond, *Squandered Victory*, contains useful material, but is disingenuous in claiming that only six of the new ministers had 'ties to large parties' (p.262), and that therefore Brahimi's plan was in effect realised. In fact, at least 17 of the new ministers were strongly tied to political parties: whether they were all large parties or not is irrelevant to the evaluation of Brahimi's success.

33.   Footage shot by independent film-makers Insider Films, 3 May 2003, unscreened.

34.   UN Office of the Humanitarian Coordinator for Iraq, weekly update, 26 May 2003; John Sullivan, 'Free elections hit snags in Kirkuk', Knight Ridder Newspapers, 24 May 2003.

35.   David Rohde, 'U.S. official overrules commanders, cancels Iraq's first postwar election', *New York Times*, 19 June 2003; William Booth and Rajiv Chandrasekaran, 'Occupation forces halt elections throughout Iraq', *Washington Post*, 28 June 2003.

36.   Etherington, *Revolt,* p. 22; Costello, interview, pp. 8, 15, 21; Rice, interview, p. 20.

37.   ICG, *Can Local Governance*, pp. 11-13.

38.   Personal communication, March 2004; also Synnott, 'State-building', pp. 49-50; and Costello, interview, p. 17.

39.   Anthony Shadid, 'In Iraqi towns, electoral experiment finds some success', *Washington Post*, 16 February 2004.

40.   Denver Regional Council of Governments, *Regional Report*, August 2003,

p. 1; Karen Rouse, 'Ex-mayor helps bring democracy to Iraqis', *Denver Post*, 7 December 2003; Dean, interview, p. 18.

41.   e.g., article 9(1) of the Interim Operating Instructions of the Baghdad councils, in the *Baghdad Citizen Advisory Council Handbook*, published by the CPA, Research Triangle Institute and USAID, 3rd edn, 7 November 2003. A different perspective appears in Adeed Dawisha, 'Iraq: Setbacks, Advances, Prospects', *Journal of Democracy* 15, 2004.

42.   'Baghdad neighborhood advisory council votes in new members', 9 January 2004, at: <http://www.defendamerica.mil/articles/jan2004/a010904d.html>.

43.   CPA Order no. 62, para 1(f), 1 March 2004.

44.   The contract is at <http://www.usaid.gov/iraq/contracts/pdf/RTI.pdf>; ICG, *Can Local Governance*, pp. 8-9.

45.   None of the three cases however involves northern Iraq: with the pre-existing KRG remaining in place, the evolution of relations between the northern governorates and the new authorities in Baghdad took a different form from the examples given here, a subject we considered in Chapter One.

46.   Quoted in Yitzhak Nakash, *The Shi'is of Iraq*, Princeton University Press, 1994, p. 22; also Faleh A. Jabar, *The Shi'ite Movement in Iraq*, London: Saqi, 2003, p. 64.

47.   Reidar Visser, *Basra, the Failed Gulf State: Separatism and Nationalism in Southern Iraq*, Berlin: LIT Verlag, 2005, esp. Chapter 10.

48.   Phrase used by, among others, Brigadier-General Mark Kimmitt, CPA press briefing, 21 November 2003; *Desert Rifles* (a 3rd Armoured Cavalry publication), 1 August 2003, p. 1; *Coalition Scimitar* (a US Department of Defence publication), 12 December 2003, p. 2.

49.   Jabar, 'Sheikhs and ideologues', p. 96.

50.   *Desert Rifles*, 1 August 2003, p. 1; CPA south-central press release, 31 July 2003.

51.   Anne Barnard and Farah Stockman, 'US plan angering new Iraq parties', *Boston Globe*, 18 January 2004.

52.   Quoted in Charles Clover and Roula Khalaf, 'Saddam's sectarian legacy lingers', *Financial Times*, 12 December 2003.

53.   Clover, 'US builds up tribal rule'.

54.   Jon Lee Anderson, 'A man of the shadows: can Iyad Allawi hold Iraq together?', *New Yorker*, 24 January 2005.

55. Barnard and Stockman, 'US plan'; Wisam M. Karim al-Jaf, 'Governorate west of Baghdad shrugs off instability and insurrection to hold peaceful ballot', Institute for War and Peace Reporting, 23 February 2004.

56. Chandrasekaran, 'In a hostile land'; also, Rory McCarthy, 'Troops find talk is key to earning trust of Iraqis', *Guardian*, 11 November 2003.

57. John F. Burns and Erik Eckholm, 'In western Iraq, fundamentalists hold U.S. at bay', *New York Times*, 29 August 2004.

58. Dexter Filkins, 'Bombing is blow to Iraq city that has plan to police itself', *New York Times,* 21 November 2003; Dexter Filkins, 'Amid attacks, Iraqis relish new liberties', *New York Times*, 16 February 2004; Anderson, 'A man of the shadows'.

59. Burns and Eckholm, 'In western Iraq'.

60. Edward Wong, 'Provincial capital near Falluja is rapidly slipping into chaos', *New York Times,* 28 October 2004; Ann Scott Tyson, 'To the dismay of local Sunnis, Shiites arrive to police Ramadi', *Washington Post*, 7 May 2005; al-Jazeera.Net, 'Governor of Iraqi province seized', 11 May 2005; Jonathan Finer and Omar Fekeiki, 'For Anbar's rookie governor, it's one tough day at a time', *Washington Post*, 30 June 2005.

61. Cole, 'United States and Shi'ite religious factions', p. 563.

62. Philippe Gélie, 'La ville sainte sous l'emprise des Islamistes', *Le Figaro*, 21 April 2003; Khalil Khalaf, 'Supreme Council condemns the assassination of al-Khu'i and Islamic delegation meets Muqtada al-Sadr', *al-Ra'i al-'Am*, 13 April 2003; AFP, 'Governor elected to head up Iraqi holy city of Karbala', 16 April 2003; Associated Press, 'Shi'ite clerics on the rise in Iraq's holy cities', 17 April 2003.

63. Nakash, *Shi'is*, pp. 23, 95-6; Salman Hadi al-Tu'mah, *The Tribes of Karbala*, Beirut: Dar al-Muhajjah al-Bayda, 1998, p. 231.

64. Ziad H. Fahmi, 'Sistani quits Karbala council', *Iraq Today*, 10 November 2003.

65. Quoted in ICG, *Can Local Governance*, p. 18. Also, 'al-Karbala'i opposes lack of consultation with the marjaiyyah in his Friday sermon', *al-Zaman*, 21 February 2004; 'al-Karbala'i rejects suggestion to put Karbala' Governorate council to the vote', *al-Rafidayn*, 28 February 2004; Aamer Madhani, 'Clerics flex political muscles in Iraq', *Chicago Tribune*, 25 March 2004.

66. Mariam Fam, 'Clout of Iraq's Shiite clergy growing', Associated Press, 25 February 2004.

67. Quoted in Kathleen Ridolfo, 'Iraq Report', RFE/RL, 27 February 2004.

68. Toby Harnden, 'Americans intensify offensive as Shias denounce Sadr', *Daily Telegraph*, 7 May 2004; *Boston Globe*, cited in Juan Cole, *Informed Comment*, 13 May 2004.

69. Results from the Independent Electoral Commission of Iraq (IECI) website, 'Results from 12 governorates', 11 February 2005, via <http://www.ieciraq.org>, p. 5.

70. Al-Iraqiyah TV, Baghdad, 14 March 2005.

71. Michael Knights, 'Battle for Iraq Lies in the South', *Jane's Intelligence Review*, June 2005, p. 12.

72. 'Announcement of the formation of a Karbala' commando unit', *al-Sabah al-Jadid*, 1 June 2005.

73. *Al-Sharqiyah*, Baghdad, 14 June 2005; 'Karbala' governor: the interior minister did not order the governorate's chief of police to stay in his post', *Al-Mada*, 20 June 2005; Aqil Abu-Gharib, 'Karbala' governor: we have formed committee to study federation among Karbala', Babil, and Wasit', *al-Sabah al-Jadid*, 6 June 2005.

74. Rod Nordland, 'Basra melee', *Newsweek*, 10 April 2003; Yaroslav Trofimov and Farnaz Fassihi, 'Struggle for order begins in Iraq as rival forces jockey for power', *Wall Street Journal*, 11 April 2003; 'New Basra leader has links to Saddam', Associated Press, 12 April 2003; Julian Coman, 'Chalabi army flies in to get lead over rivals', *Daily Telegraph*, 13 April 2003.

75. Al-Jazeera website, 'British dissolve council in Basra; elections held in Samarra', 25 May 2003; BBC NewsOnline, 'Basra protests against UK leader', 1 June 2003.

76. Al-Jazeera TV, news report, 6 July 2003.

77. Ahmad Jawdah, 'Oil and drug smuggling raises prices of commodities and real estate', *al-Sharq al-Awsat*, 28 December 2003.

78. Brigadier Nick Carter, quoted in Melissa Kite and Alex Thomson, 'Violence in Iraq will get even worse, says Blair', *Daily Telegraph*, 18 April 2004; also Matthew Parris, 'What the f*** are we doing here?', *The Times*, 31 March 2004.

79. Ashraf Khalil, 'A loss of faith in the city of Shiites', *Los Angeles Times*, 25 January 2005; Steven Vincent, 'The Islamists who patrol Basra's streets', *New York Times*, 1 August 2005.

80. General Hassan al-Sa'adi, quoted in Rory Carroll, 'Basra out of control, says chief of police', *Guardian*, 31 May 2005.

81.   Ian Cobain and Richard Norton-Taylor, 'No more softly softly after army's difficult day', *Guardian*, 21 September 2004; Adrian Blomfield, 'UK troops left isolated as Mahdi Army weaves a web of official corruption', *Daily Telegraph*, 22 September 2005; Michael Howard, 'Continued anger on the streets of Basra as marchers denounce "British aggression"', *Guardian,* 22 September 2005 ; Robert F. Worth, 'Anger grows in Basra after British raid', *New York Times*, 22 September 2005; Anthony Loyd, 'Taking a screwdriver to the truth', *The Times*, 23 September 2005.

82.   Steve Negus, 'Tensions grow in Basra as militias vie for supremacy', *Financial Times*, 20 September 2005; Anthony Loyd, 'Murder, violence and politics: how rogue police can live outside law', *The Times*, 22 September 2005.

83.   Rory Carroll, 'Liberal Basra pushed to the right', *Guardian*, 13 June 2005; Louise Roug, 'Islamic law controls the streets of Basra', *Los Angeles Times*, 27 June 2005; Edward Wong, 'Shiite theocracy takes hold in Iraqi oil city', *New York Times*, 8 July 2005; Steven Vincent, 'Shiites bring rigid piety to Iraq's south', *Christian Science Monitor*, 13 July 2005; Anthony Shadid and Steve Fainaru, 'Militias wresting control across Iraq's north and south', *Washington Post*, 20 August 2005.

84.   Catherine Philp, 'Death at "immoral" picnic in the park', *The Times*, 23 March 2005; Kathleen Ridolfo, 'Militiamen push their version of Islam in absence of rule of law', *RFE/RL Iraq Report*, 28 March 2005; Anthony Shadid, 'Picnic is no party in the new Basra', *Washington Post*, 29 March 2005; Gethin Chamberlain, 'Students escape war zone', *Scotsman*, 14 May 2005.

85.   Peter Spiegel, 'Rivalry between Badr and Sadr militias worries U.K. forces', *Financial Times*, 14 December 2005.

86.   IECI, 'Results from 6 governorates', 13 February 2005, via <http://www.ieciraq.org>, p. 3.

87.   Edmund Sanders, 'Power struggles stall Iraqi provincial councils', *Los Angeles Times*, 6 April 2005.

88.   Nancy A. Youssef, 'Proposal to divide Iraq into semi-autonomous states gains ground', Knight Ridder Newspapers, 24 May 2005; Steven Vincent, 'In the south, a bid to loosen Baghdad's grip', *Christian Science Monitor*, 28 June 2005.

89.   Wong, 'Push for autonomy develops in Iraqi south', *New York Times*, 30 June 2005; Vincent, 'In the south'.

90. Thomas Wagner, 'Iraqis protest British rescue mission', Associated Press, 21 September 2005; Kim Sengupta, 'Basra governor ends co-operation with British', *The Independent*, 23 September 2005.

91. Costello, interview, p. 13.

92. Telephone interview with Lt-Col. Joe Rice, 5 May 2004.

93. ICG, *Can Local Governance*, p. 15.

94. Costello, interview, pp. 14, 21.

95. Memorandum from Rubin; Etherington, *Revolt*, pp. 128-9, 226.

96. Etherington, *Revolt,* pp. 158-9; ICG, *Can Local Governance*, pp. 24-5; Costello, interview, pp. 14-15.

97. Etherington, *Revolt*, pp. 155-6, 225-6 *et passim*.

98. Shadid and Fainaru, 'Militias wresting control'; Knights, 'Battle for Iraq', pp. 12-13.

99. 'Ala al-Tamimi is no longer in office', *al-Sabah al-Jadid*, 10 August 2005; James Glanz, 'Baghdad mayor is ousted by a Shiite group and replaced', *New York Times*, 10 August 2005; Rory Carroll, 'What has Hussein al-Tahaan got to smile about?', *Guardian*, 7 September 2005.

100. Al-Mendhar website, 'Ministers' council grants Al Tamimi a compulsory leave', via <http://www.almendhar.com>.

101. Quoted in Michael Georgy, 'Ousted Baghdad mayor says gun, not vote, rules Iraq', *Reuters*, 12 August 2005.

102. Kurdistan National Assembly, political programme of October 1992: see Falaq al-Din Kakai, 'The Kurdish parliament', in Hazelton, ed., *Iraq since the Gulf War*.

103. Articulated, e.g., by Costello, interview, p. 15; Raphel, interview, p. 11; and in Kim Sengupta, 'British forces face push by Shias for autonomy in south', *The Independent*, 30 November 2003.

104. e.g., Guenther Roth, 'Personal Rulership, Patrimonialism, and Empire-building in the New States', *World Politics*, vol. 20, no. 2 (1968), pp. 194-206; S.N. Eisenstadt, *Traditional Patrimonialism and Modern Neopatrimonialism*, Beverly Hills: Sage, 1973; Christopher Clapham, ed., *Private Patronage and Public Power*, London: Frances Pinter, 1982, esp. pp. 1-35, 162-92; Michael Bratton and Nicolas van de Walle, 'Neopatrimonial Regimes and Political Transitions in Africa', *World Politics*, vol. 46, no. 4 (1994), pp. 453-89; Javier Auyero, '"From the Client's Point(s) of View": how Poor People Perceive and Evaluate Political Clientelism', *Theory and Society*, vol. 28, no. 2 (1999), pp. 297-334.

105.   Jean-François Medard, 'The Underdeveloped State in Tropical Africa: Political Clientelism or Neo-patrimonialism?', in Clapham, ed., *Private Patronage*, p. 181.

106.   Dodge, *Iraq's Future*, p. 42; also, Andreas Wimmer, 'Democracy and ethno-religious conflict in Iraq', *Survival*, vol. 45:4 (2003), pp. 111-34.

107.   Memorandum from Rubin. The Ministers of the Interior and Water Resources were selected by their brothers-in-law; the Minister of Trade was selected by his uncle; the Foreign Minister was selected by his nephew; and the Oil Minister was chosen by his father.

108.   Dermer, interview, p. 29. Dermer did not specify which parties he used.

109.   Oliver Poole, 'Student extremism brings violence and chaos to Iraqi universities', *Daily Telegraph,* 9 January 2006; Khalilzad, 'Snapshots from the office', p.2.

110.   Relaying a negative assessment of the Ministries of Defence, the Interior, Oil and Electricity, see Eric Schmitt, 'Iraq facing hurdles, U.S. general warns', *New York Times*, 4 January 2006.

111.   Hashim Hamid, 'Electricity ministry accuses oil ministry and some governors of not cooperating', *al-Mu'tamar*, 25 June 2005; also articles in *al-Bayan*, 10 April 2005; *al-Mashriq*, 22 May 2005 and 9 June 2005; *al-Sabah al-Jadid*, 6 August 2005; *al-Adalah*, 13 August 2005.

112.   Joel S. Migdal, 'The State in Society: an Approach to Struggles for Domination', in Joel S. Migdal, Atul Kohli and Vivienne Shue, eds, *State Power and Social Forces*, Cambridge University Press, 1994, p. 27.

113.   *al-Bayyina*, 23 August 2005.

114.   Salwan Binni, 'Iran, Turkey to boost energy exports to Iraq', Agence France Presse, 29 May 2005; Steven Vincent, 'On again, off again: a power problem in Basra', *National Review*, 2 August 2005.

115.   Haifa Zangana, 'Why Iraqi women aren't complaining', *Guardian*, 19 February 2004; interview with Haifa Zangana, 11 March 2004.

116.   The *Washington Post* reported that a letter of *tazkiyya* in southern Iraq cost between $100 and $1000 in mid-2005: Shadid and Fainaru, 'Militias wresting control'.

117.   Rory McCarthy, 'How freedom from repression has brought frustration and fear', *Guardian*, 15 March 2004.

118.   George Packer, 'The next Iraqi war', *New Yorker*, 4 October 2004.

119.   Interview with senior Coalition military official, May 2004.

120.   GAO, 'U.S. water and sanitation efforts', p. 27.

121.   Rajiv Chandrasekaran, 'U.S. to form Iraqi paramilitary force', *Washington Post*, 3 December 2003; ICG, *Iraq: Building a New Security Structure*, 23 December 2003, pp. 20-1.

122.   CPA Order no.27, s.2: Organization of the FPS; DoD weekly report, 5 January 2004, p. 16.

123.   Nicolas Pelham, 'Rival former exile groups clash over security in Iraq', *Financial Times*, 11 December 2003; Knut Royce, 'Start-up company with connections', *Newsday*, 15 February 2004.

124.   'Allawi quoted in AFP, 'De-Baathification hampering US reconstruction', 28 December 2003; David Ignatius, 'A big man to watch in Baghdad', *Washington Post*, 1 February 2004; monitoring of the INA's radio station, al-Mustaqbal, February 2004; Kathleen Ridolfo, 'Allawi's dangerous game', *RFE/RL Iraq Report*, 22 October 2004.

125.   Dana Priest and Robin Wright, 'Iraq spy service planned by U.S. to stem attacks', *Washington Post*, 11 December 2003; Edward Wong, 'New Iraq agency to hunt rebels', *New York Times*, 31 January 2004. For the INA's history, see Dilip Hiro, *Neighbours, Not Friends: Iraq and Iran after the Gulf Wars*, London: Routledge, 2001.

126.   Shadid and Fainaru, 'Militias wresting control'.

127.   Richard Oppel, 'Iraq vote shows Sunnis are few in new military', *New York Times*, 27 December 2005.

128.   CPA Memo no.7 (4 November 2003); IGC Decree 94 (11 January 2004). The press conference at which Chalabi announced the new procedures was covered by Dubai TV (11 January 2004).

129.   Interview with Mithal al-Alusi, Director of the Commission, in *RFE/RL Iraq Report*, 8 April 2004.

130.   Jon Lee Anderson, 'Out on the street', *New Yorker*, 8 November 2004; Associated Press, 'Baghdad resumes purging Saddam party members', 11 May 2005; Thanassis Cambanis, 'Outspoken pro-Israel politician finds few allies', *Boston Globe*, 28 April 2005.

131.   Sameer N. Yacoub, '9 dismissed from tribunal trying Saddam', Associated Press, 20 July 2005; Tom Lasseter, 'De-Baathification of special tribunal may imperil Saddam's trial', Knight Ridder Newspapers, 1 August 2005.

132.   Mariam Karouny, 'Saddam trial judge "once a member of Baath party"', Reuters, 19 January 2006; Ross Colvin, 'Saddam's chaotic trial set to resume', Reuters, 28 January 2006.

133.   Decision of the Board of Commissioners, IECI, 11 December 2005, and

Clarification from the IECI Board of Governors, 12 December 2005, both via <http://www.ieciraq.org>.

134.   Royce, 'Start-up company'; also, Rod Nordland and Michael Hirsh, 'The $87 billion money pit', *Newsweek*, 3 November 2003.

135.   Interview with senior official in Iraq, September 2003.

136.   *Al-Hayat,* 21 July 2005.

137.   Ma'ad Fayad, 'Interview with deputy PM Ahmed Chalabi', *al-Sharq al-Awsat*, 25 October 2005.

138.   Examples from Wasit province are in Etherington, *Revolt*, pp. 79, 82, 144.

139.   Interview with senior Coalition military officer, February 2005.

140.   Alan Sipress, 'Shiites make up for lost time', *Washington Post,* 6 December 2003; Tom Lasseter, 'Cleric's army quietly takes control', Knight Ridder News Service, 14 July 2004; Anthony Shadid, 'Sadr's disciples rise again to play pivotal role in Iraq', *Washington Post*, 30 August 2005.

141.   Isam al Khafaji, 'A Few Days after: State and Society in a Post-Saddam Iraq', in Toby Dodge and Steven Simon, eds, *Iraq at the Crossroads: State and Society in the Shadow of Regime Change*, London: International Institute for Strategic Studies, 2003, pp. 77-92; Philippe Le Billon, 'Corruption, Reconstruction and Oil Governance in Iraq', *Third World Quarterly*, vol. 26, no. 4-5 (2005), pp. 690-3.

142.   Donald Rumsfeld, DoD operational briefing, 7 April 2004; Doug Struck, 'Official warns of Iranian infiltration', *Washington Post*, 26 July 2004; John F. Burns and Robert F. Worth, 'Iraqi campaign raises question of Iran's sway', *New York Times*, 15 December 2004; 'Iraq defense chief: Iran is "number one enemy"', Associated Press, 15 December 2004; 'Iranian intelligence officer: Tehran is deploying its agents in Iraq from north to south', *al-Sharq al-Awsat*, 3 April 2004; 'Iran deploys four military divisions near border', *al-Sharq al-Awsat*, 15 June 2004.

143.   Ewen MacAskill, 'Iranian arms intercepted at Iraqi border', *Guardian*, 11 August 2005; Kim Sengupta, Ben Russell and Terri Judd, 'Anger as Britain admits it was wrong to blame Iran for deaths in Iraq', *Independent*, 5 January 2006.

144.   Scott Peterson, 'Shadows of Tehran over Iraq', *Christian Science Monitor*, 19 April 2004; Robin Wright, 'U.S. wary as Iran works to increase influence in Iraq', *Washington Post*, 12 June 2004; Edward Wong, 'Iran is in strong position to steer Iraq's political future', *New York Times*, 3 July

2004; interview with senior Coalition military officer, May 2004.

145.   First disclosed in Michael Hirsh, Scott Johnson and Kevin Peraino, 'The new way out', *Newsweek*, 5 December 2005.

146.   Adnan Ali al-Kadhemi, deputy to Ibrahim al-Ja'fari, quoted in ICG, *Iran in Iraq: How Much Influence?* 21 March 2005, p. 14.

147.   Ahmad Salamatian, 'Iran and Iraq: the limits on Shia power', *Le Monde Diplomatique*, July 2005.

148.   ICG, *Iran in Iraq*, pp. 15-19; for al-Da'wa, Yaroslav Trofimov, 'Journey of an Islamist party', *Wall Street Journal*, 28 April 2005.

149.   Borzou Daragahi, 'Sadr's mentor distances self from young firebrand', *Daily Star*, 17 April 2004; Juan Cole, *Informed Comment*, 12 July 2004.

150.   ICRSS, 'Public opinion poll in Iraq', June 2004, p. 15; similarly, Oxford Research International (ORI), 'National Survey of Iraq', June 2004, pp. 9-11.

151.   IIACSS, 'National Public Opinion Survey of Political Attitudes in Iraq', June 2004, p. 15.

152.   Dexter Filkins, 'Top Shiite cleric is said to fear voting in Iraq may be delayed', *New York Times*, 23 September 2004; Ashraf Khalil and Paul Richter, 'US is said to urge its Iraqi allies to unite for election', *Los Angeles Times*, 25 October 2004; correspondence with UN official in Baghdad, September 2004.

153.   For the constituent parties of the UIA in the two elections, see IECI, 'Final list of coalitions and their constituent entities certified to contest the 30 January 2005 elections', 20 December 2004, pp. 2-3, and 'Final list of coalitions', 5 November 2005, p. 2, via: <http://www.ieciraq.org>.

154.   Erik Ekholm, 'Ally of militant cleric is on the stump in Sadr City', *New York Times*, 5 January 2005.

155.   Private communication from a US official closely involved with the electoral process, November 2004. These figures have never, to our knowledge, been formally communicated by UIA officials. A preliminary set of proportions was reported in Dhiya Rasan and Steve Negus, 'Sadr's men to stand for election in Iraq poll', *Financial Times*, 8 November 2004, but SCIRI later objected to this distribution. See also Hamza Hendawi, 'Shiites seek to ensure win in Iraq vote', Associated Press, 17 November 2004; Anthony Shadid and Karl Vick, 'Candidate slate shows Shiites closing ranks', *Washington Post*, 7 December 2004; Robert

F. Worth, 'Shiite groups unite to run in Iraq elections next month', *New York Times*, 9 December 2004.

156. Reidar Visser, 'SCIRI, Daawa and Sadrists in the certified Iraq elections results', 11 February 2006, at <http://historiae.org/SCIRI.asp>; Charles Levinson, 'Ballot-box win boosts Iraqi radical', *Christian Science Monitor*, 30 January 2006.

157. Calculated from national election results broken down by governorate: IECI, 'Results from 12 governorates', p. 20.

158. Fully tabulated and sourced at Glen Rangwala, <http:// middleeastreference.org.uk/iraq051215results.html>.

159. Seymour Hersh, 'Get out the vote', *New Yorker*, 25 July 2005.

160. RFE/RL, *Iraq Report*, 4 November 2005 and 9 December 2005.

161. Robert Worth, 'Democracy is most attractive for Shiites leading in the polls', *New York Times,* 14 December 2005.

162. Batatu, *Old Social Classes*, pp. 13-36; Jabar, *Shi'ite Movement*, pp. 33-7.

163. ICRSS and Gallup polls, reported in State Department Office of Research, 'Iraqi public has wide ranging preferences for a future political system', 21 October 2003, p. 6.

164. IIACSS, 'Political Attitudes Survey of the Iraqi Electorate', August 2004, p. 27.

165. ORI, 'National Survey of Iraq', March 2004, p. 32.

166. IIACSS, 'Political Attitudes', August 2004, p. 21.

167. IRI, 'Survey of Iraqi Public Opinion', October 2004, p. 22.

168. ABC News Poll, 'Where things stand', 12 December 2005, at: <http:// abcnews.go.com/images/Politics/1000a1IraqWhereThingsStand.pdf>, p.13.

169. Nancy A. Youssef, 'Democratic debate bursting out all over Iraq's university campuses', Knight Ridder Newspapers, 19 October 2004; also, Oliver Poole, 'Student extremism'.

170. An example is the Independent Iraqi Democrats, which had a secular liberal leadership from both major sects. Despite being awarded a seat in the IGC and securing a high international profile for its leader, Adnan al-Pachachi, it received just 0.15% of the vote in the January 2005 elections.

171. e.g., Ali Kais al-Rubai, 'Islamists pledge continued war on Coalition', Institute of War and Peace Reporting, 14 May 2004; Nir Rosen, 'Home rule', *New Yorker*, 5 July 2004; Rod Nordland, Tom Masland and Christopher Dickey, 'Unmasking the insurgents', *Newsweek*, 7 February

2005; Patrick Cockburn, 'Stop killing Iraqis, nationalists warn religious fanatics', *The Independent*, 11 April 2005.

172.   Jonathan Steele and Rory McCarthy, 'Sunni and Shia unite against common enemy', *Guardian*, 10 April 2004; also Jon Lee Anderson, 'The uprising: Shia and Sunnis put aside their differences', *New Yorker*, 3 May 2004.

173.   e.g., Sadiq Rahim, 'A new sectarian apportionment divides out positions among Iraqi deputy ministers', *al-Zaman*, 27 January 2004; 'Iraqis without sectarian apportionment', *al-Zaman*, 1 September 2004; other references in ICG, *Reconstructing Iraq*, p. 23.

174.   State Department Office of Research, 'Iraqi Kurds and Arabs living in two different worlds', 8 November 2004, p. 9. 'Mid-Euphrates' generally refers to the areas south and south-east of Baghdad but north of Samawa, and includes Karbala', Hilla, Najaf, Diwaniyya and Kut.

175.   ABC News Poll, 'Where things stand', pp. 4-5.

176.   IRI, 'Survey of Iraqi Public Opinion', December 2004, p. 11.

177.   IRI, 'Survey', October 2004, p. 16.

178.   State Department, 'Iraqi Kurds and Arabs', 8 November 2004, p. 9.

179.   UNDP/MOPDC, ILCS 2004, Vol. II, pp. 145-9; also Merza, 'Reconstruction under Uncertainty'.

180.   *USA Today*/CNN/Gallup, administered by the Pan Arab Research Centre of Dubai, 'Nationwide Survey of 3,500 Iraqis', 28 April 2004, question 7B.

181.   e.g., Daniel Byman, 'Five Bad Options for Iraq', *Survival*, vol. 47 no.1 (2005), p. 12; Reuel Marc Gerecht, 'Don't Fear the Shiites', *American Enterprise*, April/May 2005; Bathsheba Crocker, 'Checking the Rising Tide', in *Iraq: Reconstruction and Future Role*, Abu Dhabi: ECSSR, 2004, pp. 58-9.

182.   Sarah Graham-Brown, *Sanctioning Saddam: the Politics of Intervention in Iraq*, London: I.B. Tauris, 1999, p. 184; Khafaji, 'The Parasitic Base'; Ayubi, *Over-Stating the Arab State*, pp. 362-6.

183.   *USA Today*/CNN/Gallup, 'Nationwide Survey', 28 April 2004, questions 7A and 7B.

184.   *USA Today*/CNN/Gallup, 'Nationwide Survey', 28 April 2004, question 7F.

185.   *USA Today*/CNN/Gallup, 'Nationwide Survey', 28 April 2004, question 19.

186.   *USA Today*/CNN/Gallup, 'Nationwide Survey', 28 April 2004, question

8.

187.   IRI, 'Survey', October 2004, p. 44.

188.   Abu Dhabi TV/Zogby International, 'Elections in Iraq', question 7.

189.   Quoted in Sabrina Tavernise, 'Many Iraqis see sectarian roots in new killings', *New York Times*, 27 May 2005.

190.   Christopher Clapham, 'Clientelism and the State', in Clapham, ed., *Private Patronage*, pp. 6-7.

191.   Rajiv Chandrasekaran and Anthony Shadid, 'Ethnic and religious fissures deepen in Iraqi society', *Washington Post*, 29 September 2003. 'Wahhabi', a derogatory term for a follower of the puritanical teachings of Muhammad ibn 'Abd al-Wahhab (1703-92), has become a catch-all term among many Iraqi Shi'i for Sunni Arabs perceived as extremist.

192.   e.g., Nicholas Blanford, 'Baghdad blast brings sectarian divide to surface', *Daily Star*, 13 December 2003; Dhiya Rasan and Steve Negus, 'Iraq's Sunni accuse Shia of selling out Islam', *Financial Times*, 24 November 2004; Richard Beeston, 'Fear of civil war grows as Shia start to retaliate', *The Times*, 23 May 2005; Sabrina Tavernise, 'One by one, killing off of Sunnis', *New York Times*, 5 July 2005.

193.   Ghaith Abdul-Ahad, 'Two years ago Shia and Sunni lived happily alongside each other; now they are divided by fear and hatred', *Guardian*, 3 May 2005; Juan Cole, 'Melting pot of blood', Salon.com, 6 May 2005.

194.   'Shi'is are bought and sold in Latifiyya', Karbalanews.net, 21 November 2004, at <http://www.karbalanews.net/artc.php?id=1457>.

195.   Juan Cole, *Informed Comment*, 12 July 2004.

196.   As'ad Rashad, 'Why the Sunni Arabs are working to sabotage the Iraqi elections', Alnajafnews.net, 3 January 2005.

197.   e.g., Salah Hemeid, 'A nation divided', *al-Ahram Weekly*, 26 May - 1 June 2005; CBS News, 'Undeclared civil war in Iraq', 26 September 2005, via <http://www.cbsnews.com>; Sinan Salaheddin, 'Government accused of death squads in Iraq', Associated Press, 7 October 2005; James Rupert, 'Some see U.S.-backed Iraqi guards as death squads', *Newsday*, 16 November 2005; Roel Meijer, 'The Association of Muslim Scholars in Iraq', *Middle East Report,* vol. 237 (Winter 2005).

198.   Brought out well in Tom Lasseter, 'Sectarian resentment extends to Iraq's army', Knight Ridder Newspapers, 12 October 2005.

199.   Reported in Dhiya Rasan and Steve Negus, 'Iraq's Sunni accuse Shia of selling out Islam', *Financial Times*, 24 November 2004.

200. Quotes from Kathleen Ridolfo, 'Operation in Tal Afar a success, but for how long?', *RFE/RL Iraq Report*, 12 September 2005; Colin Freeman, 'Troops blitz Iraq's "funnel of death"', *Daily Telegraph*, 11 September 2005.

201. Talib al-Shatri, 'Funeral of the state', at <www.alnajafnews.net>, 21 July 2004.

4. INSURGENCY AND COUNTER-INSURGENCY

1. John Nagl, *Counterinsurgency Lessons from Malaya and Vietnam: Learning to Eat Soup with a Knife*, Westport, CT: Praeger, 2002, especially pp. 30, 205; Thomas Hammes, *The Sling and the Stone: On War in the 21st Century*, London: Motorbooks International, 2004; William S. Lind, 'Understanding Fourth Generation War', *Military Review*, Sept.-Oct. 2004, pp. 12-16; G.I. Wilson, 'Iraq: Fourth Generation Warfare (4GW) swamp', 10 March 2004, via <http://www.military.com>; Stephen J. Hedges, 'Critics: Pentagon in blinders', *Chicago Tribune*, 8 June 2005; Bruce Hoffman, *Insurgency and Counterinsurgency in Iraq*, Santa Monica: RAND, June 2004, esp. p. 6; Mary Kaldor, 'The "New War" in Iraq', *Theoria*, vol. 108 (March 2006).

2. Syria offered to engage in joint border patrols with US forces along the Syrian-Iraqi border in 2003, an offer the US rejected. It also provided detailed intelligence to the US. According to a senior US official who had been directly involved in policy-making on Syria in 2003, this intelligence 'exceeded CIA expectations in quality and quantity', and directly prevented attacks that would have endangered US lives. Interview, 25 May 2005. See also Eric Schmitt and Thom Shanker, 'Estimates by U.S. see more rebels with more funds', *New York Times*, 22 October 2004; Robert Baer, 'The devil you think you know', *Newsweek*, 15 August 2005; Ghaith Abdul-Ahad, 'From here to eternity', *Guardian*, 8 June 2005; Anthony Cordesman, *Iraq's Evolving Insurgency and the Risk of Civil War*, Washington, D.C.: CSIS, 23 March 2006, pp. 133-4, 167-8, 187-8, 211-7.

3. Interview with senior Coalition military officer, February 2005; Mike Barber, 'WMD? Iraq is teeming with conventional arms', *Seattle Post-Intelligencer*, 14 June 2004.

4. Centcom press briefing, 13 November 2003.

5. AP, 'Iraq insurgency larger than thought', 9 July 2004; Schmitt and

Shanker, 'Estimates by U.S.'; O'Hanlon and Kamp, p. 18.

6.   Scott Johnson and Melinda Liu, 'The enemy spies', *Newsweek*, 27 June 2005; AFP, 'Iraq battling more than 200,000 insurgents: intelligence chief', 3 January 2005.

7.   Reuters, 'Top U.S. general: 15,000 insurgents killed or caught', 26 January 2005; Department of Defence regular briefing, 26 July 2005.

8.   Reported in GAO, 'Rebuilding Iraq: preliminary observations on challenges in transferring security responsibilities to Iraqi military and police', Testimony to Congressional Committees, 14 March 2005, p. 11.

9.   Rory McCarthy, 'Beside the ruined valley of peace, Sadr's men wait for martyrdom', *Guardian*, 12 August 2004.

10. Cordesman, *Iraq's Evolving Insurgency*, pp. 180-1; Jonathan Finer, 'Among insurgents in Iraq, few foreigners are found', *Washington Post*, 17 November 2005.

11. CPA, 'Disclaimer', no date, accessed 5 July 2004, at <http://www.cpa-iraq.org/arabic/prisoners/index.html>. See also Peter Eisler and Tom Squitieri, 'Foreign detainees are few in Iraq', *USA Today*, 6 July 2004.

12. Cordesman, *Iraq's Evolving Insurgency*, p. 180.

13. ABC News, 'Official: some Iraqis forced to be bombers', 23 July 2004.

14. ICG, *In Their Own Words: Reading the Iraqi Insurgency*, 15 February 2006, especially pp. 1-2, 12-13.

15. Middle East News Line, 'Al Qaida presence drops in Iraq', 24 March 2006.

16. Quoted in Toby Dodge, 'Cake Walk, Coup or Urban Warfare: the Battle for Iraq', in Toby Dodge and Steven Simon (eds), *Iraq at the Crossroads: State and Society in the Shadow of Regime Change*, London: International Institute for Strategic Studies, 17 January 2003, p. 59.

17. Richard Sale, 'Iraq's new war', UPI, 24 December 2004.

18. See for example the Iraq Committee's website, <http://comitesirak.free.fr/>. ICG, *In Their Own Words*, p. 6.

19. Hashim, 'Sunni Insurgency', p. 5; Dodge, *Iraq's Future*, pp. 15-16; Chehab, *Iraq Ablaze*, Ch. 1; ICG, *In Their Own Words*, pp. 5-6.

20. Kevin Woods, James Lacey, and Williamson Murray, 'Saddam's Delusions: the View from the Inside', *Foreign Affairs*, May/June 2006.

21. O'Hanlon and de Albuqerque, *Iraq Index*, p. 4.

22. This and the following two paragraphs draw extensively on the ICG report

In Their Own Words.

23. Anthony Shadid, *Night Draws Near: Iraq's People in the Shadow of America's War*, London: Henry Holt, 2005, pp. 197-9, 217-8.

24. On Salafism, see Olivier Roy, *Globalised Islam: the Search for a New Umma*, London: Hurst & Co., 2004, esp. pp. 232-89; also, Fawaz Gerges, *The Far Enemy: Why Jihad went Global*, Cambridge University Press, esp. pp. 131-4; Bassam Tibi, *The Challenge of Fundamentalism: Political Islam and the New World Disorder*, Berkeley: University of California Press, 1998.

25. US Department of Defence, 'Measuring Stability and Security in Iraq', Report to Congress, 13 October 2005, p. 23, and 17 February 2006, p. 27.

26. Calculated from Kaldor, 'The "New War" in Iraq'. A monthly categorisation of attacks by target is presented in GAO, 'Enhancing security', p. 10.

27. US Department of Defence, 'Operation Iraqi Freedom (OIF) US Casualty Status', <http://www.defenselink.mil/news/casualty.pdf>.

28. O'Hanlon and de Albuquerque, *Iraq Index*, 29 August 2005, pp. 8-9.

29. O'Hanlon and de Albuquerque, *Iraq Index*, 29 August 2005, p. 13.

30. USAID, 'Focused stabilization in strategic cities initiative – request for application', 2 January 2006, annex F, p. 60; Paul Schemm, 'Allawi: Iraq in low-intensity civil war', Middle East Online, 20 March 2006.

31. Beverley Milton-Edwards, 'The Rise of Islamic Insurgency in Iraq', *Journal of Conflict Studies*, vol. 25, no. 2 (2005), pp. 48-71; Roel Meijer, 'Association of Muslim Scholars'.

32. DoD, 'Coalition forces will pacify Fallujah'; Lt-Gen. Ricardo Sanchez, CPA briefing, 8 April 2004.

33. For example, Professor Ahmed Hashim of the US Naval War College in Newport, Rhode Island, had published in August 2003 a paper on the insurgency: Hashim, 'Sunni Insurgency'. It resulted in Hashim gaining the attention of the Pentagon, and he spent December 2003 to June 2004 with the CPA. See his *Insurgency and Counter-Insurgency in Iraq*, London: Hurst, 2005. Also Warren P. Strobel and Jonathan Landay, 'Intelligence agencies warned about growing local insurgency in late 2003', Knight Ridder newspapers, 28 February 2006.

34. Interview with senior Coalition military officer, May 2004; email correspondence with Coalition military officer, August 2005.

35. The Coalition has also looked to a wide range of other conflicts for lessons such as France's defeat in Algeria and Israeli methods against Palestinians

and the US's own support for the government of El Salvador in the early 1980s. See Hoffman, *Counterinsurgency*; Adam Entous, 'Israel quietly helps US in Iraq, aides say', Reuters, 11 December 2003; Seymour Hersh, 'Plan B', *New Yorker*, 28 June 2004; Michael Hirsh and John Barry, 'The Salvador option', *Newsweek*, 8 January 2005. In the preparation of the initial plan, lessons drawn from the US experience in the Philippines in the 1980s were given as much weight as those from Malaya. Email correspondence, Coalition military officer, August 2005.

36.   For example, it is on the curriculum of the US Marine Corps. US Marine Corps, 'Infantry officer course, insurgency/counter-insurgency operations', June 1999.

37.   Robert Thompson, *Defeating Communist Insurgency: Experiences From Malaya and Vietnam,* London: Chatto & Windus, 1974, pp. 50-62. Thompson attributed Britain's success in Malaya to what he saw as its adherence to these principles and the US's failure in Vietnam to its violation of them. On his prominent role in Vietnam, see Douglas Valentine, *The Phoenix Program*, Lincoln, NE: iUniverse.com, 1990, pp. 73, 74, 79, 85, 92, 299-301, 345, 363, 391, 406; and Mark Curtis, *Unpeople: Britain's Secret Human Rights Abuses*, London: Vintage, 2004, pp. 210-3, 221, 232.

38.   Nagl, *Counterinsurgency Lessons*.

39.   Peter Maass, 'Professor Nagl's war', *New York Times*, 11 January 2004; Nicholas Blanford, 'Insurgent and soldier: two views on the Iraq fight', *Christian Science Monitor*, 25 February 2004; Headquarters, 3rd Armored Cavalry Regiment, Department of the Army, 'Brave Rifles Reading List for Operation Iraqi Freedom', 25 April 2005; presentations by Nagl, 28 April and 17 March 2005, at <http://www.cfr.org/bio.php?id=11087>.

40.   Nagl, *Counterinsurgency Lessons*, pp. 29-30.

41.   US Department of the Army, *Counterinsurgency Operations*, Field Manual-Interim FMI 3-07.22, October 2004; Douglas Jehl and Thom Shanker, 'For the first time since Vietnam, the Army prints a guide to fighting insurgents', *New York Times*, 13 November 2004; Department of the Army, *U.S. Army Counterguerrilla Operations Handbook*, Guilford, CT: Lyons Press, 2004. The Army produced a manual in 1990 – FM 3-20 – on 'low intensity' conflict, but this included only one section on counter-insurgency.

42.   Army, *Counterguerrilla Operations*, pp. 1(1), 1(5) – 1(7).

43.   Army, *Counterinsurgency Operations*, pp. viii, 2(2)-2(3), 4(1). See also pp.

1(3), 2(13). 4(1), 4(8). It defines counter-insurgency as 'those military, paramilitary, political, economic, psychological and civic actions taken by a government to defeat insurgency.' See p. vi.

44. Army, *Counterguerrilla Operations*, pp. 1(1), 3(6).

45. Army, *Counterguerrilla Operations*, p. 3(6). Emphasis in the original.

46. Army, *Counterinsurgency Operations*, Appendix E.

47. Army, *Counterinsurgency Operations*, p. 1(1).

48. Army, *Counterguerrilla Operations*, pp. 1(1)-1(2), 2(1).

49. On US use of these techniques, see Noam Chomsky and Edward S. Herman, *The Washington Connection and Third World Fascism*, Boston: South End Press, 1979; Michael McClintock, *Instruments of Statecraft: U.S. Guerrilla Warfare, Counterinsurgency, and Counterterrorism, 1940-1990*, New York: Pantheon Books, 2002 and Doug Stokes, *America's Other War: Terrorizing Colombia*, London: Zed Books, 2004. On Britain's record in this area, see John Newsinger, *British Counter-insurgency: From Palestine to Northern Ireland*, London: Palgrave, 2002; and David Anderson, *Histories of the Hanged: The Dirty War in Kenya and the End of Empire*, New York: W.W. Norton, 2005.

50. Army, *Counterinsurgency Operations*, pp. 3(2)-(3).

51. Army, *Counterguerrilla Operations*, pp. 4(4), H(68)-H(11).

52. 'Army's insurgent manual author speaks', November 2004, via <http://www.defensetech.org/>.

53. 'Army's insurgent manual'. Attacks by insurgents in Samarra' soon resumed: see, for example, Caeser Ahmed and Raheem Salman, 'Gunmen storm northern Iraq city', *Los Angeles Times*, 30 June 2005.

54. Etherington, *Revolt*, p. 220.

55. Valentine, *Phoenix Program*; Chomsky and Herman, *Washington Connection*, pp. 322-8. Thompson was a major player in the Phoenix Programme.

56. Hersh, 'Moving targets'; Hirsh, Barry, 'Salvador option'; Douglas Valentine, 'Preemptive manhunting: the CIA's new assassination program', *CounterPunch*, 11 December 2003; Douglas Valentine, 'Echoes of Vietnam: Phoenix, assassination and blowback in Iraq', CounterPunch, 8 April 2004.

57. Army, *Counterguerrilla Operations*, pp. 3(5)3(8)-(9)

58. Army, *Counterinsurgency Operations*, pp. 2(13)-(15).

59. Quoted in Mark Oliva, 'Marines suspend Fallujah offensive, push humanitarian aid', *Marine Corps News*, 13 April 2004, via <http://www.

usmc.mil>.

60. Iraq Body Count, 'No longer unknowable: Falluja's April civilian toll is 600', 26 October 2004, <http://www.iraqbodycount.net/press/index. php#pr.9>.

61. See, for example, the eyewitness accounts from Falluja of sniping by US Marines at <http://www.aqwo36.dsl.pipex.com/fallujah.htm>, especially those of human rights activist Jo Wilding, and the documentary film *Letter to the Prime Minister: Jo Wilding's Diary From Iraq*, Bristol: Year Zero Films, 2005, <http://www.alettertotheprimeminister.co.uk/>.

62. Jack Fairweather, 'Biggest threat to Iraq is from outside, says US general', *Daily Telegraph*, 3 July 2004.

63. Etherington, *Revolt*, p. 219.

64. Rowan Scarborough, 'U.S. declared insurgency "broken"', *Washington Times*, 19 November 2004.

65. UNAMI Emergency Working Group, *Fallujah Bulletin Update*, 18 January 2005, via <http://www.uniraq.org/>.

66. Daud Salman, 'Slow progress in battered Falluja', Institute for War and Peace Reporting, 19 April 2005.

67. Bing West, 'Return to Fallujah: the emerging Iraqi Army', *Slate*, 27 September 2005, via <http://slate.msn.com/>

68. Dahr Jamail, 'Life goes on in Fallujah's rubble', Inter Press Service, 24 November 2005.

69. Sean Rayment, 'Trigger-happy US troops "will keep us in Iraq for years"', *Daily Telegraph*, 15 May 2005; Rory Carroll and Richard Norton-Taylor, 'RAF joins US forces in Iraq assault', *Guardian*, 20 June 2005.

70. Quoted in Tom Lasseter, 'Officers say arms can't settle Iraq war', Knight Ridder Newspapers, 13 June 2005.

71. Tom Lasseter, 'US military air strikes significantly increased in Iraq', Knight Ridder Newspapers, 14 March 2006.

72. 'Army's insurgent manual'; discussed critically by Brigadier Nigel Aylwin-Foster, 'Changing the Army for Counterinsurgency Operations', *Military Review*, Nov.-Dec. 2005, pp. 4-5.

73. Eric Schmitt and Robert F. Worth, 'Marines' Falluja report is gloomy', *New York Times*, 19 November 2004.

74. 'Army's insurgent manual'.

75. For example, Meg Jones, 'For troops on patrol, threats lurk at every step', *Milwaukee Journal Sentinel*, 16 June 2005.

76. ICRC, 'ICRC concerned about the plight of civilians in Iraq', 16 May 2005, Press Release 05/26, via <http://www.icrc.org/>.

77. Dahr Jamail, 'A town becomes a prison', Inter Press Service, 21 January 2006.

78. Quoted in Tom Lasseter, 'Officers say arms can't settle Iraq war', Knight Ridder Newspapers, 13 June 2005.

79. Quoted in AP, 'Death toll mounts in Tal Afar', 11 September 2005.

80. Rory Carroll, 'Iraq bombings and shootings leave 150 dead', *Guardian*, 15 September 2005.

81. Les Roberts, Riyadh Lafta, Richard Garfield, Jamal Khudhairi and Gilbert Burnham, 'Mortality Before and After the 2003 Invasion of Iraq: Cluster Sample Survey', *The Lancet*, vol. 364, no. 9448 (20 November 2004), pp. 1857-64. For a survey of the debate on and defence of the methodology of the study, see Michael Lewis, 'The Lancet Iraq mortality survey: the UK Government's response is inaccurate and misleading', 1 November 2004, <http://www.casi.org.uk/briefing/041101lancetpmos.html>.

82. IBC, 'A Dossier of Civilian Casualties 2003-2005', July 2005, <http://www.iraqbodycount.net/press/pr12.php>.

83. Calculated from IBC, 'Dossier'.

84. Quoted in Aylwin-Foster, 'Changing the army', p.4.

85. Thompson, *Defeating Communist Insurgency*, pp. 52-3.

86. US Army, *Counterinsurgency Operations*, pp. 3(4), J(1).

87. While the Security Council did not pass a resolution specifically on the issue of the legality of the invasion itself, the occupation was placed into a legal framework of the laws of occupation by Security Council Resolution 1483 (22 May 2003). The Coalition thus had the opportunity to act within the laws of occupation, even if many – including the UN Secretary-General Kofi Annan – believed the invasion itself to have been illegal.

88. Jonathan Steele, 'Iraq council was regarded with scorn – but now it has found its voice', *Guardian*, 12 April 2004.

89. Seymour Hersh, *Chain of Command*, London: Penguin, 2005; Karen Greenberg and Joshua L. Dratel (eds), *The Torture Papers: The Road to Abu Ghraib*, Cambridge University Press, 2005; Mark Danner, *Torture and Truth: Abu Ghraib and America in Iraq*, London: Granta Books, 2005; and Human Rights Watch, *Leadership Failure: Firsthand Accounts of Torture of Iraqi Detainees by the U.S. Army's 82nd Airborne Division*, vol. 17, no. 3(G), September 2005, <http://www.hrw.org/reports/2005/us0905/>.

90.   Major General Antonio Taguba, *Article 15-6 Investigation of the 800th Military Police Brigade*, March 2004, esp. p.8.

91.   ICRC, *Report of the International Committee of the Red Cross (ICRC) on the Treatment by the Coalition Forces of Prisoners of War and Other Protected Persons by the Geneva Conventions in Iraq During Arrest, Internment and Interrogation*, February 2004, pp. 3-4.

92.   ICRC, *Report of the Red Cross*, pp. 11, 13.

93.   ICRC, *Report of the Red Cross*, p. 3.

94.   ICRC, *Report of the Red Cross*, p. 13; Center for Economic and Social Rights (CESR), *Beyond Torture: U.S. Violations of Occupation Law in Iraq*, June 2004, p. 12, <http://www.cesr.org/beyondtorture.pdf>; Charles Hanley, 'Documents show army seized wives as tactic', Associated Press, 27 January 2006.

95.   ICRC, *Report of the Red Cross*, pp. 7-8, 20-2.

96.   ICRC, *Report of the Red Cross*, pp. 8-9, 24.

97.   Kirsten Scharnberg, 'US raids test Iraqis' patience', *Chicago Tribune*, 15 June 2005; BBC Newsnight, 19 June 2006; 'The Torture Question: Interview - Tony Lagouranis', PBS Frontline, edited transcript of interview conducted on 25 September 2005.

98.   Figures calculated from UNAMI, 'Human rights report, 1 January 2006 – 28 February 2006', p. 6.

99.   Taguba Report, *Article 15-6 Investigation*, 'Findings and Recommendations' section 24.

100.   Amnesty International, 'Iraq: human rights protection and promotion vital in the transitional period', 28 June 2004, via <http://web.amnesty.org/>.

101.   UNAMI, 'Human rights report, 1 September – 31 October 2005', p. 3.

102.   See successive UNAMI human rights reports: '1 September – 31 October 2005', p. 3; '1 November – 31 December 2005', p. 5; '1 January – 28 February 2006', p. 6.

103.   CPA Order Number 13 (Revised) (Amended), 'The Central Criminal Court of Iraq', 22 April 2004.

104.   Headquarters US Central Command, 'Iraq's central criminal court convicts AIF [Anti-Iraqi Force] members', News Release 04-08-08, 2 August 2004, <http://www.centcom.mil/CENTCOMNews/news_release.asp?NewsRelease=20040808.txt>.

105.   Rory Carroll, 'Courts resort to rushed justice', *Guardian*, 19 July 2005.

106.   Jeffrey Fleishman, 'Justice is swift and deadly in Baghdad', *Los Angeles Times*, 6 June 2005.

107.   Quoted in Nicholas Pelham, 'Prisoner 27075 learns the limits of sovereignty', *Financial Times*, 28 June 2004.

108.   CPA Order Number 99, Joint Detainee Committee, 27 June 2004; AFP, 'Iraqi prime minister to co-chair Detainee Committee', 30 June 2004.

109.   CPA Order Number 98, Iraqi Ombudsman for Penal and Detention Matters, 27 June 2004.

110.   Doug Smith and Raheem Salman, 'Long jailings anger Iraqis', *Los Angeles Times*, 29 May 2005.

111.   Amnesty International USA, *Iraq: One Year On the Human Rights Situation in Iraq Remains Dire*, 17 March 2004. There are many reports of the indiscriminate use of force by the Coalition, especially by US forces, in addition to those contained in this Amnesty International report. For example, Paul Rockwell, 'Atrocities in Iraq: "I killed innocent people for our government"', *Sacramento Bee*, 16 May 2004; CESR, *Beyond Torture*, pp. 11-12.

112.   The regulations permit the immunity from Iraqi legal process to be waived by the state of which the individual is a citizen, but there appear to have been no cases of this occurring. CPA Order Number 17 (Revised), 'Status of the Coalition Provisional Authority', MNF-Iraq, *Certain Missions and Personnel in Iraq*, 27 June 2004; Kamal Ahmed, 'Iraqis lose right to sue troops over war crimes', *Observer*, 23 May 2004.

113.   Jeff Wilkinson, 'In Tikrit, US destroys homes of suspected guerrillas', Knight-Ridder Newspapers, 18 November 2003; AI, *Iraq: One Year On*.

114.   Alan Elsner, 'US seen as unaccountable in Iraqi civilian deaths', Reuters, 3 May 2005.

115.   Peter Singer, 'Beyond the law', *Guardian*, 3 May 2004; David Leigh, 'Who commands the private soldiers?', *Guardian*, 17 May 2004; Peter Singer, *Corporate Warriors: The Rise of the Privatized Military Industry*, Ithaca, NY: Cornell University Press, 2004.

116.   Senate Armed Services Committee, *National Defense Authorization Act for Fiscal Year 2005 Report*, Senate Report 108-260, 108th Congress, May 2004, section 864.

117.   Senate Armed Services Committee, *National Defense Authorization Act*, section 864.

118.   HRW, *Iraq: U.S. Prisoner Abuse Sparks Concerns Over War Crimes*, 30 April

2004, via <http://www.hrw.org/>.

119.   CCR, *CCR Files Lawsuits Against Private Contractors for Torture Conspiracy*, accessed 22 January 2005, via <http://www.ccr-ny.org/ >.

120.   Senate Armed Services Committee, *National Defense Authorization Act*, sections 864-865.

121.   AI, *Iraq: Killings of Civilians*; Owen Bowcott, 'Inquiries into killings of Iraqis "flawed"', *Guardian*, 30 July 2004.

122.   The relevant standards are the UN Code of Conduct for Law Enforcement Officials; the UN Basic Principles on the Use of Force and Firearms by Law Enforcement Officials; and the UN Principles on the Effective Prevention and Investigation of Extra-Legal, Arbitrary and Summary Executions.

123.   Public Interest Lawyers (PIL), *PIL Reacts to Fresh Cases of Abuse of Iraqi Prisoners in Basra*, <http://www.publicinterestlawyers.co.uk>.

124.   PIL, 'Al-Skeini v Secretary of State for Defence', December 2005, <http://www.publicinterestlawyers.co.uk/>.

125.   HRW, *The New Iraq? Torture and Ill-Treatment of Detainees in Iraqi Custody*, January 2005, via <http://hrw.org/>; State Department, *Iraq: Country Reports on Human Rights Practices – 2005*, 8 March 2006, via <http://www.state.gov/>.

126.   Jeffrey Fleishman and Asmaa Waguih, 'Detainees in Iraq suffer abuse, says government', *Los Angeles Times*, 19 June 2005.

127.   UNAMI, 'Human rights report, 1 September – 31 October 2005', p. 3.

128.   'Jonathan Steele, 'Iraq's interior ministry refusing to deploy US-trained police', *Guardian*, 4 April 2006.

129.   Army, *Counterinsurgency Operations*, pp. vi, 2(3). See also p. 2(1).

130.   Summarised in GAO, 'Rebuilding Iraq: resource, security, governance, essential services, and oversight issues', Report to Congressional Committees, June 2004, pp. 53-4.

131.   Interview with senior Coalition military officer, May 2004. Although not secret, the chart is not a public document.

132.   Email correspondence, Coalition military officer, 2 August 2005.

133.   US State Department, *Iraq Weekly Status Report*, successive editions from 20 July 2005 to 21 September 2005 inclusive.

134.   By January 2005, the security forces comprised the Air Force, the Army, the Coastal Defence Force, the Intervention Force (the counter-insurgency element of the Army), the National Guard (the relaunched ICDC), the Police Service Emergency Response Unit (for 'national level law

enforcement emergencies'), the Special Operations Force (for counter-insurgency), the Mechanised Police Brigade (for counter-insurgency) and the Special Police Commando Battalions of the Ministry of the Interior. Multinational Security Transition Command – Iraq, *MNSTC-I Troops Fact Sheet*, 15 January 2005, <http://www.mnstci.iraq.centcom.mil/facts_troops.htm>.

135.   GAO, 'Rebuilding Iraq: resource, security', p. 59.

136.   Etherington, *Revolt*, p. 82.

137.   GAO, 'Rebuilding Iraq: resource, security', pp. 54-5, 57-9

138.   Reuters, 'NATO clinches deal to train Iraqi Security Forces', 30 July 2004.

139.   Numbers on 18 June 2004 were 84,000 in the police, 18,000 in the Department of Border Enforcement, 36,000 in the ICDC and 74,000 in the FPS. GAO, 'Rebuilding Iraq: resource, security', p. 56; Jim Krane, 'Iraqi chief says Security Forces changes ahead', *Messenger-Inquirer*, 21 June 2004; MNFI-MNCI News Release 'Iraqi Security Forces receive materials, weapons', 6 August 2004, <http://www.cjtf7.com/media-information/august2004/040806d.htm>; Michael Howard, '"Bomb trap" kills 28 in Baghdad', *Guardian*, 30 December 2004.

140.   Todd Pitman, 'Iraq police say the job is now perilous', AP, 31 July 2004. With 710 police being killed between April 2003 and May 2004, opinion polling showed that nearly half of Iraqis would oppose a member of their family serving in the Iraqi police or the ICDC. To counteract this slide in support, payments to surviving families were increased. Jonathan Steele and agencies, 'Relatives of murdered Iraqi policemen to get wage for life', *Guardian*, 16 July 2004.

141.   David Axe, 'Down and out with Iraqi forces', Salon.com, 23 May 2005.

142.   Ewen MacAskill, Richard Norton-Taylor and Rory McCarthy, 'US and UK look for early way out of Iraq', *Guardian*, 22 January 2005.

143.   State Department, *Iraq Weekly Status Report*, 22 March 2006; Philip Sherwell, 'Americans hand front-line security to new Iraqi units', *Daily Telegraph*, 26 February 2006.

144.   ICG, *Iraq: Building a New Security Structure*, p. 21; Tom Lasseter, 'Sectarian resentment extends to Iraq's army', Knight Ridder Newspapers, 12 October 2005; Dexter Filkins, 'Sunnis accuse Iraqi military of kidnappings and slayings', *New York Times*, 29 November 2005; Sabrina Tavernise, 'As Iraqi Shiites police Sunnis, rough justice feeds bitterness', *New York Times*,

6 February 2006.

145.   State Department, 'Country Reports on Human Rights Practices, 2005: Iraq', 8 March 2006; also, Edward Wong, 'U.S. is seeking better balance in Iraqi police', *New York Times*, 7 March 2006.

146.   Calculated from NATO Update, 'NATO trains over 1,000 Iraqi officers', 18 January 2006, via <http://www.nato.int/>; and DoD, 'Measuring stability and security', 17 February 2006, p. 40.

147.   Department of State, *Iraq Weekly Status Report*, 15 March 2006, p. 26.

148.   O'Hanlon and Kamp, *Iraq Index*, 23 March 2006, p. 20.

149.   Hashim, 'Sunni insurgency'; John F. Burns and Eric Schmitt, 'Generals offer a sober outlook on Iraqi war', *New York Times*, 19 May 2005.

150.   Richard Norton-Taylor and Ewen MacAskill, 'Military anger at delay to Iraq pull-out plan', *Guardian*, 21 September 2005.

151.   'US hands over holy Shiite city Karbala to Iraq', *China View*, 29 September 2005.

152.   Greg Jaffe, 'New factor in Iraq: irregular brigades fill security void', *Wall Street Journal*, 16 February 2005; Pepe Escobar, 'Destination civil war', *Asia Times*, 30 April 2005; Maass, 'Way of the commandos'.

153.   Mariam Fam, 'Iraqis say security forces use torture', Associated Press, 6 July 2005; ABC News, 'Iraq's Wolf Brigade said to be effective, at times brutal', 13 December 2005.

154.   Hannah Allam, 'Elite Iraqi unit gains fans as it takes fight to insurgents', Knight Ridder Newspapers, 22 May 2005; Lionel Beehner, 'Iraq: militia groups', Background Q&A, Council on Foreign Relations, 9 June 2005.

155.   Mark Woodbury, 'Commandos find new stomping ground in Ramadi', *The Advisor* (Official Weekly Command Information Report for the Multi-National Security Transition Command – Iraq), 24 December 2005. Human rights violations reports include Amnesty International, 'Urgent action: Faraj 'Abdullah Mulhim et al.', AI Index: MDE 14/042/2005, 28 October 2005.

156.   On the US role in El Salvador, see Michael McClintock, *The American Connection: State Terror and Popular Resistance in El Salvador*, London: Zed Books, 1985.

157.   Leaked testimony, quoted in Thom Shanker, 'Pentagon says Iraq effort limits ability to fight other conflicts', *New York Times*, 3 May 2005.

158.   Gallup, 'Nationwide survey of 3,500 Iraqis' (March-April 2004), *USA Today*, 30 April 2004, <http://www.usatoday.com/news/world/

iraq/2004-04-28-gallup-iraq-findings.htm>.

159. State Department, 'Iraqi Kurds and Arabs', p. 3 (Figures 2 and 3), p. 10 (Tables A14-15).

160. James Zogby, 'Bend it like Cheney – polling evidence shows most Iraqis have a negative view of the US-led occupation', *Guardian*, 29 October 2003.

161. Richard Burkholder, 'Baghdad views US troops: protectors or justifiable targets?', press briefing Gallup Organization, 14 October 2003, regarding the Gallup poll of September-October 2003.

162. Gallup polls of August-September 2003 and March-April 2004: 'Baghdad: Then and Now', table 15, in USA Today, 20 May 2005, <http://www.usatoday.com/news/world/iraq/2004-04-28-baghdad.htm>.

163. Gallup poll August-September 2003 and March-April 2004, Baghdad, table 14.

164. Gallup, 'Nationwide survey' (March-April 2004), table 23.

165. Gallup poll August-September 2003 and March-April 2004, Baghdad, table 9.

166. IIACSS, 'Public Opinion in Iraq' (May 2004), 15 June 2004, p. 35.

167. IIACSS, 'Public Opinion in Iraq' (May 2004), p. 39.

168. IIACSS, 'Public Opinion in Iraq' (May 2004), p. 46.

169. The sectarianism was not simply Sunni versus Shi'a: Sunni Kurds concurred with Shi'i against Sunni Arabs on many points of opinion.

170. State Department, 'Iraqi Kurds and Arabs', pp. 3 (Figures 2-3), 10 (Figure A1), 11 (Table A17).

171. Zogby International poll 19-23 January 2005, Elections in Iraq, table 18.

172. Bryan Bender, 'Insurgency seen forcing change in Iraq strategy', *Boston Globe*, 10 June 2005.

173. Zogby International poll as quoted in Medea Benjamin, 'Withdraw U.S. troops', *Miami Herald*, 30 April 2005, via <http://www.zogby.com/>.

174. Zogby International poll 19-23 January 2005, 'Elections in Iraq', table 13.

175. Sean Rayment, 'Secret MOD poll: Iraqis support attacks on British troops', *Daily Telegraph*, 23 October 2005.

176. IIACSS, 'Public Opinion in Iraq' (May 2004), pp. 8-9.

177. State Department, 'Iraqi Kurds and Arabs', p. 11 (Table A17).

178.   WorldPublicOpinion.org, 'What the Iraqi public wants', 31 January 2006, p. 6.

179.   WorldPublicOpinion.org, 'What the Iraqi public wants', 31 January 2006, p. 8.

180.   WorldPublicOpinion.org, 'What the Iraqi public wants', 31 January 2006, p. 3.

181.   Aylwin-Foster, 'Changing the army', pp. 4 and 5.

182.   Quoted in Maass, 'Professor Nagl's war'.

183.   State Department, 'Iraqi Kurds and Arabs', p. 9 (Table A8); IRI, *Survey*, 24 November - 5 December 2004, pp. 17-18.

5. CAPITAL

1.   These themes are explored with regard to cases other than Iraq in Michael Pugh and Neil Cooper with Jonathan Goodhand, *War Economies in a Regional Context*, Boulder, CO: Lynne Rienner Publishers, 2004.

2.   Miguel Angel Centeno and Alejandro Portes, *The Informal Economy in the Shadow of the State*, February 2003, <http://cmd.princeton.edu/papers/wp0306.pdf>.

3.   Independent Inquiry Committee, *The Management of the United Nations Oil-for-Food Programme*, vol. I, 7 September 2005, p. 35; Lawrence Kumins, 'Iraq oil: reserves, production, and potential revenues', CRS Report for Congress, 13 April 2005, pp. 1-2.

4.   Successive DoD and State Department editions of *Iraq Weekly Status Report*; also Carola Hoyos, 'Iraq oil production on the decline', *Financial Times*, 6 December 2005.

5.   Samah Samad, 'Iraqi tribes accused of oil protection racket', *Daily Star*, 21 June 2005; Robert Worth and James Glanz, 'Oil graft fuels the insurgency, Iraq and U.S. say', *New York Times*, 5 February 2006.

6.   Patrick McDonnell, 'Boat bombs hit oil station', *Los Angeles Times*, 25 April 2004; Michael Evans, 'Isolated in a ring of steel, the key to Iraq's economic future', *The Times*, 7 March 2006; similarly, 'Eight oil pipelines attacked in southern Iraq', *RFE/RL Iraq Report*, 27 August 2004.

7.   Robert Collier, 'Black market drains Iraq oil: Pentagon out to stop ships plying booming trade', *San Francisco Chronicle*, 22 October 2003.

8.   Juan Cole, 'Basra: massive drug, petroleum smuggling; Christians, musicians harassed', *Informed Comment*, 31 December 2003, via <http://

www.juancole.com/>.

9. 'Oil Ministry cracks down on smugglers', *Iraq Press*, 14 January 2004, at <http://www.iraqpress.org/english.asp?fname=ipenglish%5C2004-01-14%5C0.htm>.

10. Isambard Wilkinson, 'British troops hunt night oil raiders who are bleeding Iraq', *Daily Telegraph*, 13 July 2004.

11. Strategic Review Board, *National Development Strategy*, p. 22; Xinhuanet, 'Iraq confiscates ships for smuggling oil', 21 August 2004.

12. Abed Battat, 'Basra police crack down on oil smuggling', Azzaman.com, 9 June 2005.

13. Jill Carroll, 'Why a black market for gasoline vexes Iraq', *Christian Science Monitor*, 20 April 2005; Yaseen al-Ruba'i, 'Corruption draining Iraq's oil industry', *Environment News Service*, 21 April 2005. <http://www.ens-newswire.com/ens/apr2005/2005-04-21-03.asp>.

14. Independent Inquiry Committee, *The Management of the United Nations Oil-for-Food Programme*, vol. II, 7 September 2005, pp. 185-259.

15. Al-Ruba'i, 'Corruption Draining'.

16. Energy Information Administration (EIA), US Department of Energy, Country Analysis Brief: Iraq, 8 June 2005, <http://www.eia.doe.gov/emeu/cabs/iraq.html>; Beth Potter, 'Oil-rich Iraq wants to end gasoline imports', Middle East Online, 23 May 2005, <http://www.middle-east-online.com/english/business/?id=13556>.

17. Eric Eckholm, 'On Iraq's border, sailors of the desert smuggle subsidized gasoline', *New York Times*, 21 August 2004.

18. Worth and Glanz, 'Oil graft fuels the insurgency'.

19. UN Office on Drugs and Crime, 'Organized Crime to be a Growing Problem in Iraq UNODC Fact-finding Mission Reports', 27 August 2003, via <http://www.unodc.org/>; Wheelock and McGuckin, 'Iraqi power sector'.

20. James Glantz, 'Not all scrap metal leaving Iraq is junk', *New York Times*, 27 May 2004; James Glanz and William J. Broad, 'Looting at weapons plants was systematic', *New York Times*, 13 March 2005; UN Office for the Coordination of Humanitarian Affairs (UNOCHA) and Integrated Regional Information Network (IRIN), 'Iraq: UN concerned over suspected looting of dual use sites', 15 March 2005; James Glanz, 'Arms equipment plundered in 2003 is surfacing in Iraq', *New York Times*, 17 April 2005.

21.   Ahmed Janabi, 'Drugs trade thriving in Iraq', Aljazeera.Net, 29 March 2004.

22.   Jonathan Finer, 'Iraq used for transit of drugs, officials say', *Washington Post*, 12 June 2005.

23.   Zainab Bahrani, 'Days of plunder', *Guardian*, 31 August 2004; AFP, 'Mystery shrouds Iraq's missing artifacts', 23 June 2005.

24.   Victoria Firmo-Fontan, 'Abducted, beaten and sold into prostitution: a tale from Iraq', *The Independent*, 26 July 2004.

25.   Joshua Phillips, 'Unveiling Iraq's teenage prostitutes', Salon.com, 24 June 2005.

26.   Rick Jervis, '"Pleasure marriages" regain popularity in Iraq', *USA Today*, 4 May 2005.

27.   USAID, 'Focused stabilization in strategic cities initiative', p. 57.

28.   This system was established via CPA Regulations 5 (June 2003) and 7 (5 December 2003). GAO, 'Rebuilding Iraq: resource, security', pp. 22-4.

29.   CPA Regulation Number 3: Program Review Board, 18 June 2003.

30.   CPA Regulation Number 3: Program Review Board, 18 June 2003.

31.   PCO press release, 'PCO transition of authority', 15 August 2004, via <http://www.rebuilding-iraq.net/>. 1% of the IRRF funds ($184 million for 2005) is set aside to support US Embassy operations: CRS, *Embassy*, p. 4; Iraq Investment and Reconstruction Task Force, *Doing Business in Iraq FAQs*, 18 May 2005, <http://www.export.gov/iraq/bus_climate/faq.html>; SIGIR, *Quarterly Report to Congress*, 30 April 2005, pp. 3, 93; State Department, 'Executive summary', *Section 2207 Report on Iraq Relief and Reconstruction*, 6 April 2005; Caroline Daniel and Guy Dinmore, 'State Department takes over Iraq reconstruction', *Financial Times*, 15 December 2005.

32.   State Department, 'Executive summary', *Section 2207 Report*, 6 April 2005; Curt Tarnoff, 'Recent developments in reconstruction assistance', CRS Report for Congress, 12 May 2005, p. 10.

33.   PCO, <http://www.rebuilding-iraq.net>, accessed 9 September 2005.

34.   Tarnoff, 'Recent developments in reconstruction assistance', p. 14; M. Curtius and P. Richter, 'State Dept. criticizes focus of Iraqi effort', *Los Angeles Times*, 22 July 2004; US Department of State, 'Transcript: U.S. increases spending in Iraq for security, election preparations', 14 September 2004.

35.   SIGIR, *Quarterly Report to Congress*, 30 April 2005, pp. 39-45, 79.

36.   Interview with Larry Crandall, Deputy Head of the CPA Programme Management Office between January and June 2004 (20 September 2004), <http://www.usip.org/library/oh/sops/iraq/rec/crandall.pdf>, p. 18.

37.   Quoted in Brandon Sprague, 'The real oil war in Iraq', ZNet, 30 April 2004 <http://www.zmag.org/content/showarticle.cfm?SectionID=15&ItemID=5431>.

38.   ICG, *Reconstructing Iraq*, pp. 5, 17.

39.   Interview with CPA official, November 2003.

40.   TradeArabia, 'Iraq to Cut State Subsidies', 24 June 2005, at <http://www.tradearabia.com/tanews/newsdetails.asp?Ref=S&Article=89090&Sn=&Cnt=3>; Borzou Daragahi, 'Iraqis look at cuts in payroll', *Los Angeles Times*, 6 June 2005.

41.   ICG, *Reconstructing Iraq*, pp. 4-9.

42.   Reuters, 'US strives to privatize Iraqi state-owned firms', 13 October 2003.

43.   Klein, 'Bush's Iraq'.

44.   'Foreign firms vie For Iraq factories', *Iraq Press*, 11 December 2003, <http://www.iraqpress.org/english.asp?fname=ipenglish%5C2003-12-11%5C1.htm>.

45.   MerchantBridge, 'Iraq appoints MerchantBridge to advise on the leasing of state-owned companies to the private sector', 7 January 2004, <http://www.mbih.com/_mbih/asp/showcomment.asp?newsid=708>.

46.   Doug Struck, 'Engines of industry sputtering in Iraq', *Washington Post*, 10 July 2004; 'Tenders', Ministry of Industry and Minerals, accessed 31 October 2004, at <http://www.iraqiindustry.com/Tenders/tenders.aspx>.

47.   Greg Palast, 'Secret U.S. plans for Iraq's oil spark political fight between neocons and big oil', *Greg Palast: Journalism and Film*, 21 March 2005, <http://www.gregpalast.com/printerfriendly.cfm?artid=419>.

48.   Neil King Jr., 'Bush officials draft broad plan for free-market economy in Iraq', *Wall Street Journal*, 1 May 2003.

49.   Palast, 'Secret U.S. plans'; David R. Baker, 'Seeking Iraq's oil prize: government may allow foreign petroleum firms to invest', *San Francisco Chronicle*, 26 January 2005.

50.   CPA Order Number 39: Foreign Investment, 20 December 2003.

51.   Baker, 'Seeking Iraq's oil prize'; IRW, 'FAQ', no date, accessed 16 July

2005, <http://www.iraqrevenuewatch.org/faq/index.shtml>; Tarnoff, 'Recent developments', p. 4.

52.   Strategic Review Board, *National Development Strategy*, p. 30

53.   Walid Kadduri, Gerald Butt, 'Iraq's oil: future prospects, *Al-Ahram Weekly*, 6 March 2003; Pelham, 'Oil to be privatised'; Greg Muttitt, 'Resisting the economic war in Iraq: interview with Hassan Juma'a Awad, head of Basra oil union', *Corporate Watch Newsletter*, April/May 2005; See also Greg Muttitt, 'Iraq's other resistance: oil workers in Basra are ready to fight privatisation', *Guardian*, 3 June 2005.

54.   Eric Leser, 'Halliburton, principal bénéficiaire de la reconstruction de l'Irak', *Le Monde*, 20 June 2003; Jason Leopold, 'Defense Dept. secretly tapped Halliburton unit to operate Iraq's oil industry', ZNet, 13 May 2003; Rep. Henry A. Waxman and Sen. Byron L. Dorgan, 'Halliburton's Questioned and Unsupported Costs in Iraq Exceed $1.4 Billion', 27 June 2005, via <http://www.democrats.reform.house.gov/>.

55.   EIA, *Country Analysis Brief: Iraq*.

56.   These include agreements with Royal Dutch/Shell Group signed on 14 January 2005 to study Kirkuk using the latest technology and to draft a plan to develop Iraq's natural gas; with BP to study Rumailah; Exxon Mobil Corp to provide technical assistance and studies; with Turkey's AvrAsya Technology Engineering to develop the Khurmala Dome oil field, and an arrangement with Canada's OGI Group to develop Hamrin. EIA, *Country Analysis Brief*: Iraq; Baker, 'Seeking Iraq's oil prize'; Katzman, 'Iraq', p. 40; Laurence Frost, 'Oil companies hopeful on Iraqi politics', Associated Press, 14 March 2005.

57.   'Iraq amasses Kirkuk crude volumes for supply to Tupras', *International Oil Daily*, 12 August 2005.

58.   These contracts, whose legal status is uncertain since the fall of the Ba'thist regime that negotiated them, are estimated as being worth $38 billion. EIA, *Country Analysis Brief: Iraq*.

59.   Jonathan Steele, 'Iraqi cabinet approval ends deadlock: former US ally Chalabi to become acting Oil Minister', *Guardian*, 29 April 2005; Daud Salman, 'Iraq privatization plan drawn up: Industry Ministry hopes to persuade local and international firms to invest in state-owned concerns in Baghdad', Institute for War and Peace Reporting, 10 May 2005; Sarah Miller-Davenport, 'Iraqi officials and international experts debate future of Iraq's oil', IRW Press Release, 1 July 2005, <http://www.

iraqrevenuewatch.org/reading/pr070105.shtml>; 'UK oil conference: greater investment in Iraq', British Satellite News, 5 July 2005, via <http://www.bsn.org.uk/>.

60.   International legal challenge feared: Muttitt, 'Resisting the economic war in Iraq'. Renationalisation feared: Palast, 'Secret U.S. plans'.

61.   PSAs are controversial as they turn over control of the development of an area to a private company for 25-50 years, restricting a host country's ability to introduce new laws that would affect a company's profits. To date, oil companies do not have existing PSAs with any of the major Middle Eastern oil producing countries. Former Interim Prime Minister 'Allawi voiced support for PSAs in September 2004. See Greg Muttit, 'Resisting the economic war In Iraq' and *Crude Designs: The Rip-off of Iraq's Oil Wealth*, PLATFORM, November 2005.

62.   CPA Order No. 37: Tax Strategy for 2003, 19 September 2003.

63.   Dana Milbank and Walter Pincus, 'U.S. administrator imposes flat tax system on Iraq', *Washington Post*, 2 November 2003.

64.   CPA Order Number 38: Reconstruction Levy, 19 September 2003. Its implementation was delayed from 1 January 2004 until 1 March in Order Number 47, until 1 April in Order 54 and until 15 April in Order Number 70.

65.   CPA Order Number 39: Foreign Investment, 19 September 2003.

66.   CPA Order Number 40: Bank Law, 19 September 2003.

67.   CPA Order Number 94: Banking Law, 6 June 2004.

68.   Kofi Annan, *Report of the Secretary-General Pursuant to Paragraph 24 of Security Council Resolution 1483 (2003)*, 17 July 2003 (S/2003/715).

69.   Annan, *Report of the Secretary-General,* paragraphs 84, 88, 90.

70.   Annan, *Report of the Secretary-General*, paragraph 89.

71.   ICG, *Reconstructing Iraq*, p. 19.

72.   Curt Tarnoff, 'Iraq: recent developments in reconstruction assistance', CRS, 2 October 2003.

73.   Quoted in Jim Krane, 'Analysts say market-based economy in Iraq is reckless', *Daily Herald*, 23 November 2003.

74.   ICG, *Reconstructing Iraq*, p. 6.

75.   OPIC Press Release, 'Allawi and Connelly sign agreement opening way for more U.S. investment in Iraq', 11 July 2005 and 'OPIC and Citigroup establish lending facility to revive SMEs in Iraq', 16 March 2005, <http://www.opic.gov>.

76.   Trade Bank of Iraq, <http://www.tbiraq.com/>.

77.   In addition to the US (via OPIC and the Export-Import Bank) and a pan-Arab consortium, the countries involved include Austria, Belgium, the Czech Republic, Denmark, Germany, the United Kingdom, the Netherlands, Italy, Poland, Spain, Sweden, Switzerland, Luxembourg, Australia and Japan.

78.   IIG, *Iraq – Letter of Intent, Memorandum of Economic and Financial Policies*, and *Technical Memorandum of Understanding*, 24 September 2004, <http://www.imf.org/external/np/loi/2004/irq/01/index.htm>. The same themes are contained in the Iraqi Strategic Review Board's *National Development Strategy, 2005-2007* of June 2005.

79.   IG, *Memorandum*, para. 36.

80.   IG, *Memorandum*, para. 37.

81.   IG, Memorandum, para. 48.

82.   Jubilee Iraq, <http://www.jubileeiraq.org/iraqiviews.htm>.

83.   RightWeb, 'Profile: Zalmay Khalilzad', <http://rightweb.irc-online.org/ind/khalilzad/khalilzad.php>.

84.   Juan Cole, 'The Iraqi Constitution: DOA?', Salon.com, 26 August 2005.

85.   On its outreach programme, see CIPE, 'Iraq field update', June 2005, <http://www.cipe.org/regional/mena/Resource_1.pdf>.

86.   CIPE, 'The Iraqi Constitution from an economic perspective – interview with Noah Feldman, New York University School of Law', 1 August 2005, <http://www.cipe.org/pdf/publications/fs/080105.pdf>.

87.   IRI, *Survey of Iraqi Public Opinion, 24 November – 5 December 2004*, p. 44.

88.   IRI, *Survey, 24 November – 5 December 2004*, p. 40.

89.   Zogby International, 'Business Leader Attitudes Toward Commercial Activity, Employee Relations, and Government in Post-Saddam Iraq', December 2004, <www.cipe.org/CIPE_Zogby_Iraq_survey.pdf>.

90.   Citigroup, 'How Citigroup is organized', <http://www.citigroup.com/citigroup/business/index.htm>; Stephen Timewell, 'Top 1,000 banks', *The Banker*, 2 July 2004, via <http://www.thebanker.com>.

91.   US Department of Commerce, 'Iraq Investment and Reconstruction Task Force', accessed 16 June 2005, <http://www.export.gov/iraq/>.

92.   Peter Finn and Peter Baker, 'US decision on Iraq contracts irritates excluded war critics', *Washington Post*, 11 December 2003.

93.   PCO, 'Programme Management Office Concept of Operations'.

94.   For a survey of all US firms with Iraq-related contracts, see the Windfalls

of War project of the Center for Public Integrity, <http://www.publicintegrity.org>.

95. PCO, 'PCO Transition of Authority', 15 August 2004.

96. 'FY2004 reconstruction contracts and grants', US Department of Commerce website Export.gov/Iraq, <http://www.export.gov/iraq/market_ops/contracts04.html>.

97. Parsons, <http://www.parsons.com/about/default.asp>.

98. Heartington Invest and Trade Inc (Portal Iraq), 'Egypt: Orascom Construction and Contrack International win $325 million contract', 27 March 2004.

99. Tarnoff, 'Recent Developments in Reconstruction Assistance', 12 May 2005, p. 20; Bechtel Corporation, 'Bechtel's outreach to Iraqi subcontractors', <http://www.bechtel.com/sample_iraq_supplier_information.htm>.

100. Bechtel Corporation, 'Bechtel's outreach to Iraqi subcontractors'.

101. Parsons, 'Taji military base renovation, Iraq', 21 September 2004, <http://www.parsons.com/about/press_rm/potm/09-2004/index.html>.

102. Sheila Anne Feeney, 'Dangerous Business', *Workforce Management*, June 2004, pp. 32-40, <http://www.workforce.com/section/09/feature/23/74/38/>.

103. Pratap Chatterjee, *Iraq, Inc.: A Profitable Occupation*, New York: Seven Stories Press, 2004, pp. 15-29; Feeney, 'Dangerous business'.

104. IRW, *Disorder, Negligence and Mismanagement: How the CPA Handled Iraq Reconstruction Funds*, Revenue Watch Report No. 7, September 2004, p. 2. See also Ariana Eunjung Cha, '$1.9 billion of Iraq's money goes to U.S. contractors', *Washington Post*, 4 August 2004; and Chatterjee, *Iraq, Inc.*

105. T. Christian Miller, 'US contractor pulls out of reconstruction effort in Iraq', *Los Angeles Times*, 22 December 2004.

106. PCO, 'Welcome to PCO', via <http://www.rebuilding-iraq.net/>.

107. SIGIR, *Quarterly Report to Congress*, January 30, 2005, p. 106; Tarnoff, 'Recent developments in reconstruction assistance', 12 May 2005, p. 21.

108. Sue Pleming, 'U.S. reviews rebuilding, gives more power to Iraqis', Reuters, 1 February 2005.

109. Forrest Laws, 'Rebuilding Iraq's agriculture will be a major challenge', *Southeast Farm Press*, 21 May 2004; Glen Rangwala, 'Senior advisers of the Coalition Provisional Authority', <http://middleeastreference.org.uk/

iraqcpa.html>.

110. Reuters, 'Australia eyes more Iraq wheat sales', 14 October 2004;
      Reuters, 'Iraq: battle for $500-million wheat market heats up', 6 May
      2005; TradeArabia, 'Iraq buys Australian wheat', 29 March 2006, via
      <http://tradearabia.com>.

111. CPA Order No. 81: Patent, Industrial Design, Undisclosed Information,
      Integrated Circuits and Plant Variety Law, 26 April 2004, p. 22; Bill
      Rammell, Foreign and Commonwealth Office, Written answer, 3 March
      2005, *Hansard*, Column 1385W.

112. Focus on the Global South and Grain, 'Iraq's new patent law: a declaration
      of war against farmers', October 2004, <http://www.grain.org/
      articles/?id=6>.

113. UPOV, <http://www.upov.org/>, accessed 5 November 2004.

114. Strategic Review Board, *National Development Strategy*, p. 35.

115. IAMB, <http://www.iamb.info/>. See also GAO, *Rebuilding Iraq:
      Resource, Security, Governance*, pp. 27-35; SIGIR, *Quarterly Report to Congress*,
      30 April 2005; Katzman, *Iraq: U.S. Regime Change Efforts*, p. 40.

116. UN Security Council Resolution 1483 (22 May 2003).

117. Tarnoff, 'Recent developments in reconstruction assistance', p. 4.
      Katzman, *Iraq: U.S. Regime Change Efforts*, p. 40.

118. State Department, 'Executive summary', *Quarterly Report to Congress* (2207
      Report), April 2005, pp. 11-12.

119. SIGIR, *Report to Congress*, 30 April 2005, p. 89.

120. Tarnoff, 'Recent developments in reconstruction assistance', p. 5.

121. Tarnoff, 'Recent developments in reconstruction assistance', p. 5;
      Katzman, *Iraq: U.S. Regime Change Efforts*, 5 April 2005, p. 40.

122. Tarnoff, 'Recent developments in reconstruction assistance', p. 6; IRW,
      Disorder, Negligence and Mismanagement, p. 8.

123. US Army Corps of Engineers, 'Engineer support to Operation Iraqi
      Freedom: frequently asked questions', 7 October, <http://www.
      hq.usace.army.mil/CEPA/Iraq/March03-table.htm>;   Suzanne
      Goldenberg, 'Pentagon 'hid' damning Halliburton audit', *Guardian*, 16
      March 2005.

124. IAMB, 'Statement: release of the KPMG audit reports on the Development
      Fund for Iraq', 15 July 2004, <http://www.iamb.info/auditrep/
      pr071504.pdf>.

125. KPMG Audit and Risk Advisory Services, 'Development Fund for Iraq',

Appendix, June 2004, <http://www.iamb.info/auditrep/r123104. pdf>; KPMG Audit and Risk Advisory Services, 'Development Fund for Iraq: management letter on internal controls', 6 April 2005, <http:// www.iamb.info/auditrep/r123104b.pdf>.

126. KPMG Audit and Risk Advisory Services, 'Development Fund for Iraq: report of factual findings in connection with disbursements for the period from 1 January 2004 to 28 June 2004', September 2004, <http://www. iamb.info/auditrep/disburse101204.pdf>.

127. T. Christian Miller, 'Worries raised on handling of funds in Iraq', *Los Angeles Times*, 22 June 2005.

128. SIGIR, *Quarterly Report to Congress*, 30 January 2005, p. 4.

129. KPMG, 'Development Fund for Iraq: report of factual findings in connection with disbursements for the period from 29 June 2004 to 31 December 2004', 6 April 2005, <http://www.iamb.info/auditrep/ r123104e.pdf>.

130. KPMG, 'Development Fund for Iraq: report of factual findings', 6 April 2005, p. 17.

131. SIGIR, *Quarterly Report to Congress*, 30 July 2005, p. 46.

132. Ed Harriman, 'Where has all the money gone?', *London Review of Books*, vol. 27, no. 13, 7 July 2005.

133. IRW, *Disorder, Negligence and Mismanagement*, September 2004, pp. 2-3, 8.

134. Neil King, Jr. and Yochi J. Dreazen, 'Amid the chaos in Iraq, tiny security firm carved out opportunity', *Wall Street Journal*, 13 August 2004.

135. Dexter Filkins, 'Accusations of corruption fly over cash deal for weapons in Iraq', *New York Times*, 24 January 2005.

136. James Glanz, 'Iraqis tallying range of graft in rebuilding', *New York Times*, 24 June 2005.

137. Khaled Yacoub Oweis, 'Iraq confronts "disastrous" corruption', Reuters, 21 June 2005.

138. Ed Vulliamy and Richard Norton-Taylor, 'Millions embezzled at Iraqi ministry', *Guardian*, 22 August 2005; Patrick Cockburn, 'What has happened to Iraq's missing $1bn?', *The Independent*, 19 September 2005; Michael Howard, 'Ex-Iraqi defence minister wanted over $1bn fraud', *Guardian*, 20 September 2005.

139. Tarnoff, 'Recent developments in reconstruction assistance', p. 2 (Table 1).

140. This was known as IRRF1. SIGIR, *Quarterly Report to Congress*, 30 April 2005, p. 91.

141. Tarnoff, 'Recent developments in reconstruction assistance', p. 4.

142. This was known as IRRF2. Tarnoff, 'Recent developments in reconstruction assistance', 12 May 2005, p. 2; SIGIR, *Quarterly Report to Congress*, 30 April 2005, p. 91; Katzman, *Iraq: U.S. Regime Change Efforts*, p. 41.

143. State Department, *Quarterly Report to Congress (Section 2207 Report)*, January 2006, pp. 19-21.

144. Tarnoff, 'Recent developments in reconstruction assistance', p. 3.

145. Tarnoff, 'Recent developments in reconstruction assistance', p. 4.

146. PCO, 'PCO transition of authority', 15 August 2004.

147. Tarnoff, 'Recent developments in reconstruction assistance', p. 10; SIGIR, *Quarterly Report to Congress*, 30 April 2005.

148. SIGIR, *Quarterly Report to Congress*, 30 April 2005, p. 5-6; IRW, *Disorder, Negligence and Mismanagement*, p. 11; Pratap Chatterjee, 'Controversial commando wins Iraq contract', CorpWatch, 9 June 2004, <http://www.corpwatch.org/article.php?id=11350>; Sue Pleming, 'U.S. audit criticizes Aegis security work in Iraq', Reuters, 22 April 2005.

149. SIGIR, *Quarterly Report to Congress*, 30 July 2005, p. 58.

150. Rep. Henry A. Waxman and Sen. Byron L. Dorgan, 'Halliburton's questioned and unsupported costs in Iraq exceed $1.4 billion', 27 June 2005, <http://www.democrats.reform.house.gov/Documents/20050627140010-82879.pdf>, pp. 3-4.

151. Halliburton Watch, 'About Halliburton: LOGCAP military contract', <http://www.halliburtonwatch.org/about_hal/logcap.html>; Henry A. Waxman, 'The complex task of coordinating contracts amid chaos: the challenges of rebuilding a broken Iraq', 11 March 2004, via <http://www.house.gov/>

152. Waxman and Dorgan, 'Halliburton's questioned and unsupported costs', p. 6.

153. Waxman and Dorgan, 'Halliburton's questioned and unsupported costs', p. 7; DCAA, 'Audit report of Kellogg Brown and Root, Inc. billing system internal controls', Audit Report No. 3311-2002K11010001, 13 May 2004.

154. Waxman and Dorgan, 'Halliburton's questioned and unsupported costs', p. 17.

155. DCAA, 'Report on audit of proposal for Restore Iraqi Oil Task Order

No. 5', 8 October 2004, p. 1. See also Halliburton Watch, 'About Halliburton: Iraqi oil infrastructure contract', <www.hallliburtonwatch. org/about_hal/about.html>.

156.   Waxman and Dorgan, 'Halliburton's questioned and unsupported costs', p. 13; DCAA, 'Report on audit of proposal for restore Iraqi Oil Task Order No. 5', p. 1.

157.   Waxman and Dorgan, 'Halliburton's questioned and unsupported costs', pp. 24-6.

158.   Waxman and Dorgan, 'Halliburton's questioned and unsupported costs', p. 1.

159.   Waxman and Dorgan, 'Halliburton's questioned and unsupported costs', p. 14.

160.   Waxman and Dorgan, 'Halliburton's questioned and unsupported costs', p. 1.

161.   Sue Pleming, 'Army gives Halliburton $72m bonus', Reuters, 11 May 2005.

162.   Waxman and Dorgan, 'Halliburton's questioned and unsupported costs', pp. 15-23; Halliburton Watch, <http://www.halliburtonwatch.org/>.

163.   Steven R. Weisman, 'U.S. seeks help with Iraq costs, but donors want a larger say,' New York Times, 14 July 2003; Esther Pan, 'Iraq: Madrid donor conference', Council on Foreign Relations, 30 October 2003, <http://www.cfr.org/publication.html?id=7682>.

164.   United Nations/World Bank, United Nations/World Bank Joint Iraq Needs Assessment, October 2003; IRFFI, 'Estimated cost of the projects proposals recommended by the Iraqi Strategic Review Board for negotiation with donors as classified by clusters', <http://www.uniraq.org/documents/Estimated project costs.doc>.

165.   An additional two rotating seats at the Donor Committee Meetings are granted to non-member states, while representatives from the World Bank, the IMF and other International Financial Institutions (IFIs) plus the UN have been granted observer status.

166.   State Department, Section 2207 Report, January 2006, Appendix II.

167.   State Department, Section 2207 Report, January 2006, Appendix II, pp. 8-9.

168.   GAO, Rebuilding Iraq: Resource, Security, Governance, pp. 18, 23.

169.   IMF, Iraq: 2005 Article IV Consultation, p. 15-16.

170.   Jubilee Iraq, <http://www.jubileeiraq.org/debt_today.htm>.

171. The UNCC website has a comprehensive bibliography of academic research on its operation. UNCC, 'Selected publications', <http://www2.unog. ch/uncc/publicat.htm>.

172. Jubilee Iraq, <http://www.jubileeiraq.org/debt_today.htm>; Associated Press, 'Jews who fled Iraq to get compensation', 20 April 2004; Justice for Jews from Arab Countries, via <http://www.american sephardifederation.org/>.

173. IRNA, 'Iran will press ahead for war reparations from Iraq: says Kharrazi', 20 October 2004.

174. IRNA, 'Iran will press ahead'.

175. Iranian.ws, 'Iran: Iraq payment of war reparations still on', 20 May 2005, <http://www.iranian.ws/iran_news/publish/article_7007.shtml>.

176. Quote from Reuters in Jubilee Iraq, 'Iranian reparations', 18 December 2003, <http://www.jubileeiraq.org/blog/2003_12.html#000100>.

177. Al Jazeera, 'Iraq to launch military co-operation with Iran', 7 July 2005.

178. Portal Iraq, 'Iran: $1 billion pledge for Iraq reconstruction from Iran', 27 July 2005.

179. UNCC, <http://www.unog.ch/uncc/governin.htm>.

180. UNCC, Press Release, 'Governing Council of United Nations Compensation Commission has concluded its fifty-sixth session', 30 June 2005, <http://www2.unog.ch/uncc/pressrel/pr_56c.pdf>.

181. UNCC, <http://www2.unog.ch/uncc/theclaims.htm>.

182. Stephanie Nebehay, 'Iraq wants to end U.N. compensation scheme', Reuters, 28 June 2005.

183. Brian Whitaker, 'Damage claims spiral into the realm of the futile', *Guardian*, 1 August 2000.

184. UN Office of Internal Oversight Services, 'OSIS audit number AF2003/820/02 - audit of UNCC E1 claims: 10th installment', 16 December 2004, via <http://www.iic-offp.org/>; Jubilee Iraq, 'More on UNCC overpayment scandal', 11 January 2005, via <http://www. jubileeiraq.org/>; Claudia Rosett, 'Another trail to follow', *Opinion Journal*, 12 January 2005. For all audits and UNCC responses, see UNCC, 'Audit documents' <http://www2.unog.ch/uncc/oiosdocs.htm>.

185. See the breakdown in Jubilee Iraq, 'Debts today', <http://www. jubileeiraq.org/debt_today.htm>.

186. IMF, 'IMF Executive Board approves US$436.3 million in emergency post-conflict assistance to Iraq', Press Release No. 04/206, 29 September

2004,   <http://www.imf.org/external/np/sec/pr/2004/pr04206.
htm>. See also Interim Government, *Letter of Intent*.

187.   Paris Club, 'Iraq debt treatment', 21 November 2004, via <http://
www.clubdeparis.org>. The permanent Paris Club members are the US,
Canada, Japan and Australia plus the European countries Austria, Belgium,
Denmark, Finland, France, Germany, Ireland, Italy, the Netherlands,
Norway, Russia, Spain, Sweden, Switzerland and the United Kingdom.
Additional creditor states are sometimes involved in rescheduling
sessions.

188.   David Shelby, 'United States forgives 100 percent of Iraqi debt', US
Department of State, 17 December 2004, <http://usinfo.state.gov/
mena/Archive/2004/Dec/17-210699.html>.

189.   IMF, *Iraq: 2005 Article IV Consultation*, p. 51.

190.   Islamic Development Bank, 'IDB allocates US$500 million for Iraq
reconstruction', 7 January 2004, <http://www.isdb.org/english_docs/
idb_home/content.htm?content=include/iraqpress.inc>.

191.   IMF, *Iraq: 2005 Article IV Consultation*, p. 13.

192.   Colin Powell, 'Remarks at signing ceremony for bilateral debt agreement
with Iraq', 17 December 2004, <http://www.state.gov/secretary/
former/powell/remarks/39933.htm>.

193.   BBC Monitoring Middle East, 'OIC backs Iraq's new government', 17
June 2004; Organisation of the Islamic Conference, <http://www.oic-
oci.org/index.asp>.

194.   Jubilee Iraq, 'Jordan-Iraq meeting', 18 January 2005, <http://www.
jubileeiraq.org/blog/2005_01.html#000767>.

195.   Jubilee Iraq, 'Arab response is cool', 23 November 2004, <http://www.
jubileeiraq.org/blog/2004_11.html#000696>.

196.   European Union, Press Release, 'Iraq International Conference –
Conference Statement', 22 June 2005, <http://jpn.cec.eu.int/home/
news_en_newsobj1234.php>.

197.   Jubilee Iraq, 'Arab response is cool', 23 November 2004; 'Riyadh pledges
$1bn for Iraq reconstruction', *Arab News*, 23 June 2005.

198.   Jubilee Iraq, 'Romania refuses Paris Club terms', 14 December 2004,
<http://www.jubileeiraq.org/blog/2004_12.html#000737>;
PortalIraq, 'Legal: Romania cancels 80% of Iraqi debt', 24 August 2005.

199.   IMF, *Iraq: 2005 Article IV Consultation*, p. 17.

200.   IMF, *Iraq: 2005 Article IV Consultation*, p. 19.

201.   IMF, *Iraq: 2005 Article IV Consultation*, pp. 9-10.

202.   State Department, *Section 2207 Report, January 2006*, Appendix I, p. 20; GAO, 'Rebuilding Iraq: U.S. water and sanitation efforts'.

203.   Quoted in T. Christian Miller, 'Some Iraq projects running out of money, U.S. says', *Los Angeles Times*, 8 September 2005.

6. CONCLUSION – THE OCCUPATION AND ITS LEGACY

1.   This is the abiding theme of four keynote addresses by President Bush: speeches of 30 November, 7 December, 12 December and 14 December 2005, accessible via <http://www.whitehouse.gov/infocus/iraq/>.

2.   See, for example, Phebe Marr, 'We might prevent a failed state', *Washington Post*, 11 December 2005.

3.   Juan Cole, 'Informed Comment', 8 May 2005.

4.   See, from very different perspectives, Fukuyama, *State Building*, ch. 1; and Noam Chomsky, *Failed States: The Abuse of Power and the Assault on Democracy*, London: Hamish Hamilton , 2006.

5.   For example, Sebastian Mallaby, 'The Reluctant Imperialist: Terrorism, Failed States, and the Case for American Empire', *Foreign Affairs*, March/April 2002.

6.   Drawing upon Jennifer Milliken, ed., *State Failure, Collapse and Reconstruction*, Oxford: Blackwell, 2003, pp. 10-13.

7.   Cf. William Zartman, ed., *Collapsed States: the Disintegration and Restoration of Legitimate Authority*, Boulder, CO: Lynne Rienner, 1995, pp. 5-11

8.   Drawing upon Michael Mann, *States, War and Capitalism*, Oxford: Basil Blackwell, 1988, pp. 1-32; and Peter Evans, *Embedded Autonomy: States and Industrial Transformation*, Princeton University Press, 1995.

9.   Generally, see Patrick Dunleavy and Brendan O'Leary, *Theories of the State*, London: Macmillan, 1987; David Runciman, 'The Concept of the State: the Sovereignty of a Fiction', in Quentin Skinner and Bo Stråth, *States and Citizens*, Cambridge University Press, 2003. On Iraq specifically, see Eric Davis, *Memories of State: Politics, History, and Collective Identity in Modern Iraq*, Berkeley: University of California Press, 2005.

10.   Most famously, in Graham Allison and Philip Zelikow, *Essence of Decision: Explaining the Cuban Missile Crisis*, 2nd edn, Harlow: Longman, 1999.

11.   PCO, *Capacity Development: A Foundation for a Sustainable Future*, April 2006.

12. State Department, 'Provincial stability assessment', 31 January 2006, p.2; leaked to the *New York Times* in April 2006, and available via <http://www.nytimes.com>.

13. Articulated most forcefully by Ali Mazrui, e.g., in 'Africa Entrapped: between the Protestant Ethic and the Legacy of Westphalia', in Hedley Bull and Adam Watson, eds, *The Expansion of International Society*, Oxford: Clarendon, 1984.

14. State Department, 'Iraqi Kurds and Arabs', 8 November 2004, pp. 4, 12.

15. Jonathan Steele, 'Baghdad mosques become vigilante forts as sectarianism divides suburbs', *Guardian*, 21 April 2006.

16. Nick Olivari, 'US envoy urges crackdown on Iraq militias', Reuters, 26 March 2006.

17. Ellen Knickmeyer, 'U.S. has end in sight on Iraq rebuilding', *Washington Post*, 2 January 2006; USAID, 'Focused Stabilization', 2 January 2006, annex F, p. 60.

18. Paul Richter, 'Staffing, security issues stall provincial program', *Los Angeles Times*, 2 April 2006.

INDEX